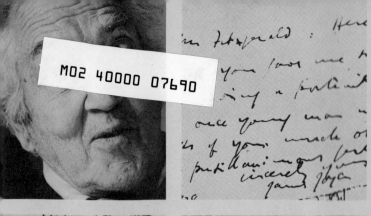

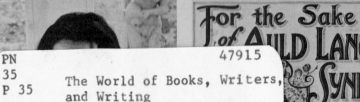

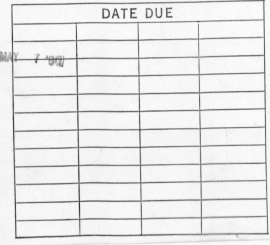

PN
35
P 35

47915

The World of Books, Writers, and Writing

Pages

DATE DUE

MAY 7 '97			

Pages

1

O Captain! dearest Ca[ptain]

Get & hear the bells

Wake up & see the st[ars]

~~flags a flying~~;

For you it is the Ci[ty]

shores are crow[ded]

red-rose

For you the ~~very~~ ga[rlands]

of women;

O Captain! O my ba[ck]

~~beneath~~ you;

~~[illegible]~~ is some Dream

~~soft, slumber~~

you ~~[illegible] & cold~~

Pages

THE WORLD OF BOOKS, WRITERS, AND WRITING

1

MATTHEW J. BRUCCOLI
Editorial Director

C. E. FRAZER CLARK, JR.
Managing Editor

GALE RESEARCH COMPANY · BOOK TOWER · DETROIT, MICHIGAN 48226

Pages

1

Matthew J. Bruccoli, *Editorial Director*
C. E. Frazer Clark, Jr., *Managing Editor*
Joan Paterson Kerr, *Picture Editor*

Irwin Glusker, *Art Director*
Kristen Reilly, *Associate Art Director*

Fred M. Kleeberg, *Production Supervisor*

Published by
Gale Research Company
Book Tower, Detroit, Michigan 48226

Frederick G. Ruffner, *Publisher*
James M. Ethridge, *Associate Publisher*

Subscriptions and additional single copies of *Pages* are available from Gale Research Co., Book Tower, Detroit, Michigan 48226. $24 per volume.

A country, finally, erodes and the dust blows away, the people all die and none of them were of any importance permanently, except those who practised the arts, and these now wish to cease their work because it is too lonely, too hard to do, and is not fashionable. A thousand years makes economics silly and a work of art endures forever, but it is very difficult to do and now it is not fashionable.

— Green Hills of Africa

Ernest Hemingway wrote these words in 1935 reacting to assertions that the importance of literature had diminished. In our time we hear that literature is no longer relevant.

Writing is the most important endeavor, and the most enduring. But general readers have been quarantined from the profession of authorship and from bookmanship. Hence the rationale for *Pages*—which involves readers with books, writers, and writing. *Pages* is concerned with literary history—construing that term to encompass publishing, librarianship, bibliography, the book trade, book-collecting, as well as the non-printed media which generate writing. Ultimately, the worth of *Pages* will depend on its contributors. We are proud of the writers represented here who share our conviction that literature should belong to its readers.

Table of Contents

Pages is honored to open its first number with an inside look into the gestation of a major work by a major writer. The editors share James Dickey's hopes for his new fiction: "When people talk about the futility of war and the arrogance of men, coupled with a strange, terrible kind of mystagogy, they will surely remember Alnilam. *If they read it, they will never forget it."*

"If I can bring this off, Tolstoy will seem a minor writer"

NOTES FOR WORKS IN PROGRESS

By JAMES DICKEY

The plan now is to write two novels simultaneously. The first of these will be *Alnilam,* and the second will be called *Crux.* The general plan here is to take the material in *Alnilam* and expand it into a much longer work dealing with the Pacific War as it was fought at night. The two central figures of *Crux* will be Harbelis and Shears, from *Alnilam.* I wish to write the latter novel in a way that would make people able to understand *Crux* without having read *Alnilam,* but if the reader *has* read *Alnilam,* the meanings will be clearer than if he had not.

What happens, essentially, is this. We pick up these two characters, Harbelis and Shears, as they leave San Francisco for a New Guinea replacement depot. We follow them for two years, until the end of the war, with Harbelis on occupation duty in Japan.

They are both assigned to the same night fighter squadron. We take them from Northern New Guinea up through the Philippines campaign, through Okinawa and the end of the war, with a slight coda having to do with Harbelis on occupation duty in Japan.

The general thread of action is this. Shears is still under the influence of Joel, and Harbelis also, but less so. Harbelis becomes increasingly mature, less romantic, more practical. Shears becomes more and more fanatical and more and more successful. During the Okinawa invasion, and the campaign for the air supremacy over Japan, he is in command of the squadron. Everyone hates him, and is in awe of him. He is the stuff of which heroes are made, and he draws almost everything from Joel, and the Alnilam plot. Harbelis is a little bit like Colonel Ross in Cozzens' *Guard of Honor*. He is still in awe of Joel, but he has come into a broader humanitarianism than Joel, with Joel's youthful fanatical approach to life, would have permitted. We might have a short series of letters between Joel and Frank Cahill, who is now living in Atlanta with Hannah, and these could be very moving. Frank Cahill is still confused, but accepting. Hannah reads Harbelis' letters to him.

In the meantime, Shears has become one of the legends of the South Pacific. He is what Joel might have been. The central conflict of the novel turns on Shears' insisting to the General of Fifth Air Force Fighter Command, as the tide and the balance of power turn from the Japanese to the Americans, on the squadron which he now commands being converted from a night fighter—that is, essentially a defensive group—into a night intruder outfit, which goes out over the enemy airfields, does light bombing, harassing, sampan strafing, and so on. This entails the making of enormously long, dangerous missions, and the loss of many lives. The General is as much under the sway of Shears as Shears is under the sway of the dead or disappeared Joel. The novel swings on the conversion of the squadron from a night fighter unit into a night intruder unit, the consequences, and the rest. It should probably be, as a conservative estimate, around 400 pages.

One of the consequences of Shears' actions as he attempts to show the General what his squadron can do is that several—at least two—of his people, the most likeable of them all, are captured by the Japanese and beheaded. We need to show this scene, as the two men are bound by wire and wait all night in an abandoned Philippine school house, guarded by Japanese. We need to have an interior monologue here on two levels: one the level of the brave guy who is not afraid to die, and the craven, desperate boy, 21 years old, who is. We need to show this, and to show the actual moment of beheading. Shears is not only outraged by this, but sees it as a tremendous opportunity for aggression; the kind of thing that Joel had always believed in. He has every plane in the squadron go on a dawn strafing strike against the place where these two crewmen have been executed. They shoot up everything in sight. Is there any evidence that this has done any good? No; it is questionable. But it is a gesture that the General at Fifth Fighter Headquarters likes. Shears becomes, progressively, the stuff of which legendary heroes are made. At the beginning he is not an exceptional boy until he encounters Joel and the Alnilam plot. He then becomes progressively more impressive, more learned, more intellectual, and more fanatical. He is something of an airborne Lawrence of Arabia. I mean to show, here, the fascination of power and mystery simultaneously. That is, the fascination of power and personal mystery: mystiques. Mystiques, both in their absurdity and their grandeur, and their lending to the personal dramatic significance that human events and human beings so desperately need and respond to. Shears is a hero and the manner of his death is heroic. Or is it? There may be developed some parallelism between the death of Shears and the death of Joel Cahill. I'm not quite sure how I will have Shears killed, but he is killed.

The death of Shears is an occasion not only for general squadron and Air Force mourning, but even of national mourning. He is killed just before he plans to spring the Alnilam plot full-scale through the whole Air Force. He has become more and more convinced that Joel is a kind of secular messiah, and that he is the Peter to Joel's Christ.

Harbelis, on the other hand, grows progressively away from the Alnilam plot and the baleful and wonderous influence of Joel Cahill into a broader humanitarianism. He survives.

We must have a great, hideous gala scene of the night of the signing of the peace treaty, with the ships in Buckner Bay shooting off their artillery, the fire hoses going off, all this resulting in the death of several dozen Americans from falling, spent bullets, bomb fragments, and so on.

This is a very difficult business, this projection in fiction, of the quality of the fabulous, insofar as the human personality is concerned. I want, in these two novels, to project that quality insofar as I can find the objective correlatives by which to do it. The reader must not constantly be *told* that Joel Cahill was fabulous, that he could, in a sense, influence a whole war, or even a segment of it, but things must be recounted of him that would cause the reader to accept this quality in him. That is going to be one of the tough things.

One of the qualities I would like to show, in these two novels, is the dangerousness—

the sheer *dangerousness*—of ideas. Their applicability can result in the deaths and mutilations of many.

The concept of the *fabulous* death: Joel has had one, and may in fact not even be dead, even now. Shears has another, and this, I must invent. It should also be shown, or at least implied, that Shears dies in order to *be* fabulous. Death is part of this sort of mystique, as was T. E. Lawrences'. The only person that Shears can entrust Joel's Alnilam plot to is Harbelis, and the last part of the novel will be to show Harbelis rejecting, dazedly and reluctantly, this gambit. This might take place in the scene with the Japanese school children, or it might take place somewhere else, but it should be implied that it *does* take place. Fanaticism, with all its allure, glamor, sense of consequentiality, must, in the end, go. It is terribly sad to be humdrum, efficient, honest, loving, and human. But we imply that these are the necessary conditions, despite the attractions of the other.

These two novels are conceived, essentially, as a study of power, and its relationship to personal fascination and mystery. It is important that Shears' body is never found, though it is searched for almost desperately by all that the U.S. military forces possess: Air Force, Navy, Seabees, Marines, civilians, everybody. It is never found. The living legend has become, simply, a legend.

Overall structural note, including health possibilities. I will start out on *Alnilam* and *Crux* as though I was going to carry out my original plan of making *Alnilam* a slightly longer-than-average novel and *Crux* an enormous, Tolstoyan, panoramic book about the Pacific air war at night. However, if there is anything seriously wrong with me, and I am told that I won't make it for more than, say, a few years, I will then abandon that plan, and write *Crux* as a much shorter book in brief scenes, something like Joan Didion's *Play it as it Lays*. If time is *very* short, I will do them both that way. It would be easier to do, and I could get them both done, even if I had only a couple of weeks to live. And I think, no matter what, I will have a little more than *that!*

I have everything I need, now, for *Alnilam,* except the plot that Joel is trying to bring off, or leads people to believe he is. The question that must either be answered or left creatively up in the air is whether or not he wants to effect *anything,* beyond causing havoc. The way I see this now is to throw out some hints—and they must be startling, unheard-of ideas, and yet curiously boy-like—as to what he hopes to effect. This may take some reading and a lot of thinking on my part. But I have some great scenes in this damn book, and I think it can be an awfully good novel if I could just find this one missing part of the puzzle. I would like it to serve as a blueprint for other wild-thinking young fellows, though I hope they would never carry the notions as far as Joel seems to have wished to do.

There may be some *very* sketchy notion of some kind of hierarchy such as is in Plato's *Republic,* where people are divided into classes according to some method of classification or other, but on no account must Joel's mad scheme of the rejuvenation of the human race have anything to do with books. He makes a point of not reading books; he has only this one text-book that the aphorisms and the plan are outlined in. This Harbelis describes to Cahill. Harbelis, in his own, half-educated way, is also rather eloquent, though naturally in quite a different manner from Mac-Caig's "country surrealism."

To almost everyone among his own peers who knows him, Joel represents the thing that stands for them against the military bureaucracy. He is more man than any of them, or of all them put together. He can outdo them at their things, and disdains both the things and the men that do them. He will not take anything at all that he does not wish to take off any superior. He has a kind of lordly contempt for military people and military things, especially officers. But he is always just this side of being washed out for "attitude." The point about Joel is not so much himself as his *influence*. It should be more or less left up to the reader to decide whether he is a kind of military saint, an egotistical young phony, a confused boy, a person who puts himself above the law, above his country, and so on, in the name of something that is never fully explained, or what.

Joel's influence. The influence that he exerts comes out in other people in many, many ways, at many times, and under many different kinds of circumstances, from love making to flying combat. We want to get this firmly implanted in *Alnilam,* and then carry it on out into the Pacific war, where many heroes are created by it, and many men killed.

In regard to Joel's plot. He evidently has some notion of a society which he calls, "circulatory," or "cyclic." The society would depend very heavily on *role-playing,* and on *lying.* Joel believes that lying exercises the creative and imaginative faculties, and, when indulged in on either an individual or a group basis, raises the consciousness of the party or parties concerned. The process is what Joel calls "continuous invention," and he believes, apparently, that such systematic practice of fabrication will create a new human consciousness where there is really no difference between the actual world and the transfigured world of the human ability to fabricate. There is a kind of sketchy notation to the effect that there will be "truth areas," where empirical fact is rigorously adhered to and communicated truthfully. This is the area that will enable the state to function. All the citizens are indoctrinated both to truth and invention, so that they can be circulated in and out of both areas, as the state desires. It might even be a kind of law that one must spend equal time in both, or perhaps more time in the "invention area" than in the "truth area," but surely, some time in both. The real basis for the *mind* or imagination of the state will be in the invention area, where people are constantly exercising their creative abilities by making up stories about themselves, about their neighbors, about anything and everything there is. People would soon learn to live with this, Joel says, exploit it, and rejoice in it. It is a kind of freedom human beings have never before had on a large-scale, systematic basis. There might be a kind of hierarchy of lying here where one class of "inventors" would be compelled to enter the truth area or indicate by some sign or other, in case vital or necessary information was required, that this was indeed truth. The rest could be lies, but the highest group of all, the group that corresponds to the philosopher-kings or sages, are those that need make no sign as to whether what they say is true or whether it is fantasy. These are the master inventors, and the state reveres them.

In regard to Joel's theory of the new state based on role-playing and lying, there are hints that he has conferred on some of the cadets and other people the privilege of training for the top class: i.e., those who do not have to distinguish between the truth and "invention," so the reader ends up not knowing who is telling the truth about what, or what piece of information is an "invention."

If we're going to use aphorisms here, we'll have to contrive some way of making aphorisms which are nonbookish: that are not based on Heraclitus or on any of the other famous aphorists. This will have to sound absolutely spontaneous, deriving from no one. That is going to be tough. But I am on the right track here; I *know* it.

Perhaps it would be a good idea not to reveal too much of the plot of Alnilam in the first novel. Or perhaps it would be best to make it look, maybe, a little *too* amateurish and boyish, and, with the aircraft wrecking scene would have seemed to have come to an end. Shears somehow—figure out how—protects himself and avoids being washed out and court-martialed, and goes on. So does Harbelis, through a fluke. Some of the fellows are deliberately set up to get caught and kicked out. But the key men go on. That would be about all that is revealed about the Alnilam plot in the first book: tantalizing hints.

It would then be in *Crux* that the full diabolical scope of the Alnilam plot takes place, and culminates in a holocaust somewhere in the Pacific wherein Shears and a number of the other key fellows—the first echelon men, those from the base where Joel trained, the second and third echelon men, who had gotten into the plot by various means—all are killed.

The take-over succeeds on a couple of islands, flares up briefly, and then subsides. But are these incidents, too, *planned?* Is Shears' death part of the plot? Will it go on? Joel has said that it will never end, and that it will take many forms, most of them unknown, unfathomable, and undetectable. Harbelis is left in the end wondering if it is in fact the end, as he looks on the remote and yet very close whiteness of Fujiyama: inaccessible, moving into the room, untouchable, impossible.

The main thing I want to do with *Alnilam,* is write the ultimate novel of fathers and sons; the mysteries, the frustrations, the revelations, and, at the end, the eventual renunciation and reconciliation.

Great joy in creation. Great joy in having the story moving. I truly believe that

Alnilam and *Crux* will create a new sensibility for mankind. Of *course* this is extravagant and immodest as one applies it to oneself. Nevertheless, it is true. If I can bring this thing off, Tolstoy will seem a minor writer.

The trouble with *Alnilam* and *Crux* at this stage of composition is that I have got so many balls to juggle in the air that it is almost impossible to keep them all in motion. There are so many different themes and so many different people, that I am really not sure as to the implications or personal relationships, military, artistic, social, and so on. I am not sure of what I am really trying to say. I think that the crux of the matter lies somewhere in the definition of what power does to a man, and also charlatanry, and also love.

The whole point of my two novels is that the story should open out from a small incident at a primary training base into a vast Tolstoyian vision of the Pacific night air war. That is going to be very difficult to do, but it can be done. Maybe not by me; but if not by me, by no one.

Shears' excuse to get all the planes of the night fighter squadron, heavily armed, in the air would be the execution of Davison and Barnwell by the Japanese. I dread writing this scene, but I must describe in detail the castration and beheading of these two average American boys, who know nothing at all of Alnilam. But the Japanese play into the hands of Shears. They castrate and behead both of the American flyers, fly over the American base where Shears' squadron is encamped, and throw out the heads. Davison's head bounces into the weeds, and is found there with the genitals stuffed into the mouth, bound into it with barbed wire. The other boy's head hits on the runway, bursts open like an egg. Shears seizes the opportunity to mobilize the whole squadron and go on a revenge raid. This is the signal for the breaking of the Alnilam plot. Shears has men on convoys and as air controllers, and in several other of his own squadron's aircraft. They take off and swing toward the island where Davison and the other boy have been mutilated. Shears looks at his watch, and then breaks into the Alnilam special language. Consternation. General Smith, who adores Shears, and thinks him the finest young man in the Pacific, has authorized the strike. The erstwhile blood-thirsty commanding officer of the squadron has become increasingly mystified and horrified by hints of what Shears has been doing, or, even worse, might plan to be doing, and the end is a kind of air holocaust, comparable to the ground holocaust in *Alnilam*. Massingale, the commanding officer, deliberately rams Shears to wipe an evil thing out of the life of mankind. This is written so that most of the aircraft either run together or are incapacitated. A few minutes of confusion, and the whole Alnilam plot has come to nothing. Should it have come to anything? Who knows? But at any rate we end with the only survivor of the Alnilam group is Harbelis. And we end *Crux* with him on rest leave in Japan, getting drunk and looking out through a picture window at Fujiyama, and mumbling to himself in the secret language. Perhaps meanwhile, Cahill has died in Atlanta, and the only one who knows anything about the plot is Harbelis, and, perhaps, Hannah back in the little cotton mill town that has been commandeered as a training base. Harbelis, a good-hearted, rather gullible man, talks to himself with a thick tongue about returning to the States and going to college, at which idea he begins to laugh uproariously. He then mumbles to himself in the now-forgotten tongue of the Alnilam plot. He takes a sheet out of his pocket and looks at the basic kinds of words that all the members must commit to memory. But there is no word there for sorrow, and the novel ends where he invents the word, and writes it into the code. And he raises his glass of whisky, perhaps even a martini, to Fujiyama, and his eyes, unaccountably, or perhaps accountably, fill with tears, drunken tears, tears of comprehension, and he drains the glass, so that there will be more water in his eyes so that Fujiyama, symbol of peace, remote, intimate, indescribable, impossible, can dance for him there after all these strange circumstances have taken place. Harbelis is the Ishmael of the whole enterprise: "I alone have returned to tell thee." But he will never tell anyone. No one would believe it. We end with the image of Fujiyama, dancing and glittering in the rainbows of his eyelashes, with the last part of his drink being drunk, the glass being put down, and Fujiyama dancing on, dancing on.

All I need now is the utopia part, the hint of what Joel hopes, or says he hopes to accomplish by all this disruption: the future. What is it? It must be something stranger than men have ever conceived of, or ever thought of living, but which might be good, might be better than anything we have ever had. There must be only hints, because the core of the Alnilam plot is its mystery and its feeling of: "it will all be revealed at the proper time." On the other hand, there must be a powerful stimulation of hope and belief and daring to make men do these things. It must be more than just youth and dissent and dissatisfaction. It must be the ultimate social mystery. Again, what *is* it? When I get this, I have the key to the whole thing, for I can write the details and the scenes easily once I know what the plot *might* be. The ghost scene, which impels Cahill full-bodily into the plot, is a thing which may very well have been staged, as I said earlier, by Shears. But Cahill also, on the basis of this, and on the basis of the possibility of the survival after death, gets religion in some way, which would enable us to tie up the sense of bloodthirstiness in the military and the religious sense between which I am convinced there is a profound tie. We would have, perhaps, in the strange invented language of Joel and Shears, a good many letters of Cahill's, and we would print a glossary at the back of the book, so that the reader could decipher what they meant. These letters of Frank Cahill's would be a strange mixture of military shrewdness and mystical Christianity. They would include strange chunks of poetry, scripture, interpretations of Cahill's of these things, and a good many weird and undecipherable aphorisms and Heracletian sayings, which would indicate that the father has fallen very much under the spell of the son. These would be clumsy and obvious at first, but would become, toward the end of the letters, just before Cahill dies, increasingly profound, or, as Heraclitus would have said, "dark." They would be cryptic, strange, and disturbing indeed.

But the device of having the reader decipher the letters would be rather unique in fiction, I would think. Many a businessman and housewife would spend time deciphering the key messages that go into the Pacific night air war. The point is that there is no way to crack a code that consists of a private language, which the adepts know the meaning and significance of but no one else but them does. This Joel has diabolically seen, and has concocted what little he was able to make of the language with a great glee. Shears furnishes the rest. This is what will give force to the invention of the last word of the language, by the last survivor of the Alnilam group, Harbelis, as he sits drunk, looking at Fujiyama, and invents, as the rest of the language has been invented, just by random association and syllabification, the word that is lacking from the whole language of conquest and mystery and power: the word for sorrow and pity.

I wish now to concentrate on developing a character in *Alnilam* who is known only as "the Navigator." He is a man who has been in combat and has been terribly mutilated in some way, perhaps even castrated, and is in town to give to the cadets a series of lectures on the importance of navigation and its techniques. But the lectures are now over, and he stays on. Why? No one knows. He has had these terrible, hideous mutilating wounds, and the feeling begins to be among the cadets who love him, and the townspeople that don't know him or what he is doing there, that he has no place to go. Now, what I want to do very *lightly* is to implant the notion in the mind of the reader that the Navigator may indeed be the devil.

Let us begin to block the novel out in scenes, proceeding very, very slowly. I need notes on what I hope every scene will accomplish, and we will do these into the tape recorder, and write the scenes and the novel on the typewriter. We need to go very slowly through this. I know, essentially, what form the novel is going to take, and what is going to happen. But we also need to link this up with what is going to happen in the *second* novel, and so it would be a good idea to work on the second one at least *somewhat* while the first one is being written, so this conjunction can be made. Also read Melville's *The Confidence Man,* for hints as to the character of the Navigator. This might be extremely helpful, for I intend him as the ultimate Mysterious Man, inexplicable and diabolical, and also very down-to-earth and easy-going.

The Navigator and his obsession with times, spaces, distances, stars, and so on gives me the kind of all-encompassing character that I would like to have. The devil must have this information.

Might it not be possible to have the Navigator recount some incident which would in some way duplicate Satan's flight through Chaos in the second book of *Paradise Lost*? This could be immensely thrilling and powerful, weird, strange, unforgettable.

I've got it, or what may be part of it. The great secret thing that Joel is always talking about is what happens when "Orion leaps free," and releases "the energy." This idea is seized upon by Shears. He has never ceased saying this, through all his correspondence with his minions all over the Air Force and the armed services, that something of this sort was going to happen. Shears halfway believes that something of this sort of thing is in the offing, but he is not sure that it is not pure bluff. When the atomic bomb strikes Hiroshima, he realizes his opportunity, and seizes it. This is Joel's prediction, now at last made manifest in the killing of hundreds of thousands of people. Shears takes off on this, and the others follow.

I wish to project the idea, that, in the smoke and flames of the brush fire where his plane crashed, Joel Cahill contrived to lose his own body, so that the legend might be perpetuated. Therefore, other people keep saying they have seen him, and we, among the living, may have seen him, too. He may emerge as a political figure, for example. But I really do believe that Joel Cahill contrived to lose his own body, to become a legend, so that the legend and the Alnilam plot should be perpetuated.

Now what this leads to is this. Joel has worked out an elaborate system for coding the E6B computer. This is central to the plot, for it is the way he gets his messages to his people who are off the base. He is expanding to several other training bases, and is planning to go into the Infantry and the Navy as well. The way the system works is this. He sends out, by chain letter, an E6B formula. The people who are in on the plot, plus those who are *being* let in on the plot, have a list of words in a private language that Joel has concocted—give some of this—and when they receive this, they get the computers and work the formulas out. When they work the formulas out—they are mostly time-distance problems—perhaps it would be better to give a set of formulas for different words and phrases and so on. When they work the formula out, say, the speed arrow will point to the correct designation of the word. The code works in words rather than letters, but they are the words of the private language of the Alnilam people. The private language is known only to initiates. What is on the goggles is the final coded message which Joel will release to no one except his two or three top aides, with them swearing on their own blood never, never to decode it unless he is dead, or unless he gives the word. That is the formula on the goggle strap. He wears this inside the goggles, which is one of the reasons it is still legible. He has these two things on the strap, but nobody sees them. Nobody knows that they're there. He has them for his own mystique, and because he wants them there as he flies. This same inscription, this formula, is the one at the end of *Crux* where the last survivor of the Alnilam plot, after so many people have died, and so much meaningless violence has happened, and so much violence done to the enemy by means of, is left in the mind of the last survivor, the decent guy, Harbelis, who always carries his E6B with him, even after he has come out terribly burned from the war, and is on rest leave at Fujiyama, or just under Fujiyama. He plays in a ping pong tournament, and goes to a Japanese school, where the children dance and sing around him, and give him American flags, and he is told by the schoolmaster about the strafing of the children before the peace was signed, when they came running out of the school waving American flags, and the A-26's shot them down. Anyway, Harbelis feels that as the last repository of the message, he can finally decode. He takes his E6B out of his pocket and turns it to the formula. It is only one word. It is the word of the twenty-five or so in the secret language that has never been used on any message. The word is *nothing*. Harbelis then goes out into the glittering cold and looks at the mountain, but it is too remote. He has some GI field glasses, and he goes with his eyes slowly up the trunk of a pine tree until he hits the crest, and he stands looking at it, locked in with it. It is not in the direction of the school, but in the opposite direction. But he knows how to get back to the school if he wants to. Probably he never will, but he enjoys knowing that he could. He stands looking with rapt attention at the top of the tree moving a little in the wind, then swings his binoculars to Fujiyama, but it blinds him. He comes back to the bottom of the tree, and goes up it again, because he wants it to be the right one. The last sentence of the second novel is, "It was not impossible, like the mountain."

When people talk about the futility of war and the arrogance of men, coupled with a strange and terrible kind of imaginative mystagogy, they will surely remember *Alnilam*. If they read it, they will never forget it.

These two books will attempt to show the existence of the Alnilam plot gives hope to some, arrogance to others, a mystical feeling of belonging to a select group to others, revulsion, in secrecy, to others, and so on. Alnilam is, to coin a phrase, all things to all men; it is the future of mankind, or the destruction of it; or it is a joke.

In the scene in *Crux* where the two fliers are beheaded and the first one has been tortured and chopped up with a hatchet or an ax and then beheaded, the Alnilam man, alone, is standing there in relative calm, saying nothing. His plan is to infuriate the Japanese captain until he flies into a rage and kills him quickly. This he does. The Japanese captain is beside himself with anger when Malone spits in his face, and cannot control himself and runs Malone through with his sword, and again, and again, and again. Malone takes all this, slowly falling to the ground. The last things he says— it takes all his effort to raise his head—he says, with the blood running out of his mouth, his last words: "I know something you don't."

End of *Crux,* as Harbelis is looking at the top of the tree through the field glasses. "It drew what it needed from the earth, and so possessed the movement of life."

Pursuant to the last entry, or, "It drew what it needed from the earth, so the movement of life was in it."

The Graves Of Academe

Serving as writer-in-residence can be like working as the playground director in the Kremlin.

Dear Professor J—:

How very kind of you to write!

Yes, there have been inquiries from other colleges concerning my plans for 1970. But after reading your letter, I truly cannot imagine a climate more congenial, a chairman more sympathetic to the very special needs of writers. . . .

All right, I confess that the only other inquiry I'd had was from some coaltown college located between nothing and nowhere. On the other hand I wasn't aware that I should have gotten another $1289 per annum plus a lighter teaching load or that for all of Professor J-'s heavy hints about tenure—"a strong likelihood, perhaps even a powerful possibility"—negotiations with next year's writer were already nicely underway.

To be sure, I started suffering spasms of heartburn when my program arrived and it turned out that the free-wheeling seminar I'd been promised was prefixed with a zero and designed "for students who, after having completed their basic composition course, desire or need further training in precise and coherent expression." At around the same time I ran into the late Harvey Swados, who shook me up with his first-hand accounts of academic perfidy and pettiness, his sinister analogies to the Kremlin and the kindergarten. As I remember, he quoted Jesse Unruh at me ("The appalling viciousness of academic poli-

By WALLACE MARKFIELD

...the best-selling novelist and the poet celebrated only by his wife are nowadays shoving at the same academic trough.

tics is in inverse proportion to the size of the stakes"), then David Rousset ("Human beings do not know that everything is possible"), then Dostoyevsky ("The right to dishonor exerts an irresistible fascination").

Well, I needed the money, of course, but it wasn't the money, it wasn't even the prospect of all those nubile nineteen-year-old girls which whipped my imagination to a froth. To tell the plain, stupid truth, I was absolutely wild to teach; touch me, touch any writer, I suppose, and you're touching a performer, a pundit, a prophet—which is hardly big news, though it may help explain why the best-selling novelist and the poet celebrated only by his wife are nowadays shoving at the same academic trough.

It turned out that if I wasn't exactly the best teacher since Socrates, I nevertheless did have a few good days. And on one such day I came out of a short story workshop shining with contentment, hailed a colleague in the corridor and tried to tell him how I'd just nailed down a powerful point about the strains and pains of writing. "First I took six similes from James Agee," I said. "I wrote them on the blackboard, I left out the word or phrase which would complete them, then—oh listen, listen to this—"

"Agee," my colleague murmured, nicely overstressing the "g." A moment passed, then he went on to say, *"Actually, I haven't read him yet."*

I underscore this line because it became for me the quintessential academic line, one which I would hear in every possible permutation and combination from most of the hundred-odd members of the English faculty. What's more, when I spoke of a novel, they'd answer with something about The Novel, decline and death of; when I praised a novelist, they placed him somewhere to the rear of Henry James; when I switched to the movies, they switched to cinema and started asking me how many horses Eisenstein had killed. At such times I felt heavy-handed and big-footed; in effect, a clown. And for once in my life I started regretting the lack of advanced degrees, the years and years wasted reading *Partisan Review* instead of *PMLA,* the inability to beat those under-

nourished overspecialists at their own scholarly games.

So I tried not talking to my colleagues of things that mattered; in fact I tried not talking to them altogether. The more I tried, however, the more I provoked their sympathetic remarks about "the writer's temperament" or "the plight of the creative artist in America" or "the isolation, the *essential* isolation of the literary man." In a mingled state of disbelief and despair I started needling, shafting, bludgeoning, saying things like "Publish *and* perish" . . . "May your contract be terminated and your thermos jug shattered" . . . "If it is the privilege of all academics to write badly your last memo nevertheless abuses the privilege." On and on and worse and worse until at last I was imitating the department's topgun scholar to his face.

But as my chairman used to say with a chuckle or a chortle, "One must, perforce, become an actor in the academic drama."

And pretty soon I answered a knock at my cubicle door and beheld the impoverished scalp and luxuriant beard of the man I'd most often fantasied belting with a pig bladder.

"Markfield," he began, looking into my eyes like a dog begging to be walked.

Then he fumbled with the clasps of a battered portfolio and in a voice pitched for the Academic Senate spoke of "a small problem and a minor difficulty."

Now since there's no quick way to explain what I found so engaging about the man's absolute charmlessness, I'll report simply that I spent the next day-and-a-half on "a bit, only and merely and no more than a bit of light editing" of a sixty-three-page monograph explicating the place names mined by Mark Twain during his Hartford Period, 1874-1891.

Word of my *Gemütlichkeit* got out and, during the weeks that followed, I must have been handed more petitions than a tzar—petitions calling stridently and, it seemed to me, simultaneously for open enrollment and more rigorous entrance requirements; for expanded on-campus parking facilities and the construction of a new theater on the one spot where these facilities could be expanded; for additions to the junior staff and elimination of the required courses they taught; for less attention to publications as a criterion for advancement and the immediate funding of a university press. I remember my mail box all at once blooming with twofers, take-out menus, subscription blanks for the *Consumer's Research Bulletin* and the *I. F. Stone Newsletter;* I remember coming across my books on the library's *Recent Acquisitions* list; I remember the Modern American Fiction man pumping and pumping my arm as he informs me that he's just reserved them.

And by and by my chairman, and after him three full, and after them three associate professors invite me to dinner. Seven academic households in all, and in five of those households I heard what sounded, to my ear at least, like the same meandering monologue.

"We took a side road, a secondary road outside of Utica, St. Paul, Iowa City, Boulder, San Diego—this is when we owned our 1962 Opel with 239,000 miles on the odometer which never had its engine touched, which during my sabbatical, my Fulbright, my Guggenheim took us, without our having to add water, oil, gas, from Central Appalachia to Arabia Deserta—and we pulled over at a farmer's market to pick up some summer squash, winter lettuce, spring corn. Well, Tisha, Fern, Rosetta, Prudence, Carla, Mimi, Natalie noticed this hutch cabinet, coffee mill, harpsichord, Franklin stove, Khalabar rug, Shaker chair. But all we had between us was nine dollars and thirty-seven cents. 'Say, all we have between us is nine dollars and thirty-seven cents,' I said to the mildly eccentric, slightly daft, absolutely deranged farmer who was at that very moment engaged in ploughing under what turned out to be an authentic Empire couch, a Luddite spinning wheel, a Salem whipping post. . . ."

But whatever it was, my colleagues knew the truckman to haul it at ox-cart rates, the Old Country craftsman to restore and refinish it at two dollars an hour

less faculty discount. They knew, for that matter, which factory reject discontinued model appliance would last till the millenium, which ninety-nine dollar charter-flight would be likely to serve the best Salisbury steak, which scholarly journal gave out the most expensive books for review, and which departmental secretary would type that review for a few kind words and a jar of dry roasted peanuts, the four-ounce size. "What do you pay your baby sitters?" I was once asked by a colleague whose anthology must have been in its fourth or fifth edition. When I answered, "Sometimes a dollar, sometimes a dollar-and-a-quarter," his wife, the author of nine children's books still in print, laughed musically and said, "Yes, fine, but how much by the hour?"

In fairness, though, I found that academic couples strove to make contact with me, to find my wavelength. But if the enormity, even, at times, the pathos of their striving wasn't lost on me, neither was their consummate ineptitude—an ineptitude invested with a certain style which drew its unique flavor and savor from the total absence of flavor and savor. I had my first knowledge of this style on the night when, after the instant espresso, after the Kraft Cracker Barrel cheese, after the talk of Ralph Nader and Mark Lane, I heard, like a panelist in a dream, "What—in the sense, that is, of thematic content and narrative thrust, the thrust of your narrative, that's if you have a narrative—what is your work-in-progress about?"

"In the sense of thematic content and narrative thrust," I said, "well, in that sense I'd have to say—"

Whereupon I was warned that writers should never talk about a work-in-progress.

Several seconds later. "Do you know Katherine Anne Porter?" There was grumpy silence when I shook my head. Then, "Say, even if you don't know her—and I am surprised you don't know her, though perhaps Katherine Anne Porter is so well known that she doesn't move in the same circles, your circles—I imagine you will get *something* out of this story. . . ."

The story, condensed here, has stayed with me all these years.

"I was at a party in Boston, Massachusetts, making what might be termed 'frequent visits' to the punch bowl. During one visit a woman smiled at me and said, 'Hello, there.' I answered either 'Well, hello to you' or 'Well now, hello to you' and either 'You bear quite a close resemblance to Katherine Anne Porter' or 'You bear quite a marked resemblance to Katherine Anne Porter.' The woman smiled. I said, 'Say, I notice you're smiling. Don't tell me you *are* Katherine Anne Porter.' She said, 'Indeed I am.' I said, 'I hope you are not pulling my leg.' She said, 'I am not pulling your leg.' And—and, by gosh, she *wasn't!*"

All the same I had to have him back, likewise my chairman, likewise the three others who sat on the Budget and Personnel Committee. And once having had them back, what was gained by avoiding their table in the faculty coffee room? By excluding myself from their talk? By holding down an occasional human impulse? If, as it happened, a colleague needed a catchy title for a course on themes of alienation in literature I couldn't, just couldn't be so mean-spirited as not to suggest Literature and Alienation.

And so my chairman appointed me to fill a vacancy on the Curriculum Revision Committee.

At its third meeting he introduced me to the Dean of Liberal Arts, who was filled with plans for symposia, discussion groups, dialogues, rap sessions, readings. But, one needed—and this was said after checking the experiences of other colleges—people. Did I know of, could I suggest some people?

"Not a one!" I hastened to say.

And so he named me an adjunct member of the Speakers' Resource Bureau.

It presently hit me, and with awful force, that I was spending little time reading, virtually none at my typewriter, and hadn't once managed to violate the moral turpitude clause.

"Look," I finally said to my chairman, "I was hired on because I'm a writer. Whatever distinction I might give this department will come from my writing, not my committee work."

But the more my teeth were set on edge, the more did his smile increase. In fact he positively beamed as he explained that "A writer is . . . a writer. His concerns, however, are ultimately . . . a writer's concerns."

Never mind, no matter, I used to console myself. If I wasn't meant to make it with the intellectual Rotarians I'd at least compel the discipleship and deepest admiration of my students, I'd have them speaking my name—my first name—as though it was spelled out in letters of flame. After all, I intended giving them—but what did I *not* intend giving them?

For openers, everything that was on my mind and undermind: evocations of old movies, anecdotes about the lives and wives of writers, bits of realpolitik, metaphysical speculation about the human condition, mots and aperçus culled from candy stores and cafeterias. I wanted primarily to put myself across, to come on as my own non-academic man, as one who had gone to school to Joyce and Kafka and Celine and Marx and Louis B. Mayer. Then, then I could with absolute justice impose upon each class a standard of excellence—my standard!

And the very highest standard was to be imposed upon my Expository Writing class; it consisted, I reasoned, of somewhat older students, a few of whom were in fact close to my own age and a good many of whom were working toward a Master of Fine Arts degree, said degree awarded upon "completion and acceptance of an original and creative work evidencing signal achievement, individual merit, and distinctive skill in the selected field/discipline/medium."

So on the sixth or seventh meeting of the class I announced that it was the sixth or seventh meeting of the class, that I intended at this time to start conveying some notion of "the discipline of letters." And yes, oh yes, it was a discipline, albeit a joyous discipline; make no mistake about it, people. But come, find out for yourselves; let's start to work on some "rigorous exercises in close observation and meticulous expression."

Therefore the first thing I wanted of this class was the beginning—"a few hundred words, a page or so" —of a book review.

"And what," I inquired emotionally, "is a book review?" I caught a buzz and a hum.

"Who, for instance, are some of your favorite book reviewers?"

"Professor Markfield—"

"Edmund Wilson, think of Edmund Wilson—"

"Professor Markfield, when you say 'a book review' do you mean we'll have to read a book?"

I said that it would not go unappreciated.

Could they review a short book? Because right now *every* teacher was piling on the reading lists and it didn't seem fair that they should *have* to do additional reading for a writing class; wasn't this a *writing* class?

I suggested Saul Bellow's *Seize the Day*. "It's a novella," I crooned. "Big type, generous margins. . . ."

But even so, nearly all present were greatly annoyed with me next time.

For one thing, there had been long lines at the college book store.

For another, they'd found *Seize the Day* quite sad and terribly depressing as an emotional experience. Also, the principal character or protagonist was such a boring personality type and so unable to find the inner resources with which to overcome his neurotic handicaps that—and this didn't mean the book lacked literary merit—he, Tommy Wilhelm, was impossible to identify with and relate to.

"Tell your own truths, then," I said. I also said something very close to, "Give your response fully and human and directly. Ask what Bellow's vision is. Go as far as you can into the center of that vision. How does that vision square with the vision of your own life as you lead it from day to day? What is it, what could it be you find in Tommy Wilhelm that's so ungenial and unsettling and plain boring?"

They had hoped that was what I wanted.

And so I got, *A full response to* Seize the Day *is beyond me in human and direct terms. . . .*

And, *The life I personally lead from day to day cannot to my mind be squared with Mr. Bellow's vision of life. For to tell my own truth, I find too much in that vision unnecessarily unsettling and uncongenial and plain boring.*

And, *Careful reading of* Seize the Day *leaves me convinced that the Bellowesque vision of Tommy*

"...the academic community is...a community."

Wilhelm lacks at its center what I would call full human directness.

When I handed back the papers there was a clamor for direction.

Direction and purpose.

Purpose and motivation.

Then how about another assignment? A more compelling, fulfilling, creative assignment? Some high-class writing about low-brow stuff? About, say *Gunsmoke?*

That would be fine.

I went to work, willingly, gladly, chronicling the history of the Western in general and *Gunsmoke* in particular.

I mimeographed pieces by Manny Farber and Gilbert Seldes and Barbara Deming and Dwight Mac-Donald.

I exhorted the class to observe what seriousness each of these writers brought to the popular arts, what finesse of tone and temperament.

And so I got, *"Wal," as the bearded and disheveled Festus might say, "that there episode of Gunsmoke last night was a real old scudder. . . ."*

And, *Miss Kitty was her customary radiant self when Marshal Matt Dillon strode through the swinging doors of the Long Branch saloon and used his blazing six-shooter on her paying customers. . . .*

And, *As the villainous gunslinger, enacted by Steve Forrest nearly outdrew heroic Matt Dillon, enacted by James Arness, I found myself virtually crying aloud, "Lotsa luck, villainous gunslinger. . . ."*

When I handed back the papers there were expressions of mild disapproval.

"Could you define your terms when you say 'this has a slipshod, tossed-off, scratch-pad quality?' "

" 'I'm not grabbed by this, Miss Goodfriend,' doesn't tell me what to do in terms of self-improvement."

" 'Mindless, pointless, and thoroughly hopeless,' Professor Markfield, is *your* subjective negative reaction."

Then a moon-faced, sweet-tempered woman who nearly always brought me a container of coffee and two Hydrox cookies, turned in her chair and addressed the class.

She said that Professor Markfield was a professional writer new to teaching and therefore somewhat unfamiliar with the totality, the *gestalt* of what faced a graduate student who carried sixteen and eighteen and twenty credits, who had exams in Middle English, who minored in Sociology and therefore continually confused the sociological style with more creative styles. She was sure that there was misunderstanding on both sides, but that once basic rapport was established the class would be able to get many valuable professional writing tips.

They felt that way too.

And I gave the next assignment: a memoir.

I had brought along an essay of Robert Warshow's —*An Old Man Gone*—and I asked if they would like to listen to a few passages. "It's an extraordinary work. It's truly"—on the verge of saying marvelous I said instead—"a model of the genre."

I read to them, *There is no doubt that he wanted more than he got. But how much more and more of what? . . . He concealed himself behind a screen of restless, purposeful industry which did indeed bear fruit; but the sum of his activity in its very clarity never seemed to answer to the great unclear, unspoken demand which hung upon him like some faintly disturbing bodily effusion. . . .*

I read to them also, *He asked everything and nothing; what he asked was never just what he wanted and he knew it, even if he did not know what he wanted. Money itself was almost too specific an object. . . . Perhaps his demands were at bottom so enormous that he did not dare to define them.*

They could see why this was a model of the genre and a very nice memoir. But they needed more explicit guidelines.

Guidelines and background.

Background and information.

I told them to open their notebooks.

Then I instructed them to double space; to maintain one-and-a-half-inch margins; to put their names and student identification numbers on the lower left or upper right of the title page; to number all subsequent pages; to use paper clips or, if stapling was preferred, to so place the staple as to allow for the easy turning of pages; to go over their papers once, and once again, for typos; to make their corrections neatly, using standard proofreader symbols which could be found in most any good dictionary.

Thanksgiving recess passed and Christmas recess and the twelve days of intersession, and then I found on my desk an unsealed number ten envelope. It held a badly hectographed letter which thanked me for my contribution to and services on behalf of the college and wished me all good fortune in my academic undertakings.

When I took the letter to my chairman he agreed that it had been, indeed, badly hectographed. "As for its contents," he said, "remember that the process of reappointment is . . . a process. For the academic community is . . . a community."

John Shaw Billings
and Henry Luce
editing photos.

Henry Luce

From the diaries of
John Shaw Billings,
the first Managing Editor
of Life.

Starts A Picture Magazine

Remembering John Shaw Billings

By JOSEPH KASTNER

The crisis that brought John Shaw Billings in as managing editor of *Life*—a move crucial to the huge success of the magazine—was apparent to all of us on the staff in those pre-publication days of 1936. But we were too busy with our own troubles to pay much attention to Henry Luce's. Trying to master the new art of photojournalism, we stumbled through stacks of photographs, hoping to find coherent stories in haphazard collections. All of us—Joseph Thorndike and David Cort from *Time,* myself from *Fortune,* Paul Peters from the theatre—were disciplined to write with the greatest economy of words. Now we were desperate with layouts that gave us forty words to tell a whole story and dozen-word captions to explain half a dozen pictures. Our confusion would be compounded when Luce would come around, blow through our pictures, throw off contradictory instructions and go off leaving chaos behind—but also, in his subliminal way, rubbing some of his ideas off on us.

Our work was made more uneasy by the conflicts between our two working bosses, John S. Martin and Daniel Longwell. Martin, a cousin of Briton Hadden, the co-founder of *Time,* had been with that magazine almost since its beginning. A worldly, sardonic man, he had lost one arm as a child and spent his life making up for it—he was a fine athlete (golf in the 80s) and a ladies' man. Longwell, a comparative newcomer to the organization, was effervescent and thin-skinned, completely committed to the new magazine. He had a genius for seeing good stories in the most obvious subjects and could spin off more ideas for us in ten minutes than we could think up in a week—or execute in a year. Martin had no respect for working hours; Longwell worked his head off.

There was excitement in all the uncertainty. No one knew whether or not we would really publish or even what we would call the magazine. *See, Pic, Showcase, Look* (later bestowed on Cowles) were among the hundreds of names proposed. *Dime* was Luce's original choice but he finally gave it up, in part because someone pointed out that if he ever wanted to change the price he would also have to change the name. The first pre-publication trial issue we put out was called, inelegantly, "This is a DUMMY." It was terrible. The second try, called *Rehearsal,* was so much better that Luce decided to go ahead and publish.

By that time, as these diaries tell, Luce had bought the old *Life,* the humor magazine, to get its title. And he had replaced Martin with *Time's* managing editor John Shaw Billings. Like us, Billings had trouble with Luce and photo-journalism. It was only after a few months that he really asserted himself as managing editor. Our jobs as writer-editors of the magazine departments, which made

Joseph Kastner, one of the original editorial associates on *Life,* became the magazine's Copy Editor.

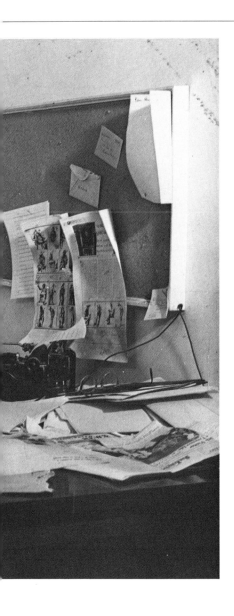

us responsible for thinking up, assigning and writing our stories, brought us into everyday contact or confrontation with Billings. We found him a formidable, unassailable boss, cold-eyed, laconic. His face was impassive, his manner remote, his decisions unchangeable and his efficiency awesome. He looked at every picture in the big sets we brought him, chose the ones he wanted after a couple of quick run-throughs, indicated how he wanted them laid out, edited every word we wrote, herded us mercilessly towards our daily deadlines and went home every night at 6:10.

When we handed in our copy, he would call us to his office, stand us beside his desk to watch as he moved his thick pencil over the carefully-wrought words, crossing out ours and substituting his in large blunt handwriting, counting length as he wrote so that the story would fit the assigned space. Under the pressure of space and Billings' pencil, *Life's* prose style became simple declarative. Articles and conjunctions were a luxury and punctuation consisted largely of periods. If there were a choice between a fine phrase or a plain fact, the phrase went. If it were a case of cropping a picture or cutting copy, the copy was cut. All this produced concise, muscular, superbly functional prose—though it did sometimes sound like "See Dick, See Jane." For the most part, Billings left the assigning of story subjects and photographers to others but by what he accepted and rejected, he governed the magazine's content and approach.

The cold way he rebuffed our disagreements with him, the cruel way he treated laggards on the staff, the impersonal relationships he imposed—all these kept us away from Billings. Then, as he gradually permitted it, we approached and warmed to him. When our work pleased him, he doled out measured praise. If he liked a story particularly, he would come by our office, copy in hand, poke his head in to say it was fine and carry it down to the typists himself. It was the ultimate flattery to have the managing editor act as your copy boy.

We came to see—as the magazine itself showed—what an extraordinary editor Billings was. He had a sharp feeling for photographs, a clean sense of design, a mind whose remarkable control disguised its subtlety. Luce gave *Life* its inspiration and direction. Billings, as the man in practical command, shaped its character—and the character of American photo-journalism. Luce more and more surrendered authority to Billings, in part because he could not cope with the intricate schedules that *Life's* ever-increasing circulation forced on us. When Billings was on vacation, Luce liked to come down and edit the issues himself. We would suffer as he grew unbearably frustrated by the fact that he had four or five different deadlines to meet in each issue, that he could not indulge his habit of tearing up stories he had already closed and start all over again, that a photograph was what it was and could not be changed by an editor's pencil. He would leave after a few weeks with his frustrations multiplied and the rest of us unnerved. Coming back to a shambles, Billings—with grumpy self-satisfaction—would quickly set everything straight and listen happily to Luce's complaints that he had created a monster.

He was, so far as he let us see, utterly loyal to Luce, vastly admiring Luce's journalistic perceptions, willingly following his lead. I took it for granted that Billings' personal feelings paralleled this professional respect. I am astonished to find the contrary in these diaries. In fact, I find many surprises. In years of working with Billings, I knew warmth beneath his dour exterior and true friendliness behind his distant manner. The diaries seem to show that it was even darker below the dourness and that the distance was set by distaste. Most surprising of all is the fact of the diaries themselves—not just that he kept them so laboriously and fully but that he placed no posthumous restrictions on their publication. Here at the end he has opened himself to the world verbatim.

It was hard to argue with Billings when he was alive but I find myself arguing with him now. Remembering his loyalty and his concern for me and others on the staff, I can't accept his self-portrait of an almost unmitigated misanthrope. This is, I realize, Billings letting others see him as he saw himself. Yet I wonder if what a man says is altogether believable just because he is talking to himself.

Billings with *Life* editor Daniel Longwell in the Chrysler Building, June 1937.

From the Billings diaries: the launching of Life

John Shaw Billings was born at Redcliffe Plantation, Beach Island, S.C. in 1898. Although he attended Harvard and made his career in the North, he retained a devotion to Redcliffe, eventually acquiring and restoring it. Billings was Managing Editor of Time *(1933-36), Managing Editor of* Life *(1936-44), and Editorial Director of Time, Inc. (1944-54). A compulsive diarist from boyhood, in 1973 Billings turned over to the Caroliniana Library at The University of South Carolina some 70 volumes of diaries and 200 scrapbooks, as well as thousands of pages of manuscript covering his career at Time, Inc. He died at Redcliffe in 1975. These excerpts from the Billings diaries chronicle the launching of* Life *during the period from February 1936 to November 1937.*

1936

Feb. 27
Thur
Luce took me to lunch at the Cloud Club with Ingersoll & Larsen in a private room. The subject up for discussion: starting a new picture magazine. Larsen was doubtful, wanted more pictures in TIME. I agreed to that but argued that such a supplement would not prevent others from starting a picture mag. Luce was all for a picture mag; he's got it in his blood. He seemed hard & cold and impersonal — & some of his remarks were cuttingly critical. I despise him in such moods when he seems contemptuous of me and my views . . . .

Feb. 28
Fri
Luce is completely absorbed in new magazine. He came prancing happily into my office and cried: "I'm pregnant" — i.e. with ideas on picture mag.

Mar. 6
Fri
Luce took me to lunch at the Cloud Club with Goldie, Thorndike & Longwell to talk about story ideas for the new picture magazine. (Luce liked Goldie's Blum cover story — but not his Jap assinations story). Various ideas were put up & discussed — but I notice that Luce never listens to what I have to say. Hence I say little. A mean dog who, I suppose, has no idea how much I dislike him personally . . . .

May 17
Sun
Luce came in, to salute, say "How's tricks" and walk out. Longwell, Martin and Ingersoll gave him hell for not doing more work on the new picture magazine — so now he is in working on Sunday . . . .

May 18
Mon
(I hear Luce worked from 9 to 6 on the new magazine, after being criticized for loafing on the job) . . . .

*"I hear the
new picture
magazine
upstairs is
fairly
churning."*

May 25
Mon
Luce came in, said he was sorry I was going away now because the picture magazine was just coming to a critical decision. He took me up to the Experimental Dept to show me sampler of Dummy No. 2. I had seen most of the material before — but was quite impressed with what they had been able to make out of it. The magazine I hope will be a picture record of our times . . . .

July 3
Fri
Luce held a full staff meeting in the library, to outline how Time writers would feed news ideas to the new picture magazine. I tried to sit in the back row but he called me up to the head table with him. All I wanted to hear him say was that work for the new mag. would not serve as an excuse for neglecting Time work — & he said it . . . .

July 24
Fri
I went to lunch with Luce at the Waldorf Grill. He was all full of talk about the new magazine for which they are now getting up a sample dummy. He pumped me dry of all the stories I have for my next issue. A pleasant meal — but of course coldly impersonal . . . .

July 30
Thur
I hear the new picture magazine upstairs is fairly churning. It is taking all of Luce's time and attention. It hampers me by cutting down the flow of news photos across my desk . . . .

Aug. 3
Mon
Luce came in with his text for the front cover of the Dummy — "Let's pretend this is a regular magazine and you are a regular reader" —a most disarming approach — . . . . Dummy copy going to Chicago on our teletype slowed up TIME considerably.

Aug. 8
Sat
I got my first look at the dummy of the new magazine. It was fair but not exciting — in fact not as good as I expected. Not enough big pictures, not enough original pictures. I also found the captions hard going. Others also thought it was lousy — and I hear Luce is in the dumps at the general critcism. Can't he take it? He is giving a big week-end party at his Greenwich estate on the subject of the dummy . . . .

Aug. 17
Mon
I went to lunch at the Cloud Club with Luce, Larsen, Ingersoll, Martin, Hodgins & Longwell on the new mag. Feeling like a rank outsider, I had little to say while Luce discussed editorial organization — and the necessity for getting in the best pictures. Time men are getting middle-aged and stuffy — and their talk has lost its snap &

bouyancy. I left early, to get back to the reality of *Time*. . . . I took the Jacobs color cover to Luce. It was very bad and he hit the ceiling. Well, it wasn't my fault. . . . Later I saw pictures of the Luces & their guests (mostly Timesters) at their Greenwich place on a Sunday party. They depressed me, for no special reason: I guess I hate to see other people have a good time while I have to work & make the money for them.

Sept. 14
Mon
Out to lunch with Luce at the Ritz. He was in an easy agreeable mood — wanted to talk about the new magazine and asked me nothing more than my off-hand opinions about titles & possible picture stories. It was pleasant & nice . . . .

Sept. 19
Sat
I am having a tough time getting pictures which are all being stolen & lost by the picture magazine boys. They are getting out their final dummy — & going through hell, I gather from a distance.

Oct. 9
Fri
TIME has brought *Life* to give its name to the new picture magazine. Luce was in to show me the ads to be used. I must have a big *Life* story in *Time* . . . .

Oct. 11
Sun
At office I rewrote the story of our purchase of LIFE for name of new picture magazine. (Farr did first draft). It turned out well — and I got compliments on it from all sides. (Perhaps I haven't lost my old writing touch after all) .

Oct. 12
Mon
Luce was carried away with the Life story — until he heard I had written it. That let him down because he had hoped it was new talent. (He evidently expected such work from me).

Oct. 23
Fri
At 5:00 Luce called me to his office, shut the door and proceeded to tell me that a great crisis had arisen on Life — a crisis due to Martin's behavior. Luce and Martin just don't pull together as a team, and as a result Life is still badly disorganized and nowhere near ready to go into publication. Martin, said Luce, had contributed little or nothing to the experimental issues, had been off on his own — and was just irresponsible. What precipitated the crisis was a Cloud Club lunch today at which Martin had appeared drunk & proceeded to criticize and abuse Luce before staff juniors. It must have been a bad scene. Now Luce wants to put Martin back on Time & make me Managing editor of Life. He thinks he & I could work well together, etc. I was

John Martin was replaced by Billings.

surprised and startled at this proposal. I know nothing of the philosophy of Life — and am devoted to Time which is clicking along well. I hate to think what Martin will do to the morale of my staff. Yet Life is a new job, with fresh excitement — & much harder work, I suppose. My answer to Luce: I was ready to do whatever Luce thought best for the organization. If he wanted me with him, I would come & do my level best. If there was to be a change, it should come at once . . . . Luce is leaving tonight for a week-end at his South Carolina place where he will think over his decision. He believes that if he puts Martin in as TIME M.E., Martin will soon bust himself out with liquor — and we will then have another crisis. . . . Hence, consideraby upset and unsettled in my mind. I am not picture-minded (Luce says Martin isn't either). Can I make a go of it? I told F. & Ma about my talk with Luce. The only feature of it that really interested them was whether my new hours would be longer or shorter. (I thought that was a narrow selfish view of a major change in my work). . . . I am sorry for Martin who for three years has been a high-paid ($33,000) super-numerary, whose career is being wrecked by liquor — who now may get another chance. I am sorrier still for my staff at whom he will bark and curse and mistreat and bully. But the decision is Luce's: to wreck TIME to launch LIFE.

Oct. 24
Sat
To the office, still disturbed in mind about the shift Luce has in mind.

Billings wrote the caption for this photo in his scrapbook: "The Managing Editor is fussing with a Newsfront spread of a Friday afternoon when Luce comes to help for half an hour. . . ."

I talked to Longwell about it. He is in Luce's confidence — and says conditions on Life at this point are desperate, that someone must take hold of them and organize them. We are right under the guns — and must get going. . . . I went to lunch with Larsen at the Cloud Club to discuss the Martin matter. Larsen takes a hard-boiled, non-sentimental attitude toward Martin whom he considers impossible to work with. He says Martin must rule or ruin. Martin is evidently drinking as hard as ever . . . — all pretty disgusting! Larsen is for busting him clean out of Time. Larsen said his job and mine was to keep Luce's backbone stiff in dealing with Martin. (I always have thought Luce was half-afraid of Martin) . . . . Back to work as usual. Great changes are in prospect but my routine does not show it. Picking pictures — copy — home for dinner and back to work. Maybe this is the last issue of TIME I will edit. I really hate to leave my present job, because I have it running smoothly and know it thoroughly. . . .

Oct. 26
Mon

Luce got back from South Carolina at 12:15 — & called me in at 12:30. Yes, he had decided on the shift from TIME to LIFE for me. He would talk to Martin late in the day and let me know officially after that. I registered a complaint about Martin's name in editorial box as M.E., declaring he took all the credit. Luce said Martin made him appear as the fourth assistant editor outside the office. . . . Back to work, my head in a not altogether happy whirl. Work — work — and waiting for Luce to phone me the official news so I could tell the staff. . . . Finally he came in at 7 — and said everything was off until tomorrow. He had talked to Martin who had put up a great plea for a second chance on LIFE, promising to cooperate etc. Luce had evidently got cold feet. He did not want to bring up Martin's drinking as one of the real reasons for the shift. Hence he told Martin he'd let him know tomorrow — & he would then let me know. . . . I felt let down & flat, because Luce failed to carry through. Now I can't tell anyone about the shift until after it occurs.

Oct. 27
Tue

At 4 p.m. Luce telephoned: "It's done. It was brief and painful. It made me sick." That meant that he had seen Martin, had ordered him back to TIME as M.E. — and had ordered me to LIFE as M.E. A blow to Martin who has boasted widely about the picture magazine he was putting out and who will lose face with all his friends. It also means a great change & upheaval in my life — with something new for something old.

Oct. 28
Wed

Because I am far behind on what LIFE is doing (and because LIFE itself is also far behind), I went to the office at 10 a.m. — and straight in to spend an hour with Luce. He made a speech to me on LIFE's principles and purposes, explained the departments, etc. My job is to pick up

LIFE

Vol. 1, No. 1

Nov. 23, 1936

REG. U. S. PAT. OFF.

his ideas as quickly as possible — & carry them out, without too much criticism. (I think Luce is damned smart — & I have little or no criticism of his ideas) . . . . Longwell is ill with grippe — a sad circum-since because he is to initiate me into the LIFE personnel and machine. Back to my old office (I hate to swap it for Martin's smaller one), looking over layouts and captions, to get acquainted with material in the works. Luce & I went to lunch at the Ritz where he continued to explain and expound (he talked in such a low voice I had to strain to hear him.) This last for an hour & a half. Back to Chrysler Bldg. I was assigned a gas mask story for the first issue and went to work on it in Longwell's empty office. There was nobody around to do a thing — and I had a horrible sense of disorganization. In two weeks we start to press & everything is now chaos: no office space, no worthwhile help, no system.

Oct. 29
Thur
To the office and officially moving into Martin's 51st floor office — with Miss Bradley just outside. I collected the gas mask material — and got Raveren to start laying it out for me. Tons of stuff were dumped on me. Martin came in, friendly & nice. Later we ate a sandwich lunch together in my office while he went over stories & ideas he had been working on and is now transferring to me. . . . I had to see map-makers, see this or that thing, discuss the art schedule with Eggleston, go over the dummy & press schedule with Harry Luce & his brother Sheldon . . . Luce detailed stories on hand, Cort brought me the Curry captions to edit (I never did get around to it). . . . Miss Albertson was tied up with a printer's test run of 16 pages, hence was of no help to me in learning my way around. Everything was rush & confusion — & nothing was really accomplished. Longwell is still home sick — which puts a crimp in everything. I don't even know where to order pictures. . . .

Oct. 30
Fri
On TIME I used to sit still and everything came to me at my order. On LIFE I must run around at a great rate to get anything I want. . . . Longwell is still ill — damn him! I read & edited some captions, a slow job until you get the swing of it. Looking at this layout & that — and probably making very little sense amid such complete disorganization. Poor Miss Albertson is just swamped! Luce & I went to lunch at the Biltmore where he talked of his LIFE ideas. . . . Approving the gas mask layout & turning it over to Murphy of Fortune to write the captions over the weekend. Going over a La Guardia layout with Kastner, and a Florida girlies layout with Furth. . . . Copy read — sense of rush. Home at 7. After dinner I edited "Overweather," "Chinatown School" & "Paintings by Rembrandt". . . .

Oct 31
Sat
To lunch with Luce at the Cloud Club, in a private room. He had a

batch of story lists, which he read off, elaborating his ideas on the development of each story. We adjourned to his office at 3 where he divided up future stories with me. (He took two for every one he assigned to me.) A good NBC story fell in his lap — & he was very excited about it. Later I took in some final captions for him to read. He liked Curry & the Chinatown School but ordered "Overweather" rewritten. He himself took over the Helen Hayes piece to rework. . . . An hour clearing my desk. All other LIFErs away for the last week-end before the grind begins. (Ingersoll, Luce said, was off doping out a picture magazine which can be put out in three days.) . . .

Nov. 2
Mon
My life on LIFE is now too full for more than notes here. Hence just notes: Office. So many people in and out of my office that I could not settle down to real work. Longwell back after his cold. Also a new art director named Richmond, from Macy's. A very nice fellow and capable. Luce gave a Cloud Club lunch to talk problems — & jumped on Longwell for butting in with his ideas. Layouts & captions. I'll go crazy trying to do them.

Nov. 3
Tue
Luce & I talked over movies, getting nowhere. Also an art meeting with Luce, but no decisions. Lunch alone. Layout is getting to be good fun. Captions are the devil — and Luce makes me do them over.

Nov. 4
Wed
All morning I worked on captions for the gas mask story. Cloud Club lunch with Luce, Kastner & Breasted, an old guy who is going to dig up science stories for us. The gas mask story to Luce. It didn't come out — that worried me. What was wrong? Running around on make-ups. Starting things but never getting time to finish them. I can't remember all I did but I was steadily busy. Layouts & talks with Luce. He is being very nice and treats me well. . . . Home at 6:30. After dinner I looked over miscellaneous pictures — & worked on Hitler Art.

Nov. 5
Thur
Still no gas mask story out of Luce's office. He talked over Vol. 1, No. 1 with me, assigned me certain jobs to take care of. We lack a good opening story — a smash! And then Bourke-White's pictures of Whoopee at Fort Peck came in, as if in answer to our prayer. Now the first issue is all set! This story went to Ingersoll & MacLeish to work out & I had nothing to do with it. This & that. I have charge of art & color, with Eggleston. Lunch at the Cloud Club with Martin, Longwell and Grantland Rice. Martin thinks Rice can help us on pictures. I doubt it. Luce went over the gas mask story with me, explained where my captions were wrong. I worked like mad rewriting them. They went off to the printer at 6:45. They won't be in the first issue, though.

The cover and (opposite) the table of contents of the first issue.

Nov. 6
Fri

Copy to read. Loose ends to clean up. I got pretty sore because all the writers were out somewhere; I couldn't get them for chores. People in & out — I have a whole new staff to learn. Luce picked Life's first cover in the library: Fort Peck Dam. At Luce's request I dashed off some ideas for the "Introduction". (He used a good many of them later) .

Nov. 7
Sat

Office work is getting to be a routine. I am called into Luce's office half a dozen times a day on this or that job. He makes all the decisions — & I must carry all questions to him. Also layout sessions with Richmond in layout room. Lunched with Luce & Longwell at the Cloud Club to discuss back-of-book ideas. We are set on Vol. 1, No. 1 — but are short of stuff thereafter. . . . Longwell is a nice fellow and easy to work with. All p.m. on this & that. We got a "party" — a French hunting party with the Comte de Fels. Luce turned it over to me to handle — which means I'll do it myself. Home at 7 for dinner. Back to the office at 8:30 for two hours. It was time wasted because I had nothing to do but watch Luce & Cort mull over foreign pictures.

Nov. 8
Sun

Working with Luce on "Beautiful Robert Taylor." A session on type for LIFE. Neither Luce nor I know anything about it, really. No great drive. I thumbed through some U.S. pictures. Lunch alone at the Grand Central. This & that. Fitting text to a 100% measure is a tiresome bore. . . . The editorial box was made up by Luce and he used my suggestion: "Editors: Luce, Billings, Longwell." Ingersoll was in & out with ideas — a great kibitzer, but he has no vote.

Nov. 9
Mon

This is our last week to get out the first issue. Office. Up to see Van Doren at Pan-American to get a release on the Gooney Golf pictures. Working on the French shooting party. Lunch at the Cloud Club with Luce and Longwell to discuss Vol. 1, No. 2. Our big problem is to get future feature material banked up. At 3 I dash over to the Modern Museum to meet Eggleston and pick out samples of surrealist paintings we are going to use in full color later. It was a breathless selection and I was back inside an hour. We began to make up the dummy on No. 1. To see Luce with it — and Larsen & others came in to look it over. Everybody had a different idea. Soon Luce was pulling it all apart.

Nov. 10
Tue

Rush! Rush! The first forms of the first issue must go off today. All morning I wrote the copy to go with the French hunting party. Took it to Luce. O.K.! Lunch alone. The first two forms got safely off on the 20th Century. LIFE on the American Newsfront and the President's

Album with Thorndike. Pretty poor material to work with. I complained to Longwell. Home at 7. F in dumps. I knew something worried her but she wouldn't tell me at first. At 10 she cut loose and gave me hell for giving all my time and interest to LIFE and not to her. She felt very bad about it — talked wildly of divorce, etc, etc. But there was no quarrel because I just listened and agreed with her. She'll feel better now this is out of her system.

Nov. 11
Wed
An easy day for copy going out. I jumped Gurney Williams (from the old LIFE) hard for his poor writing on art. Luce deep in thought on the introduction. Lunch with him on Vol. 1, No. 2. He gets all the ideas, makes all the decisions. I have contributed practically no original ideas to the magazine so far. . . . Working with Thorndike on Rembrandt (movie for second issue) , Prex & News. These latter are my special departments — Luce doing foreign stuff. . . . I made some layouts but Luce went into a brown study and remade them completely. I don't know how to do it to satisfy him. It is pretty discouraging. Luce doping out the dummy — trying to get "unity and flow."

Nov. 12
Thur
President's Album was no good the way Luce did it last night. We got Richmond in to do it over — and he turned out a nice job in short order. A great rush of copy to make the train. Thorndike had much to write and I kept pressing him hard for copy. Even then he wasn't done in time. . . . I went back to the office for an hour and a half, to edit Thorndike's Prex. Album copy. Luce was there, too. Home at 11.

Nov. 13
Fri
Not much to do. As Luce says, you can't make any forward passes the last quarter, on this magazine. I got the Newsfront pages laid out and approved. A spontaneous and informal lunch with Martin & Luce in the basement Schraffts. Copy. With Luce I went over ideas for Vol. 1, No. 2. We are still shy on serious feature material. There is so much discussion with Luce, so much philosophizing, before anything is done. . . . Took Luce to his River House apartment, and on home, late for dinner. . . .

Nov. 14
Sat
All done but three news pages. Then went through & Thorndike wrote the text. I worked over Williams captions on Muirhead Bone — and next week's stuff: party (American Petroleum Institute,) Speaking of Pictures (Brain Operation) . I was through by 5. Vol. 1, No. 1 is now behind us — and we get tomorrow off.

Nov. 16
Mon
Luce in dumps when he saw mistakes in the proofs. I worked on

*"Vol. I, No. I was
a sellout yesterday —
...What worries
me is the stuff for
next week."*

"Tiger! Tiger!" and Brain Operation. A Cloud Club lunch with Luce & Eggleston to discuss color. We must keep four weeks ahead on this. Writing & editing. Luce was in a bad humor — as if issue No. 1 had gone sour on the presses. He passed back-of-book filler to me. . . . Longwell is in disgrace because he was late getting in this morning. . . . Luce seemed so down & out when I left him that I decided to volunteer to go back to the office and help him out tonight. I called two or three times but got no answer.

Nov. 17
Tue
Ingersoll told me that he & Luce had been up until 3 a.m. battling with Ross over a profile about Luce to run in the New Yorker. It was a malicious insulting piece & Luce had tried to get the facts straight. There was much drinking and bad temper. Luce didn't get in until about 11, looking red-eyed and bum. Realizing that he was useless he went home to sleep it off, returned about 4 in better shape. . . . The first complete issues of LIFE were in — & they looked pretty good to me. Congratulations & cheer began to roll in and we all felt pretty good. But one issue doesn't make a magazine. I rewrote the brain operation text running under "Speaking of Pictures." Eggleston was in on color problems: we have to keep so far ahead on that stuff. We got a day's grace on the schedule which meant we don't have to send the first off until tomorrow. Home at 6:30, with copies of LIFE. Ma & F. fairly devoured it after dinner. I did a little editing.

Nov. 18
Wed
Luce changing signals on the back-of-the-book. He seems to throw my stories to put in his. I was assigned West Point — & put Peters to work on it. Luce asked me again to write notes for the Introduction. I did — and to my surprise he used most of it as the Introduction itself. — With Thorndike I mulled over Newsfront pictures. Harry brought Mrs. Luce II in to say how much she liked the first issue. (She looked washed out and unpretty — perhaps the result of hard work on her play). I went over Science material with Breasted — all pretty barren and he is a fluttery agitated hulk whom I dislike.

Nov. 19
Thur
At 9:30 I stopped by Pix on Park Ave. to see what Eisenstaedt had got on the embarkation of Roosevelt on the Indianapolis at Charleston for South America. That is our lead story for the second issue. To office. Working on Peter's West Point story and driving Thorndike to get newsfront done. Lunch with Luce and Longwell at the Biltmore: we had a huge private dining room. Under discussion was material for Issue No. 3. With Luce later we did a layout on the Indianapolis lead story. He always has his ideas on playing a story — and uses them. . . . I had to go back to the office for three hours. Luce was there. Together we pondered various stories in the issue — and then he changed signals again, kicking out some, putting in others. I got the A.F. of L. layout

through. Home at 11.

Nov. 20
Fri
Luce was late coming in which slowed down the whole works because he has to approve layouts made overnight. I got his O.K. on some things — & started Wood to work on the Yukon Expedition. What worries me most is the lack of good future material — lots of it. By a fluke I took Luce & Norris to lunch at the Cloud Club which gave Norris a chance to tell Luce that he wanted to quit Martin & come up on Life. Luce said he would ponder the matter. . . . Editing copy, etc. Home for dinner. F. came back to the office with me for an hour. I had to edit Thorndike's lead story captions. Longwell was also on deck.

Nov. 21
Sat
Vol. 1, No. 1 was a sellout yesterday — but even so Luce was nervous & fidgety as [to] the public reaction to his magazine. He rewrote some text I had passed (his heel joggling frantically under the desk). He looked at two skimpy pages of Newsfront, said: "I don't like this." His gloom increased as he saw some of the first blat letters to come in. About 5 he left me to wind up the issue & went on home. We waited to see if we could get a good Harvard-Yale football picture but none came in — so we did not make over. Home at 7. So sleepy I couldn't even read. Early to bed. What worries me is stuff for next week.

Billings cuts *Life's* first birthday cake. Joseph J. Thorndike, at right, became Managing Editor in 1946.

Poets Revisited

By HILARY MILLS

For more than twenty years Rollie McKenna has photographed—and rephotographed—several hundred modern poets, building a cultural portrait gallery which is becoming increasingly known for both its documentary value and human interest. Few photographers have had Mrs. McKenna's success in capturing such intensely internalized people, for few own her uniquely "non-directive" approach: "I like to picture people as *people,* not merely as subjects for my camera. It's the individual's personality that should come through, not the photographer's preconception."

Her study of poets began in 1950 when the then-director of the New York YMHA Poetry Center, John Malcolm Brinnin, asked her to photograph several guest poets. Mrs. McKenna was thirty at the time and photographing Italian Renaissance architecture. "I was apprehensive," she recalls. "Architectural photography has its hazards, but photograph-

ing poets is demanding in a different way. One has to be more intuitive, more mobile."

When Brinnin decided to do a comprehensive anthology, *Modern Poets* (New York: McGraw-Hill,

Rollie McKenna

1963), Mrs. McKenna took the photographs. "She had an immediate, human rapport with her sitters," Brinnin remembers. "She works fast, but waits for the right moment to descend. She doesn't do Cinema Verité-type photography, and her sitters tend to trust her instincts."

In 1952 *Mademoiselle* sent Mrs. McKenna to Wales to do a study of Dylan Thomas. One of her most affecting bodies of work, an acutely moving chronicle of the poet's life, the study later evolved into both a book and a movie.

In 1973 McGraw-Hill issued an updated version of the *Modern Poets* anthology, for which Mrs. McKenna rephotographed many of the poets. In some cases the contrast was startling to the photographer; in others, time seemed to have had little effect. The following paired photographs speak for themselves—or, rather, Rollie McKenna's lens lets each poet speak *of* himself.

W. H. Auden

Stravinsky once said of W. H. Auden's face, "Some day we'll have to roll it out and see who it is." The visual change here is startling: from the classically arrogant, unkempt stance of 1952 (at left), to the devastatingly complex landscapes of the face in 1969. At the second session Rollie McKenna felt she was "looking at a suffering person."

Robert Graves

An impersonal shooting of Robert Graves in the YMHA dressing room in 1961. Far right: Graves suffering from an illness at his house in Majorca eight years later. Rollie McKenna was told by a friend to bring a special non-manufactured present to ensure a good reception. She presented a small Indian bead to the ailing poet, and his face immediately brightened into a smile.

Richard Eberhardt

Richard Eberhardt in 1951, while he was teaching in Cambridge (below) a genial, tweedy, pipe-smoking man. Rollie McKenna refers to him as "the Santa Claus of poetry." Left: Photographing him 18 years later at his Undercliff colony in Maine, McKenna found Eberhardt essentially unchanged.

John Hollander

Left: John Hollander at 32, photographed in James Merrill's Stonington, Connecticut home. Hollander was teaching at Yale during this period and had just been awarded the Yale Younger Poet Prize. Mrs. McKenna was able to rephotograph him in the same location in 1969, eight years later. This was a few years before the poet became a Senior Fellow for The National Endowment for the Humanities, and his stance was more casual and relaxed.

Robert Lowell

The classic image of the young aristocratic New England poet (below), captured in Florence, Italy in 1950. Right: As Robert Lowell reached a certain stature 18 years later, his hair style and dress became less conventional, demarking a change in his work from high formality to a more open expression.

Alan Dugan

Alan Dugan in 1962 in the relaxed, personal atmosphere of Rollie Mc-Kenna's Stonington, Conn. home. Below: Five years later at The International Conference of Poets in Stonybrook, Long Island. Dugan was having problems at the time and broke down on the speaking platform.

W. S. Merwin

Below and right: Both pictures were taken in New York, eight years apart. Rollie McKenna finds W. S. Merwin a consistently comfortable and handsome sitter, shucking off rigid formality in his life much as he does in his verse.

C. Day Lewis

C. Day Lewis at his businessman's desk in his London publisher's office in 1950 (below). Rollie McKenna found him a reserved, remote man. Left: The same setting 19 years later, not long before his death. Despite the ongoing conventionality of his lifestyle, McKenna found him much more relaxed and personable at this sitting.

Elizabeth Bishop

At Lauren MacIver's studio in New York in 1955 (right). Elizabeth Bishop, who is often self-conscious about her looks, usually won't sit for photographers. Rollie McKenna has found this generally true of all female poets. Above, at her home in Brazil in 1961. McKenna found her much more relaxed in this setting, a place Bishop would go to find peace.

51

John Berryman

John Berryman at 38 in Rollie McKenna's New York studio. Full of life, he roguishly chased the photographer around the room. Lower left: The poet at 55 in a Minneapolis hospital for treatment of alcoholism and a neck injury. McKenna felt a new gravity in his demeanor, as if the "fire had dwindled." Berryman committed suicide in 1972.

Anne Sexton

Anne Sexton in her Boston home in 1961 (below). Rollie McKenna remembers her quippy humor and vitality. Right: Seven years later in John Brinnin's Massachusetts house. Both Brinnin and McKenna found her vibrant and more alive to things beyond herself, although her *Death Notebooks* were at the same time defining the raw material of misery. Her breakdown occurred two years later.

Exactly at 11:00 a.m. on an October morning, another day at Sotheby's began. In contrast to the usual British casualness about business time schedules, just before the hour specified on the catalogue, Lord John Kerr entered the sales room in New Bond Street. Decisive, brisk movements brought him to the rostrum. He recited a few words of preamble about this sale of books formerly in the library of William Beckford. And, with an amiable but no-nonsense air, the first item in the day's sale was presented. "I'll have to ask twenty pounds to open the bidding." A director of Sotheby's and head of the Book Department, Lord John started one more day of a sale at Sotheby's.

* * *

In 1744, a bookseller, Samuel Baker, founded this establishment for the primary purpose of selling his own and other people's books through a series of auctions. The idea quickly caught on, and the business prospered. By 1767, Baker took on George Leigh as partner, and when Baker died in 1778, Leigh was joined by the founder's nephew, John Sotheby. Over the years, Sotheby's has grown and gained a wide reputation. To the librarian or bibliophile, the name Sotheby's is synonymous with books. Yet Sotheby's auctions today cover the full range of collecting fields. Art is represented by paintings, drawings, prints, and sculpture. Metalware, jewelry, glass, carpets, and furniture are among the antique items prepared for sales. Special events are created by the auctioning of a cellar of vintage wines, the "motorama" of antique cars, or something as unique as the drawings, letters, music, production -sketches and costumes for Diaghilev's Ballet Russe.

Today such a range of objects cannot be handled under one roof in London alone. The already diversified New Bond Street building can no longer house all of Sotheby's activities. There is now a Belgravia Sotheby's to conduct sales specializing in Victorian paintings, drawings, prints, ceramics, furniture, silver, and early photographs. And in Chancery Lane, amid the savor of Fleet Street and London's Inns of Court, there is a second room for the disposal of books.

Although London is its home and headquarters, Sotheby's has now branched out into the Continent, South Africa, and Australia and crossed the Atlantic. 1964 was an important year for the firm, when it purchased the New York business of the Parke-Bernet Galleries. Today, under the tri-name of Sotheby-Parke-Bernet, its rooms are in Rio de Janeiro, Toronto, and California. Yet, although Sotheby's is represented in the United States, American bookmen journey to London to attend the book sales in the New Bond Street room they have grown to know over the years.

Sotheby's first saw a portion of the Beckford library when he decided to clear part of his collection in 1808. At his death, Beckford's material effects went to Hamilton Palace, and the remaining part of his library was later auctioned by Sotheby's during 1882-1883. Lord Rosebery patiently put together what books he could obtain from these former sales. One portion of Lord Rosebery's Beckfords saw the Sotheby's sales room in 1933, but the last substantial allotment from the original library has been reserved for this two-day sale of 517 lots.

After the descriptions of the books have been digested from the catalogue, the London collector then has the opportunity to associate himself directly with them. For two days prior to each sale, the books are displayed at Sotheby's for inspection. The basic descriptive details for an item may not be impressive, whereas actual sight of it will prove the book's rightful significance. No amount of catalogue space can ever supplant the physical reality of the books themselves. Their true worth can only be ascertained by examination.

To the uninitiated, the inner sanctum of Sotheby's Hall of Prints, Books and Manuscripts is but a single,

By DONALD WEEKS

"It's Yours, Sir"

A Day At Sotheby's

Lord John Kerr, Head of the Book Department, in the rostrum at Sotheby's.

The St. George Street
entrance to Sotheby's
as sketched by Donald Weeks.

unpretentious room. For the purpose of the auctioneer's nomenclature, the room is divided into four
portions: "at the table," "to my left," "to my right,"
and "at the back of the room." Behind the auctioneer
there is a wall of shelves on which rest the books to
be auctioned that day. In front of this wall stands the
auctioneer at his rostrum. To his right sits the recording clerk. Jutting out before and just below him is
a U-shaped table. Around this sit the privileged few,
the men who have combined their own names with
the books they have handled over the years during
which they have been in the trade. Winifred Myers,
dealer in manuscripts, has the place of honor, sitting
closest to the auctioneer. The other names circling the
table ring in association with books going to collectors
and libraries throughout the world: Thorp, Weinreb,
Quaritch, Peter Murray Hill, Pickering & Chatto,

Sotheran, Francis Edwards, Stanley Crowe, Traylen,
Dawson, Heywood Hill, Alan Thomas, Sawyer, Dawson, Maggs, Blackwell, Parker, and Charles Rare
Books. (For a sale of modern books, the list of dealers
is augmented by Rota and George Sims.) To one side
of this table is a row of chairs against a wall. Another
row is opposite, in front of several large windows. On
these chairs sit the "American cousins" and less-
renowned English dealers, together with dealers from
the Continent. Whoever else attends a book auction
sits "at the back of the room"—although there are some
S. R. O. days. Such were the two days of the sale of the
Lord Rosebery/William Beckford books.

* * *

"I'll have to ask twenty pounds to open the bidding."
The auctioneer had begun the day. Lot 1 was up for
sale—a book of travel, history and politics, printed in
France in 1665. A voice from the floor opened the
bidding at £20—a voice which sounded like the first
soft audible breath in the morning. A second—
or longer?—went by. Then: "Twenty-two." From
"Twenty-five" to "Twenty-eight," the sounds of these
figures were breaking the inertia of the audience watching a salesclerk walk within the inner confines of the
table, displaying the book to be sold. A chain reaction
was beginning to set in, and bids soon rose to the last
figure for this item: £85.

The second lot—an Italian book printed in 1780—
again opened for £20. Slowly it reached the selling
price of £70. The first two lots combined sold for
£35 over their estimated value. When a collection
of books is being considered for a sale, Sotheby's
appraises the value of each item. They then publish a
list of these estimated prices. In most cases these appear
in two figures as "£60/80"—meaning that Sotheby's
places a value of at least £60 on the item, which could
also be sold as high as £80. Usually, these estimated
prices are accurate and can be assumed to approximate
the selling prices. The estimates are particularly helpful in the dealings between a bookman and a customer
before a sale, each then having an idea of the value of
some wanted book.

The first prize lot of the day was *Antiquities of the
Russian State,* printed in several volumes in Moscow
at the expense of the Emperor of Russia between 1849
and 1853. It went to Weinreb, perhaps the leading
London dealer in rare illustrated books and prints.
The volumes are lavishly illustrated with 515 litho-
graphic plates. (Although exceedingly rare items,
printed for presentation purposes only, the books did
not belong to Beckford. They were with his library at

the Hamilton Palace sale and later acquired by Rosebery.) Sotheby's estimated price on this lot was £1,500 and Weinreb secured it for an additional £100.

In his library, and in his own binding, Beckford had copies of his novel, *The History of the Caliph Vathek*. It originally appeared both in English (in London) and in French versions (in Lausanne) in 1786. One was included in this sale as lot 11. This was the first English edition of the French text, printed in 1815. Sotheby's had appraised it at £30. The opening bid was £10. Then £12, £14 . . . £60, £65. *Vathek* in any early edition is highly sought after, and the bidding for this exceptional copy came from all quarters, especially from Francis Edwards, Traylen, Pickering & Chatto, Thorp, and Maggs. The £65 bid brought the sound of the hammer and the auctioneer's words: "It's yours, sir." Maggs was the winner of this book for £35 over the pre-sale estimated price.

There is one question in the mind of a novice viewer at Sotheby's. Sitting "at the back of the room," this person can only see the backs of heads in front of him, some profiles "at the table," the auctioneer and the clerk who exhibits each lot at the time of its bidding. But what of the bidding? How is it done? The backs of heads tell this tyro little, if anything. Yet, through all this precious time, the auctioneer's head is quickly moving, his eyes adjusting and meeting some sign for a bid made only to him. A newcomer to the Book Sales Room may well be puzzled at the swiftness with which business is conducted, especially when he himself has no idea who the bidders for a particular lot may be. Of course, it is not really a question of "Who?" but rather "How do they do it?"

The dealers gathering at Sotheby's are individuals, each having mannerisms to set him apart from his fellow bookmen; these mannerisms spill over into the act and art of bidding. The styles of bidding are therefore quite individual. Lew David Feldman, from The House of El Dieff of New York, uses a simple method. When he wishes to bid, he merely raises his eyebrows. (He did miss a bid one day. Wearing glasses, he rests them on his forehead during a sale. On this one day, evidently with too much eyebrow raising, his glasses

fell down into their ordinary position. He was startled but recovered himself in time to bid on.) A finger held to one side of the forehead in salute fashion is another signal. An upraised pencil tells the auctioneer one dealer is bidding. Another dealer has his felt hat on the table before him. When his hand touches it, he is bidding. A pair of glasses taken away from the head of one dealer indicates a bid from him. A casual wave of a catalogue is the sign with which Stanley Crowe catches the eye of the auctioneer. Among others, there are two clear ways of bidding. An oral figure can be given by anyone. And, in contrast to the whims of his co-bookmen, Bryan Maggs merely raises his hand to sanction his bid. These, then, are the signals, the flares from the floor, to be sighted by and interpreted by the auctioneer.

A dealer has to know not only the value of the book but how it can be related to his business. Of course, there is the dealer who bluffs. There is the dealer who hopes. But, far more often, there is the dealer who knows. During the second day of the Beckford Library sale, Bryan Maggs was using his knowledge. When he first saw the catalogue, lot 293 struck him: *Ceremonies et Coutumes Religieuses de tous les Peuples de Monde,* an enormous work in several volumes compiled and written by Bernard Picart and printed in Amsterdam, 1723-1736. (On the title pages of this edition in French, the author's name is spelled "Picard," changed to "Picart" in the Englished edition beginning a year later.) The book is a monument in the descriptions of ancient and "modern" superstitions. (The third volume is on the Americans.) Handsomely engraved illustrations abound through the volumes, from full-page size to "pull-outs." Grand in appearance, its esoteric information is of enormous value. A scarce item anywhere, here was a set with Beckford's own annotations.

Bryan Maggs had to compass several fields to decide the value of *Ceremonies*. Totally apart from everything else, what was the book alone worth? What was its worth to have as stock? Once in stock, would there be a customer for it, and what price would that person care to pay for it? Of course, Bryan Maggs may already have been approached by a customer. If so, he had to set a value on the book to tell his customer. A book dealer can be friendlier than the family doctor or lawyer, but, like them, he has certain professional ethics to maintain. Whatever reason he may have for bidding on a book—for his own stock or for a specified customer—that reason is secret.

Bryan Maggs had read the lot's description in the

WILLIAM
BECKFORD
AND
FONTHILL
ABBEY

The Great Western Hall of Fonthill Abbey.

William Beckford (1760-1844) was styled "The Caliph of Fonthill" by linking his novel, *Vathek*, with Fonthill Abbey, the most elaborate monument of a house ever built for one person in England. The City of London's Guildhall is graced by only two statues in its huge banqueting hall. From opposite walls, Sir Winston Churchill's features look across at the senior William Beckford's, who was twice Lord Mayor of the City. Cocoa and coffee had just been introduced into England, which created a need for sugar. This newly acquired taste for the sugar of Jamaica brought to the Beckford family means to reign high in society. In 1770, the elder Beckford died, leaving young William at ten half-orphaned and a millionaire. And, as "England's wealthiest son," William Beckford maintained his individual tastes throughout a long life.

A precocious youth who had been tutored by Mozart,

at twenty Beckford wrote his *Biographical Memoirs of Extraordinary Painters*. Appearing in 1786, *Vathek* was a Gothic novel of the highest order and influenced all such tales thereafter, including *Frankenstein*. As widely published as *Vathek* has been, Beckford's eccentricity overshadows his literary activity. His master dream was the building of Fonthill Abbey. A few miles from Bath, the Abbey's every book and picture were gems. Its gardens were unrivaled by any in England. A recluse by this time, Beckford surrounded his "palace of art" by a formidable wall, twelve feet high and seven miles in circuit. But, recluse as he had become, Beckford was also a patron, and the greatest artist of the day, J. M. W. Turner, was a one-time guest, whose talent brought forth the towering magnificence of the Abbey in a series of paintings.

Beckford traveled throughout Europe with a retinue

Fonthill Abbey, southwest view.

of servants, musicians, and companions. These travels are detailed in his *Dreams, Waking Thoughts, and Incidents; Italy With Sketches of Spain and Portugal;* and *Italy, Spain, and Portugal, With an Excursion to the Monasteries of Alcobaca and Batalha.* In Geneva, he bought Edward Gibbon's enormous library, intending to read each volume. He was an avid but discerning collector of books and paintings, the latter of which now form part of the national art heritage in Britain's galleries. London was the capital for books, and he would order through his "agents" there, sending one a note at times such as: "I shall wait patiently as I can for the Sotheby Cat."

But Beckford was no mere acquirer of books. He read each one in his vast library, as his annotations attest. (His notes at the end of the three-volume *Frankenstein* read: "This is, perhaps, the foulest Toadstool that

has yet sprung up from the reeking dunghill of the present times.") Not only were the books lovingly handled for reading, but almost all were bound in leather and gilt-tooled to his personal designs.

Beckford's life spanned a quickly changing world. He was in France during its Revolution. And he lived in England from the first glimmer of the Industrial Revolution until the time of his last friend, the then rising young novelist, Benjamin Disraeli, who later was to shape Britian's empire.

Over the years, three major collections have been made of the books once belonging to Beckford. Two Americans individually sought out books from Fonthill: James T. Babb and Ray Livingston Murphy, whose "gatherings" are now at Yale University. The third collection was brought together by Lord Rosebery, a British prime minister.

catalogue and had viewed the volumes prior to the sale. Sotheby's pre-sale valuation for lot 293 had been £200/250. And, immediately after lot 292 had been sold, the echo of the hammer had hardly faded away before the auctioneer spoke: "I am bid two hundred pounds for this lot." The bids raced around the room —£250, £300, £350, £400, £450, £500. Dealers in sumptuous editions, books both rare and beautiful, competed for this lot. Francis Edwards, Quaritch, and Weinreb kept pace with Bryan Maggs' bids. In the crowded room, in the tense air of competition, it was impossible to know who was offering each bid for this prized work. Bryan Maggs was seated "at the back of the room," his left arm held firmly in the air. There was no confusion of several dealers bidding at once. But there was no time lost between one bid and the next. The auctioneer's head was almost immobile, yet his eyes flashed and darted across the table below him, to the left, to the right, to "the back of the room." The lower figure of Sotheby's estimated price was the opening bid. And already, within seconds, the bids had more than doubled that figure. This was the point where Bryan Maggs' knowledge had to balance itself against the fever in the room at that moment. Even at a sale where all the books can be special, there has to be tension when the bids race away, outstripping the suggested prices — £550, £600, £650, £700, £750. Only Maggs, Weinreb, and Edwards stayed. Each second saw a renewed movement to boost the price—£800, £850, £900, £950. Bryan Maggs was still bidding, but there was keen competition. There was hardly a sound above the slight rustle of a sleeve around an upraised arm in a bid. £1,000. Weinreb raised the bid to £1,300, an action prompting Bryan Maggs to spring up, his arm waving in the air. "At one thousand four hundred pounds," the auctioneer declared, adding with the sound of the hammer: "It's yours, sir."

On the opening day of the sale, the books were purchased for nearly 30% more than the estimated prices. The fine quality and condition of the books demanded such attention. And then there was their provenance. A third factor may have also entered into the matter: the fact that this was probably the last large disposal of books from Beckford's celebrated library. One main theme in Lord Rosebery's collecting habits was books on travel and history, especially those with fine illustrations and maps. One such book with numerous woodcuts was Francisco Hernandez's *Nova Plantarum Animalium Mineralium Mexicanorum Historia,* printed in Rome in 1651 and an outstanding example

of the artistic production of a book. Estimated at £200/250, it went, after heated contention, to Quaritch for a final price of £1,100.

Among the curiosities of the sale was a group of six French seventeenth-century pamphlets of a horrific nature, bound into one volume, and including such titles as *Histoire Merveilleuse et Horrible d'un Fils de Famille, qui apres avoir meschamment meurtri son propre Pere & naturel, en fin le pendit & l'estrangla* and *Supplice d'un Frere et Soeur decapitez en greve pour adultere et inceste.* This work found a "natural" home in going to P. Beres, a French dealer, for £650— £300 over the estimate.

B. H. Malkin's *A Father's Memoirs of His Child* is a book of average value. However, this particular copy, appraised for £200/250, was sold to Alan Thomas for £320. The interest of this copy is heightened by a page of Beckford's notes bound in. The *Memoirs* contain some poems by William Blake, and Beckford commented on them as "some splendid specimens from that Treasury of nonsense—Mr. Blake the mad draughtman's poetical compositions—

Tiger, Tiger burning bright
In the forests of the night—&.

Surely the receiver & Disseminator of such trash is as bad as the Thief who seems to have stolen them from the walls of Bedlam."

The books of early dates and with luxurious bindings, of course, fetched the highest prices. Not all lots had a dramatic display of bidding. But each lot did have its particular flavor of respect and love. For the 244 lots sold during the second day of the sale, the opening bid most popular was £20. Forty-three lots did open for less. The first bid of this sort was for a relatively nondescript French book of 1645, *La Vie de la Mere Terese de Jesus,* bound in calf but with only one illustration, an engraved frontispiece. When the first bid was made, the room was hushed, but not with any overtones of tenseness. It was just that no one wished to bid for it. The auctioneer did manage to ply £22 from the table for it, and the book went to Alan Thomas. Eighty-two lots opened the bidding to figures above £20. And sixty-two began at £100 or more, including several opening at £1,000. Francis Edwards purchased the greatest number of lots for the day. For forty-one he paid £4,733. Weinreb's nine books cost him £4,488. Quaritch paid £4,320 for thirteen lots. The thirteen books going to Maggs came to £4,280. Haywood Hill successfully bid for eight lots, at a price of £1,585. Foyle, Blackwell, Thorp, Alan Thomas, and Stanley Crowe paid an average of £483 for what they took away. Goodspeed's of Boston bought one book—John Speed's *Historie of Great Britaine Under the Conquests of the Romans, Saxons, Danes and Normans* of 1632 and with numerous woodcut illustrations in the text—for £95. A group of twenty-four views of Florence and its environs by Giuseppe Zocchi, published in Florence in 1744 and once belonging to Horace Walpole, made £2,600, a price paid by Dawson, almost double Sotheby's estimated valuation. Another collection of Zocchi's views, this time fifty of Tuscany, made £2,400, going to N. Israel at exactly double the suggested price.

The top seller of the day was a book estimated at £800/1,000. Printed in Milan in 1508, this *Libro de la Ventura overo de la Sorte* was printed in three columns to the page and included exemplary woodcuts filling the large pages of spiritual and astronomical features. A full-page woodcut of the wheel of fortune on the verso of the title page is the initial introduction into the artistic wonders of this beautiful work. Written by Lorenzo Spirito, this work is a gem of the first magnitude. Its opening was £500, which triggered serious contention in the interplay of bidding. At the hammer, the book went to Breslauer, a Continental dealer, for £3,500.

"Nothing second-rate enters here," Beckford once wrote to a friend about the books in his library. But this was said by a man who could pick and choose when and where he wished. To receive a Sotheby's catalogue is a different matter today. A desired item may be the last remaining copy of the book to come on the open market. The delight of knowing Sotheby's lies with the pleasure of being able to discover—and acquire—some treasure, no matter how slight. This delight in unearthing some little, even if tarnished, gem for £10 can parallel the honor of being the owner of a £3,500 book. But the greatest moment for each lot comes not when the final bid is made. There is a universal pronouncement, almost sacred, which is something reserved between only two people—the auctioneer and the successful bidder. This highest bidder has made his final bid. Then comes gratification of hearing the auctioneer say: "It's yours, sir."

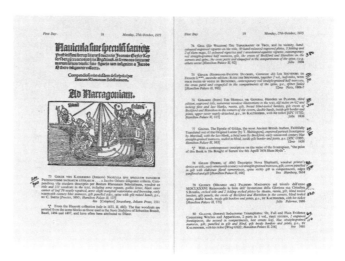

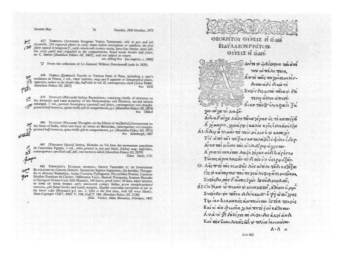

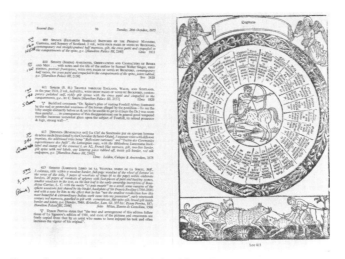

Pages from *Catalogue of Valuable Printed Books formerly in the library of William Beckford of Fonthill. . . .* (sale of 27-28 October 1975). The presale estimates and auction prices are noted in pounds.

Georgia Boy

A retrospect of Erskine Caldwell

By MALCOLM COWLEY

During the early Depression years I was book editor of *The New Republic* and hence was a minor source of income to young writers who were trying to keep alive in New York. Many of them had found that other sources were limited in those bleak days before the Federal Writers' Project. I felt involved in their problems, which were even worse than my own problems had been a dozen years before, when I had sat on the other side of that big, battered desk and tried to explain why I should be given a book for review. Now younger men and women were making the same worried explanations, and usually I did find a book for them if they showed intimations of having talent or if they merely looked hungry; at least they could sell the book on Fourth Avenue and buy a meal. For Erskine Caldwell, however, I didn't find a book, even though he impressed me as having more promise than almost any of the others.

I had read some of his stories in little magazines and later when they were collected in a first book, *American Earth,* published in the spring of 1931. Clearly he had a natural gift for story telling and he had a subject, too, in the small cotton farmers of East Georgia. Sometimes he wrote as if he were one of them; as if he had dropped the plowlines that very morning, stabled the mule, and rushed to the typewriter. There were other stories about Maine country people, in which his tone was that of a quizzical observer, and the book also contained a long prose poem in numbered paragraphs, "The Sacrilege of Alan Kent." This impressed me even more than the stories, for it revealed what seemed to be a new sensibility, with hints of remembered pain, cruelty, hunger, and savage longing. Some of the paragraphs were single sentences as tough and springy as an axe handle: "A man walked into a restaurant through the front door and ate all he wanted to eat."—"Once the sun was so hot a bird came down and walked beside me in my shadow." That sentence about the bird I kept repeating to myself, each time admiring its utter simplicity and rightness.

So I was curious about the author and pleased when he appeared at *The New Republic* with other candidates for books to review. Caldwell, as I afterward learned, had lately finished *Tobacco Road,* which had been accepted by Scribners for spring publication; now he planned to spend the winter in New York while writing a second novel. He was a big young man with a square-cut head, broad shoulders, and enormous hands, but with little flesh on his bones. His orange hair was cut short and lay forward close to his scalp, so that he looked like a totem pole topped with a blob of orange paint. When we talked about his stories he complained that people thought he was a humorist. "I have never tried to be funny,"

he said, making a wooden gesture. His features were as solemnly inexpressive as those of an Indian chief or a backwoods farmer.

"He's not as innocent as he seems," I said to myself, but what did I say to Caldwell? Though I can't set down the words, I remember feeling experienced and almost patriarchal. I must have told him that he had a truly exceptional gift for story telling, but that he didn't impress me as having a critical mind. When he volunteered that he had written a lot of reviews for the *Charlotte Observer,* I brushed aside the information. "Keep away from book reviews," I must have said. "They wouldn't earn you a living and they would interfere with your real business, which is writing stories." He clumped down the stairs without a book, while I sat in the editor's chair feeling ashamed of myself for having pontificated. I didn't know until much later that he had been living mostly on rye bread and rat-trap cheese, with a ten-cent bowl of soup in the evening.

Still, I had given Caldwell sound advice, even if books for review would have been more appreciated. That winter was to be his last really hard one. *Tobacco Road* came out in February 1932 and was not a commercial success, but it had more than a few enthusiastic readers. One of them was Jack Kirkland, who later asked for permission to dramatize the book. In March Caldwell went back to Maine, where he lived with his wife and three children in a big drafty house belonging to the wife's family. He had finished his second novel, but, after some hesitation, Scribners turned it down (that book has never been published). Then spring came to Kennebec County and everything seemed brighter. Caldwell started a new novel for which he already had a title: *God's Little Acre.* He had acquired a literary agent, Maxim Lieber, who was selling a few of his stories to magazines that paid for them. The new novel had gone well in the writing; it was finished in August and was promptly accepted by the Viking Press. With the advance against royalties, Caldwell bought a new typewriter, having battered away at the old one until it was beyond repair. He also bought three identical dictionaries, to have a copy always at hand, and the first roast of beef his family had eaten in a year. He was still poor, but he would never again go hungry for want of money.

"A man walked into a restaurant through the front door and ate all he wanted to eat." Caldwell could now be the man.

The next time I remember seeing him—though there were other times now forgotten—was in the winter of 1936-37, at a meeting held in a midtown hotel to advance some worthy left-wing cause. Caldwell appeared late and in the company of a spirited young woman, the photographer Margaret Bourke-White. They had lately traveled together through the Deep South, she taking pictures and he recording conversations for a book that was to become a classic record of the Depression years: *You Have Seen Their Faces.* Now, the wife in Maine forgotten, they were radiantly in love, so that their presence transformed the crowded room. Suddenly I thought of Wallace Stevens and his "Anecdote of the Jar":

> I placed a jar in Tennessee,
> And round it was, upon a hill.
> It made a slovenly wilderness
> Surround that hill.

Those two, absorbed in each other, gave focus and form to the slovenly meeting, while we others had become the wilderness in which they gleamed.

Bourke-White was bright, gallant, ambitious, and hard-working, with a habit—not displayed that afternoon—of surveying a room to pick out celebrities, then marching straight up to them. In Caldwell she had found her dearest celebrity. By that time *Tobacco Road,* in Jack Kirkland's Broadway version, had been running for three years—with four more years to come—and it was yielding as much as $2000 a week in royalties to each of the collaborators. One of Caldwell's stories, "Kneel to the Rising Sun," had made him a hero of the left-wing press, which extolled him as a spokesman for the dispossessed. He was published and praised in Russia. *God's Little Acre* had just appeared in a French version by Faulkner's translator, Maurice Coindreau, and with a preface by André Maurois. In this country a respected critic, Joseph Warren Beach, had written of Caldwell (or was soon to write), "He was destined to follow in the footsteps of Chaucer and Dickens, of Balzac and Gorky." That was heady praise, but, in those days, it did not seem implausible.

II

Erskine Caldwell was a preacher's boy raised in genteel poverty. His father, Ira S. Caldwell, had once been secretary of the Home Missions Board of the Associated Reformed Presbyterian Church, an impos-

Tobacco Road ran for 3,182 performances on Broadway in 1933-1941—
establishing a new record in long-run performances.

ing title with little or no income attached to it. The
A.R.P., as the boy learned to call his father's church,
is one of the smaller and stricter Presbyterian sects,
with few rich men among its members, and for some
years his father's occupation was to travel through
the rural South, from one struggling congregation
to another, and minister to each of them for a few
months, perhaps for a year or more, until its rifts
were healed and it could afford a minister of its own.
Sometimes, however, he caused a new rift by taking
the liberal side on racial questions. His salary wasn't
always paid. Even after 1919, when he accepted a
permanent post with the A.R.P. church in Wrens,
Georgia, his income was less than $2000 a year.

By that time his only son was a gangling boy of
sixteen. Born in Coweta County, Georgia, in December 1903 (or perhaps in 1902; there is some argument about the year), Erskine had attended school
intermittently—a few months in Staunton, Virginia,
four years in Atoka, Tennessee—but he had also been
tutored at home by his mother, who had once taught
Latin and French at a fashionable school for girls.
After one year at the Wrens high school, the boy was
given a diploma. He wanted to attend the University
of Georgia, and instead he went rebelliously to
Erskine, a small denominational college named like
himself for the Scottish founder of A.R.P. He was
there for three years and played football on the freshman and varsity squads, but he had a miserable
academic record and was often away from campus.
Once he went to New Orleans and tried to get a job
on a freighter bound for South America, but he was
jeered off the ship. Later in the same month—it was
February 1922—he was arrested for vagrancy in
Bogalusa, Louisiana, then a sawmill town, and spent
nine days in jail. He might have spent three months
there, but he smuggled out a letter to his father, who
wired money enough to pay his fine and buy a ticket
back to Georgia.

In 1923 he got away from Erskine College by applying to the United Daughters of the Confederacy
for a scholarship to the University of Virginia. He
spent four semesters at Virginia, in all, but they were
scattered over four academic years. He did well in
English, as one might expect, and sociology, but in-
differently in his other studies, and he took to writ-

ing stories. In March 1925 he secretly married Helen Lannigan, the daughter of an athletic coach. Forgiven by the bride's parents, the Caldwells spent another semester at the University; then Erskine talked himself into a job as cub reporter on the *Atlanta Journal*. He gave up the job in the late spring, determined as he was by then to earn a living by writing fiction. With his wife he went to Maine, where the Lannigans owned a house and a hundred acres in the town of Mount Vernon, near Augusta. Erskine fell into the routine of hoeing potatoes or chopping wood all day, in preparation for winter, then writing through much of the night. His stories went out to magazines and came back with rejection slips. In 1929 he received his first letter of acceptance; it was from Alfred Kreymborg, who was then helping to edit a distinguished yearbook, *The New American Caravan*.

That is a bare record of Caldwell's early years, based on information kindly supplied by Dr. William A. Sutton, the author of *Erskine*, an unpublished biography. His account differs at various points from those offered by Caldwell himself, which in turn differ with each other (except in their common quality of being romanticized). I quote from a letter that Caldwell wrote to the compiler of *Twentieth Century Authors* (1942):

When I was eighteen, I enrolled at Erskine College, Due West, S.C., but remained only a short time. I went to sea on a boat that was running guns for a revolt in a Central American republic, and ended up several months later in Mexico. My next attempt to complete my education was when I entered the University of Virginia after having won a scholarship offered by the United Daughters of the Confederacy. I remained there almost a year, working nights in a poolroom for room and board. I had begun to write short stories, though, before I left, and continued writing while working in a variety store in Pennsylvania, playing professional football, managing a lecture tour for a British soldier of fortune, and selling building lots in Alabama under three feet of water. I attended the University of Pennsylvania for a short time, making my expenses, and more, as a bodyguard for a Chinaman....

The article in *Twentieth Century Authors* goes on to summarize information offered by Caldwell on other occasions. It says, "Anyone who doubts Mr. Caldwell's close personal knowledge of the underdogs of whom he writes should note that in addition to the jobs he mentions he has also been a cotton-picker, a lumber-mill hand, a hack-driver, a stage-hand in a burlesque theater, a soda-jerker, and a cook and waiter." Some of those jobs he really held, if briefly, while others are as improbable as his running away to Central America. Dr. Sutton said in the course of a long letter, "Perhaps I have left you with the impression that no Caldwell statement about himself can be taken as necessarily true. Exactly right. As one of his old friends told me, 'He is a put-on artist.' "

It would be more accurate to say that he is simply an artist, one who assigns some of his own adventures to a fictional character named Caldwell. That sort of yarning is not at all unusual among poets and novelists. Whitman, Sherwood Anderson, Hemingway, Faulkner, and Nathanael West—to mention only a few names—all created imaginary selves and thereby made trouble for their biographers. In Caldwell's case the process can be broken down into three stages (though I suspect that these developed almost simultaneously). *First stage:* He wrote a great number of stories (often late at night or when he was tired and hungry). Some of the stories surprised him by the feelings they revealed, which were different from those of the daytime Caldwell. *Second stage:* He therefore adopted a persona, that of the man who might logically be supposed to have written the stories. *Third stage:* Even a persona must have a past, so Caldwell constructed it, yarned it out, using a mixture of episodes from his early life with impulses he had never acted upon.

In "The Sacrilege of Alan Kent," the early prose poem that corresponds on a lesser scale to Whitman's "Song of Myself," one notes the beginning process of self-dramatization. Here is what happens to the nine days in the Bogalusa jail:

I went to a town where lumber was planed, and lay in jail two or three years or more. There was nothing to do at any time other than listen to a Mexican file his pointed yellow teeth and to feel my growing beard.

And here is the episode of his asking for a job on a freighter docked at New Orleans:

One night I crawled aboard a coaling tramp and begged a man for a job. He heaved a cask-bung at my head and shouted, "Get the hell off here, you God-damn rat!" Before the tramp and the man got half way across the Atlantic, they went down and no one knows where.

Perhaps Caldwell was taking a fictional revenge on the bo's'n who jeered him off the ship. By 1942, however, the episode was to grow into that mythical voyage to Central America on a gun runner. Here is another paragraph, wholly imagined and not pretending to be anything else, that foreshadows a deep feeling expressed in his later work:

The night when he heated the iron pokers and began burning the Negro girl with them, one of the Negro men and I took two shotguns and killed him. After we had broken the chain around the girl's waist, we walked all night until we reached the town.

The feeling is that blacks and whites of the oppressed classes should join forces against the oppressors. It is a feeling mingled with dreams of miscegenation—as note the presence of a Negro girl—and the dreams become clearer in still another paragraph:

For a week on the top floor of a seven-story warehouse, a brown-limbed girl fed me every day and warmed me at night. She even helped me lick my wounds. When I threw my cigarette butts out of the window, they fell into the ocean; and I could see all the way across it. Then I went away for two years and came back to get her, but she was not there; and I can't find her now.

That "brown-limbed girl who fed me every day" was to reappear often in Caldwell's novels. Of course "The Sacrilege of Alan Kent" is a fantasy, not a novel, much less a factual memoir. There is, however, a similar dramatization or pure invention of episodes in Caldwell's purportedly true story of his life, *Call It Experience* (1951). I thoroughly enjoy the book, which is full of lively incidents, and have never felt an impulse to separate the fact in it from the fiction. Whether Caldwell really worked on the night shift of a cottonseed-oil mill in Wrens, Georgia, during the spring of 1920 is a question that I gladly leave to Dr. Sutton. A much more interesting subject is the persona he created for himself: its function, its nature, and its effects on his writing, which were good at first, but ultimately disastrous.

III

I should guess that the primary function of the persona was simply to make the author an interesting figure. At one time he must have told himself a continued story in which he was the hero; that is a boyhood practice of many or most authors. Now—again like many authors—he was embroidering the story for others. But the persona also had a secondary function

Caldwell with his second wife,
photographer Margaret Bourke-White.

that became always more important, and this was to validate his fiction. Caldwell was presenting himself as, in his publisher's words, "the spokesman for simple people, good or evil, vicious or oppressed," but there might be those who doubted his "close personal knowledge of the underdogs of whom he writes." The obvious answer was that he had been one of the underdogs; that he had worked or looked for work or starved among them as a field hand, a sawmill hand, a carnival roustabout, and a vagrant —not to mention other occupations—and that he had shared their brief pleasures of drinking, gambling, and whoring. One remembers how "Song of Myself" presented its author to the public; he was

Walt Whitman, an American, one of the roughs,
  a kosmos,
Disorderly fleshy and sensual . . . . eating drinking and breeding.

In constructing a public image, Caldwell had less to conceal than Whitman and stayed closer to his true self. He was truly a wanderer, truly a listener, truly used to working with those big hands. He withstood hunger and cold like an Indian brave. He truly raged against injustices to Negroes and sufferings endured by the poor whites. On the other hand, he was less of a Deep Southern primitive than he pretended to be, had more schooling than he acknowledged, and had read more contemporary fiction, at least in the days when he was reviewing books for the *Charlotte Observer*. His pose of gullible innocence was combined with a good deal of shrewdness in dealing with editors and in calculating how long his money would last.

One has doubts about a famous telephone call that he received from Maxwell Perkins, who was the Scribners editor in chief. For months—according to Caldwell's account in *Call It Experience*—he had been bombarding Max with stories, usually a new one every week. When he came to New York in the spring of 1930, Max phoned him at his cheap hotel to say that he needn't send any more, at least for the time being. Two of the stories were being accepted, and what about the price: "Would two-fifty be. all right? For both of them."

CALDWELL: Two-fifty? I don't know. I thought maybe I'd receive a little more than that.

PERKINS: You did? Well, what would you say to three-fifty then? That's about as much as we can pay. . . .

CALDWELL: I guess that'll be all right. I'd thought I'd get a little more than three dollars and a half, though, for both of them.

PERKINS: Three dollars and fifty cents? Oh, no! I must have given you the wrong impression, Caldwell. Not three dollars

and a half. No. I meant three hundred and fifty dollars.

It is a good story, for all one's doubts about Caldwell's perfect financial innocence. Another good story is how, shortly after his return to Maine, he gathered together all his rejected manuscripts, including novels, novelettes, short stories, essays, poems, and jokes; he says that they nearly filled three suitcases. He spent the night paging through them in a lakefront cabin; then in the morning he carried them to the beach and burned them all, adding for good measure a seven years' accumulation of rejection slips. It was a ceremonial bonfire that marked the end of his apprenticeship, and it serves as evidence of his wild fecundity. Dr. Sutton rather spoils the story by noting that the manuscripts of two unpublished novels survive from the same period. They weren't part of the image that Caldwell was trying to project.

The image was that of a man driven to write fiction by "an almost uncontrollable desire," he says, "that seeks fulfillment at any cost . . . as overpower-

A scandalous book in its time, *God's Little Acre* was one of the first paperback best-sellers—more than a million copies in its first six months.

ing as the physical need for food and drink." Or warmth or sleep, he might have added. "Upstairs in an unheated room," he says in speaking of his first Maine winter,

I wore a sweater, a leather jerkin, and an overcoat while I sat at the typewriter. I kept a blanket wrapped around my feet and stopped once in a while to blow on my numbed fingers. . . . For ten and twelve hours a day, and often through the night, I wrote story after story, revising, correcting, and rewriting . . . trying over and over again to make a story sound to the inner ear the way I wanted to make it sound.

Caldwell went south in January when he had burned the last of his firewood and eaten almost the last of his potatoes. He tells us:

For several weeks I lived in a one-room cabin in the piney woods near Morgana, Edgefield County, South Carolina, eating a can of pork-and-beans three times a day and writing for sixteen or eighteen hours at a time. After a while I went to Baltimore and lived on lentils and wrote short stories in a room on Charles Street. When money gave out, it was spring. I returned to Maine.

This time . . . I would cut wood during the day and hoe potatoes in the long purple twilight, and, when night came, I would sit down and work on a short story. At that time of year, in that latitude, it was broad daylight at three o'clock in the morning when I went to sleep for a few hours. Time seemed to go so swiftly and there was so much to do that some nights I would stop the clock or turn the hour hand backward while I was at the typewriter.

And what was the purpose of all this labor, beyond the gratification of his physical need for writing? On that point Caldwell has less to say, but still he makes one specific statement:

I wanted to tell the story of the people I knew in the manner in which they actually lived their lives from day to day and year to year, and to tell it without regard for fashions in writing and traditional plots. It seemed to me that the most authentic and enduring materials of fiction were the people themselves, not crafty plots and counterplots designed to manipulate the speech and actions of human beings.

In those early days his writing was never impeded by the want of subjects to write about. He had known hundreds of persons in the Deep South, and later in Maine, whose moments were clamoring to be recorded. If memories failed him, he could always continue his travels around the country making new observations. "Often I would find myself wonder-ing," he says, "what people might be doing at that moment elsewhere in America, in hundreds of villages and small towns." He was so busy at all times observing, experiencing, and recording that he had no leisure for reading books. "Many years ago," he was to say on various occasions, "I divided the population into two parts, those who read and those who write. I wished to belong in the latter category." The one book he carried with him on his travels—besides his typewriter and a cigarette-making machine—was a collegiate dictionary. "I not only consulted it frequently," he says, "but in my free time I read the dictionary instead of reading novels and magazines." Once he went through it striking out every word of more than four syllables.

Such is the image of *homo scribens,* the writing man, that Caldwell presents to the world, and to himself as an ideal. It is a radically simplified picture that omits the problems encountered by others who follow the trade. Caldwell's idealized writer has no problems except material ones; no doubts of himself, no hesitations, no fears of losing contact with his subliminal wealth. He is impelled to write by a physical need that makes him forget the need for sleep; turning back the clock, he goes on working. His only aim is to set down, in the simplest words, a true unplotted record of people without yesterdays. Past literature does not exist for him, and he is scarcely aware of having rivals in the present. As with Adam in the garden, every statement he makes is new. His only mentor is *Webster's Collegiate Dictionary;* his only acknowledged judge and critic is the inner ear.

So far as the author himself accepted that simplified image, he was limiting his possibilities of development. Writers learn from life, if they are lucky, but they also learn from other writers, and Caldwell was learning less than his contemporaries. In the beginning, of course, he had learned somewhat more than he confessed to himself. I suspect that most of his early stories could not have been written without the encouragement offered by *Winesburg, Ohio,* which served as a beacon light to many new talents of that age, including Hemingway and Faulkner. I also suspect that Caldwell owed a debt to Hemingway's Michigan stories, though he never wrote Hemingway prose; and he must have been affected by the experimental spirit of the little magazines that published his early work. But once he stopped reading—except for "half a dozen novels a year," as he tells us—he deprived himself of models to shape his critical sense (that "inner ear") and also lost what Henry James called "the stimulus of suggestion, comparison, emulation." There was no one he cared to emulate—not James, most certainly; not Proust or Joyce or Conrad; he never mentions them. Although he lived in an age of experiments, including his own, he refused to profit from the experiments of others, which he dismissed, in fact, as "crafty plots and counterplots designed to manipulate the speech and actions of human beings." He wanted to depend on his own technical resources. In the proud way of many American writers at the time, conscious as they were of speaking for a new age, in a new country, he wanted to be completely his own man, owing no debt to anyone else's work. All he asked was that his own work be recognized—and recognized it was, after he had served an arduous but relatively brief apprenticeship.

Early recognition—perhaps at a cost to be paid later—is not unlikely to be the fortune of those who cling to a simple image of themselves. So it was with Caldwell, and the bands were already playing in his honor during the winter of 1936-37, when I saw him at that meeting in a midtown hotel. But I wondered even then what his next literary step was to be.

IV

In those days his name was very often coupled with that of William Faulkner, and we have forgotten that the two authors had many things in common. Especially in subject matter: both of them dealt with a society that appeared to be in a violent stage of decay. They came from different, but not strikingly different, sectors of that society. Caldwell's forebears were less prominent than Faulkner's, and he took less pride in them, but they were educated persons, some of whom had fought for the Confederacy. The real difference here was one of election. Faulkner elected, we might say, to speak as an heir of the cotton planters, even while deploring the crime of slavery. Caldwell chose the side of the cotton tenants, especially the blacks, and he painted such an angry picture of their lives that he was often abused as a traitor to his section. Both men, however, were intensely conscious of having roots in the Deep South.

Where Caldwell was outraged, Faulkner was saddened by injustices to Negroes. Both men were fascinated by the theme of miscegenation, with the difference here that Caldwell admired his quadroons and octoroons, while Faulkner portrayed his with sympathy, but still with the feeling that most of them were damned souls. Both wrote about Southern gangsters and prostitutes. One might say that Caldwell's early novelettes *The Bastard* (1929) and *Poor Fool* (1930) are his versions of the material that Faulkner uses in *Sanctuary* (1931). There is no possibility of literary influence, since *The Bastard* and the first draft of *Sanctuary* were being written at the same time, one in Maine, the other in Mississippi, but still there are curious similarities. Other parallels might be noted among short stories, again without any likelihood of literary derivation. "Saturday Afternoon" is Caldwell's "Dry September," "Candy-Man Beechum" is his "Pantaloon in Black," and "Meddlesome Jack" is his "Spotted Horses." Again, in reading novels by both men, one might think of Caldwell's Darling Jill, in *God's Little Acre,* as the sister of Faulkner's Eula Varner and might regard the people on Tobacco Road as the still more ignorant and destitute cousins of those in Frenchman's Bend.

Just as in their work, it is easy to find resemblances in the early careers of the two authors. Both were proud of having taken odd jobs, of which they both exaggerated the number. Both had early moving-picture assignments, and in the spring of 1933 they worked successively on the same picture, never released, which had *Bride of the Bayou* for its studio title. Director Tod Browning was shooting it on the Gulf coast south of New Orleans. Faulkner was fired by MGM, and Caldwell took his place with so little lapse of time that both must have been bitten by the same mosquitoes. Later, during World War II, both men worked in Hollywood without becoming part of the movie colony (and apparently without meeting each other).

Even in the beginning, when they were regarded by the studios and by the public as almost interchangeable values, there were tremendous differences between them. "Faulkner's genius," one says immediately, but genius is hard to define and one has to look for its manifestations in an author's life and works. There is a clue, perhaps, in the image that Faulkner had formed of himself, which was different from Caldwell's self-image and provided more incentives to growth. Very early in his career, Faulkner showed that he wanted to be not only a writer but among the greatest writers. Shakespeare, the Bible, Dostoevsky, Conrad, Joyce: we know that he read all these intensively. A spirit of emulation kept driving him ahead to study and surpass his own contemporaries, then to surpass himself. Some of his good stories became great stories only on revision, as note "That Evening Sun" and *Sanctuary* and "The Bear." Caldwell, with an immense natural gift for story telling, made fewer demands on it. He depended less on imagination and invention than Faulkner did, though both qualities were richly present in his early work. More and more he came to rely on simple observation of what people said and did.

That self-image of Caldwell's was not the best of auguries for his future as a novelist, but still he was to have an amazing career.

For nine years after the publication of his third novel, *Journeyman* (1935), he wrote comparatively little fiction. Instead he traveled to collect material, first by himself and later with Margaret Bourke-White (they were married in 1939 and divorced in 1942). They were in Moscow preparing to do a book of photographs and text on the Soviet Union when Hitler's armies crossed the border in June 1941. For the next few months Caldwell was fantastically busy as one of the first American correspondents on the scene, then later, in Connecticut, as an author rushing books into print to record his impressions. He was summoned to Hollywood as an adviser on the film *Mission to Moscow*, with other assignments to follow. It was not until 1944 that he terminated a studio contract (at four times the salary then being paid to Faulkner) and went back to writing fiction.

His project was to finish a series of roughly a dozen novels dealing with various aspects of the Deep South; "a Southern cyclorama" was his name for it. Perhaps he had looked up "cyclorama" in his favorite *Webster's Collegiate*, where, in the edition he must have owned, he would have found the word defined as "a pictorial view extended circularly, so that the spectator is surrounded as if by things in nature." That came close enough to Caldwell's purpose, which was to encircle the reader with a series of accurate representations. The publisher promised that each of the novels would present a facet of Southern life "seen through the eyes of a sociologist who is also an artist and a humorist. . . . The sum total will give a picture of a society as detailed and complete as Tolstoy's panorama of Czarist Russia."

Grandiose as the project sounds when translated into publisher's talk, it was a mere extension of Caldwell's self-image as a writer. He was simply planning to tell more stories about more and more of the people he knew, "in the manner in which they actually lived their lives from day to day." He was making the most of his travels and his skill as a reporter while neglecting his subconscious resources, including his imaginative power and his talent for transforming the ordinary into the grotesque and apocryphal. He was substituting extensity for intensity, at the risk of exhausting his material and of re-using the same plots as he moved from one Southern background to another. He pushed ahead with the series, however, and a new novel appeared each year without adding to his literary reputation. As late as 1946, Faulkner spoke of him as one of five contemporaries who were interesting to read (the others being Wolfe, Hemingway, Dos Passos, and Steinbeck). A year later Faulkner was quoted as saying to a group of students "that he had once had great hopes for Erskine Caldwell, but now he didn't know."

Great hopes were being realized at the time, but they were of a different and unexpected nature. Caldwell was becoming a central figure in a new branch of American publishing.

Early in 1946, *God's Little Acre* had been the first of his novels to appear as a 25-cent mass-market paperback. His reprint publishers, Kurt Enoch and Victor Weybright, informed him six months later that its sales had passed a million copies, then an unprecedented figure, and were expected to reach two million by the end of the year. Enoch and Weybright had started as American representatives of Penguin Books, but now they had founded their own company, Signet Books (later the New American Library). Of course they were eager to reprint Caldwell's other novels and to promote them vigorously. The rest of the story can be told in phrases and figures that appeared on the back covers of those other

The dean of American literary critics, in a recent photograph. One of the notable survivors of the literary movements of the Twenties and Thirties, Malcolm Cowley has shaped literary opinion for more than fifty years.

books as they were published in Signet editions year after year.

1949. "It is only recently, with the publication of his work in 25-cent editions, that Caldwell has emerged as one of the most influential and bestselling authors of all time. Eleven million copies of six novels have been sold in Signet editions alone (over four and a half million of *God's Little Acre*)."

1949. (There was a second book that year.) "Fifteen million copies of seven books."

1950. "Over 23,000,000 copies."

1952. "Erskine Caldwell is America's favorite author. His books have sold over 25,000,000 copies in Signet editions alone, with *God's Little Acre* topping the list with sales over 6,000,000."

1952. (Again there was a second book for the year.) America's bestselling novelist. Almost 30,000,000 copies of his books have now been sold."

1956. "The world's most popular novelist . . . has written a brilliant succession of novels and volumes of short stories which have sold over 37,000,000 copies in their paperbound Signet editions alone and have been published in twenty-six countries and languages."

1957. ". . . the world's bestselling novelist . . . has achieved international fame as one of the greatest writers of the twentieth century. . . . His books have topped 40,000,000."

1963. "His books have been translated into 27 languages, with over 61,000,000 copies of all editions in print."

As late as 1967, Caldwell was still being advertised

Erskine Caldwell: "A man walked into a restaurant through the front door and ate all he wanted to eat."

as "the world's bestselling novelist," but his publishers had stopped giving figures of "copies in print"; perhaps these weren't growing fast enough. The figures, incidentally, are not the same as for the number of copies actually sold, since they do not allow for unsold books returned to the warehouse. Might one guess that forty million copies would be closer to the actual sales? That is still an impressive figure, though later it was to be surpassed by the total sales of a few younger novelists. Even the unprecedented record of *God's Little Acre* was to be left behind. Caldwell's "unsparing realism" seemed less unsparing in a later age of total sexual candor, and his "earthy, robust" country humor was replaced by kinky urban humor. Still, during a period of fifteen years or more, the demand for his novels had increased the sales of paperback books in general and had helped to establish mass-market publishing as the most flourishing branch of the industry. After being a literary force in a somewhat limited field, Caldwell thus became a commercial property that, for a time, had its national importance.

It should be added that those sales to a vast public were unexpected in the beginning and were never a reflection of his self-image. Unlike many of his successors in the mass market, Caldwell never became a manipulator of plots and characters. He did offer concessions, sometimes in a rather awkward fashion, to what he thought the public expected of him, but even in the weaker novels of his Southern cyclorama, he still was telling honest stories about people he had known from youth or had observed in his travels.

During the 1960s he made some efforts to write more serious books without much thought of whether they would reach a wide audience. *In Search of Bisco* (1965) is an account of how he traveled through the Deep South looking for a black playmate remembered from his childhood. The search, however, is only a framework for his reflections on racial bigotry and for dramatic monologues by others. Caldwell, always an ear-minded writer, is good at catching their voices. Another nonfiction book, *Deep South* (1968), is a report on fundamentalism as he observed it in various white and black congregations. A few of the white ones, always in small towns, had the Reverend Ira S. Caldwell as their pastor. The best passages in the book are tributes by a wayward son to his father's tolerant and courageous Christianity. Some of Caldwell's later novels also treat his material more seriously and even, in one or two cases, with a hint of affection. The best of them is *Weather Shelter*

(1969), which is based on two themes that appeared in his earliest writing: miscegenation and the search for a lost son of mixed blood. This time they lead to a happy ending. The son is found; he is rescued from an attempted lynching; and he will inherit his white father's estate.

I read these three of his later books with sympathy and respect for the author, but, it must be confessed, with none of the troubled surprise I had felt on reading his early work. It is the early books—say the first three novels and the stories up to *Georgia Boy* (1943)—on which Caldwell's reputation will stand or fall. Today there is an unfortunate tendency to let it fall; to dismiss the books as having been too popular. We should not forget that they made a contribution to American letters, not to mention their having added a chapter to American folklore.

In a way they continued the tradition of what used to be called Southwestern humor, though more of it was Georgian or Alabamian. What they added was a new vision, combined with new characters and a new sensibility. Caldwell was taking chances and was giving rein to his subconscious feelings. The result in his work was that homely objects or events— a crushed strawberry, a sack of turnips, a crown fire in the piney woods—became charged with emotion and made themselves remembered as symbols. There was a vein of poetry beneath the surface of his early writing; it was laid bare in "The Sacrilege of Alan Kent," but he made no effort to exploit it, and later it disappeared. There was also a hint that many of his "unplotted" stories fall into ritual patterns corresponding to racial memories. In *God's Little Acre,* for instance, why does Will Thompson tear the clothes from Griselda and reveal her "rising beauties" before he turns on the power in the closed-down cotton mill? There is nothing logical in the sequence of events, but still we sense that it is right. In *Tobacco Road,* when the grandmother is dying of hunger with her face in the dirt, why does Jeeter Lester feel that the soil is right for planting, and set a fire to clear his overgrown fields, and die in the flames? "All this is magic," Kenneth Burke said long ago in the best essay that anyone has written on Caldwell's early work. ". . . the plots are subtly guided by the logic of dreams." It is no wonder that Jeeter and Sister Bessie and Will Thompson have become figures in American folklore. The magic is there, and it must have cast a spell on the millions who bought the novels in paperback long after the critics had forgotten them.

By ALDEN WHITMAN

Photographed by HANS NAMUTH

Something Always Happens On The Way To The Office: An Interview With Joseph Heller

Most literary artists, as distinguished from Grub Streeters, have evolved very personal methods of accretion in constructing their fictions. Some, like Jules Romains, the French master, plot it all out in advance on precisely arrayed index cards, as was the case with *Les Hommes de bonne volonté,* the multivolume, panoramic novel of French and European life from the turn of the century through World War I. Others, like John O'Hara, start with an idea, do industrious research, but do not pull it all together until their fingers hit the typewriter keys. Still others, like Herman Melville, begin with a theme and a character and painfully intertwine the two through many revisions.

Unlike all these, Joseph Heller of *Catch-22* and *Something Happened* follows a "process that seems to be different, because when I try to describe it people tend to be surprised." Heller and I talked about the

flow of his creative juices earlier this year in his Manhattan studio, a small but comfortable furnished apartment, high over West 57th Street, that contains, in addition to the obligatory desk and typewriter, a couch, easy chairs, a refrigerator (for noshing and beer), a gas range, a small library of reference works, and a dictating device.

A stubby man just under medium height, Heller at 53 has a darkish complexion and a marvelously untamed crest of tightly curled iron-gray hair. Restive with kinetic energy, he found it difficult to relax in a chair, for he constantly changed his position, as if sitting went against his grain. His dress was casual—a shirt open at the collar, a gray sweater, dark slacks, and nondescript shoes.

Hunching up in his chair, Heller sought to explain what is "different" about himself. "For one thing, I

Joseph Heller at his office.

don't think of the book consecutively," he said. "I have an idea for each of my novels, sort of a general idea, but even as I'm writing, working on a certain section, my mind will roam around almost in a free-association way, just thinking of characters or episodes that are new. I might get a page of dialogue, a paragraph of description, a humorous trait assigned to a character, which I'll then write down."

Heller, who talks rapidly, sometimes to the point of appearing to mumble, pressed on, remarking:

"And as happened with *Catch-22* and *Something Happened,* three, four, six years might pass before I come to the point in the book at which I use certain sections. The same thing is happening to the book I'm doing now. I'll get an idea. I never start with a subject. I start with something that goes through my mind that gets larger and larger. Then, by the end, I'll have

a general idea of the journey a character will take, that the book will take, and some notion of the main characters. Then I will think for a long time before I do a draft.

"Then when I sit down and face the typewriter, I will have, either hand-written or typed very loosely, perhaps two or three hundred pages, most of which will find their way into the book, all of which are written down because there is a possibility. But they are not in sequence; they did not occur in sequence."

Heller's methods help to explain the thirteen-year gap between *Catch-22* and *Something Happened.* Not only is there a sense of perfectionism at work in him, but also a belief that ideas, like humans, tend to be reproductive.

Heller himself likes to call it "a kind of free reverie within a very rigidly confined space." His most pro-

Joseph Heller leaving his home at the Apthorp, Broadway and 79th Street.

ductive reverie period these days is the twenty or twenty-five minutes it takes him to walk from his home at Broadway and 79th Street to his studio. Essentially a morning person, Heller awakens early, breakfasts, showers, and heads briskly for 57th Street, a little more than a mile distant.

"Just this morning," he recalled, "I was thinking about one character in my new book as I walked. A number of lines came to me that won't go into the chapter I'm writing today. But I wrote them out. I have no idea where they will fall in the book, but maybe in a couple of months or years they'll fit in."

The helter-skelter of Heller's creative process produced a *Catch-22* that baffled reviewers. Published late in 1961 by Simon and Schuster, the 443-page novel evoked less than favorable responses. "Emotional hodgpodge," R. C. Stern called it in *The New York Times Book Review,* while *Daedalus* described it as "pretentious, immoral [and] poorly written." *The New Yorker's* critic, Whitney Balliett, said "Heller . . . wallows in his own laughter, and finally drowns in it." "What remains," Balliett went on, "is a debris of sour jokes, stage anger, dirty words, synthetic looniness and the sort of antic behavior children fall into when they

know they are losing our attention." More moderate, but also negative, was Orville Prescott in the daily *New York Times,* who began his review by saying *Catch-22* "is not an entirely successful novel . . . not even a good novel by conventional standards." Although he found it realistic and funny, he concluded on an equivocal note by writing that it "will not be forgotten by those who can take it."

The only strongly positive American review was by Nelson Algren in *The Nation.* He termed the book the strongest repudiation of our civilization to come out of World War II. It is "the best American novel that has come out of anywhere in years," he wrote in summary.

Early sales were spotty, and while the first printing, priced at $5.95, limped along at fewer than 100 sales a week for a couple of years, Heller felt he was lucky to teach fiction at Yale and the University of Pennsylvania, to grind out some television scripts under a pseudonym, and to work on screenplays in Hollywood. About 1964, *Catch-22* began achieving an underground reputation on college campuses across the country, and as the Vietnam War escalated, it took on the dimensions of a sacred text. Dell, which had pub-

lished the book in paperback in 1962, suddenly found it could hardly keep up with the demand. Modern Library issued the novel in 1966 for a more general audience now alerted to the book's significance. By mid-1971, more than seven million copies had been sold in the United States, with the total through 1975 estimated at ten million. In addition, a Delta critical edition, edited by Robert M. Scotto and published in 1973, continues to sell briskly, chiefly among students.

The cumulative result, quite apart from showing Nelson Algren's perceptiveness as a critic, has been to elevate Heller to the ranks of major American writers and ordain *Catch-22* as an indisputable modern classic. The phrase "catch-22" has also passed into accepted speech as meaning, according to the Second College Edition of *Webster's New World Dictionary of the American Language,* "a paradox in law, regulation or practice that makes one a victim of its provisions no matter what one does."

For Coney Island-born Joseph Heller, who worked variously as a blacksmith's helper, advertising writer, promotion manager for women's magazines, and flack for Remington Rand, success has made him neither cocky nor arrogant. For one thing, his literary efforts

since *Catch-22* have not been unqualified triumphs. A play, *We Bombed in New Haven,* laid a small egg on Broadway, closing in December, 1968, after eighty-six performances. Moreover, his second novel, *Something Happened,* has been neither a commercial nor a critical success. But Heller is far from being dismayed, for he is one writer who can objectify himself and who can recall his creative experiences without apology, as he did for me in describing the long genesis and peculiar gestation of *Catch-22.* "While I was planning that and writing it, I had an office job unconnected with writing," he told me, adding:

"As with most office jobs, there are periods in the day when there is no work. In these times, most people go out shopping or make personal phone calls or write letters or sit around the office with their girlfriends. But once I had the idea for *Catch-22* I would spend those periods thinking about the book—not writing it, but just making notes. I would think in my reverie, fantasizing, idle speculation; but it was all concentrated in the area of *Catch-22.*

"I made notes because memory slips sometimes, very distressingly as a matter of fact. Also, I find that more often than not the way a sentence occurs to me

77

the first time is the best way. Nowadays, instead of writing it out, I sometimes speak it into the dictating machine."

But because Heller has put so much time and effort into thought, have his books been subject to change in the middle, once he starts his coherent draft?

"The changes that do take place," he replied, "are generally amplification, as new possibilities for actions or clarifications occur to me. In *Catch-22,* certain qualities or attributes of the characters were changed, or, better, reconciled, once I was deep into the actual writing. But basic changes, I think not."

Heller works in his studio not so much for seclusion and privacy as for change. "There's no reason why I couldn't work at home," he said. "The children have all left the nest, but I like some demarcation between my personal life and my work life. In the summer, on Long Island, there's a part of the house where I work. In New York, though, there's a certain renewal of the imagination that comes from getting out of the house and walking to the studio. Most of the time I'm walking I'm working. It's psychological, I suppose."

Heller's working day—his time in the studio—is from 10:00 to noon, in which he crafts about three handwritten pages, "which will fill up one typewritten page." "That will take me between one and two hours," he went on, "depending on how much I have in my mind before I begin. Now, some days I'll do nine in one or two hours, and sometimes I'll barely get through a hand-written page."

In a novel's final stages, however, when Heller is conflating his material and burnishing it for publication, his day's output is more bulky. Then his fingers work the typewriter keys with fair speed, but he is by no means a rapid writer. O'Hara, at the top of his form, could turn out a flawless short story between midnight and dawn—his working day—but by comparison Heller, even with all his episodes in place and his characters stabilized, feels lucky if he produces a thousand words by lunch time.

In the afternoons in previous years Heller taught a course in creative writing at City College. This year, he just walks around Manhattan many an afternoon or goes to the gym at a nearby YMCA to jog and swim. His evenings are devoted to a social life with his wife, who is careful to forebear asking, "How did things go today, Joe?" Instead, the couple attend the theater, concerts, the movies, or dine casually with friends.

Since *Catch-22* turns on its use of irony, satire, and humor to suggest that Yosarian, Heller's Candide, is

tongue-in-cheek naive, I asked Heller about his conception of the comic imagination.

"I get on weak ground," he confessed. "I have an idea of the things that go into mine, but I'm not as clear in analyzing it the way most critics do. For one thing, I don't know the source of humor per se. There have been numerous treatises on humor, and in reading these you come away with the feeling that there's no such thing as humor—it does not stand that type of analysis.

"There was a magazine article a few years ago on the types of humor included in *Catch-22*. It was very informative, very true, but in writing the book I was not conscious of them. And yet the author of the article was correct. Nonetheless, I understand how the patterns of humor were formed only after reading that article."

"But you must have a basic sense of the ludicrousness of American society and the way it's run," I said. "I do," Heller replied, "but one can have that sense and not be able to make, to achieve, any comic effects out of it. The fact that I have been able to in *Catch-22* and in *Something Happened* (with a different kind of humor), the fact that I have been able to be funny and display a comic imagination to people who themselves

recognize and respond to it—but who themselves might not be capable of writing satire or parody or creating comical situations—I think illustrates my point. Most people will respond to humor, yet most people can't be comic.

"I don't know. One could take something out of *Catch-22,* or out of *Something Happened*—a line. The one that comes to mind now is, 'Women don't suffer from penis envy, men do.' Now it's a humorous line, and one can try to find where the humor lies. Well, there's the surprise and there's a certain amount of embarrassment, there's a certain truth about human nature, and it's phrased pithily. All these elements contribute. Yet it is only one type of humor, like a Woody Allen one-liner."

"What are some of the other sorts?" I asked. "The extended situation is one other, I think," Heller said. "If I may cite *Catch-22* again, such a situation has to do with Doc Daneeka trying to prove he's alive and then finding that it's hopeless because of all the form letters involved. I say 'extended' because very early in the book it's mentioned that Daneeka, if he wants to get flight pay without actually going up in a plane, has to put his name on the register. The humor in this, I think, arises from his 'death' by a foxy greediness."

Heller reiterated, however, that the source of his comic inventiveness eludes him. It certainly cannot be explained fully in psychoanalytical terms, he said, adverting to his own experiences with analysis, but he allowed that psychology and a writer's past history have a lot to do with it. Then, he added, there is the overlay of his perception of the absurdity of American social conventions and ways in which institutions are organized.

"In *Catch-22*," he remarked, "the Army is used symbolically for the whole government structure. The humor lies in the way human beings—the victims of the structure—seek to manipulate it or circumvent it by employing the institution's rules and regulations. To be sure, the situations in the book are exaggerated, but that is how fantasy is often used to demonstrate reality. There are very big similarities and big differences between *Catch-22* and *Something Happened*. The similarities are in my commentary on society, the differences are in literary form.

"In general about humor, I think on reflection that there's probably a high degree of exhibitionism involved, whether it's as a performer or being funny as a newspaper columnist or being funny as a novelist.

The motivation is psychological, but it still doesn't explain why some people are funny while others are not. In my own case, I was interested in writing from an early age—in elementary school, in fact, at a time when we all like to excel in what we know we can do well. I found early on that I could be humorous, but the why remains beyond me."

"How much in your work is autobiographical?" Heller was asked. "Both books originated in experiences that I had," he said, "or from environments in which I lived. My Army experience is obvious in *Catch-22*. The corporate atmosphere I perceived in my office jobs is handled through *Something Happened,* but I am not a thinly disguised character in either book. My point of view is there in both books, and not in the slightest concealed, I hope. I am not writing, however, to achieve a personal catharsis—a replaying of a family or personal trauma.

"So my books were not written out of some profound psychic need to let it all hang out, to resolve a conflict. I am writing to continue as a novelist, a good one, I hope, who gets better with time. And I think there is a similar motivation for many novelists I know.

"Although Erica Jong's *Fear of Flying* and Alix

Joseph Heller arriving at his office on 57th Street.

Kates Shulman's excellent *Memoirs of an Ex-Prom Queen* seem almost totally autobiographical, I think that in both instances the books were written because their authors wanted to write and thought they had a good idea for a book. And in each case they were right. Both Erica Jong and Alix Kates Shulman are young. When you are young and want to write a novel, you have limited autobiographical experience to draw upon, and this may be employed without necessarily making the novel an autobiography.

"*Catch-22* contains some autobiographical material, but its purpose was not the same as that of Jong or Shulman. My book, by the way, is not really about World War II, but about the Korean War and the Cold War in this country; but the environment was autobiographical. This is true of my first creative writing, when I was twenty-three and a student at New York University. Almost without exception, my short stories were located in Brooklyn or Coney Island, where I came from. And they were all imitations, incidentally, outright imitations of John O'Hara or Irwin Shaw. By the time *Catch-22* was started I was thirty years old, and I had gained a lot of experience, and I was distant enough from the Army in time to put it into focus and

to create characters who are types and persons at the same time."

At this point, Heller was twisted into what I can best describe as a bagel position in his chair, and it seemed wise to let him uncoil with a final question, the subject of his current novel. "It's about politics," he said, straightening up to a slouch, "presidential politics and college professors. I don't know how else to describe it at this point. It's based on the phenomenon we have that is almost characteristic of presidential politics, of a president coming in who finds a college professor already in Washington. It has created in my mind a comic situation. Henry Kissinger, yes?"

"A bleeder," as slow writers are often called, Heller has no promise of when his completed manuscript will fall on his publisher's desk. It probably won't take thirteen years, though, for this novel is scheduled to be shorter than his previous two.

As the interview ended and I prepared to depart and talk turned to chitchat about Long Island where Heller and I are near-neighbors, I was struck by a remarkable fact about the afternoon. As pleasant and cordial and outgoing as Joseph Heller had proved to be, not once did Joseph Heller crack a joke, not once did he laugh.

F. Scott Fitzgerald Appraises His Library

A writer in need of money considers selling his books—but doesn't

Commentary by ANTHONY ROTA

Not even F. Scott Fitzgerald's genius as a writer of fiction was sufficient to produce a regular income that kept pace with his expenditure. We know that his financial affairs were often at a low ebb, and we can learn from the three pages of manuscript reproduced here that at one stage—probably in 1936-37—Fitzgerald was driven to contemplate selling his library. In his own calculations he valued the books at a total of $486.50 and estimated that at a forced sale he would probably receive no more than $300 for them. Whether that sum was insufficient to make a major impact on the needs of the moment or whether a royalty cheque or publisher's advance came in the nick of time and saved the day is not clear. But happily Fitzgerald and his books were not parted.

When exactly did the crisis occur? Such clues as the list gives us are misleading. None of the books which can be specifically identified was published later than 1923. Almost all of them were published in the decade immediately before that. In some cases Fitzgerald does not list titles but merely gives us some such indication as "Mencken (9 books autographed, some firsts)." H. L. Mencken had in fact published a dozen books by 1923. George Jean Nathan, of whose books Fitzgerald claimed eight, had similarly published at least ten by the year in question. Yet the evidence, drawn partly from records of Fitzgerald's earnings, is that it was actually much later. In 1936, the last full

year for which the author kept a detailed financial record, his income had fallen from some $37,000 (in 1931) to a low of $10,180. At that time, during the period of "The Crack-Up," Fitzgerald's affairs reached their nadir, and it must have been then that he contemplated the desperate remedy of selling his books. Yet he must have added contemporary publications to his library between 1923 and 1936. Why those later volumes were not listed remains an intriguing question.

Looking at other people's libraries is always a rewarding occupation, if only for the insight we are given into the owner's tastes. Fitzgerald's library contains few surprises. The books he identifies comprise a fair sprinkling of the British and American writers fashionable in the early twenties. In terms of fashion we might remark that Fitzgerald was luckier with his British authors than with his American. This is especially true if we use the word "British" to include Joseph Conrad who made England the land of his adoption. The limited signed edition of Conrad's *Notes on My Books* which Fitzgerald valued at $20 is worth three times as much today. Aldous Huxley's book of essays, *On the Margin,* might sell for $25 now. Bernard Shaw's *Back to Methuselah* would bring the same price. John Masefield, represented here by a signed copy of *Rosas,* and George Moore, represented by the limited signed editions of *Memoirs of My Dead Life* and *Abelard and*

Heloise, are currently in something of a decline. It is interesting that in the case of John Galsworthy's *Forsyte Saga* Fitzgerald had the American rather than the English edition. The American edition was actually published before the English, and in logic it is the earlier form which the first-edition collector ought to want. Yet in the nineteen-twenties the practice among book collectors was to "follow the flag," i.e. to collect only the English editions of English authors and the American editions of American authors, regardless of priority, and in this instance Fitzgerald was swimming against the tide.

If some of the American books Fitzgerald collected are temporarily out of fashion (Joseph Hergesheimer's *Cytherea* and the works of Mencken and Nathan are good examples), *The Enormous Room,* E.E. Cummings' account of internment in the First World War, is at the other extreme in critical attention and demand. Valued by Fitzgerald at $2, the 1922 first edition is worth a hundred times that today. James Branch Cabell's *Jurgen* has slipped a little from the pinnacle it occupied in the nineteen-twenties but this celebrated fantasy still has its claim to fame. Sherwood Anderson (*Winesburg, Ohio, Poor White, Triumph of the Egg,* and *Many Marriages*), John Dos Passos (*Three Soldiers* and *A Pushcart at the Curb*), Eugene O'Neill (*The Emperor Jones*), and Theodore Dreiser (*The Genius* and *A Traveller at Forty*) are all good, solid names, not at the peak of demand but represented in the collection by major works no longer easy to find in the first editions. In the cases of Willa Cather and Sinclair Lewis, Fitzgerald had a really famous book by each writer, *My Antonia* and *Main Street* respectively. Fitzgerald's copy of *Main Street* contained an autograph letter from the author. Indeed it is pleasing to see what a high proportion of Fitzgerald's books are, like *Main Street,* association copies—in other words, copies which bear signatures or presentation inscriptions by their authors or which contain letters from them. The presence of these inscriptions or letters naturally increases the value very greatly.

Fitzgerald's annotation, "autographed," is not in point of fact a sufficiently precise description in bibliographical or bookselling terms. It does not tell us all that we need to know. According to Webster it means literally that it bears a person's own signature, or something "written in a person's own handwriting." It does not tell us who that person is, although Fitzgerald clearly implies that the signature is that of the author. It certainly does not tell us what he has written. Cabell's *Jurgen,* mentioned above, is a case in point. Fitz-

gerald's copy was inscribed: "For F. Scott Fitzgerald with cordial and admiring regard James Branch Cabell 20 December 1920." Today it would command perhaps $300 as against the $15 at which Fitzgerald originally assessed it. We know that in the case of *Jurgen* "autographed" meant with a signed autograph presentation inscription from Cabell to Fitzgerald. If we do Fitzgerald the courtesy of assuming that he was consistent in the use of the term, then the desirability and value of all the books marked "autographed" in the list is enormous indeed.

Near the foot of the first page of his inventory Fitzgerald lists *The Natural Philosophy of Love.* This is a translation by Ezra Pound of a work by Remy de Gourmont. The note Fitzgerald has made against it—"Restricted Sale"—tells us enough to identify the edition. It was clearly the New York printing of 1922, of which every copy bore the legend: "This work is supplied to the Bookseller on condition that all discretion shall be used in its sale or distribution." The book was not published in London until 1926, when the Casanova Society brought out an edition limited to 1,500 copies. The need for "all discretion" was occasioned by the accounts of bestiality, men coupling with animals, that the work contained. It is strange that Pound, now recognised as one of America's most gifted and influential poets, should have been represented in this collection only by this one translation.

Fitzgerald's notes about his T. S. Eliot items do not tell us very much, but as is the case with so many of his authors, Fitzgerald once again had the key book. In this case it is *The Waste Land,* which has been described as a poem of six hundred lines containing a distillation of two thousand years of Western culture. It is arguably the most important and influential poem of the twentieth century. Fitzgerald had a copy of its very first appearance in America, which was between the covers of the magazine *The Dial* in November 1922 (it had been published in England in *The Criterion* in the previous month). The poem's first appearance in book form was in the Boni & Liveright edition in New York in 1922. The book comes in two states and in the earlier of them it commands at least fifty times Fitzgerald's figure of $5. Below *The Waste Land* on the list Fitzgerald has written "Poems (Elliot) (first)." It seems safe to assume that it was indeed T. S. Eliot who was intended. Fitzgerald's first American printing of Eliot's *Poems* (New York: Knopf, 1920), signed, "T. S. Eliot 3.ii.33," is worth about $500 today.

From other sources we can be certain beyond peradventure about Fitzgerald's copy of James Joyce's

Possibly Valuable Books

2.00	Laus Veneris	(first american edition)
5.00	Colvin's Keats	(Binding)
5.00	Rosas (Masefield)	(1st autographed)
5.00	Memoirs of my Dead Life	(Privately Printed)
20.00	Notes on my books	(limited + autographed)
2.00	Notes on Life + Letters	(First edition)
100.00	Ulysses	(First + limited)
3.00	On the Margin	(First)
2.50	Back to Methuselah	(First)
5.00	Forsyte Saga	(First American with autograph letter)
5.00	Leslie [5 books]	(all autographed)
5.00	Boyd, Earnest [2 books]	(all autographed)
5.00	Abelard	(limited edition)
2.00	The Natural Philosophy of Love	(Restricted Sale)
5.00	Vandover + the Brute	(1st)
3.00	Blix	(1st)
5.00	The Waste Land	(1st)
5.00	Poems (Eliot)	(1st)

Total 184.50

Above and on the following two pages: Fitzgerald's appraisal of his library.

3.00	Vachel Lindsey	(3 books all 1st)
5.00	Winesburg	(1st with autographed letter)
5.00	Poor White	(1st with autographed letter)
3.00	Triumph of the Egg	(1st)
3.00	Many Marriages	(1st)
5.00	Three Soldiers	(with autograph Card)
3.00	A Push cart at the Curb	(autographed)
4.00	East & West Poems	(1st)
2.00	Undertakers Garland	(1st)
2.00	Enormous Room	(1st)
2.00	Emperor Jones	(1st)
15.00	Jurgen	(1st autographed)
5.00	Figures of Earth	(1st autographed)
5.00	The Genius	(1st)
4.00	A Traveller at Forty	(1st)
3.00	Main Street	(1st with autograph letter)
2.50	My Antonia	(1st)
5.00	Seventeen	(autographed)
4.00	Cytherea	(autographed
4.00	Norris, Charles	(two books autographed)
2.00	You know me Al	(autographed)
2.50	Thru the Wheat	(1st autographed) Total
		89.00

2.00   Being Respectable   (1st autographed)
2.00   Married Life of Fred Carrol   (1st)
25.00   Mencken   (9 books autographed
                                          some 1st)
17.00   Nathan   (8 books autographed
                                          some 1st)
4.00   Stewart   (2 books autographed)
         Weaver   (1 book autographed)
         Towne   (3 books autographed
         Saunders
         Cale Young Rice   }   Autographed
         De Souza

3.00   The Dial ~~Wonton~~
                (including Wasteland)

                                      Total $53.00

         53.00
         89.00
        184.50
        326.50
        160.00   (400 books range 10¢ to $1.50, average 40¢)
        486.50
Probable value of library at forced sale $300.00

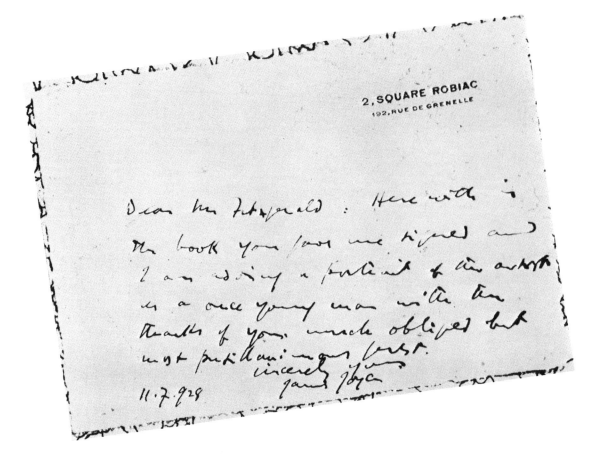

Ulysses. The first edition comprised 1,000 copies published by Shakespeare & Co. in Paris in 1922. The first 100 copies were signed by the author. The next 150 copies were printed on special paper, "vergé d'arches," and the final 750 on an unspecified handmade paper. Fitzgerald possessed this third form, his copy being No. 980. Following the custom for books published in France, all of the thousand copies were issued in paper wrappers. Because of the size and weight of *Ulysses* (740 pages) the paper binding was particularly liable to break and tear, and copies still in the original wrappers and in really fine state command high prices today. A signed copy might bring as much as $10,000, and even the ordinary form could command $1,500. Fitzgerald's copy, like most, was at some stage put into a more durable binding, and this would have reduced its value. On the other hand, pasted into this copy is a letter from Joyce to Fitzgerald. Valuing manuscript material is never easy, but book and letter together could well be worth $2,500. It is perhaps fair to say that *Ulysses* is to the modern novel what *The Waste Land* is to modern poetry. Both books were published in the same year, but *Ulysses* was banned in the United States on the grounds of obscenity until Judge John Woolsey's famous judgment in 1933.

I have said that Fitzgerald's collection contains few real surprises, although one is agreeably struck by the very high proportion of authors represented by their key books. It would be interesting to speculate on books that Fitzgerald did not have, but the bottom of the third page of manuscript rules out such speculation. We see that Fitzgerald had some 400 other books which he did not consider worthy of mention. Without knowing what they were we cannot begin even to guess at a current value for them. What treasures, one wonders, did those 400 items include? Be that as it may, we can say with a reasonable degree of assurance that the books to which Fitzgerald attributed specific values, adding up to a total of $326.50, would command at least twenty times that sum today.

Anthony Rota is managing director of Bertram Rota Ltd, the London firm which is internationally recognised as the leading specialist in the world of first editions and manuscripts of modern English and American literature. Great-grandson of the scholar-bookseller Bertram Dobell, Anthony Rota entered the family business in 1952 and in 1966 he succeeded its founder, his father, Bertram Rota, at its head. In 1971 be became the youngest-ever President of the Antiquarian Booksellers' Association, an organisation of which he remains an officer. He has written, lectured, and broadcast on book-collecting and bibliography, both in England and the United States.

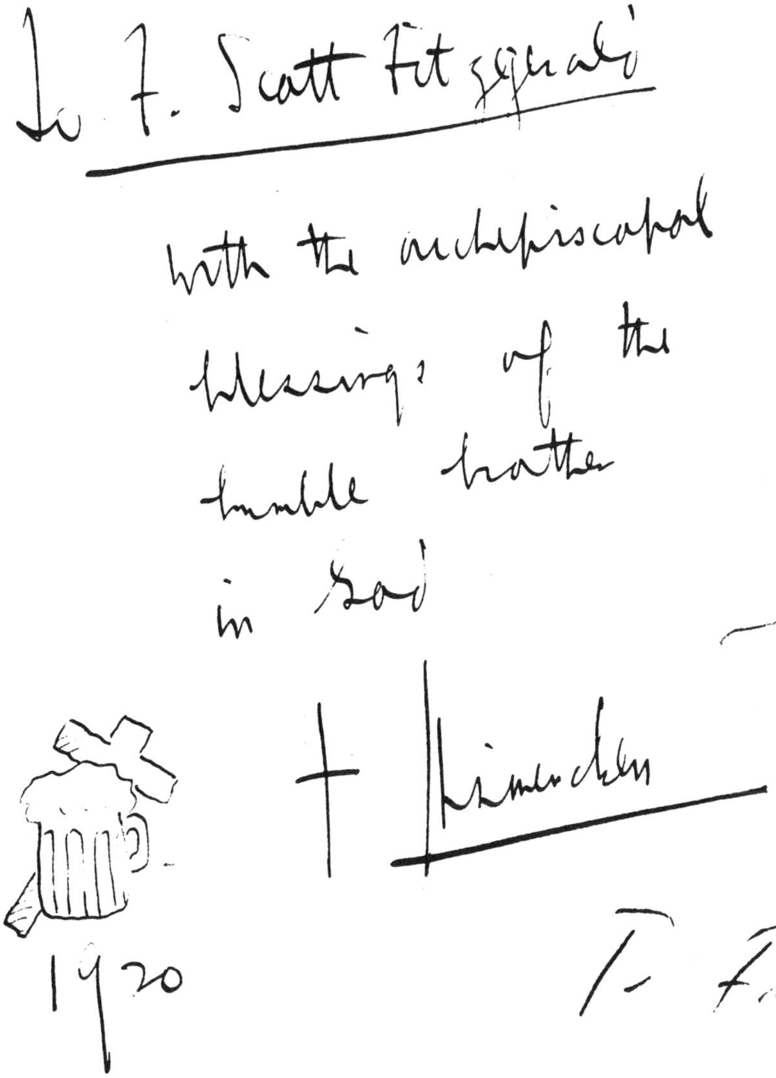

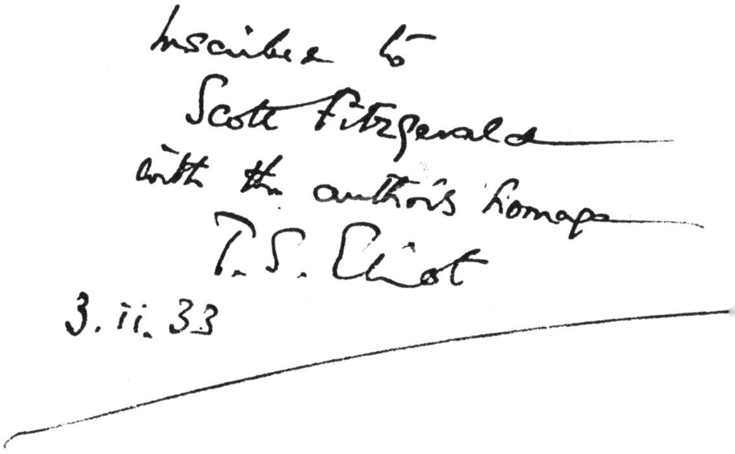

To F. Scott Fitzgerald

with the archiepiscopal
blessings of the
humble brother
in God

inscribed to
Scott Fitzgerald
with the author's homage
T. S. Eliot
3. ii. 33

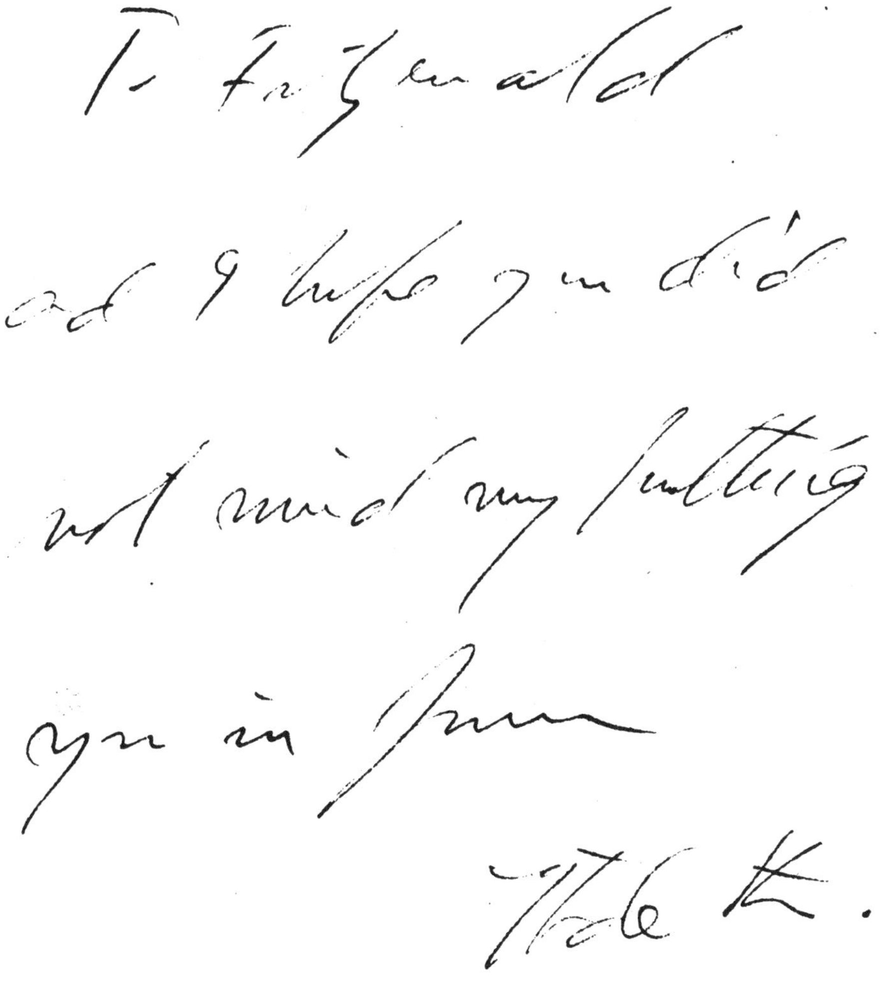

† H. L. Mencken
1920

To Fitzgerald

and I hope you did
not mind my putting
you in

Gtde St.

Inscriptions to Fitzgerald
from H. L. Mencken, T. S. Eliot,
and Gertrude Stein. At left:
James Joyce returns
Fitzgerald's copy
of *Ulysses* with a note.

Three Teachers
And A Book

*"I found a book on the floor where the custodian kept his
supplies... I thought perhaps invisible hands had placed that book there for me
and opened the custodian's door so I could find it."*

By JESSE STUART

Blue Ridge Range of the Appalachians

When people in America or any country in the world get one of my books in English or translation from a library, they do not know, probably do not care to know, the man behind the book. They'll read a few excerpts from the dust jacket, enough to know I'm an American, that I live in rural America (Appalachia, a rural original part of America—much larger in land area than many foreign countries—including all of the British Isles), and that I write of rural, village, small-town (there are no large cities here) people of my area.

But how did I become a writer from the time I was able to put words on paper? I could do this at six. I went to a one-room school where one teacher taught all grades from first to eighth. My teacher taught fifty-six classes in six hours. He assigned older pupils to teach the beginning classes. All this went on in the same little room where there were about fifty pupils. And don't smile upon this! The idea has become, for the most part, the ungraded school of today, which has become very popular in America.

I deviated from the little assignments in my texts and wrote about my classmates and people. My teacher let me read my efforts in class. All the pupils would listen when I read. And they would laugh loudly. I had only twenty-two months of schooling at Plum Grove. Then I went to work for twenty-five cents (ten, twelve, fourteen hours) per day for a farmer on whose farm my father was a tenant. But my education continued, for I worked with men who told stories that couldn't be told in public gatherings. I never told Mom about these, for any mother

wouldn't have wanted her son to have been subjected to these raw tales told by farm laborers who couldn't read and write. Later I wrote many of these, but I cleaned them up and some are in textbooks today. I was the only boy working with them. I dropped strawberry plants over acres of ground. I learned to set plants. Later I picked berries and carried water to the crew of farm laborers. I did all kinds of work from the age of ten to fourteen.

At fourteen I got a job that paid me seventy-five cents for ten hours. I walked five miles to and from my work. I was water boy for a crew of men who were paving the streets of Greenup, Kentucky. This is where the first of our three public libraries is now located. I was only water boy three days in Greenup. During these three days, I watched our boss, Mr. Pancake, hire a new man each day to carry hundred-pound sacks of cement to the concrete mixer. Each man said in the summer heat the cement did something to his skin. I was a strong boy for my age. And this job paid $3 per day. I asked Mr. Pancake if he'd let me try the job. He did. And I did the work until the streets were paved in Greenup. I've told people in lectures that not many or even one of my books might be a monument to me; but that if and when they ever travel over the streets of Greenup, Kentucky, I helped put all the cement in that concrete. The same streets with minor repairs have withstood the years, and they're a monument to me.

Here something happened that changed my life. We'd just finished the streets. I saw young boys and girls my age and older, cleanly dressed in the best clothes of that time on their way to pre-register for Greenup High School, which had perhaps an enrollment of 125. I wanted to join these young people and enter Greenup High School. I went to see the top man, Superintendent of Greenup City Schools. I had to take an examination on eleven subjects, and five of these subjects I'd never studied. I had to make an average of 75 and not below 60 on any one subject. I made an average of 78 and on one subject I made 59, but the three examiners of my papers raised it a point and let me enter Greenup High School. I made the 59 on English Composition. One can never tell about grades.

The only book in my father's and mother's one-room shack where I was born, near a coal mine on a mountain top, was the Bible. My father had never gone to school a day in his life. He couldn't read and write. He never wrote a letter, never read one, never read a newspaper or a book in his life. My mother could read a book slowly and write a letter. She had finished the second grade. In their day schools of any kind were few and far apart in the Eastern Kentucky Mountains.

Now, to have a son in high school, September 1922, my parents were proud. I was proud to walk five miles over a mountain and five miles back. I was in a new world where youth wore better clothes, and where there were books. There was a whole room full of books called the Greenup High School Library. Here I read my first book called a novel, *Silas Marner,* and I liked it! Here I read Emerson, Hawthorne, Thoreau, Dickens, Scott and many others. I think in my four years I read all the books in the Library plus many more.

I never read a book there but that I didn't wonder if I would not be able to write one someday. I'd look at the author's picture in his or her book, admire the picture and wonder if my picture wouldn't be in a book I'd write someday. I'd sit in the Library or my assigned seat in the study hall and dream.

Fortunately for me, I was lucky to have a great high-school English teacher who was a graduate of the University of Missouri's School of Journalism. She had also majored in English and Music. She was Mrs. R. E. Hatton. Her husband with a Ph.D. was Superintendent of Greenup City Schools. Mrs. Hatton before her marriage was Hattie McFarland and was of Scottish descent. So was I. My father's people had come from Scotland. She was great on a poet named Robert Burns. I'd never heard of him. She gave me a collection of his poetry which set me on fire. I read Robert Burns all the way through and cried for more. I knew if Robert Burns, a plowboy poet of Scotland, could write poems that would endure and go around the world, then Jesse Stuart, a plowboy poet in the Kentucky hills, could do the same thing.

In all of my own teaching since I left Greenup High School and college I've used Mrs. Hatton's formula for teaching. It has worked—even in American University in Cairo, Egypt. She had one day for themes, stories, poems—whatever we chose to create. We could choose our subject. What we did had to be original. But she did tell us to write about the subject we knew the most about. Many of my classmates wrote about picture shows they'd seen. When I entered Greenup High School I'd never seen a picture show. I wrote poems and themes about wildlife, snakes, domestic animals, fowls, and about some of my neighbors.

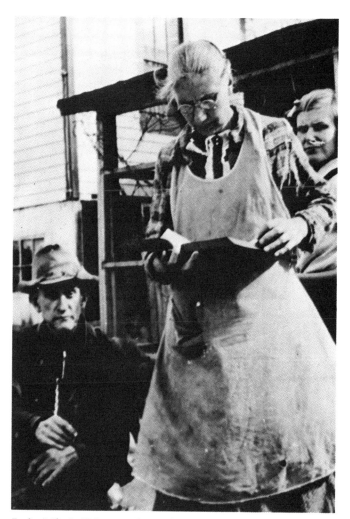

Left: Mitchell Stuart, the author's father, c. 1935. Above: Mrs. Stuart reading from the *Bible* to Mitchell and Glennis Stuart, 1932.

One of these was about a rooster, hatched from a nest egg, raised by the hen who hatched this egg. I told of the exploits of this rooster, how he killed the other roosters and stole their hens—and how one night an owl flew on to the tree where my rooster sat upon a tree branch among his many hens. The owl singled him out while he sat there asleep and killed him. I was almost in tears when I read this theme, but my classmates laughed, and Mrs. Hatton laughed loudest of all. She showed me there in class the grade she gave me—an A+.

Mrs. Hatton wasn't the only teacher to give "Nest Egg" an A. Twenty-seven other teachers did. I took "Nest Egg," plus other themes, poems, stories, articles with me to Lincoln Memorial University, to Peabody College for Teachers, and to Vanderbilt

Birthplace of Jesse Stuart
on the hill overlooking
W-Hollow and Shackle Run
Valley. The cabin was burned
by a forest fire in 1956.

University. Not all the twenty-eight A's "Nest Egg" made went to me. I loaned it to students along the way who said they couldn't write a theme. Editors of the *Atlantic Monthly,* twenty years later, gave it an A, too, and I got a nice check. It was reprinted in Homer A. Watt's college reader, and students in colleges and universities read "Nest Egg." This story has gone around the world. The chicken is a universal subject. I suppose there are chickens in all countries. I've found them everywhere I've been. When I wrote this theme for my English class I'd had twenty-two months of schooling in one-room rural Plum Grove and not quite one year in Greenup High School. I didn't know a chicken was a universal subject. I'd not been anyplace.

In Greenup High School I knew I had one of the greatest English teachers in the world. I said so. But many of my classmates didn't agree with me. On my five-mile walk, and sometimes run, to and from Greenup High School, Robert Burns, who had been dead 124 years and was buried in Scotland, walked with me. Ralph Waldo Emerson, long deceased and buried in Concord, Massachusetts, walked with me. I had great companions. I'd stop along the way, sit on a stone or a stump and read Burns' poetry or one of Emerson's essays. Everywhere I went, I carried Robert Burns' poetry. Even when I plowed mules on a steep hill on my father's farm, I carried Burns' poems until I wore the volume out and Mrs. Hatton gave me another one. Now, Mrs. R. E. Hatton, my Greenup High School teacher, is one of the reasons why my books are in libraries over America and in other countries on six continents in English and in translations.

While at Greenup High School a most unusual thing happened. This didn't concern any teacher or student. I found a book on the floor where the custodian kept his supplies. I picked it up from the floor and wiped the dust with my hand. This book wasn't marked as property of the Greenup High School Library. It didn't have a name in it. It was a stray book. And after I got into reading *The Odd Number,* a collection of stories by Guy de Maupassant (a French writer whom I'd never heard of) I thought, perhaps, invisible hands had placed that book there for me and opened the custodian's door so I could find it. I'd never read anything as fresh and fine as these stories. Each story was a plotless colorful slice of life, one this reader couldn't forget.

The popular short story writers whose stories we had been studying in American Literature were Poe, O. Henry, Hawthorne, Mark Twain. Poe I thought might have invented the detective story, while O. Henry did the story with the unnatural trick ending. But de Maupassant was a natural writer. What one book can do for a high school student! *The Odd Number* changed my life regarding the way a story should be written. I told Mrs. Hatton the way I felt about his stories compared to the American authors' stories. She disagreed with me.

After working for a street carnival and doing military training at Fort Knox, Kentucky, I worked at the American Rolling Mills, which is now Armco. Here I learned to be a blacksmith. While working in the steel mills, I did many poems, continued to buy a good book and see a movie each week. I had a small library in the blacksmith shop where I worked with good men in steel, but so many couldn't read and write.

Finally, on a day in early September I packed my belongings, taking with me what I thought was the best of what I'd written. I had more manuscripts in my cheap suitcases than belongings. I actually didn't have time to apply and get enrolled in a college. In a matter of days all colleges and universities would be opening. And I didn't have money and decent clothes. I couldn't choose a college. One had to choose me. I had to go present myself and explain my resources. I'd taken a sudden notion to leave the steel mills where I'd advanced from stand-by labor to a blacksmith with good pay for that time. I could have stayed on indefinitely at the American Rolling Mills. I was one of the best workers in my department. I also wrote many of my boss's letters, and I certainly did his figuring in steel when this had to be done.

Hitchhiking, I came to one college with some new buildings. It looked too big for me. I moved on to a Methodist college. My father was Methodist. I talked only to a student, who was working part of his expenses there. I told him what I wanted. Then I asked him how much money it would take. He replied: "At least $300!" "I don't have that kind of money," I told him.

"What is the matter with your face and hair?" he asked me.

"I've been working in the steel mills," I told him. "I quit working there day before yesterday. I worked with hot furnaces and over hot fires where we heated pieces of steel large enough for railway car axles. My face is the color of burnt bacon and my eyebrows are singed off—also hair up half way of my head."

"I think you'd better go on," he said.

I found out who this man was in later years. He has my books now in his library.

Now, I hitchhiked on to Berea College. I'd never been to Berea College in my life. This was the first place I'd ever set foot on a college campus. I knew one man there who was from Georgia. He traveled one summer selling Bibles to defray his Berea College expenses. My mother bought one which she didn't need and paid him with chickens.

"He's some mother's son from the far-away state of Georgia out trying to get an education," Mom said.

Now my mother's son was out hitchhiking with a burnt-bacon discolored face, lost eyebrows, and singed hair trying to find a college that would take him.

On the Berea College campus a young man directed me to the Y.M.C.A. after I told him I wanted to see Will Sears.

"Has Will Sears returned yet?" the young man asked the director of the Y.M.C.A., an elderly man, with a round face, thinning brown hair, large round china-blue eyes, who was modestly dressed in gray suit, white shirt, and black bow tie.

"No, he'll be back from Georgia tomorrow," replied the director. "He's been in Georgia selling Bibles this summer."

"What's your name?" the student who'd taken me to the Y.M.C.A. asked me.

"Jesse Stuart."

"Mr. Stuart here knows him and wants to see him."

"What I want is to try to enroll in Berea College."

"Well, you'll want to see Dean Hendrix," replied the director.

"I'll take you to his home," said the friendly young man who was trying to help.

Both friendly college student and Y.M.C.A. director eyed me suspiciously.

"I'd like to wash my face and change my shirt," I said.

After a general cleanup I followed him under the oaks where dozens of squirrels played.

"Dean Hendrix, here's a young man who wants to enter Berea College."

"Stuart's my name," I told him.

"Why do you want to come to Berea?"

"Well, I can work my way through school here."

"Do you drink?" he asked me, after looking at my face and hair.

"No, sir."

"Do you smoke?"

"No Sir."

"Dean, I've just come from the steel mills," I explained. "I've worked with hot furnaces and over hot fires. My face will change color and my hair will grow back."

"But we have 105 students on the waiting list for this school. Apply for next year."

"There'll be no next year at Berea College for me," I said. "I'm going somewhere to college."

"Since you're so positive and determined," he said, "there's a small school south of here at Harrogate, Tennessee, where one of our Deans, Dr. Charles D. Lewis, is Acting President. Go down and tell him I sent you. You'd better hurry. Tomorrow is the last day of their registration."

"How's the fastest way?" I asked.

"There's a passenger train through here at ten this evening and it will get you there early in the morning," he told me.

"Goodby and thank you, Dean Hendrix."

"Goodby and good luck, Mr. Stuart."

Dean Hendrix gave me a last suspicious-looking glance as we shook hands in parting.

"We'll pick up your suitcase and smaller bag at the Y.M.C.A. and I'll take you to the railway station," said the student who could not have felt more remorseful because I'd been rejected at Berea College.

In years to follow I recommended, and Berea College accepted, many of my high-school graduates, good students without money, and here they obtained college educations. In 1955 Berea College awarded me the Berea College Centennial Award for Literature. In 1966, forty years after my trying to enter college there, Berea College gave me an Honorary Doctor of Literature degree. I have the longest list of titles in their famous Weatherferd-Hammond Mountain Collection. In addition, Berea College Bookstore has always been stocked with my books. They sell there.

When I rode a slow night train around curves through the East Kentucky mountains, I had a

Plum Grove School, 1917; Miss Elta Cooper, teacher.
Jesse Stuart at far right in front row.

thought: It wasn't my destiny to attend Berea College. I looked forward to going to a new school where I didn't know anyone and to be in Tennessee, a state where I had never been.

I arrived at Harrogate in the morning. When I got off, a girl inquired where was Lincoln Memorial. I said I was going there, too. A young freckled-faced man told us he'd met the train for Lincoln Memorial students. Two young women got up on the truck seat beside him. I and three other boys stood up in the back and held to the cab. All of us had our belongings in the truck bed.

"Better take you where they're registering, for this will be the last day," said the driver.

He took us near the old auditorium-gymnasium (combined) where we joined a line of students. There were teachers and Dean Charles D. Lewis, Acting President of Lincoln Memorial University. He was making decisions for the students who had problems. I was one.

"Your name?"

"Jesse Stuart."

Dr. Lewis went through a sheaf of papers on his table.

"You don't have an application."

"No, I don't."

"When did you decide to come to Lincoln Memorial University?"

"Yesterday evening. I was in Dean Hendrix's home. I tried to get in Berea College. They have 105 students on the waiting list. Dean Hendrix must have been impressed with me. He told me about you and Lincoln Memorial University. He told me to tell you since he couldn't take me in Berea College for you to take me in Lincoln Memorial University."

I'll never forget how President Lewis, an average-sized man, blue eyes, chubby round face, nice smile, hair parted in the middle, in his middle forties, looked at me and said: "Stuart, you've got an honest face!"

I got in college on my face.

Jesse Stuart as Superintendent
of Greenup County Schools at age 24.

In years since, when I lectured in nine foreign countries, I often told this story. And the students wanted to come to America. I think this is the only country in the world where that could have happened.

"Now, Mr. Stuart, how much can you pay?" President Lewis asked me.

"I can pay $10.00," I told him.

"Then, you'll be a full work student, and you'll probably be permitted to take only a half schedule of classes," he said.

"Oh, no," I told him.

I actually came onto the campus with $29.30. But I was alone and without anyone to help me. I thought I might need a little emergency fund.

"Do you think if your schedule is arranged so you can go to school a half day, work a half day and perhaps work after each meal, you can carry a full load?" he asked me. "Remember we have quality teaching and a high standard here!"

"Well, let me try it," I said. "I don't want to spend eight years instead of four finishing college."

This schedule was arranged for me. I worked mornings until noon. In the afternoons I had my classes. After each meal, I dried the pots and pans. College work was easy for me after ten-hour days in the steel mills. I did any work at LMU I was asked to do. I was one of the crew to help dig the water line from Cudjo's Cave in Cumberland Gap over a low Cumberland Mountain foothill to Harrogate, Tennessee. This furnished all the water for Lincoln Memorial University and a great portion of the village of Harrogate. I worked on the farm. I assisted in bricklaying for one of the dormitories. I was often called out, even sometimes on a Sunday, to unstop a sewer line. I didn't mind. I was in college. I had been given a chance.

Sitting beside President Lewis at the next registration table was a big man I couldn't help but notice. He had ruddy cheeks, twinkling blue eyes, a pear-shaped head with the little end up. He was Harry Harrison Kroll, Head of LMU's English Department. I didn't know it then, but he was to be my teacher of destiny at Lincoln Memorial University. Mr. Kroll was a Dunkard, pure German; his family had moved from Indiana to be cotton sharecroppers. He often boasted that he had less formal education than Abraham Lincoln. He had entered Peabody College as a special student, after three months of elementary schooling in a one-room school. He was self-taught. He passed an exam for an eighth grade diploma, which he had to have. He passed the high school subjects examination and received his high school diploma, his B.A., and M.A. degrees at Peabody College at the same time.

I thought Lincoln Memorial University, with 320 students, was fabulous. To be there, among young people, going to classes and working on the campus was such a contrast to being a blacksmith in the American Rolling Mills. Also, I had in my suitcase when I arrived at Lincoln Memorial over 500 poems, plus themes, and essays which could be called stories. I also had a wire clotheshanger which was filled to capacity with rejection slips for my poems.

Thomas Tillman, editor of *The Blue and Gray*,

our college paper, was preparing his last paper he would edit before the school would elect a new editor. I selected twenty-five of my best poems and sent them to him. When the paper was published, I grabbed a copy and looked. Not one of my poems was published. I had another idea. I had my room-mate Mason Gardner, who planned to be a minister, nominate me for the editor of *The Blue and Gray*. He was a fine speaker and told the student body I could write. But someone nominated a beautiful girl; later she was to be chosen Miss Lincoln Memorial University. When the votes were counted she won by a 5-1 margin. She got nervous and couldn't keep the editorship. Another election was held. Gardner nominated me again. Another beautiful girl was nominated who beat me 4-1. She, too, got nervous and couldn't be the editor. Then, the faculty members interfered and gave me the editorship of *The Blue and Gray*. First thing I put in the paper was my poem, "Cumberland Call." I published my own first poem the first time I was ever in print. My poem looked good. I enjoyed it. So did the students.

In Mr. Kroll's class, which was called Journalism, he asked us to write 30,000 words per quarter.

"Don't you know any old scandals that happened around your homes?" he asked us. "If you do, write these up but be damn sure you change the names!"

Now, Mr. Kroll was writing, too. He was selling stories and articles. He tried poetry, which he didn't do well. He was also writing a novel. He called it "Peckerwoods." A peckerwood is what a poor white used to be called in the south.

"It's a terrible title, Mr. Kroll," I told him.

He did change his title to *Cabin in the Cotton*, a novel that sold to the movies, and Richard Barthelmess and Bette Davis played in it. He was to follow this with about twenty more published books, among these, *I Was a Share Cropper* and *Their Ancient Grudge*.

In Mr. Kroll's classes I found plenty of competition. I wanted Mr. Kroll to say I was a "genius." He never did. He said Callis McCall was the genius of our class.

"Mr. Stuart, you're going to be a great poet," he said. "But you can't write a short story."

"Why can't I write a short story?" I asked.

"You're too damned scatter-brained," he replied quickly. "And your endings are terrible. Tie them up like Poe and O. Henry."

"I'll take Guy de Maupassant's way of writing colorful slices of life," I said.

"Who's Guy de Maupassant?"

Mr. Kroll inspired us! He lifted us to new heights! We went beyond the hours he was to teach and the hours we were taking. We had extra classes in the evening when weather was warm out under a campus street light or under a tree. If the weather was cool, we went in to a classroom. Each student read a story or poem or excerpts from a book.

Because of the unorthodox way that Mr. Kroll taught English, there were students and teachers against him. When his first book was published while he was at LMU, one professor ripped it apart and put it on the fire. Some of the students who were against him had another teacher to teach them creative writing. They sat under a eucalyptus tree in warm weather while we sat with our H. H. Kroll under a larger eucalyptus tree not a hundred feet away. When I returned to Lincoln Memorial University, I used to go and have a look at those trees. On my last visit to LMU I saw the opposition tree had died. I wrote a story about this which has been published.

Mr. Kroll taught two years at Lincoln Memorial University, then he was fired. Over the years, since his teaching there, he and his students have published more than 100 books, published by reputable houses on a royalty basis, while one student from the opposition tree had four books published.

While at Lincoln Memorial, I didn't get a scholarship. I worked all of my way, except for two one-dollar bills my mother sent me. I'm the only one of five children ever to get money from home. My brother and three sisters all worked their ways through college without a scholarship. Our family is one-hundred percent college graduates with twenty-six years of college and university training. I finished college in three years and two summers with 2.2 out of a possible 3. I left owing Lincoln Memorial $100.50, which I paid two summers after graduating.

Of what I'd written for my great teacher, Harry Harrison Kroll, my stories that bothered him, forty-three later made quality magazines, including *Atlantic, Harper's, American Mercury, Story,* and *Esquire*. I wrote a story about Mr. Kroll, "The Crazy Professor," that was later published in *Esquire*. I told how he taught creative writing.

Now from the material I did on this campus,

also, came three books which are somewhere on library shelves over America. *Head of W-Hollow,* my third published book, is a collection of these stories. I wrote a long short story, "Kim," published in a magazine called *The Little Man,* which today is a collector's item. I did it all at LMU, an assignment for H. H. Kroll. I also selected poems I'd done, some in high school, some in the steel mills, but mostly at Lincoln Memorial, into a volume titled *Harvest of Youth,* which I had privately published in 1930. When only three copies were left, it was reprinted in an edition of 2000. A copy of the original printing has sold for $1,000.

My great teacher is now deceased and doesn't know this. I have had 470 stories published in quality magazines. About one-third of these are in my eight collections. They're in libraries over America. They're in foreign schools and libraries in English and in translation. They're taught in textbooks of more than thirty countries. Was this because I found a book which I loved, and kept because it gave me a dream?

When I returned to my home, a college graduate in 1929, I was one of a dozen there with college degrees. There still weren't any hard roads in Greenup County. Only Russell and Greenup, towns in Greenup County, had independent high schools. Greenup County didn't have a high school. I taught in a small high school branch of the Greenup Independent Schools located at Winston. I taught fourteen first- and second-year pupils in a little building that had been used to stable horses. These students had not seen movies, had not read many books. I carried them my books in a suitcase, walking seventeen miles each way.

Here were the best students I have ever taught. They waded through my copies of *War and Peace, Anna Karenina,* and *Resurrection.* They read all the books I could take them and wanted more. We won six scholastic honors out of seven against Greenup High School that had close to 300 pupils. We rode mules, on a cold winter day, from Little Winston High to Greenup High and we conquered them—scholastically!

The following year Greenup High School's principal resigned, and I, now called a "genius teacher," (I had genius students who nearly worked me to death) was offered the principalship of Greenup High School. I grabbed it, never asking how much I was to receive. My pupils from Winston High School followed me to Greenup. We won football

games and scholastic events in a state competition. But before the year was over a friend learned of my salary and prompted me to ask for a raise, which I did. I was fired. I never asked for another raise in my life. When I accepted a teaching position, I let the administrators set my fee in the United States and in foreign countries.

I had received $100 per month for nine months at Winston High, but from each monthly check I paid $25 for room and board. In the summer of 1930 I paid, not a large fee, to have *Harvest of Youth,* my first book, published. Then I'd gone to Peabody College by bus for summer school to improve my teaching. I'd purchased myself a new suit, reasonably priced, shirts, socks, neckties, underwear, shoes, and a light gray overcoat, which I always liked. I'd made my dollars count. I didn't smoke. I didn't drink intoxicating beverages. I didn't waste a dollar.

As principal of Greenup High School, I received $1,000 a year. I asked to be raised to $1,200. In the meantime I'd contracted for a 50-acre farm which joined my father's farm, and I had almost paid for it. Near the end of the school year when I was fired, I was almost without money.

In early September 1931, I packed my trunk, mostly manuscripts and special books, books that were my friends, books that I loved. I bought a bus ticket for Nashville, Tennessee. I hadn't applied to enter Vanderbilt University. But I had a strong feeling I would be going there. I didn't know as I rode on a lonely bus over rough roads through the night that I would find that teacher who would shape my writing destiny. Next morning when I arrived in Nashville, I had $130. This wouldn't get me far toward paying expenses for a graduate student at Vanderbilt University, where a minimum fee in 1931-32 would be $1,500.

Now to the Vanderbilt Campus where I looked up Dr. Edwin Mims, a well-known lecturer, educator, writer, head of the English Department.

"Dr. Mims, I'm here," I said.

"But who are you?" he asked.

"I'm Jesse Stuart, and I've come here to do graduate work in English," I said. "I've heard of you! My first introduction to you was in the Camp Knox Library. I found your introduction to Thomas Carlyle's essay on Robert Burns. I was the first soldier to read it. I thought it was excellent."

"But where did you go to school?" he asked.

"Lincoln Memorial University," I said.

Dr. Mims wasn't impressed. The mentioning of the name Lincoln to a dyed-in-the-wool Confederate in 1931 was, to say the least, not impressive.

"But my problem is money," I said. "I've got only $130. I don't have any financial support from home. I'll have to work a half day maybe—"

"Your financial difficulties are not my worries," he said. "My work is to handle this English Department."

"Said to be one of the best of any school in the nation," I said. "The Fugitives, the Agrarian Writers such as Tate, Ransom, Warren, Davidson, Merrill Moore, Andrew Lytle, yourself, and many more. When I was a student at Lincoln Memorial I used to read Donald Davidson's literary page in the *Knoxville News Sentinal*."

Dr. Mims had a pair of black eyes, and his steady gaze at me was piercing.

"I've brought a trunk half-full of manuscripts," I said. "If things get too tough for me, I could sell a few of these here—perhaps to students."

I knew I'd said the wrong thing.

"Stuart, I hadn't planned to let you enter the graduate school," he said. "I've changed my mind. We'll accept you. I want to observe you."

I paid all I could to enter Vanderbilt, but I kept back a few of my $130. I went to the Y.M.C.A. director, Mr. Hart. He helped me get a janitorial job, which was almost a half day's work of sweeping the Science Building. Then I worked in Wesley Hall cafeteria, where the elite of Nashville came. I waited tables and dried silver. First I received my meals for doing this. Since we were in the Depression, and people didn't come out to eat as in the past, our work time was cut down. We pro-rated time, and I was cut down to eleven meals per week.

I roomed with the ministerial students of Vanderbilt's College of Theology in Wesley Hall. I worked with them in the cafeteria. A room was much cheaper here. Only one other student in Wesley Hall wasn't a ministerial student. He was an undergraduate in Math and Science. His mother brought him bread and fresh eggs from the country, and he shared some of his food with me. We also purchased

molded bread, cut the mold off and found it better than fresh bread.

I took the Novel under Robert Penn Warren, American Literature under John Donald Wade, Victorian Literature under Dr. Edwin Mims, Elizabethan Poetry under Donald Davidson. All classes in Vanderbilt ranged from six to a dozen students. Clem Carson, from Tifton, Georgia, shared his textbooks with me, and now his daughter is teaching my books in her high school English classes. I couldn't buy textbooks.

My first semester at Vanderbilt was the hardest time I'd ever had in school. I didn't have time to study. Working took my time. I was one of two white student janitors; the other one was a ministerial student.

And when my grades came through first semester, I wrote a poem to "Three Low Grades Vanderbilt," which is in *Man With a Bull-Tongue Plow*, a long sequence of poems I began before leaving Vanderbilt. I wasn't given a grade in Dr. Mims' class. I made the second-to-the-lowest marks in American Literature. In the Novel course under Robert Penn Warren where students discussed writing novels and the great American novel, I made for three quarters grades of C, C+, B—; grades low for an undergraduate, but not passing for a graduate. I had no interest then in thinking I might write a novel. But I'm the only one from that class, with the exception of the teacher, who has written one. I've written nine novels. Three have had foreign publications; one has gone around the world, translated into many languages. It has sold over two million hardback copies.

In Donald Davidson's class I received A. Here I had found a man, a spirit that went beyond teaching. He was the last man to shape and mold me as much as anyone could—and all for the better. I found so much in him. He must have seen much in me. I showed him poems I'd been writing in the tradition of the period. I was following the school of the imagist poets. I had imitated others, one was Carl Sandburg. Then I had written poems about people, scenes, and moods of my country—rural Appalachia. I let him see two batches of my poems.

When he reported to me, fire danced in his eyes.

"Stuart, don't imitate anybody," he said in a loud voice. "You don't have to! Write of your country when you go back home! Write of your country as the Irish have written of Ireland and the Scots have written about Scotland! Your Appalachia is bigger than either Scotland or Ireland. It's larger than both with England and Wales added—in area but not in population!"

"Here, send this poem of yours to H. L. Mencken, editor of *The American Mercury*," he said.

He handed me "Elegy for Mitch Stuart," a poem about my grandfather, and he'd made three or four slight changes.

"That big magazine," I said. "I can't make the little magazines."

"You're not cut out for the little magazines," he said. "You belong to the big ones."

"But I've just read a syndicated article in *The Tennessean* where Mencken said there wasn't any poetry written in America worthy to be published."

"His bark is bigger than his bite! Send it!"

And I did send it. The poem was accepted. Unfortunately, I was not paid for it until after I left Vanderbilt.

My second semester at Vanderbilt University was a different story.

Wesley Hall burned, and the cafeteria burned where I was getting eleven meals a week. Everything I had—my trunk, over 500 poems, all other manuscripts, including my thesis I'd nearly finished, my old Oliver typewriter, which I'd bought for $25, all my clothes but the ones I had on—perished in this fire. Then I really wondered about my future. Finally, I decided to stay and build on the ashes. All ministerial students, including me, not a ministerial student, were transferred to Kissam Hall. One person, a student, tried to get me to enroll as a ministerial student so I wouldn't have to pay for my room. Not me. Clothes came in for all of us. Being the largest man in the group, I got the finest suit. A teacher, who had taught for me in Greenup High School, sent me one of his suits. I had a change of clothes.

Then Dr. Mims said to his class: "I want you to write for me a personal story about yourselves, not under eight typewritten pages and not over eighteen—"

This I wanted to do. Katherine Atherton Grimes on the old *Southern Agriculturist* gave me paper, and I rented a typewriter for 75¢ from Patrick, a

Jesse Stuart, the author of 47 books, in his study at W-Hollow.

ministerial student. I had eleven days to do my paper. Now I was living on one meal a day. A classmate from Lincoln Memorial had paid for this out of his meager earnings.

I never cut a class. I did my janitorial work. I lived on a noon meal. The Depression was on us. I never want another one. And on the eleventh day I had my paper. Dr. Mims had sat just across from me, although this was imaginary, and I told him how I got from the one-room shack where I was born to Vanderbilt. I told him my story. The paper was written from margin to margin, for I didn't have much paper. It was 322 pages. To hell with eight or eighteen pages. But I put the manuscript on heavy cardboard, bound it down with two heavy rubber bands that almost cut the paper but compressed it to make the manuscript look smaller.

Students quipped about their important lives when they handed their papers to Dr. Mims. They had passing grades. I didn't. But I believed the life of any human being was important in America and in the world. I knew my life was important. It was all that I really had.

I was the last one in my class to go up with my paper to Dr. Mims.

"There you go, Stuart," he said, feeling the weight of my paper, "you're failing in my class and you hand me a paper like this. You know I read every word of the papers handed in to me by my students."

Three days later Vanderbilt was a new place for me.

"I've been teaching for forty-three years," Dr. Mims said. "Stuart, your 'Beyond Dark Hills' is the finest paper ever handed to me by a student. It's crudely written. Yet so beautiful, and it needs punctuation!"

Beyond Dark Hills was published six years later as my fourth book, in America and England. An excellent review in the *New York Times* questioned why a man of thirty would write his autobiography. The reviewer didn't know I'd written it six years before for a term paper in an English course which I was failing.

Also, I was offered two scholarships at Vanderbilt, not big in those Depression years, but quite substantial; one for continued graduate work in English, another for football. I'd gone out for some spring practice, but a meal a day wasn't sufficient food. I didn't have a trunk to take home. I had myself and a small suitcase. I said farewell to my teachers and fellow students. Donald Davidson clasped my hand, his black eyes sparkling, "I hope you have a million readers!"

In the years that have followed, I don't know how many million readers I've had. There is no way to measure. My books have sold, and they've been worn out in libraries and reordered. I've had over a million French readers, Arabic readers, Spanish readers, German readers, Scandinavian readers, English readers, Czechoslovakian readers, and Japanese readers.

I borrowed two one-dollar bills and I hitchhiked the long way back, 450 winding road miles, living mostly on tomatoes from gardens and early apples from orchards.

My mission had been completed. I knew what I was going to try to do. I would send my Appalachia over America and to the world. Since I left Vanderbilt, spring 1932, until this present hour, February 14th, 1975, I have had forty-seven books published, 470 stories, 2,100 poems, 400 articles, over 3,000 publications listed by Dr. Hensley Woodbridge in his bibliography of my work. I've traveled in forty-nine states and lectured extensively in forty-five. In a dozen states I've spoken no less than 100 times.

I've traveled in ninety-one countries. I've lectured over and worked in nine foreign countries. My wife Naomi and I lived and taught in Egypt. One of my books, *The Thread That Runs So True,* was found in the American University of Cairo Library and brought me the invitation to come there and teach. This book has since been translated into Arabic and used in schools in the Arab world.

I was born in a country that offered me a chance. I didn't ask or expect my country to pay for my chance. I spent less than $500 in cash for my higher education, almost equivalent to a Ph.D. I worked for the rest, never asking for or obtaining a scholarship. I had good, great, and encouraging teachers, all along the way. But I had three teachers that were sent for me at the right place and at the right time.

I had Mrs. R. E. Hatton, Greenup High School; Harry Harrison Kroll of Lincoln Memorial University in my undergraduate days; and Donald Davidson in my graduate days at Vanderbilt University. I've read so many of the world's great books, but not one has been as influential as that dust-covered one placed on the floor with the door ajar so I could see it in the Greenup High School janitorial room, Guy de Maupassant's *The Odd Number*. Three teachers and a book have been the great influences to send my books to libraries, schools, and homes over America and to countries and peoples on six of the earth's continents.

The American Antiquarian Society

There is no other collection like it on earth

By ELLIOTT B. KNOWLTON

First building of the American Antiquarian Society, at left, from an 1836 woodcut. The Society's third building and current home on Salisbury Street in Worcester, Massachusetts, below.

The American Antiquarian Society at Worcester, Massachusetts is the premier research library for early American civilization. It preserves and makes available for study the largest single collection of printed source material relating to the history, literature, and culture of the first 250 years of what is now the United States. Its holdings of materials printed before 1821 are pre-eminent, and its collection of 1821-1876 material among the strongest anywhere. Of the estimated 100,000 books and pamphlets printed in this country between 1640 and 1821, AAS, remarkably, holds 60,000. Today, this collection totals more than 600,000 books and pamphlets, half a million manuscripts, an equal number of maps, prints, broadsides, and ephemera, and close to three million newspapers (the newspaper collection occupies two floors in three bookstacks which contain five miles of shelving).

In his diary for June 23, 1828, Isaiah Thomas, aged seventy-nine, wrote laconically—"Cut the grass at AAS Library." There is nothing too unusual about a seventy-nine year old mower of lawns, but when he turns out to be the president of the institution whose grass he is cutting, then explanation is needed.

One of the giants of a period in American history which produced a remarkable number of talented and farsighted men, Isaiah Thomas (1749-1831) became in 1812 the principal founder, first librarian, and first president of the American Antiquarian Society (AAS).

Successor to his hero and friend Benjamin Franklin

Oil portrait of AAS founder Isaiah Thomas (1759-1831) by Ethan Allen Greenwood. Marcus A. McCorison, below, was appointed Director in 1967. An AAS treasure is the first book printed in this country, *The Whole Booke of Psalmes*—the famous "Bay Psalm Book"— printed in Cambridge by Matthew Day, 1640. One of eleven copies known.

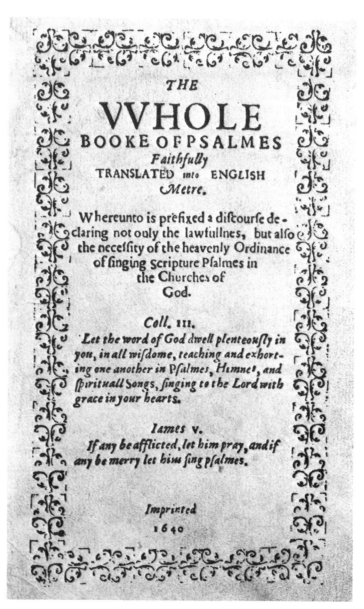

THE
VVHOLE
BOOKE OF PSALMES
Faithfully
TRANSLATED into ENGLISH
Metre.

Whereunto is prefixed a discourse declaring not only the lawfullnes, but also the necessity of the heavenly Ordinance of singing Scripture Psalmes in the Churches of God.

Coll. III.
Let the word of God dwell plenteously in you, in all wisdome, teaching and exhorting one another in Psalmes, Himnes, and spirituall Songs, singing to the Lord with grace in your hearts.

Iames v.
If any be afflicted, let him pray, and if any be merry let him sing psalmes.

Imprinted
1640

as the most distinguished printer-publisher-bookseller of his generation, Thomas was self-taught and could, in fact, set type before he could read. At the age of six he was apprenticed by the overseers of the poor to a Boston printer where one of his first jobs, mounted on a stool, was to set type for a lewd broadside ballad, *The Lawyer's Pedigree, Tune, Our Polly is a Sad Slut.* Ten years later, at sixteen, he ran away to Nova Scotia and worked on the *Halifax Gazette* until his repeated denunciations of the Stamp Act forced him to leave. Thomas's final act for this official newspaper of the provincial government was to print the stamp upside down next to a woodcut of his own carving showing the devil jabbing at the stamp with a pitchfork.

Drifting between Maine and South Carolina, Thomas returned to Boston early in 1770. He immediately laid plans to start his own newspaper, *The Massachusetts Spy,* which first appeared in August 1770. The fervor of this sheet made him even more of an anathema to British authorities and their Tory lieges than he had been in Halifax. As a chief protagonist of the rebel cause in the Bay Colony, his vigorous advocacy of revolution forced another retreat. On the night of April 16, 1775, Thomas ferried his press and types across the Charles River. Thence they were taken by ox-cart to Worcester, forty miles inland. On the 19th, with Dr. Joseph Warren, he went to Charlestown to urge that town to arms. The next day, the twenty-six year old printer followed his press to Worcester where he re-established the *Spy* and remained for fifty-six

Richard Mather's manuscript for "A Modell of Church-government" (1646), acquired with the Mather Library in 1814. The three men appointed to draft the Cambridge Platform were John Cotton, Ralph Partridge, and Richard Mather. Mather's version prevailed. The Society also holds the Ralph Partridge draft, although that of Cotton has disappeared.

The Boston News-Letter, 1704. One of three known copies of the first regular newspaper in North America. Founded by Boston postmaster John Campbell, it was a staunch Tory paper. Suspended twice during its first six years, it continued publication until February 1776, and during the last few years of its life was published by a woman, Margaret Draper.

years. In Worcester, Thomas developed the most successful printing and publishing business in the Colonies which included newspapers, books, a paper mill, bindery, and bookstores. The editions which he published were the best in every field, and were marketed through interlocking partnerships from Maine to Georgia.

In 1802 Thomas retired and turned over the business to his son and turned his own attention to collecting, with an eye to preserving, the recorded origins and growth of the nation which he had helped to create. He was very much aware of the history he had helped to make, and of the importance of the printed word. Regarding the art of printing as the preserver of all other arts, he set about gathering a large and varied assortment of printed materials which might otherwise have been lost. He bought up files of colonial newspapers, and began to build a library of books, broadsides, pamphlets, sheet music, and other printed sources illustrative of life in the New World.

In 1810 Thomas completed and published his *History of Printing in America*—still considered the standard work on that subject. By then he was more convinced than ever that there was a need for a library or learned institution to house his own and other American historical sources, to keep them safe, and to make them available to historians. With a group of like-minded men, all of whom had participated in the Revolution, Thomas petitioned the Great and General Court of Massachusetts for the establishment of

107

the American Antiquarian Society, a name patterned after the Society of Antiquaries in London. A charter was granted in October 1812. At its first meeting at the Exchange Coffee House in Boston on November 19, Thomas was elected president, a post he held until his death in 1831.

Thomas described the new Society in this fashion: "[It] is, in some respects, different from all other societies in the United States. Membership is restricted to no state, or party. There are no members merely honorary, but all have an equal interest and concern in its affairs and objects of this institution, whatever part of the United States they may reside in. It is truly a national institution." And so were to be the collections: ". . . every variety of book, pamphlet and manu-

> "If the American Antiquarian Society had not come into existence, our knowledge of the origins of this nation would, for a long time, have been composed of myths and legends. In a sense, the American Antiquarian Society gave us our past."
>
> —*Willard Thorp*

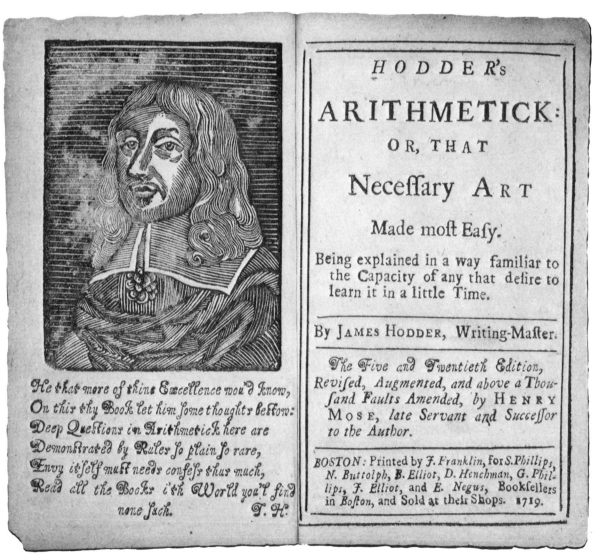

Another AAS strength is the collection of early children's books. Shown is the first American printing of *Hodder's Arithmetick: or, That Necessary Art Made most Easy,* printed by James Franklin (Boston, 1719.)

script that might be valuable in illustrating any and all parts of American history." Although AAS was the third historical society to be founded in the United States, following the Massachusetts Historical Society (1791) and the New-York Historical Society (1804), it was the first to be national in purpose, membership, and in the scope of its collections.

The founders chose Worcester as the site of the new Society. For one thing, Thomas lived there and had offered his house as temporary repository for the library; for another, the War of 1812 was in progress and an inland town forty miles from the guns of the British fleet, then in Boston harbor, was considered by the founders to be safer "for a place of deposit for articles intended to be preserved for ages."

The following year Thomas gave his own library of nearly 8,000 volumes to the Society. In 1814, he bought and gave to AAS what his diary records as "the remains of old Library of the Mathers which belonged to Drs. Increase, Cotton and Samuel. This is unquestionably the oldest in New England. The Remains are between 600 and 700 vols. Worked hard all day with Lawrence [his coachman] and other assistance in packing and removing it." Two weeks later when the books were safely in Worcester, he wrote: "Have been engaged in taking a Catalogue and putting the books in order of the Mather Library for the last 8 days, have not been abroad for the last six days." The next day he skipped a bank meeting to continue cataloguing, and the day after Christmas reported: "Still at work on

The title page from *Pamela: or Virtue Rewarded,* by Samuel Richardson, the first novel published in America. Reprinted by Benjamin Franklin in Philadelphia.

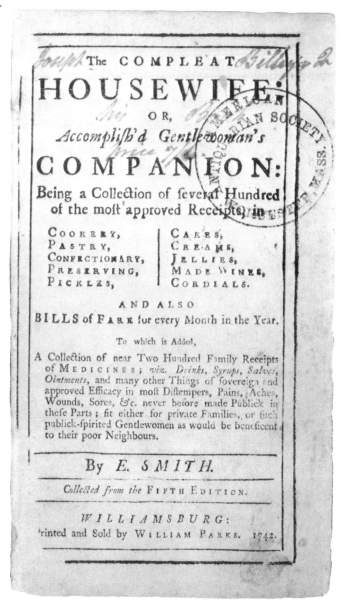

The Compleat Housewife: or, Accomplish'd Gentlewoman's Companion by E. Smith (Williamsburg, 1742,) is the only perfect copy of the first cookbook printed in America.

the Mather Library—very assiduously—have been only to bank and to church for a month past. Have got through with the bound books—now engaged on the mss." The seventy-five page folio catalogue Thomas compiled is still available at AAS, including the price he paid for each item.

Always resourceful and imaginative, Thomas was ahead of his time even as a fund raiser. In 1816 he presented the Legislature with a scheme for a lottery with a grand prize of $25,000. The public would buy $110,000 worth of tickets and, after prizes were paid, the Society would receive $30,000. But the Legislature disapproved. Eventually, he built the first Antiquarian Hall at his own expense. In the spring of 1817 he contributed the site, $2,000, and 150,000 bricks. The building was dedicated in August of 1820. That month he

notes in his diary: "Settled with the master workmen for building the American Antiquarian Society Library. This building cost, the mere building cost, without Land, or fences, or fixing the grounds, etc., 6752 dollars 84 cents. The building only.—Extra Labour on the Cellar, 11 dollars in all 6763 dollars 84 cents."

When the collections were moved from his house to the new building, he and "4 or 5 members attended all day" packing, unpacking and arranging. Small wonder he "Cut the Grass at AAS Library." Not only did Thomas give liberally of himself in time, talent and treasure, but he expected every member (114 in 1831) to contribute something of value to the Society's collections at least once a year. And most of them did.

Isaiah Thomas's death in 1831 could have left an unfillable void but for the emergence of Christopher

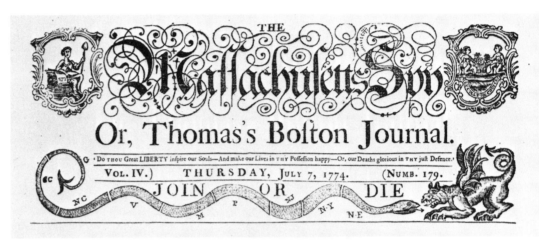

Masthead of Isaiah Thomas's *Massachusetts Spy* for Thursday 7 July 1774. Thomas started the *Spy* in Boston in 1771, and began printing it in Worcester 3 May 1775. The masthead was engraved by Thomas's friend, Paul Revere.

One of two known copies of a 1768 political cartoon engraved by Paul Revere. The verse, by Dr. Benjamin Church, consigns to hell those seventeen members of the Massachusetts General Court who cravenly voted to rescind an official protest against British tax levies.

Sensational journalism! A 1772 broadside condemning judges and jury (in most intemperate language) because Ebenezer Richardson, convicted of "most barbarously murdering" one Christopher Seider in 1770 was as yet "unhanged" on 5 March 1772. This rare broadside is notable for the reproduction of Paul Revere's "Boston Massacre" in the upper left corner.

Columbus Baldwin who, at a salary of $600 a year, became librarian of AAS in 1832. A member of the Harvard Class of 1823, expelled in his senior year for involvement in a famous Harvard riot, Baldwin came to Worcester to study law. Somehow he got sidetracked, fell under an Antiquarian spell, and worked with Thomas on a volunteer basis until his appointment. Like his predecessor, Baldwin was ready and willing to do anything that would improve upon the AAS collections. His success in adding to the newspaper collection and in acquiring the private library of Thomas Wallcut, regarded today as one of the most important assemblages of Americana acquired in the nineteenth century, are still remembered with awe and reverence. In 1835, Baldwin was killed in a stagecoach accident near Norwich, Ohio on his way to examine Indian

mounds on behalf of the Society's interests in archaeology. In four years, this thirty-five-year-old librarian added enormously to the American Antiquarian Society's growing stature. Baldwin's short tenure shaped no model for subsequent librarians. Samuel Foster Haven succeeded for forty-three years, and Clarence Saunders Brigham, who arrived in 1908, held office for fifty-one years.

Books, manuscripts, statuary, and artifacts strained the physical confines of the 1820 Antiquarian Hall. A new and larger library and cabinet museum was built in 1853. Enlarged in 1877, this, too, was replaced in 1910 by the present library building, thanks to the generosity of Stephen Salisbury, 3rd, Worcester merchant, philanthropist, and president of AAS from 1887 to 1905. Subsequent additions to the book stacks

A MONUMENTAL INSCRIPTION

ON THE

Fifth of March.

Together with a few LINES

On the Enlargement of

EBENEZER RICHARDSON,

Convicted of MURDER.

AMERICANS!
BEAR IN REMEMBRANCE
The HORRID MASSACRE!
Perpetrated in King-ftreet, BOSTON,
New-England,
On the Evening of March the Fifth, 1770.
When FIVE of your fellow countrymen,
GRAY, MAVERICK, CALDWELL, ATTUCKS,
and CARR,
Lay wallowing in their Gore!
Being bafely, and moft inhumanly
MURDERED!
And SIX others badly WOUNDED!
By a Party of the XXIXth Regiment,
Under the command of Capt. Tho. Prefton.
REMEMBER!
That Two of the MURDERERS
Were convicted of MANSLAUGHTER!
By a Jury, of whom I fhall fay
NOTHING,
Branded in the hand!
And difmiffed,
The others were ACQUITTED,
And their Captain PENSIONED!
Alfo,
BEAR IN REMEMBRANCE
That on the 22d Day of February, 1770.
The infamous
EBENEZER RICHARDSON, Informer,
And tool to Minifterial hirelings;
Moft barbaroufly
MURDERED
CHRISTOPHER SEIDER,
An innocent youth!
Of which crime he was found guilty
By his Country
On Friday April 20th, 1770;
But remained Unfentenced
On Saturday the 22d Day of February, 1772.
When the GRAND INQUEST
For Suffolk county

A WAKE my drowfy Thoughts! Awake my mufe!
    Awake O earth, and tremble at the news!
    In grand defiance to the laws of God,
The Guilty, Guilty murd'rer walks abroad.
That city mourns, (the cry comes from the ground,)
Where law and juftice never can be found:
Oh! fword of vengeance, fall thou on the race
Of thofe who hinder juftice from its place.
O MURD'RER! RICHARDSON! with their lateft breath
Millions will curfe you when you fleep in death!
Infernal horrors fure will fhake your foul
When o'er your head the awful thunders roll.
Earth cannot hide you, always will the cry
Of Murder! Murder! haunt you 'till you die!
To yonder grave! with trembling joints repair,
Remember, SEIDER's corps lies mould'ring there;
There drop a tear, and think what you have done!
Then judge how you can live beneath the Sun.
A PARDON may arrive! You laws defy,
But Heaven's laws will ftand when KINGS fhall die.
Oh! Wretched man! the monfter of the times,
You were not hung "by reafon of old Lines,"
Old Lines thrown by, 'twas then we were in hopes,
That you would foon be hung with new made Ropes

111

were built in 1924 and 1950. Complete renovation of the 1910 building, a new office addition, and climate control for the entire building came in 1971 and 1972.

When Brigham arrived in 1908, with the new 1910 building in the planning stage, a carefully considered decision to specialize and limit collecting goals was reached. Ninety-six years of collecting had amassed first-rate collections of early American newspapers and imprints. But there were large numbers of miscellaneous books either in foreign languages or on subjects unrelated to American history. These, along with antiquities and curiosities were dispatched to more appropriate havens in neighboring art and archaeological museums. Only those objects of American historical interest germane to books and manuscripts, or that could serve as house decoration were retained. Those

fields in which the Library was particularly strong were clearly defined. A policy of building upon strength was adopted—a dictum which continues to this day. Since that decision there has been no question that the American Antiquarian Society is completely a research library for early American history and culture.

In the latter part of the nineteenth century notable increases were made in existing collections of genealogy, bibliography, local history, psalmody, children's books, government documents, school books, and almanacs. New collections were established and built upon: American literature, city directories, maps, political cartoons, book catalogues, song books, sheet music, lithography, bookplates, colonial currency, cookbooks, music, Hawaiiana, transportation, and western narratives. Minor ephemeral lodes were quar-

ried and polished, such as stereoscopic views, lottery tickets, valentines, miniature books, awards of merit, watch papers, advertising trade cards, circusiana, theatre posters, and watermarks.

During the twentieth century AAS initiated an aggressive publishing program to further support scholarly research. *Paul Revere's Engravings* by Clarence S. Brigham was published in 1954 after thirty years of study. R. W. G. Vail, AAS librarian from 1930 to 1939, edited the last nine volumes of Sabin's *Dictionary of Books Relating to America*. Clifford K. Shipton (librarian from 1940-1967) added a thirteenth volume to Evans' *American Bibliography* in 1955, followed in 1959 by cooperative publication of a cumulative index to the complete Evans. In the last fifteen years AAS has published each year at least one

One of the earliest editions of "Yankee Doodle," probably printed in Boston in 1775.

Journal Of My Forty-Fifth Ascension, Being The First Performed In America (Philadelphia, 1793). The first American book on aviation. Although Blanchard was full of hot air in stating that his was the first balloon ascension in America, George Washington did witness Blanchard's feat, performed in Philadelphia on 9 January 1793.

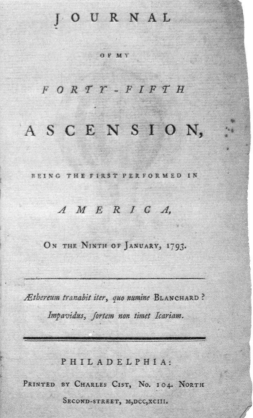

major work based on its holdings.

Beyond serving scores of scholars through its research library facilities, AAS has maintained since its founding an active publishing program to disseminate historical knowledge to a wider audience. The *Transactions and Collections,* designated as "Archaelogia Americana," published by the Society from 1820 to 1912 reflected the period interest in exploration and discovery. Reports of the meetings and papers of the American Antiquarian Society first appeared in 1813. Since 1849 its *Proceedings* have been published twice each year without interruption. The catholicity of subject matter reflects the spirit of an early statement of the Society: "The history that is hereafter to be written is not to be merely the history of government and politics, but the history of man in all his relations and interests, the history of science, of art, of religion, of social and domestic life."

The Society's most far-reaching contribution to scholarly work in American history has been the participation in an edition of *Early American Imprints,* an immensely important project making widely available in Microprint form as complete a publication as possible of all non-serial material published in the United States from 1639 to 1820. To date, 70,000 titles have been reprinted in this manner. The Society also participates in the *Early American Newspaper Series,* reproducing in Microprint form all American newspapers printed before 1821. It is safe to say that these projects have changed the whole direction of

Sir   Monticello. Jan. 9. 1814.

I have duly recieved your favor of the 13th of December, informing me of the institution of the American Antiquarian Society and expressing it's disposition to honor me with an admission into it, and the request of my cooperation in the advancement of it's objects. no one can be more sensible of the honor and the favor of these dispositions, and I pray you to have the goodness to testify to them all the gratitude I feel on recieving assurances of them. there has been a time of life when I should have entered into their views with zeal, and with a hope of not being altogether unuseful. but, now more than Septagenary, retired from the active scenes and business of life, I am sensible how little I can contribute to the advancement of the objects of their establishment; and that I should be but an unprofitable member, carrying into the institution indeed my best wishes for it's success, and a readiness to serve it on any occasion which should occur. with these acknolegements, be so good as to accept, for the society as well as for yourself the assurances of my high respect & consideration.

Th: Jefferson

Samuel M. Burnside
    Secretary of the A. A. Society

114

teaching and writing colonial history by giving teachers and scholars everywhere immediate access to the complete texts of nearly every American book, broadside, pamphlet, and newspaper published before 1801.

Allan Nevins called AAS "one of our national treasures." Samuel Eliot Morison, president of the Society from 1938 to 1952, noted that "The bibliographic treasures that the Society has in its keeping are a never-ceasing marvel." In 1968, because of its "treasures," AAS was designated a National Historic Landmark by the United States Secretary of the Interior. By special Act of Congress in 1814, AAS was made an official depository of all documents printed and distributed by the U.S. Government.

Sooner or later anyone seriously interested in American civilization from the earliest days of settlement comes to AAS—several thousand each year. To meet the needs and expectations of scholars, Marcus McCorison, present librarian, has instituted a program which will carry the Society's unique resources to a more diverse public: AAS now offers both short and long-term visiting fellowships for research in American history and culture.

Today the American Antiquarian Society continues its work as a learned society and research library in American history and culture, striving to implement the tenets set down by Isaiah Thomas over a century and a half ago to COLLECT, PRESERVE, and PROCESS for use the printed record of our past. There is no other collection like it on earth.

Thomas Jefferson's letter of acceptance to membership in the American Antiquarian Society. It was signed at Monticello 9 January 1814 and was directed to Samuel M. Burnside, Secretary of the Society. Jefferson was the second of twelve presidents of the United States who have been members of AAS.

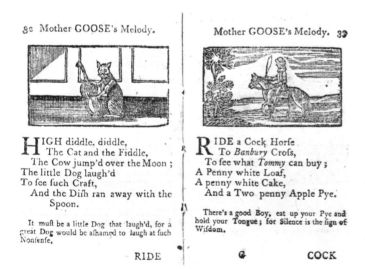

Another example from the juvenile collection: the earliest surviving American text of *Mother Goose*, 1794.

An 1849 broadside offering stock shares and passage to California for $300. It offers "A rare chance to any wishing a safe investment, good home and Large profits". No mention is made of any risk to person or funds.

WHEN THE SUN ALSO ROSE

President Calvin Coolidge

By LAWRENCE VAN GELDER

October 22, 1926. Half a century ago, almost a time out of mind—peaceful, frivolous; the Jazz Age at full flower; the Crash still three years in the future—distant, invisible, unperceived.

October 22, 1926. Publication day for a novel by a twenty-seven-year-old expatriate of some promise. His name: Ernest Hemingway. Its title: *The Sun Also Rises.* 259 Pages. Publisher: Charles Scribner's Sons. Price: $2.

1926—not a bad year for either a novel or a person to begin life, or so it seemed. At birth in New York City, a male could expect to live 52.82 years; a female 55.76. A person with a net income of $20,000 in 1925 would have paid the Federal Government about $618 in income tax in 1926. An actuary in the Treasury Department deduced from the returns that one out of 10,450 Americans was a millionaire. And it cost two cents to mail a letter first class.

It was a time of innocence, insularity, and the capacity for awe. America was observing its sesquicentennial. The telephone was fifty years old. Babe Ruth caught a baseball tossed from an airplane at a height of 300 feet. Lieut. Cmdr. Richard E. Byrd of the Navy and his pilot, Floyd Bennett, flew to the North Pole and back

from Spitzbergen in 15 hours, 51 minutes. Mussolini, known to his followers as Il Duce, was with some naiveté still accepted as the journalist-politician (and a Premier, at that) who wrote articles for the Sunday supplements and reviewed 50,000 blackshirts in Rome on the seventh anniversary of something called Fascism.

Calvin Coolidge sat in the White House (sometimes), presiding laconically over a nation almost evenly divided between the urban and the rural: 54,304,603 Americans, 51.4 percent of the population, lived in the cities: 51,406,017 lived in the country. The President earned $75,000, and in July went off with Mrs. Coolidge on a two-month vacation. His Vice President, Charles G. Dawes, earned

$15,000, the same as members of the Cabinet and William Howard Taft, the Chief Justice of the United States. Associate Justices of the Supreme Court—among them Oliver Wendell Holmes, Louis D. Brandeis, and Harlan Fiske Stone—were receiving $14,500.

But they were solid dollars, still as good as gold. (Ernest Hemingway's French francs, a good deal the worse for war, were worth only 2.98½ cents.) Being solid, however, the dollars were not that easy to come by. Girls, sought for unspecified "light" factory work, were offered $13 a week. "Chauffeur-mechanic, married, white; experienced Pierce car; steady position; $40," read a help-wanted advertisement in *The New York Times* of October 22, 1926. Still, the salary was better than that being offered the factory girls or the typists, receptionists and clerks answering the newspaper ads — $25. A personnel office near Times Square had a $30-a-week job for a secretary; one at $35 for a bookkeeper; and one at $75 for a furniture salesman who could take charge of a store. For a Ph.D. in chemistry, there was an opportunity at $2,700 a year, and perhaps more. Someone was willing to pay a machine parts salesman $2,100. There

Benito Mussolini

Ad from *Life* magazine

Ads from *The New York Times*

GIMBEL BROTHERS

Gimbel Sale—Unprecedented

Men's Famous "Imperial" UNION SUITS

⅓ OFF Regular Prices $1.95

Sensational!

CHANCELLOR PANATELA 3 for 25¢

Holeproof Hosiery

Stars and their car

Lieut. Cmdr. Richard E. Byrd

was employment for a radio repairman at $1,500. An electric draftsman specializing in marine piping could command $2,800; and a chemist with experience in plastics could look forward to $3,100.

But then as now, it was better to be rich than poor. True, $1.95 would buy one of the men's "famous Imperial union suits" (either drop seat or closed-crotch model) during the one-third-off sale at Gimbel Brothers ("eighty-four years of faithful service") in New York; and the same amount would buy a pair of Nada brand silk stockings at Best & Co. on Fifth Avenue.

How much nicer, though, not to have to worry about being able to afford, say, a packet of 20 Melachrino cigarettes (either plain or cork tip) for 30-cents or three of the new Chancellor panatella cigars for a quarter in those days before smoking was the handmaiden of disease (although alcohol, thanks to Prohibition, was legally the handmaiden of the Devil)

And why stop at cigarettes or cigars? For the individual with money and an eagerness to spend, it was a time of opportunity in housing, furnishings, clothing, entertainment and travel—to say nothing of the stock market.

But best of all, for the moneyed and carefree, there were the automobiles—Marmons, Jordans, Packards, Reos, Oaklands. "It is not by accident, surely, that Cadillac is outstripping, by two to one, all cars at its price or over," said a newspaper advertisement in October of 1926. "The growing demand for the great new Cadillac points this fact—one of the realities of American life is that success comes as the result of giving value. It is inconceivable that even Cadillac could maintain its leadership for any other reason than that it deserves its success —and that people know it." Prices began at $2,995, F.O.B. Detroit. For slightly more than a thousand dollars less, a Jordan "straight line eight sedan" could be bought. Jordan,

newspaper readers were told, is "the kind of car that women like to drive —that seasoned owners never tire of— that the small boys point to in traffic."

Not unknown were appeals to thrift and the employment of mechanically mysterious but wonderful-sounding phrases to describe automotive features. Thus, Chrysler was offering "new lower prices" on its "light six Chrysler 60 series." As a result, the club coupe cost $1,125, down $40; and the sedan was available for $1,245, down $50. The Marmon cost a good deal more—prices began at $3,195 for its series 75—but it offered a mechanical marvel: the "steering stabilizer, which produces an ease and steadiness of steering never before attained since the advent of balloon tires in combination with new four wheel brakes."

At the other end of the price spectrum, there was the Chevrolet touring car or roadster, at $510. The Overland Whippet sold for $695. The Dodge Brothers special sedan was priced at $1,040, but a touring car could be had for $881. The Flint ranged in price from $960 to $2,125. The Peerless Six-90 close-coupled sedan started at $1,895. The Oldsmobile de luxe sedan cost $1,125. Buicks

were $1,195 to $1,995. And the Pontiac Six could be had for $825. The Packard Six five-passenger sedan was still $2,781, "delivered at your door." The Reo? $1,495 and up.

The used-car market was active, too. A Rickenbacker coupe, in splendid condition, like new throughout, could be had for $350. For $865, one could buy a 1925 seven-passenger Sterling-Knight sedan, refinished and fully equipped, right down to four-wheel brakes. A Cleveland 1925 sedan (six cylinder), equipped with disk wheels, balloon tires, and four-wheel brakes, cost $595. And a 1926 Oakland sport roadster (kin to the Pontiac), with its original finish, four-wheel brakes, balloon tires and, yes, bumpers, was available for $785.

Of course, some people preferred simply to hire a car. The Grand Central Packard Renting Corporation (J. P. Carey) offered new straight-eight Packards with uniformed chauffeurs for $4 an hour for five hours or more, and $5 an hour for four hours or less. Sunday rates were $5 an hour for six hours or less and $4 an hour thereafter. All that was necessary to do was dial Murray Hill 3940.

The airplane was still largely a novelty — dangerous and unpredictable, best left to explorers and dare-devils. Civilized people traveled by train or steamship, and anyone tempted to do otherwise had only to look at the front page of *The New York Times* for Friday, October 22, 1926 to be shorn of such a fool notion. From London came word that 10 passengers—seven of them Americans—and two pilots had had a narrow but thrilling escape from drowning the preceding day when an English airplane on the London-Paris aerial route fell into the English Channel. The plane kept afloat long enough for a small fishing smack to race four miles to the rescue. The accident was the third in nine weeks on the London-Paris airline.

Of course, the plane had its uses.

The transcontinental air mail operated in both directions daily, leaving Hadley Field in New Brunswick, N.J. at 11 A.M. Eastern Standard Time and San Francisco at 8:45 A.M. Pacific Time. A small notice near the back of *The Times* said that Wednesday's air mail from San Francisco had arrived at Hadley Field at 3:21 P.M. and was forwarded to New York by rail. The westbound mail had arrived safely at 5 P.M.

Flying was definitely for the adventurous—and those with their minds on war. Tucked away on page 12 of *The New York Times* was a two-paragraph story:

London, Oct. 21—For the first time in the history of flying two high powered fighting airplanes have been successfully launched from an airship in midair. Cruising above Norfolk Downs today, two planes were slung beneath the airship R. 33. Their pilots started their engines and cut loose from the airship when they were ready.

This successful launching means that airships may now be used as floating airdromes.

Interesting, nothing more. Not even on a par, really, with a couple of other stories that day—Frank Lloyd

Clara Bow

John Barrymore

Barnstorming in the 1920's

Wright, the "widely known architect," was in jail in Minnesota, charged with violation of the Mann Act for transporting a woman to that state from Wisconsin, where warrants charged them with adultery. And in West Orange, N.J., 71-year-old Thomas A. Edison had celebrated the 47th anniversary of the invention of the electric light by listening in on an "electric night" on the radio.

So who was likely to become very excited about some tests involving warplanes? Travel—real travel—was the province of trains and steamships. As one advertisement put it:

BROADWAY LIMITED
20 HOURS TO CHICAGO

3800 passenger trains each day speed over the Pennsylvania Railroad—the largest operation of its kind in America. The Broadway Limited is the flagship of this great fleet. To make it a worthy leader, it has been equipped with every new luxury of travel.

Dining cars of new design—menus of unusual attractiveness—chefs especially trained in preparing delicious meals—the latest equipment in every car.

Traveling the shortest route to the West, the Broadway and ten other Pennsylvania trains each day set high standards of travel.

Scheduled to arrive in the port of New York on Friday, October 22, 1926, were the Cunard liner *Aquitania,* from Southampton and Cherbourg; the North German Lloyd liner *Columbus,* from Bremen, along with its sister ship, *Seydlitz,* also from Bremen, and the United States liner, *George Washington,* also from Bremen. Sailing were the White Star liner *Olympic,* for Cherbourg and Southampton; the Red Star liner *Zeeland,* for Antwerp; and the North German Lloyd liner *Berlin,* for Bremen.

Among the passengers arriving aboard the *Aquitania* were George Eastman, president of the Eastman Kodak Company, back from a seven-month hunting expedition in East Africa and warning that the big game would disappear soon; Mary Garden, prima donna of the Chicago Civic Opera Company, looking slimmer, younger, and more debonair than ever; and Sir Harry Lauder, Scotland's gift to entertainment, making what he called his fourth annual farewell tour of the United States.

Sir Harry was scheduled to open October 25 at the Century Theater, where Jeanne Eagels was in the "farewell week" of *Rain,* "The World's Greatest Drama." Entertainment seekers who cared for neither Sir

Harry nor Miss Eagels suffered from no dearth of other attractions. "The outstanding musical hit of all time," *Countess Martiza* was playing at the Schubert. *The Great Temptations,* a revue, was at the Winter Garden. Florence Reed was starring in *The Shanghai Gesture* at Chanin's 46th Street. At the Central, it was Lillian Gish in *The Scarlet Letter.* At the Bijou, it was Helen Hayes in *What Every Woman Knows;* at the Ritz, Florence Moore, in *She Couldn't Say No;* at the New Amsterdam, Marilyn Miller in *Sunny.* William Hampden was starring in *The Immortal Thief* at the theater named after him; and at the Longacre, the attraction was Dreiser's *An American Tragedy.*

There was rich fare, too, for moviegoers: *Beau Geste* at the Criterion; George Jessel and Syd Chaplin in *The Better 'Ole* at the Colony; Anna Case and John Barrymore in *Don Juan* at the Warner; D. W. Griffith's *Sorrows of Satan* at Loew's State; Emil Jannings in *All for a Woman* and *The Last Laugh* at the Cameo; and at the Broadway, Red Grange in *One Minute to Play.*

The timing was right for the Red Grange movie. Football held center stage in sports. The World Series had ended October 10, when the Cardinals

119

Gene Tunney

Red Grange

Babe Ruth

Billy Jones and Ernie Hare

beat the Yankees 3-2 in New York to take the seventh and deciding game. Notre Dame was getting silk pants and rubber hip pads and lightweight shoes to reduce the pounding and obtain more speed for the weekend game with Northwestern. (Knute Rockne's team was to win it 6-0, before 47,000 fans.) Harvard was preparing to play (and beat) Dartmouth, before 53,000 fans; Fordham was getting ready to lose to Washington and Jefferson, 28-13. Brown was preparing to play (and beat) Yale before 35,000 people. And Columbia was reaching a pitch that would enable it to run away to a 24-0 win over Duke.

Despite the ascendancy of football, there was still room for a few lines about Babe Ruth. In Atlantic Highlands, N.J., he was picking up some post-season money by barnstorming. His team played to a 6-6 tie with the North Highlands team. The Bambino hit two long home runs, resumed his pitching career, only to see the home team take the lead, and then provided the heroics with a ninth-inning hit that tied the score.

Not far away, in Atlantic City, Harry Greb, the former middleweight champion and the only man to beat Gene Tunney, who had won the heavyweight championship in Phila-

delphia from Jack Dempsey on September 23, died following a minor operation for a nose injury received a few weeks earlier in an auto accident.

Football, baseball and boxing could command their devotees certainly; but there were thousands who cared nothing for the playing fields and arenas. For their excitement, they looked to the stock market. Americans who picked up their morning newspaper on October 22, 1926, found that, in general, all was well on the New York Stock Exchange. General Motors, which would rise 22½ points during the year, closed at 147½ up 4 points on a volume of 229,900 shares. Chrysler was 33¾, unchanged. Atlantic Coast Line was 149, up 4. U.S. Steel, 138, up 2¾. Woolworth, 161⅞, up 2⅞. Hudson Motor Car, 45, up ½. Jordan Motor Car, 15¼, up ¼. Pierce-Arrow, 21, up ¼. Paige-Detroit Motor Car, 12, down ¾. Coca Cola, 147⅞, up 2⅛. International Business Machines, 49, up ⅛. American Telephone and Telegraph, 146⅜, up ⅞. Standard Oil of California, 60⅛, unchanged. Standard of New Jersey, 41⅛, up ¼. Sears Roebuck, 54, up 1⅝. Radio Corporation of America, 58⅝, up 3⅝. General Electric, 83⅛, up 1⅛.

With figures like these, one might well ponder the matter of spending one's profits. Some travel perhaps?: $245, first class aboard the North German Lloyd line flagship *Columbus* to Plymouth, Cherbourg and Bremen; $85 and up to Havana aboard one of the Pacific liners; $10 round trip to Boston aboard the *Boston* or *New York* of the Eastern Steamship line, each equipped with dance floor, dining salon, elegant furnished staterooms. Or perhaps some clothing? Lord & Taylor was offering men's hand-tailored suits, single or double-breasted sack suits, of English, Scotch, and domestic fabric, at $60. B. Altman had bowlers at $15, $20, and $25. For $33, from Wallach Brothers, one could buy all-wool overcoats or suits, in the new styles and colors, with "trustworthy tailoring" by Hart, Schaffner and Marx. For her, there was the fox scarf ("more women sanction it daily") from B. Altman, at $38 and $45. Or, during the 70th anniversary sale of W. H. Hall, the furrier at 18 West 38th Street, an extra-dark mink coat, for $1,800.

A four-piece bedroom suite, in walnut veneer, consisting of a full-size bed, dresser, chifonette, and vanity, could be had at $187.50, on sale.

Also on sale, at $197.50 was one of

Marilyn Miller

the new Radiola Super VIII 6-tube super heterodyne radios, completely equipped, requiring no ground or aeriel. Anyone who bought a new radio that October 22 would be all set to tune in that night when Queen Marie of Rumania, on a seemingly endless visit to the United States, appeared at Aeolian Hall on West 43d Street to give a talk at 8:30 to be broadcast over twenty-one stations, including WJZ in New York. Of course, there was no need to listen to the queen. If you could pick up WBAL in Baltimore, either at 246 meters or 1220 kilocycles, at 10 P.M., you could hear *Rigoletto*. And at 11 P.M., WGN in Chicago was offering Sam 'n' Henry, with songs.

But you could pass up the radio entertainment altogether if you had one of the Victor Orthophonic Victrolas and one of the new Orthophonic Victor records. "There is nothing with which to compare it, except the singing or playing of the artists themselves," the advertising proclaimed. Two dollars would buy a 12-inch recording of Leopold Stokowski and the Philadelphia Orchestra, playing the Strauss "Blue Danube Waltz" and "Tales from the Vienna Woods." For 75-cents, Victor offered Paul Whiteman and his Orchestra playing "Pre-

cious" (fox trot) and "Moonlight on the Ganges" (fox trot).

Some people, of course, would prefer always to spend money on food. Among the fancy groceries being advertised by Macy's were the 25-pound bag of extra-fancy new crop Louisiana uncoated whole head rice, at $2.97; Japanese crab meat — a large can for 74 cents; strawberry and raspberry jams, made of pure fruit and sugar, at 37 cents for 15 ounces; a one-pound carton of South American blend coffee for 49 cents; and the ginger ale—a dozen 12-ounce bottles, for $1.84

More lavish spenders might consider housing. At Fifth Avenue and 85th Street in New York City, a 12-room apartment with five baths could

be had for an annual rental of $9,500 to $12,500. On less fashionable West End Avenue, at 103rd Street, 3- and 4-room apartments were available in a fireproof building beginning at $1,800 a year.

In Rockland County, about 30 miles from Columbus Circle, a 42-acre estate was being offered. It was situated on two county roads with 2,000 feet of frontage. The estate, about 1.5 miles from the nearest village and its station, consisted of a large park with exceptionally valuable shrubbery and trees. Part of the estate was woodland; part cleared. There were a 12-acre deer park, fishing and rowing on the property, a bowling alley, tennis court, and facilities for billiards. The master house had 14 rooms and four baths. There were servants' quarters with bath and a gardener's lodge in addition to the three-car garage and other outbuildings. The price was $95,000. Of course, the advertisement noted, it was a sacrifice.

With the stock market going well, one could fall asleep with visions of such an estate dancing in one's head. It would be the morning of October 23 before one could learn from the newspapers of the great crowds that had greeted Queen Marie during her

Gertrude Ederle

Emperor Hirohito with family

visit to New York; of the three earthquakes that shook northern California on the 22nd but injured no one; that 17 Americans had died in the hurricane in Cuba on October 20; that Al Smith and Ogden Mills were still slugging it out in their New York gubernatorial campaign.

One absorbed sensation. Significance could wait until later. This was the year when Fascist youth organizations were founded in Italy and Germany; the year when Germany was admitted to the League of Nations, and Dr. Joseph Goebbels was named the Nazi gauleiter of Berlin. It was the year when Hirohito succeeded his father Yoshihito as Emperor of Japan, and Trotsky and Zinoviev were expelled from Moscow.

This was the year when Eugene V. Debs and Alton B. Parker died; and when Queen Elizabeth II of Britain was born. Rudolph Valentino died and so did Claude Monet. Kodak produced the first 16-millimeter motion picture film. Work was ready to begin on what people called the Hudson River Bridge and what would be called the George Washington Bridge. The Holland Tunnel was all but finished. The Book-of-the-Month Club began. Gertrude Ederle became

the first woman to swim the English Channel. People sang "I Found a Million Dollar Baby in the Five-and-Ten-Cent Store."

This was the year when Russia celebrated the ninth anniversary of the overthrow of czarism; when the last convict ship afloat sailed from France to Devil's Island, carrying 340 men; when millions of British laborers staged a general strike; when Sinclair Lewis laid his watch on the pulpit of the Linwood Boulevard Christian Church in Kansas City, Mo., and called on God to strike him dead within ten minutes. The incident took place a few weeks before Lewis refused the $1,000 Pulitzer Prize for *Arrowsmith* in protest to the compulsion put upon writers to "become safe, polite, obedient and sterile." This was the year the new American Hospital in Paris was completed; when evangelist Aimee Semple McPherson vanished at Ocean Park near Los Angeles and reappeared more than a month later in Mexico, where, she said she had been held for ransom after having been kidnapped by two men and a woman; when Abd-el-Krim, the Riff rebel leader, capitulated to the French in Morocco; when Robert T. Lincoln, the last surviving

child of Abraham Lincoln, died at 82 of a cerebral hemorrhage in Manchester, Vt.; when Norma Smallwood of Tulsa, Okla., was crowned Miss America; when Nicola Sacco and Bartolomeo Vanzetti, who had been convicted in 1920 of the murder of a paymaster and a guard in South Braintree, Mass., were denied a new trial. Ibn Saud became the King of Saudi Arabia. Eugene O'Neill wrote *The Great God Brown.* Sarah Lawrence College was founded. Duke Ellington's first records appeared. Robert H. Goddard fired the first liquid fuel rocket. Luther Burbank died.

The Senate Campaign Funds Committee was investigating reports of Ku Klux Klan domination of politics in Indiana. Reports filtering through the wild mountain passes to the Indian frontier said that the palace of the Grand Lama of Tibet in Lhasa, the "Forbidden City," was now illuminated with electric lights. From Paris came word that, although many inventors of the past had dreamed of harnessing the energy of solar rays to drive industrial machinery, two Frenchmen had done so. They were identified in news reports as an engineer, M. Grandillon, and M. Im-

QUEEN MARIE WELCOMED AT COLUMBIA.

Collage by
Kristen Reilly

Ernest Hemingway

beaux, a professor in the national school of civil engineers. The French government was said to be giving support to experiments on a grand scale.

But the paper of the 22d said the 40-page book review coming Sunday, October 24, would contain reviews of three important new novels. These were Willa Cather's *My Mortal Enemy,* Margaret Deland's *The Kays,* and Sheila Kay-Smith's *Joanna Godden Married,* a sequel to *Joanna Godden.*

On October 31, in an unsigned review, *The Times* did appraise *The Sun Also Rises,* calling it a work of "magnificent writing, filled with that organic action which gives a compelling picture of character." *The Times,* again anonymously, discussed Hemingway's first novel with less enthusiasm in a pre-Christmas roundup of six months' fiction. The roundup reserved its principal praise for Elizabeth Madox Roberts and said of *The Sun Also Rises* that it "is beyond question a brilliant, witty performance, but it leaves one with the feeling that the people it describes really do not matter; one is left at the end with nothing to digest."

It was left to Scribners, in an advertisement in that same issue of *The*

Times, to do the horn-tooting on behalf of its young novelist. Scribners quoted Herbert S. Gorman in *The New York World* as saying the novel was "heightened by some of the finest and most restrained writing that this generation has produced." Burton Rascoe in *The New York Sun* said: "Every sentence that he writes is fresh and alive. There is no one writing whose prose has more of the force and vibrancy of good, direct, natural, colloquial speech. His dialogue is so natural that it hardly seems as if it is written at all—one hears it."

Conrad Aiken, in *The New York Herald Tribune,* said Hemingway's novel "makes it possible for me to say of him, with entire conviction, that he is in many respects the most exciting of contemporary American writers of fiction." William Rose Benet, in *The Saturday Review,* spoke tersely of "dialogue extremely actual, superb pithy description. The book held us all the way through and we were sorry to finish it."

Scribners did not quote the *Springfield Republican,* which had reservations about the novel's "absence of structure" and "extreme moral sordidness."

Neither *The New York Times* of

October 22, 1926, or of the following day took note of the publication of Ernest Hemingway's *The Sun Also Rises.*

Among the books published that year were William Faulkner's *Soldier's Pay,* Louis Bromfield's *Early Autumn,* John Galsworthy's *The Silver Spoon,* Andre Gide's *Les Faux Monnayeurs,* Franz Kafka's *The Castle,* D. H. Lawrence's *The Plumed Serpent* and T. E. Lawrence's *The Seven Pillars of Wisdom.*

By mid-December, 1926, *The Sun Also Rises* had sold 7,000 copies.

For a first novel by a young expatriate, it was not a bad performance.

The Safe Place:

John O'Hara's Study At Penn State

By CHARLES MANN

It was the late Katharine (Sister) O'Hara's idea that her husband's study be re-created at Penn State. She first broached the matter through Marylyn Warnick, a bright young girl on the library staff who was to be very helpful with the final details of arranging the study in its new site. The suggestion was a striking one, but one that gave everyone with curatorial experience some pause. Such rooms did, of course, exist. Marianne Moore's apartment was on its way to the Rosenbach Foundation in Philadelphia. Historian Henry C. Lea's study had been set up for over fifty years at the University of Pennsylvania. Such rooms existed, but could one justify them? What would John O'Hara's reputation be one hundred years from now? Considering the situation, there were enough arguments in its favor to lead us to accept Sister's generous offer to underwrite the project. O'Hara was indeed the Pennsylvania novelist; his competition being Conrad Richter and John Updike, a writer who once pointed out how he and O'Hara could only have been nurtured in Pennsylvania, not in Boston or Brooklyn. O'Hara's Gibbsville was a town as well known as Winesburg or Jefferson, and its creator never lost track of it. Chauvinistically we could claim a logic in seeing John O'Hara honored by his own State University, even if circumstances had

The Master at his desk.

kept the undisputed master of the influence of college life on the American psyche from attending one himself. Moreover, O'Hara was more than a Pennsylvania writer; he managed to husband his creative energy to an extraordinary degree, publishing some four hundred short stories and nineteen novels.

I had first spoken to Katharine O'Hara within months of O'Hara's death in 1970 when I invited her to a memorial program at the Pennsylvania State University Library—to which O'Hara had given his manuscripts. Sister (I call her this now as did those who earned her confidence, which was not an easy matter, despite her extraordinary ability to keep groups of disparate people in harmony in her presence) had that day said in her distinctive voice—a kind of velvety tone with a bite to it—that she would not come. The occasion was for John, not for her. He had earned the honors, and she did not wish to detract from this focus on him. I was puzzled at the time; but when I knew her better, I realized that she could not have come

without breaking down, and she was too much a patrician to risk casting any such pall over the day. John O'Hara was a deeply sentimental man; this may come as a surprise to some, but indeed he was, and capable of public tears. I did not see his wife cry, but on the day we arrived at Princeton to remove the furnishings of her husband's study, she entertained us with her customary style, talking, moving about, directing the packers, and arranging for dinner. Then she disappeared, almost without a word. The next morning she apologized; the shock of seeing the study being dismantled had been too much, and, unable to face us any longer, she quickly went to her room. Four years after her husband's death she told me in a moment of strain that she missed him—missed him bitterly. It was "the strength of the guy" which had meant so much to her—and she shook a cigarette in her fingers, not wanting to say more. Again she went away. So, motivated by love, she wanted a permanent record of John O'Hara's presence to be placed somewhere. Motivated

by admiration for his work—her faith in him as a writer was as strong and unwavering as her personal feelings —she sought, I'm sure, something John had always wanted: academic recognition of his permanence and stature. That sounds a little simple and sentimental, but all I can say is that it is true.

Once our commitment was made, we labored long and hard on the arrangements for the study. The difficulties, as in all such projects, were constant, but once past were well worth it. On 5 October 1974, Sister came to Penn State with O'Hara's daughter Wylie and carloads of people to dedicate John O'Hara's study. It was her day as well as his, and she looked satisfied.

The following description of the study is taken from *The O'Hara Concern* (New York: Random House, 1975):

The study at "Linebrook" was virtually an O'Hara museum, with memorabilia from every stage of his life: his collection of antique horns; photos of daughter Wylie and Charles Addams in a Bugatti, of a coonskin-clad O'Hara in a Stutz Bearcat, of the racehorse named O'Hara, of the O'Hara Rolls-Royce, of Robert Benchley in an admiral's jacket but without trousers, of O'Hara costumed as Hitler; a photostat of the check from Yale for the Bergen lecture; the NBA award; the Donaldson award; caricatures and photos of the *Pal Joey* cast; a photo of O'Hara with Bennett Cerf and Cardinal Spellman; a John Held, Jr., drawing; the certificate of membership in the National Institute of Arts and Letters; the Gold Medal for the Novel from the American Academy of Arts and Letters; a Cape Cod lighter in the fireplace; the certificate attesting that O'Hara had crossed the equator aboard the *S.S. Kaskaskia* on 19 September 1944; a certificate from the New Jersey State Teachers of English; original Edward Shenton illustrations for *Tender Is the Night;* a horseshoe; a pottery ashtray made by Wylie; a photo of O'Hara with Senator John F. Kennedy at the National Book Award ceremony; metal artifacts; an acety-

Opposite: The dedication of the O'Hara Study at Penn State, 5 October 1974. From the left: Mrs. O'Hara, Wylie O'Hara Doughty, President John W. Oswald.

At left, closeup of pictures on the wall: O'Hara receiving the National Book Award for *Ten North Frederick,* 1955. Top, with Herbert Kubly and W. H. Auden; bottom with Auden, Kubly, and John F. Kennedy. At bottom right: Wylie O'Hara with Charles Addams in his Bugatti.

Below: O'Hara with John Hersey at the presentation of the Gold Medal for the Novel by the American Academy of Arts and Letters, 1964.

lene lantern; a mounted Stewart speedometer (set at 42983—Grace Tate's birthday); an antique purser's chest; a leather fireman's bucket for a wastebasket; a plaque carved with Joseph Conrad's credo ("My task, which I am trying to achieve, is, by the power of the written word, to make you hear, to make you feel. It is, before all, to make you see. That—and no more."); engraved silver cigarette boxes from his publishers; fire extinguishers; model cars; sabers; an Astrolite miner's lamp: decoy ducks; cuspidors; an army paymaster's chest for shoe-polishing equipment; a hurley; Benchley's banjo-mandolin; a violin; a photo of John and Sister taken against the Capitol dome in Washington; lighters; ashtrays; a buggy whip; a photo of friend Pat

Outerbridge in a Bermuda ocean race; a large American flag; a framed blackjack hand (nineteen on seven cards); storm-warning signals; a certificate of membership in the United States Naval Institute. The desk was covered with the tools of his trade, and the office model typewriter stood on its own table—with two tear-gas Pen-guns in the drawer.

The study was neither a cluttered den nor a showplace. Everything was neat, but it was a working room. It was his safe place where thousands of good words were written every week. He referred to it as his laboratory, and it was also his church—*laborare est orare*. The memorabilia served a dual purpose for O'Hara: they made him feel comfortable and helped to release the

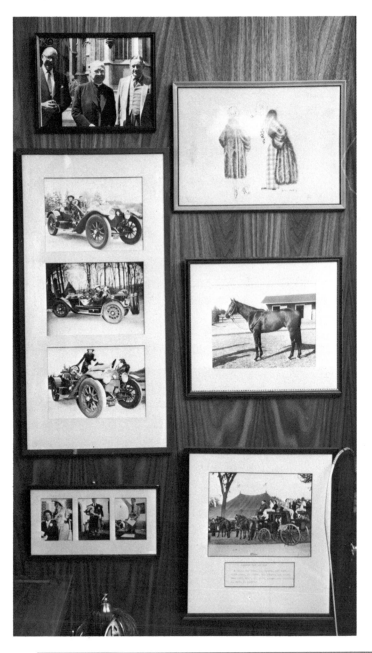

flow of memory. When he went into this room every night to do the thing he was born to do, the familiar items charged with emotions became part of the process of literary creation.

O'Hara's study was the working room of a writer who was dedicated to getting things right, so the shelves were stocked with reference books: technical dictionaries, *Who's Who in America, Who's Who, Burke's Peerage,* two editions of *The Encyclopaedia Britannica,* medical books, *Factors in the Sex Life of Twenty-two Hundred Women* (1929), histories of the auto, military reference books, works on Pennsylvania, club yearbooks, atlases, horse books, the 1902 Yale *Classbook, Baird's Manual of American College Fra-* *ternities,* the *Ayer Directory of Publications,* foreign-language dictionaries, books on music, books on sport. O'Hara's remarkable memory, verging on total recall, relieved him from the necessity of working directly from reference sources. Rather, these tools were available when he wanted to verify his memory. Like nearly everything else in the room, the reference books were comforting presences. It was good to know they were there when needed. Among the books in the "Linebrook" study was a copy of the *Yale Banner & Pot Pourri* for 1924, which may have been something more than a reference tool: if O'Hara had gone to Yale after Niagara Prep he would have entered in the fall of 1924.

Far left; details of the study as seen from O'Hara's desk. Top, O'Hara with publisher Bennett Cerf and Cardinal Spellman; middle, coonskin-coated O'Hara with a Stutz Bearcat; bottom, photos from a costume party—pantless Robert Benchley in the middle and O'Hara as Hitler at right. At right: top, a John Held, Jr. drawing; middle, the racehorse, O'Hara; bottom, a coaching party. Above: photos of O'Hara as a naval correspondent aboard the *Intrepid,* 1944.

Author Ring Lardner
cast in the leading role
by caricaturist David Levine.

Ring Lardner's
CARMEN

A Pages discovery: The previously unpublished vernacular libretto by the master of the American language.

Introduction by RING LARDNER, JR.

If there is any record of the circumstances under which my father wrote his version of *Carmen,* I have not been able to find it. I can state with complete assurance, however, that he didn't do it as an intellectual exercise or for the entertainment of a few friends. Not only is it clear from the text that he was concerned with the details of how it was to be staged, but it would be quite out of character for him to undertake such a considerable piece of work without a specific market in mind. In 1925 he was commissioned by Morris Gest to write a modern libretto for Offenbach's *Orpheus in the Underworld,* which also remains unproduced, and I think he must have had some similar encouragement on *Carmen,* which I judge from internal evidence was written a year or two earlier.

As readers familiar with the opera will observe, this is not just a case of Ring Lardner, humorist and master of American dialect, taking a classic and retelling it in New York vernacular of the 1920s, the way he did with traditional fairy stories like "Snow White" and "Cinderella." It is Ring Lardner, skilled musician and composer, working with music he loved and writing new words to fit it according to principles evolved out of many years' experience as a singer and song-writer.

Music played a very large part in the environment he grew up in. His mother, his older sister Lena, and he all had perfect pitch. Mrs. Lardner played the organ in the Episcopal Church of Niles, Michigan, of which her father was rector. My Aunt Lena succeeded her in that role and taught singing and piano. There was a pipe organ in the Lardner house as well as a piano, and when Ring began to work out two-piano arrangements for his sister Anne and himself, their parents were both obliging and prosperous enough to buy them a second piano. During the years when I was growing up in Great Neck, Long Island, my mother gave my father a different musical instrument every year for Christmas, and I can recall him playing the saxophone, the cornet, the accordion, and the French horn. These were in addition to the piano, which continued to be his main means of relaxation throughout his life. He could, and usually did, go to the opening of a new musical comedy on Broadway and play the score for us by ear the next day.

During his own youth at the turn of the century, however, his most common form of musical expression was singing, generally as part of a quartet. A natural baritone, he frequently took the bass by default. And it was to create a vehicle for himself as an amateur performer that he collaborated on his first produced or published work. In that effort, a comic opera called *Zanzibar* presented at the Niles Opera House by the American Minstrels in 1903, he is credited with authorship of the music and lyrics but not of the book.

He began to see grand opera with some regularity

During World War II a stunning black production, *Carmen Jones,* was adapted from the Bizet opera by Oscar Hammerstein II. At right, Muriel Rahn as Carmen.

during his twelve years as a Chicago newspaperman beginning in 1907. But when he wrote a short story in the first person about a visit to the opera, it was in his fictional character of a "wise boob," to whom it was a form of social climbing to go to an entertainment he and his friends weren't sophisticated enough to appreciate.

That story, published in *The Saturday Evening Post* in 1916, and as part of the book *Gullible's Travels* the following year, was called "Carmen" and a large part of it was a summary of the plot of the Bizet opera as filtered through the narrator's limited comprehension. The action takes place in downtown Chicago; Escamillo, the toreador, becomes Eskimo Bill, a slaughterhouse butcher; and other distortions are in an equally broad vein.

The New York libretto is something entirely different. Characters and plot developments are carefully chosen to represent the nearest American equivalents to the Spanish ones. Clearly the idea behind it was to bring the music to the common man without the barriers of language and traditional opera staging. That concept is quite in keeping with the rest of my father's work, for he was preeminently a popular

Ring Lardner, Jr. is the only survivor of Ring Lardner's four writer sons. His screenplay for *Woman of the Year* won an Academy Award, and more recently he wrote the screenplay for *M.A.S.H.* His novel, *The Ecstasy of Owen Muir,* was published in 1954; and *The Lardners: My Family Remembered* appeared in 1976.

magazine and newspaper writer with no pretensions to literary art and a wary attitude toward critics who professed to find it in his writing. He meant his *Carmen* for the musical comedy audience of his day.

Since it was never performed, we can only speculate about how well this version would have worked in a theater. We know the idea was theoretically sound because Oscar Hammerstein and Billy Rose and Otto Preminger proved it with the stage and screen versions of *Carmen Jones,* adapted to black America and the audience of the forties.

The change from a military guardhouse in Seville to a police precinct in New York is an obvious one since the soldiers in the original perform what we think of in modern times as essentially police functions. But it may startle readers today to note how up to date my father appears in his cynicism about "New York's Finest" as he saw them during the first half of the Prohibition era. The message comes through very clearly in "I'm Captain Moran and I get what I can," and in:

What joy, what fun
To always wear a gun
And use it any time, in any place, on anyone!

It was also quite logical to transform the toreador to the heavyweight boxing champion and the bullfighting arena to Madison Square Garden. Lillas Pastia's tavern becomes "a roadhouse on Long Island." Roadhouses were suburban speakeasies with gambling and/or entertainment. And of course the

Gypsy smugglers of the Seville area become rum-running bootleggers.

The most conspicuous change from the traditional plot is in the very ending, and I for one have no idea what effect my father had in mind. It looks as if Josephs (Don José) is about to kill Carmen as expected, using his policeman's gun instead of a knife. Then suddenly a completely new character appears, knocks out Josephs, the heavyweight champion, and the police captain, and goes off triumphantly with Carmen. He is identified with "Bill Fields' Shorty," who was a midget retainer of W. C. Fields'. My father, incidentally, had a very high opinion of Fields' talent and they contemplated breaking away from Ziegfeld (for whom Lardner had written sketches) together and doing a revue with Jerome Kern for another producer.

The distinctive feature of Ring Lardner's work as a whole is his use of common American speech. In this libretto it emerges in a special way because he is writing in the rhymed couplets of the standard French version and to the musical accompaniment added by Bizet's friend Guiraud when he rewrote a light opera failure into a grand opera hit. Most English-language versions, even though not rhymed, come up with some very awkward locutions in the effort to retain the meter of the original. "And beyond gold by a good son more prized would be" is the kind of sentence produced by this process. My father seems to have gone out of his way to keep some of this flavor and turn it to comedy effect by combining inverted word order and other forms of poetic license with slang:

Someone said that you probably with some fella to lunch had went.
  I don't know no fella who on me would spend a cent.

Or:

  I'm going where I choose! Is't anything to youse?

You find rhymes like that all the way through that are faithful to New York speech:

  Surely you ain't going to take me to prison.
  I swear to you, the fault was all his'n.

"I'll see you later" goes with "tickets to some theayter" and "Go no furder!" with "What is it? Murder!" But it was characteristic of him to save his choicest reworking of the language for a "mother" song:

  My mammy's goofy, I'll admit;
  Her brains ain't what they were,
  But where would I of been if it
  Would not of been for her?

That is first-class Lardner.

Overleaf:
Ring Lardner's Carmen

CARMEN

Characters.

DAN JOSEPHS, a Policeman.
MORAN, a Captain of Police.
CARMEN, a Working Girl.
MISS MICHAELS, a Girl from Upstate.
POLICEMEN, WORKING GIRLS, CITIZENS, ETC.

ACT I

A street in New York, running up and down stage. On the right, the exterior of a police station, with a stoop or steps in front of the door. On the left, across the street from the police station, the exterior of a United Cigar Store, in connection with which is one of its premium stores. Upstage, a little to the right of center, the entrance to a subway station. At rise of curtain, three Citizens are loitering on the street. At the end of the introductory music, the door of the cigar store opens and a chorus of girls dressed as Coupons and Certificates comes on the stage. The Citizens stand near the police station and watch them.
        Chorus.
Coupons, coupons,
Get them when you buy.
United Cigar Store coupons,
Do not them decry.
Save your coupons, get a present;
Some are useful, some are pleasant;
Some are like an English pheasant —
Grateful to the eye.
Just as one friend to another:
Don't neglect the coupons, brother.
Take them home to wife or mother.
Get them when you buy.
        First Girl.
Five whole coupons, let me state,
Equals one certificate.
        Second Girl.
Eight certificates brought in
Gets a rubber necktie pin.

        Third Girl.
Fifty of them, and you own
The mouthpiece of a saxophone.
        Fourth Girl.
For one thousand you can get
A prophylactic mah jongg set.
        Fifth Girl.
Bring five thousand, and you cop
A diamond-studded razor strop.
        Sixth Girl.
While a million of them means
A can of solid gold sardines.

        Chorus.
Coupons, coupons,
Get them when you buy, etc.
        First Citizen.
Owing to the recent rate cuts,
I've been smoking Richmond Straight cuts.
        Second Citizen.
Ah! But I don't think they seem as
Good as Piedmonts or Fatimas.
        Third Citizen.
Have you noticed that the show guls
Don't like Deities or Moguls?
        First Citizen.
That is true; the darling duckies
Much prefer Omars or Luckies.
        Trio of Citizens.
We love cigs of all descriptions —
Turks, Virginians and Egyptians,
Prices low or high,
And just like most other mammals,
We would walk a mile for Camels,
Him, and you, and I.
        Chorus.
Get them when you buy;
Get them when you buy.
Coupons, coupons, etc. (As above.)
        Solo.
(One of the Coupon Girls.)
That's the *po*-lice station,
Just across the street.
Cops of every nation
(When not on their beat),
Eager for flirtation,
Smile at us *so* sweet!

(Chorus repeats this, then goes back to first "Coupons" chorus, after which everybody offstage, the girls going into the cigar store and the three citizens into the subway station. Capt. Moran comes on stage from the police station. He wears the uniform of a New York captain of police.)

Moran.

1. Some fellas goes into the army,
   But though my old skin is so thick
   That bullets and shells couldn't harm me,
   The job don't appeal to this Mick.
   Some fellas goes into the Navy
   And spends all their life on the sea,
   But here's where a man gets the gravy,
   And gravy's a passion with me.
   Refrain:
I'm Captain Moran and I get what I can,
And what I can get gets me by.
I've a house in Montclair which is quite an affair
And a regular palace in Rye.
Two homes; and in each, there's a wife who's a peach,
And two is enough for a man.
Some guys with just one, think: "Ain't we got fun?"
But *I* am Captain Moran.

(Chorus of Policemen comes on stage from police station and repeats refrain.)

Chorus.
He's Captain Moran and he gets what he can,
And what he can get gets him by.
He's a house in Montclair which is quite an affair
And a regular palace in Rye.
Two homes; and in each, there's a wife who's a peach,
And two is enough for a man.
Some guys with just one, think: "Ain't *we* got fun?"
But *he* is Captain Moran.

Moran.

2. Some men tries to live on their sal'ries.
   Well, let them; but what is the use?
   They'll never eat too many cal'ries,
   Or need rubber shirts to reduce.
   I love wives and kiddies too dearly
   To force them to live on my pay
   When all my friends gives me just merely
   Keeps want and privation away.
   Second refrain:
I'm Captain Moran and I get what I can.
To hell with reformers and bugs!
Why should *I* waste *my* time waging war against crime
When they's some of my best friends is thugs?
The dives around here, they was pinched twicet a year

Before my régime-y began,
But now the police leaves ladies in peace,
For *I* am Captain Moran.
(Chorus of Policemen repeats this refrain, "He's Captain Moran, etc." and all are about to retire into the police station when Miss Michaels is observed, entering from the subway. Her clothes stamp her as being from out of town. She looks around nervously as if in search of some one.)
Moran.
(Note: The dialogue here and hereafter is mostly recitative.)
Well! Look who has came! A little country dame.
Chorus.
A little country dame.
Moran.
(Addressing Miss Michaels.)
Hello, there, girlie. How's everything upstate?
Miss Michaels.
Great.
Moran
What brought you to town, dearie?
Miss Michaels.
The Erie.
Moran.
I mean, are you looking for work or just for a good time?
Miss Michaels.
I'm looking for a friend of mine.
Moran.
Male or female?
Miss Michaels.
Male.
Moran.
Well, won't I do?
Miss Michaels.
To hell with you!
(Moran looks disgruntled and the other policemen laugh.)
Moran.
What is your friend's occupation?
Miss Michaels.
The same as yours is his vocation, and he travels out of this here station.
Moran.
You mean he's on the police force?
Miss Michaels.
Of course, of course.
Moran.
Maybe I know him. What is his name, kid?
Miss Michaels.

Daniel Josephs. He's a yid.

Moran.

Oh, that fella! Just a patrolman!

Miss Michaels.

(Looking Moran over disparagingly.)

Yes, but a young man, not an ol' man.

Moran.

He walks a beat. He's got flat feet.

Miss Michaels.

But Oh! He's sweet!

Moran.

Well, stick around a while. He'll be here soon.

Miss Michaels.

(Starts to exit.)

I'll be back this afternoon.

Moran.

And who shall I tell him was here?

Miss Michaels.

His sweetie dear.

Moran.

Where can he phone ya?

Miss Michaels.

At the Ansonia.

(She exits into the subway station. Moran and the policemen exit into the police station, singing one refrain of "Captain Moran." Patrolman Daniel Josephs enters from the extension of the street, up-stage left and comes down front.)

Josephs.

(To the audience. Recitative.)

I am Patrolman Daniel Josephs.

(He goes over to the police station, sits down on the stoop and takes off one shoe. He drops a large stone out of it and puts it back on again; then proceeds to manicure himself with a large pocket knife. The twelve o'clock whistles blow and the street is immediately filled with workers, out for their lunch. They enter from all directions. Included in the crowd are the Coupon Girls.)

Chorus.

Out to lunch! Out to lunch!

We're a very hungry bunch.

We have worked with all our might,

Getting up an appetite.

Some of us to Childs' will go;

Others visit Ching Lung Fo,

While a few, the plutocrats,

At Brown's Chop House check their hats.

Solo.

(A Girl.)

Schrafft's is good enough for me:

Chicken salad, toast and tea.

Solo.

(A Man.)

Takes too long; the wait is tedious.

I'll have pie at some St. Regis.

Solo.

(Another Girl.)

There's no pie as good as that

Fresh raisin at the Automat.

Solo.

(A Man Poorly Dressed.)

I'll have clams and new strawberries,

Steak and roquefort cheese, at Sherry's.

(The others laugh at him derisively.)

Chorus.

Out to lunch, etc.

Solo.

(A Man. Recitative.)

Where is Carmen today?

Solo.

(A Girl.)

I cannot say.

Solo.

(Another Man.)

Probably went to lunch with some fella somewhere.

Solo.

(A Girl.)

For the fellas she does not care. She hasn't no use for none of you bums.

Solo.

(The First Man.)

Ah! Here she comes!

(Introductory music and Carmen enters from the cigar store. She is dressed in as close an imitation to a Fifth Avenue creation as she can get with her means. She is smoking a cigarette and wears a faded rose. Josephs looks up and observes her casually and then resumes his task of manicuring.)

A Girl.

(To Carmen.)

Hello, Carmen.

Chorus.

Hello, Carmen.

Carmen.

Hello, everybody.

A Girl.

Some one said that you probably with some fella to lunch had went.

Carmen.

I don't know no fella who on me would spend a cent.

A Man.

I would! Try me!

Several Other Men.

(One at a time.)

And I! And I! And I!

Carmen.

I was just kidding. My lunch I could not let you buy.
I'm saving that privilege for my steady guy.

(She notices Josephs for the first time.)

A Man.

It's time you *had* a steady. I've often wondered why
didn't you get one already.

Several Other Men.

(One at a time.)

And I! And I! And I!

Chorus.

Why, Carmen? Why?

(During the following song, Carmen occasionally
glances at Josephs, but he seldom looks at her and
when he does, it is with seeming indifference.)

SONG—"THE RIGHT MAN."

Carmen.

You ask me why I've never got
Myself a steady guy.
Well, people, you can bet it's not
Because the boys don't try.
Since I was old enough to walk,
I've always been pursued,
But Oh! The way these dumbbells talk
And act—My God, it's crude!
"Say, listen: Ain't you lonesome, Sis?
You cert'ny are some dame!"
And then they want an endless kiss
Before they know your name.
A girl with any kind of taste
Just craves to punch their nose;
And I assure you I won't waste
*My*self on eggs like those.

Refrain:

I am waiting for the right man,
And he's got to be a bright man,
And he mustn't be a tight man,
He must spend his money free.
Yes, I'm waiting for a white man,
Who's a decent and polite man,
But a not-afraid-to-fight man,
If a fight it's got to be.
I don't care if he's a slight man,

Or a heavy man, or light man,
Or a short or middle-height man,
Or as tall as any tree,
But a seldom-out-of-sight man,
And a don't-stay-out-all-night man.
Oh, if you find my right man,
Please send him to me!

(The chorus repeats this refrain and during the rep-
etition, Carmen sings an obligato—"Oh, love!" or
"L'amour!"—as in the Flower Song of the opera and,
perhaps, following the notes of that obligato as closely as possible. At the end of the chorus, Carmen, who
has been piqued by Josephs' indifference to her, goes
to where he is sitting and throws the rose at his
feet. He starts and looks up embarrassed. Carmen
laughs and runs back into the cigar store. The chorus
disperses, some going into the cigar store, into the
subway station and others off backstage. Josephs is
left alone on the stage.)

Josephs.

(Recitative.)

Fresh kid! But a pip! I might a play for her make
if I to Jennie Michaels was not engaged. And she
throwed me a flower.

(He leans over, picks up the flower and smells it.)

Don't know what to call it, but it's mighty like a rose.
But not as sweet as the gal that throwed it. Or no-
wheres near as fresh. I hope I don't no more her see
or to forget myself I am liable.

(Miss Michaels enters from the subway station and
approaches him.)

Miss Michaels.

(Recitative.)

Dan!

Josephs.

(Starts, gets up and sees her.)

Jennie!

Miss Michaels.

(As they shake hands.)

Well, Dan, you're the same man.

Josephs.

And you, too, Jennie. You ain't changed enny.

Miss Michaels.

I got in late this morning.

Josephs.

Why didn't you give me some warning?

Miss Michaels.

That I was coming down this way, I did not know
myself till yesterday.

Josephs.

But what's the idear? Why are you here?

Miss Michaels.

Ain't you glad to see me? You don't show it in your eyes.

Josephs.

Sure, I'm glad to see you, but it's kind of a surprise.

Miss Michaels.

You act more like as if it was a shock.

Josephs.

(Jokingly.)

Oh, chase yourself around the block. But listen, dear: You ain't yet told me why you are here.

Miss Michaels.

Well, I didn't have nothing fit to wear, and I looked all over Binghamton, but couldn't find nothing there.

Josephs.

I see. And my mother, how is she?

Miss Michaels.

Worried about you, she seems to be.

Josephs.

But why should she be worried?

Miss Michaels.

She thinks our marriage ought to be hurried.

(Turns her head away and giggles.)

Josephs.

Well, you know a man can't get married these days on what a patrolman's position pays.

Miss Michaels.

Well—

Josephs.

Tell me what Ma said, and all about it.

SONG—"MAMMY SONG."

Miss Michaels.

1. My train left Bing-ham-ton
    A little after one,
    But got delayed at Goshen by a freight;
    Then, later in the night,
    A hot box stopped our flight,
    So we reached Jersey City two hours late.
    But that, as I'm aware,
    Is neither here nor there,
    And what I'm getting at is merely this:
    Before I came away,
    Your mamma, old and gray,
    Gave me, to give to you, a mother's kiss.

(She gives him a kiss which is anything but a "mother's kiss.")

Josephs.

(Recitative.)

Oh, mamma! How you can kiss!

Miss Michaels.

Refrain:

Your mammy wants you to be good,
For you're her joy and pride.
She says, Behave just like you would
If you was by her side.
Your mammy's goofy, I'll admit;
Her brains ain't what they were,
But where would you of been if it
Would not of been for her?

Josephs.

2d. Verse:

You tell my mammy dear
She needn't have no fear;
I been behaving like a model son.
I don't run round with dames
Or set in poker games.
And only oncet a week I get a bun.
And if she can arrange
To send me some loose change,
I'd like it, as it's weeks since I been paid.
Just give her the old salve,
And meanw'ile, leave us have
Another of them kisses mother made.

(They indulge in another long "mother's kiss.")

Refrain:

My mammy wants me to be good,
For I'm her joy and pride.
She says, Behave just like I would
If she was by my side.
My mammy's goofy, I'll admit;
Her brains ain't what they were,
But where would I of been if it
Would not of been for her?

(Miss Michaels joins him in this refrain, singing "Your mammy, etc.")

Miss Michaels.

(Recitative.)

Now I must go and begin my shopping.

Josephs.

When will you be through, and where are you stopping?

Miss Michaels.

I'm at the Ansonia and I'll be there about five-thirty. I'll have to put on a fresh waist, as by that time this one will be dirty.

Josephs.

Well, so long, then. I'll see you later. Meanw'ile, I'll

try and get tickets for some theayter.
(They kiss again and Miss Michaels exits into the subway station.)
    Josephs.
What a gal! What a gal!
And she'll be my lifelong pal.
We'll never brawl and we'll never fight;
She'll know she's wrong and she'll know I'm right.
A wife like she is bound to be
A help to a man's morale,
So I'll waive all claims to these Broadway dames
And marry a small town gal.
(Shrieks and yells and a big commotion from inside the cigar store. Josephs looks pop-eyed in that direction. Capt. Moran rushes out of the police station, followed by the policemen.)
    Moran.
What is all this noise and clatter?
(To Josephs.)
Josephs, find out what's the matter!
(Josephs, drawing his gun, runs into the store. He has to fight his way through the crowd of men and girls, workers and customers, who rush out, all excited. Several policemen go to Josephs' assistance and enter the store with him.)
    Chorus.
She's killed him!
    Moran.
Stop! Go no furder! What is it?
    Chorus.
Murder!
    First Girl.
It's a man named Kramer. Carmen killed him and I don't blame her.
    Second Girl.
His shrieks by me will never be forgotten. Whenever I think of them, they will make me feel rotten.
    Moran.
Don't all talk at once! I can't understand a word. Now one of you tell me just what occurred.
    A Man.
Well, if you've been in our store, you must have seen
That we have a penny weighing machine.
Well, this Mr. Kramer—He works around here—
He went up to Carmen—She's our cashier—
And he asked her if she would open the till
And give him change for a fifty dollar bill,
So he could get a penny, if you know what I mean,
And weigh himself on the weighing machine.
Then Carmen, who is stronger than Babe Ruth,

Hit him over the head with the telephone booth.
    Moran.
Well, it seems to me she was justified,
But that is a matter for the jury to decide.
(Several police come on stage from the cigar store, carrying Kramer.)
    Moran.
(To the police.)
Is he dead?
    A Policeman.
Not especially.
    Moran.
Take him in the station and lay him on the bench.
Then go to the telephone and call up Dr. French.
(The police exit into the police station with Kramer, Josephs enters from the cigar store, leading Carmen.)
    Josephs.
Here she is, Captain; and it took quite a battle to get her.
    Moran.
(To Carmen.)
Well, young lady, how do you feel about it now?
    Carmen.
Better.
    Moran·
You may not feel so good when I've put you in a cell.
    Carmen.
Oh, hell!
    Moran.
I'd like to keep you here, but for ladies we have no accommodations. I'll have to send you to one of the other stations.
(To Josephs.)
Josephs, you keep an eye on her while I go in and write a note. Then you take her to Twenty-second Street and turn her over to Captain Faurote.
(To the crowd.)
All of you get back to your jobs! Carmen will be perfectly safe with his nobs.
(Moran exits into the police station and the crowd disperses.)
    Carmen.
(To Josephs.)
Well—
    Josephs.
Well?
    Carmen.
Surely you ain't going to take me to prison. I swear to you, the fault was all his'n.
    Josephs.

I'd like to do whatever you say, cutie. But first comes duty.

Carmen.

But I know you'll let me go because I can see, that you're already wild about me.

Josephs.

Where did you get that idear? I've got a sweetie; she was just here.

Carmen.

I don't care how many sweeties you've got! You're stuck on me and there's no use saying you're not!

Josephs.

Well, shut up and say no more about it!

Carmen.

Can I talk to myself?

Josephs.

I don't doubt it.

SONG—"A ROADHOUSE ON LONG ISLAND."

Carmen.

Some like wide open spaces
In God's great out-of-doors.
I like wide open places
That's got good dancing floors.
The longer they stay open,
The better they suit me.
I know a place not far away,
Which they can't close it night or day,
'Cause no one's got a key.

Refrain:

There's a roadhouse on Long Island
Where they serve real pre-war beer.
Just a glass or two of that old-time brew,
And I call all the waiters "Dear."
There's a roadhouse on Long Island
Where they've got real pre-war rye.
Just one little shot and as like as not,
I'll hold hands with the check-room guy.
There's a roadhouse on Long Island
Where they sell real pre-war gin.
Just a sip of this and I want a kiss
From whoever has just come in.
And when I feel so cordial,
Why, my boy friends always thinks,
"Ain't I glad I came with this lovin' dame
To a place where drinks are drinks!"

Josephs.

(Recitative.)

All right. But no more of that stuff! Enough is enough.

Carmen.

(Her face close to his.)
Off to prison must I go?

Josephs.

(Weakening.)
I don't know.

Carmen.

From your eyes I'd swear that you care. Do you tell lies with your eyes? Are you that kind of a man, sir? Answer!

SONG—"A ROADHOUSE ON LONG ISLAND."

Josephs.
2d. Verse:

Well, girlie, I am frantic
To taste that old-time beer;
And when you feel romantic,
I crave to be right near.
So if you'll swear to love me
And be my sweetie-sweet,
Why, it's just possible I'll fail
To see you landed safe in jail,
And later we can meet.

Refrain:

In a roadhouse on Long Island
Where they serve real pre-war beer,
And a glass or two of their old-time brew
Makes you call all the waiters "Dear";
In that roadhouse on Long Island
Where they've got real pre-war rye,
And a little shot just as like as not
Makes you spoon with the check-room guy;
Oh, that roadhouse on Long Island
Where they sell real pre-war gin;
Just a sip of this and you want a kiss
From whoever has just come in.
And when you feel so cordial,
Why, I'll be the one who thinks,
"Ain't I glad I came with this lovin' dame
To a place where drinks are drinks!"
(Carmen and he sing this refrain as a duet, she singing the words of the first refrain.)

Carmen.

And now listen: Here is the plan: When you get the note from Captain Moran, you and me will start off that way
(Points upstage.)
and when I whisper "I love you,"

Josephs.

Yes?

Carmen.

Then I'll shove you. And you fall. That's all.

Josephs.

But where is that roadhouse where we're to meet?

Carmen.

In Port Washington, on Main street.

Josephs.

An all-night joint in Port Washington? That must be recent.

Carmen.

It is. It's an inn. It's called the Inn Decent.

(Capt. Moran enters from the police station, followed by the policemen. He hands a note to Josephs.)

Moran.

There is the note. Turn it and her over to Captain Faurote.

(The workers, male and female, come out of the cigar store to see Carmen taken away. Josephs takes Carmen by the arm and starts upstage with her. Near the subway station, she whispers something in his ear. She pushes him and he falls. She rushes into the subway station, leaving Moran and the policemen gasping with astonishment. The workers laugh and then all sing a refrain of "The Right Man.")

ACT II

*(First 3 pages Cabaret at Bloom's Roadhouse.)**

(Carmen enters and everybody looks at her. Headwaiter goes to meet her.)

Headwaiter.

(Recitative.)

Good-evening, Miss Carmen.

Carmen.

Good-evening, Pierre.

Headwaiter.

(Indicating different tables.)

Would you like to sit here or over there?

Carmen.

I do not care. But I would like to see the boss. He said if I ever wanted anything, he'd come across.

Headwaiter.

*Thus in Ring Lardner's typescript.

(Seats her at a table.)

I'll tell him you are here.

Carmen.

And I'd like a bottle of beer.

(Headwaiter goes away.)

My policeman friend ain't showed yet. I wonder if he'll forget.

(Smiles to herself. Headwaiter returns with Moe Bloom, who has been drinking.)

Hello, Moe, old pal.

Bloom.

Hello, Carmen. How's the gal?

(Headwaiter goes away. A waiter brings a bottle of beer and two glasses, opens the bottle, pours the beer and goes away.)

Pierre said you wanted me.

Carmen.

You're who I came to see. If you ain't busy.

Bloom.

No, I ain't busy. But I do feel dizzy. I've been celebrating, for this is my tenth anniversary.

Carmen.

And where is the Missus?

Bloom.

In the nursery. No matter what the weather, her and the baby always takes their bottle together. But what can I do for you?

Carmen.

Will you promise to go through?

Bloom.

I am yours to command. If it's in my power, you understand.

(They drink.)

Carmen.

I don't see why men should be so awfully nice to me.

Bloom.

Well, I see, but in my case it ain't the same. It ain't because you're a beautiful dame. It's just because— if you want the truth—you bring back the days of my youth.

Song—"You Remind Me Of My Father."

1. I look at you and think about my father.
   I seem to see him smoking his dudeen.
   The neighbors, when they came to call, he'd bother.
   By singing them "The Wearing of the Green."
   With him and mother dear and Aunt Teresa,
   How happily I lived until the day
   The landlord of our building in Odessa

141

Made up our minds that we would move away.
Refrain:

You remind me of my father, though of course you're
not as old.

A man whose name was known to fame wherever
booze was sold.

He seemed to take to everything except his wife and
work,

And but for gin, he might have been a wealthy soda
clerk.

He never bummed a drink without expressing gratitude;

He never left a place till he was absolutely stewed,

And though it sometimes took a week, he always
persevered.

You remind me of my father, though of course you've
got no beard.

2. I don't suppose you've ever been in China.
    What! Never been in China in your life?
    Well, it was there a gal named Claire (not Ina)
    Inveigled my poor father from his wife.
    We never found a trace of dear old daddy,
    Although we must have searched an hour or
    more.
    But later on we heard he was a caddy
    At Childs's restaurant in Singapore.
    Second refrain:

You remind me of my father, though of course he
was a man,

And in the war of nineteen-four, he fought for old
Japan.

They razzed him in the army, he was such a little
shrimp,

And when he'd march, a fallen arch would kind of
make him limp.

But shots that killed the taller men missed him a
foot or so,

And lameness disappeared when he was followed by
the foe,

So when he died, they placed beside his grave a citrus
wreath.

You remind me of my father, though of course you've
got more teeth.

> *Carmen.*

Well, thank you very much. Your sentiments do me
flatter. And now I will tell you what is the matter.
I got in a jam and lost my job today. And I want a
job as entertainer in your café.

> *Bloom.*

But what can you do to entertain?

> *Carmen.*

Well, you know I'm a native of sunny Spain. I can
sing Spanish songs and do Spanish dances.

> *Bloom.*

And I ain't a man that won't take chances. But what
do you want for a costume to wear?

> *Carmen.*

Nothing.

> *Bloom.*

Nothing! Well, put it on in there.

(He points offstage Right to dressing room. Carmen
goes out and Bloom visits at the different tables,
talking to his patrons.)

Dance Number— (Patrons and Entertainers.)

(At the end of the number, Capt. Moran enters the
Inn. He is still in uniform. A headwaiter shows him
to a table and a waiter comes and hands him a bill
of fare.)

> *Moran.*

(Looks at the bill of fare, then tosses it aside.)
No, no! I ain't hungry; not at them prices! Being
a sucker ain't one of my vices.

> *Waiter.*

How about a nice drink?

> *Moran.*

That's it. Let me think.

> *Waiter.*

We have all kinds of pop,—

> *Moran.*

Stop! I want a *drink!*

> *Waiter.*

But you're a cop.

> *Moran.*

What of it! I love it!

> *Waiter.*

Liquor to you I cannot sell.

> *Moran.*

Do you think I the authorities would on you tell?

> *Waiter.*

Oh, no! What if you did? We wouldn't care a bit.
But we don't sell liquor to policemen because they
cannot handle it.

> *Moran.*

(Angry.)
You give me some Scotch or I'll give you a clout.

> *Waiter.*

If you do, I'll call a policeman and have you throwed
out.

(The altercation is interrupted by introductory music and the entrance of Carmen, in a costume. Moran

recognizes her and stares at her, but she does not notice him.)

Number— (Carmen.)

(At the end of the number, Moran calls the Head-waiter.)

Moran.

Who is that gal that just done her stuff?

Headwaiter.

A nice little lady; not a bit rough.

Moran.

Tell her I want to see her. Just say it's a friend.

Headwaiter.

To you her I will send.

(He goes out toward the dressing room.)

Moran.

(To himself.)

The gal Josephs pinched today! And let her get away! What a peach when fixed up right, like she is to-night. If I'd known how she looked when not so completely dressed, I myself would of made the arrest. Thank God I came here tonight! I may not get her, but I'll put up a fight!

(Carmen comes to his table, accompanied by Myrtle and Frances. She pretends not to recognize Moran.)

Carmen.

You sent for me?

Moran.

Yes, but for you only.

Carmen.

Oh, the girlies with me were just kind of lonely, so I brought them, too.

Moran.

But I want to see *you!*

Carmen.

Well, here I am, and this is Myrtle and Frances. We won't be much of a drain on your finances.

(Carmen, Myrtle and Frances sit down with Moran.) But we were just beginning to think it was time for *some*body to buy a drink.

Frances.

And, Oh, just guess what got here today! A case of nineteen-twelve Pol Roger.

Myrtle.

I mustn't drink no champagne yet. It makes me woozy when I haven't ett.

Carmen.

If I was a man, I'd order food, rather than see a gal get stewed.

Moran.

Don't fall for that wine, 'cause I'm here to warn ya it was all made out in California. And I've always heard, and I believe it's right, that food ain't healthy this time of night.

Carmen.

Why, midnight supper is just my dish! Who wants to be healthy, you poor fish!

Moran.

I won't buy food; I've got no time to eat it. I'll buy one drink, and then I must beat it. But there's one condition.

Frances.

Well, tell us, what is it?

Moran.

(Indicating Frances and Myrtle.)

That you two go away, so's her and I can visit. (Indicating Carmen.)

Carmen.

Well, you must have already had a drink or two if you think I want to visit with you!

Moran.

(Meaningly.)

But I've got a word or two to say about what happened—you know—today.

Carmen.

(To Frances and Myrtle.)

All right, girlies, if you'll be so kind, I'll hear what's on what he calls his mind.

(As they—Frances and Myrtle—leave the table and go to another one.)

You give your order and tell the waiter to bring this guy the check. We'll join you later.

Moran.

(To Carmen, after the other girls have gone.)

They's a certain patrolman whose name I won't mention, who, on a certain lady's account, has drawed a thirty days' suspension. He's punished for letting a little bit of a slim, young girlie make a fool out of him.

Carmen.

And do your superiors punish you, too, when girlies make a fool out of you?

Moran.

Make a fool out of me? No girlie could do it!

Carmen.

Well, maybe not. Maybe God beat us to it.

Moran.

You better not get so fresh, my dear, for you belong in jail, not here.

Carmen.

Oh, Captain, I know you're too polite to want me to stay in a jail all night.

Moran.

It ain't what I want, but I'm afraid it's my duty to see that the laws is obeyed.

(He leans closer.)

But I ain't immune to sweetness and beauty, and some things makes me forget my duty.

Carmen.

For instance?

Moran.

You, my sweet patootie!

Carmen.

Speak up! What is your proposition? You'll let me go on what condition?

Moran.

I guess you know.

Carmen.

Perhaps I do.

Moran.

All right, then, gal. It's up to you.

Carmen.

I guess there's nothing more to say. But ain't you married?

Moran.

Well, in a way. But that ain't none of your affairs. Come on! Get dressed; we'll go somewheres.

(Introductory music for "Champion" song.)

Headwaiter.

(To the patrons.)

Say, listen, bunch! Let's give a cheer. The champion of the world is here.

(Battling Bam enters and bows as he is cheered.)

Chorus.

Three cheers for Battling Bam, world's heavyweight champion!

(All give three cheers. During the following song, Bam looks covetously, several times, at Carmen. She leads him on with great finesse.)

Song—"Champion."

Battling Bam.

1. I am king of the so-called ring,
   The duke of the boxing game,
   And it's just as well for the great John L.
   That he left before I came.
   Gent'man Jim, I'd of murdered him.
   And Fitz, I'd of made *him* cry,
   W'ile my first good crack at old Jeff or Jack
   Would of been like a lullaby.

The fighters in my class,
Their jaws is made of glass,
And slow? They'd stand aside to let a Sunday mornin' pass.
I've whipped the whole damn' bunch;
I've beat them to the punch,
And left them sleepin' on the floor w'ile I went out to lunch.

Refrain:

I am the champion, champion of the woild,
But a modest boy, not the least bit spoiled,
And democratic? You'll say that I'm a fool,
But I've shook hands with men that teaches school.
If I was as strong with ladies as with gents,
Then I'd sure be a high class vamp,
'Cause whenever I start in, kissin' fellas on the chin,
Why, they all fall for the champ.

(Chorus repeats refrain, singing "He is the champion, etc.")

Bam.

2. What, you ask, is the hardest task
   I've faced in my long career?
   'Twas them sixty rounds at the Polo Grounds
   With a hairy ape named Smear.
   He starts rough, which is fair enough
   If he had obeyed the rules,
   But he butts both me and the referee,
   And he kicks like a team of mules.
   The extras said that night
   That I turned deathly white
   When, in the fifty-seventh round, he catched me with his right.
   That kind of got my goat,
   The stuff them experts wrote.
   What turned me pale was his right ear a stickin' in my throat.

Second refrain:

I am the champion, champion of the woild,
But a peaceful boy that is seldom roiled.
A cool half million has got to be in sight
Or you can't make me mad enough to fight.
My rivals, they claim that I'm a yella dog,
A cheese and a no good tramp,
'Cause I ain't been in the ring since a year ago last spring—
That is why I am the champ.

(The chorus repeats this refrain, singing "He is the champion, etc." At the end of the song, Bam goes to Carmen's table. They look at one another a moment. Moran doesn't like it, but is afraid of Bam.)

Bam.

(To Carmen.)

You'll have to tell me who you are. You're wise to who I am.

Carmen.

My name is Carmen, and I'm pleased to meet you, Battling **Bam.**

Bam.

(Sits down at the table.)

Well, Carmen, I would like to say a word to you alone.

Carmen.

(To Moran.)

I think you told me, Captain, you had to use the phone.

Moran.

(Gets up.)

All right, I'll use the phone, but please remember while I'm out, that I'm in earnest in regards to what we talked about.

(He goes.)

Bam.

Who is the flat-foot, and what does he mean?

Carmen.

His name is Moran and he's loose in the bean. He's really delirious.

Bam.

Well, listen: I'm serious. My record in the ring you know. I've been in fifty fights or so. And never yet have I been beat. And never yet knocked off my feet. Them facts is in the record book. But now! You've floored me with a look!

Carmen.

Why, Mister Bam! You don't know who I am.

Bam.

Nor do I give a damn, if you'll just be my honey lamb.

Carmen.

I must be won, as you would win a fight.

Bam.

All right.

Carmen.

But not tonight.

(She sees Moran coming back.)

Here comes my friend. Please go.

Bam.

He ain't your sweetie, is he?

Carmen.

Him? Oh, no.

Bam.

And are you married?

Carmen.

I don't believe in marriage.

Bam.

Give me a ring tomorrow at the Claridge.

(Bam gets up and goes away to another table. Moran returns and is just about to sit down when Headwaiter speaks.)

Headwaiter.

Friends, you will pardon me I know, if now I ask you all to go. The boss's wife is sickly and we must close up quickly.

(Patrons all rise.)

Patrons.

For Bloom's sake, we'll let you close up quickly. We're sorry his wife is only sickly.

(Patrons start to leave.)

Moran.

(To Carmen.)

My car is here. We'll have a dandy ride. Get ready, dear. I'll wait for you outside.

Carmen.

Suppose that I won't come—

Moran.

That's up to you. But jail ain't half as nice as where I'll take you to.

(He goes. The other patrons have all gone. The orchestra leaves. The lights are turned low. The Headwaiter bolts the doors. Carmen is left alone at the table. She looks unhappy at the prospect of going with Moran. Frances and Myrtle come in and join her.)

Frances.

Ain't this exciting?

Carmen.

What? That Mrs. Bloom is sick?

Myrtle.

She ain't sick. It's just a trick. But Bloom's two partners have came, the men that's with him in the bootlegging game.

Frances.

They're starting for the South Shore right away. A ship flying the Scotch flag was sighted today.

Myrtle.

They say we can help them. They want us to go, too.

Carmen.

Not me!

Frances.

Yes, you.

Carmen.

But what can we do?

Myrtle.

Here they are. They can tell us all about it.

(Bloom comes in from an inner room, bringing Grazzi and Mario who have entered the Inn by a secret door.)

Bloom.

We want your assistance, girls. We can't do without it.

(To Carmen.)

Carmen, shake hands with my friends, Grazzi and Mario.

Grazzi.

(As he and Carmen shake hands.)

She looks like a gypsy.

Mario.

(As he and Carmen shake hands.)

A daughter of Pharaoh.

Carmen.

(Smiles and acknowledges the introduction.)

Mr. Grazzi. And Mr. Mario. I surely must have understood wrong. The girls said you wanted us to go along and help you in some big, adventurous deal. Girls help strong men? Why, it doesn't sound real!

Sextette—"Scaramouch."

(Bloom, Grazzi, Mario, Carmen, Frances and Myrtle.)

Men.

Yes, female help is wanted
Sometimes, it's understood,
Though women oft are taunted
With being not much good.

Girls.

You flatter us intensely,
But ere accepting, we
Would like to know immensely
Just what our job will be.

Men.

The ladies' job of course is
To just sit round and watch
And stall the Fed'ral forces
While we grab off the Scotch.

Girls.

(Disappointed.)

Well, fellas, if you were to
Ask us just what we think,
We'll say that we prefer to
Sit right in here and drink.

Men.

We'll promise you a thrill.

Girls.

You will?

Men.

We will.

Girls.

A thrill?

Men.

A thrill.

Girls.

You say we'll get a thrill?

Men.

You will.

Girls.

We will?

Men.

You will.

Girls.

A thrill?

Men.

A thrill.

Girls.

Well, tell us, for example

(One sample will be ample),

What thrills you had the last time out, aside from getting drunk.

Men.

Ah, girlies, it is well you
Inquired so we can tell you
The story of the morning when the *Scaramouch* was sunk.

Grazzi.

I'll tell it.

Mario.

No. Let me!

Bloom.

Why not take turns, all three?

Grazzi.

At least let me begin.

Mario.

All right.

Bloom.

Go on. Start in.

Grazzi.

With wines and liquors laden,
The *Scaramouch* left home.
They say it was her maiden
Adventure on the foam.

Mario.

Beneath bright skies she set out
From Britain's cozy isle.
Her speed, when she was let out,
Was twenty knots per mile.
    Bloom.
She made a rapid crossing:
Eleven days, no more.
Then for a night lay tossing
Abaft the Jersey shore.
    Grazzi.
And early in the morning,
A U. S. booze destroyer
Snuck up without no warning
And started to annoy her.
    Mario.
The U. S. boat's commander,
A small, moth-eaten boy
Named Captain Alexander,
First shouted: "Ship Ahoy!"
    Bloom.
The *Scaramouch's* spokesman,
Named Captain Friedrich Helf,
And something of a jokesman,
Replied: "Oy-oy, yourself!"
    Grazzi.
"I have no time to bicker!"
Said Alex with a sneer.
"Come on! Give up your liquor
And leave us go from here!"
    Mario.
Cried Helf: "Give up my liquor
So you can quench your thirst!
Not much, my fine young slicker!
I'll feed the fishes first!"
    Bloom.
Whereat, the bold rum runner
Did try to sneak away,
But the destroyer's gunner
Was shooting straight that day.
    All Three.
She's sunk, poor, inauspicious,
Ill-fated *Scaramouch!*
But, ladies, what we wish is
You could have seen them fishes
When they got all that hootch!

    Refrain (first part):
Oh, the lobsters they were boiled,
And the oysters they were stewed,
While the shrimps and eels kicked up their heels
In a dance that was coarse and lewd.

Oh, the shad forgot he had
A wife and a little roe,
And he told love's tale to a sweet young whale
Till the whale said, "Time to blow."
Oh, the flounder floundered round
Like the star of an Elks Club play,
While a blear-eyed sole sang "The Jellyfish Roll,"
In a doleful, sole-ful way.
And the bass drank Ben's ale
Till he couldn't hold no more,
When the *Scaramouch,* with a cargo of hootch,
Went down off the Jersey shore.
    Refrain (second part):
Oh, the pike and perch, you could see them lurch
Like a bear that has lost its bearings,
And the cod and scrod both cried, "My God!"
At sight of the pickled herrings.
And the crab meanwhile looked on with a smile,
Though he is a crab and knocker;
But he felt just fine when he'd had some wine
From Davy Jones's locker.
(The first part of the refrain is repeated, the three
Girls joining in this time with the three Men. At the
end of it there is a loud knock at the entrance door.
The Girls and Men are startled.)
    Bloom.
Who can that be?
    Carmen.
My God! It must be Moran. He was waiting for me.
I'd forgotten his existence.
    Grazzi.
Get rid of him! We need your assistance.
    Carmen.
I'll do what I can. But go, one and all!
If I need you, I'll call.
(Bloom, Grazzi, Mario, Myrtle, and Frances exit to
the other part of the Inn. Carmen goes to the en-
trance door and opens it. Josephs enters. He is in
plain clothes.)
    Carmen.
You!
    Josephs.
Yes, me! And I'm not too late. I was afraid you would
not wait.
(He tries to embrace her, but she eludes him.)
    Carmen.
Not now! Tell me, is there a car waiting outside?
    Josephs.
Yes, and the driver seemed anxious to hide. He shut
off his lights as I came by.

Carmen.
Did he see you?
Josephs.
Not to know me. But why?
Carmen.
(Relieved.)
Thank God!
(There is another loud knock at the door.)
There he is now!
(Grabs Josephs by the arm and drags him toward the other part of the Inn.)
Hurry! We must go!
Josephs.
But where?
Carmen.
I don't know.
(She and Josephs rush off to the other part of the Inn. After a moment, Moran opens the entrance door from the outside and enters. He looks round the room and then goes to the other doors and opens them and looks.)
Moran.
(Calling.)
Carmen!
(Suddenly a motor engine is heard starting on the side of the Inn opposite to the main entrance.)
Gone!
(Laughs bitterly.)
"And do your superiors punish you, too, when girlies make a fool out of you?"

ACT III

Scene 1

A wild spot on the Long Island Coast. Carmen, Myrtle, Frances and Josephs are shooting craps. Josephs has the dice and appears to be winning every bet. Myrtle is fading him. Bloom, Mario, Grazzi and other bootleggers stand nearby. The crap game goes on during the opening chorus.
Bootleggers.
(Addressing the girls sotto voce.)
Right soon, if you will keep close watch,
You'll see approach, from way out there, (Pointing.)

A speedboat full of ale and Scotch,
At prices more than fair.
We ask that you stay on this beach
And if a Fed'ral dick shows up,
Let out a howl, a scream, a screech,
And we'll elude the pup.
The Three Girls.
But that for us is rather tame;
Our parts just don't seem big enough.
The thrill in this rum-running game
Is helping land the stuff.
Bootleggers.
But listen, girls: We brought you here
To help as best a woman can.
The roles that we've assumed appear
Best suited to a man.
The Girls.
All right, we'll follow your advice,
Although it doesn't seem quite nice.
We'll sit right here and shoot the dice
And keep our eyes wide open.
Bootleggers.
And we'll be back here in a trice
And for your kindness, pay your price.
That you three girls would be so nice
Is what we all were hopin'.
The Girls.
Good-by, but please don't be too long,
For girls are weak as men are strong.
Bootleggers.
If youse is weak, we've got you wrong.
So long.
The Girls.
So long.
Bootleggers.
So long.
All.
So long.

(Bloom, Grazzi, Mario and the other bootleggers exit. The crap game between Josephs and the girls continues. Josephs still has the dice.)
Josephs.
(Recitative. Throwing the dice.)
What rhymes with heaven?
There it is, another eleven!
Myrtle.
That's six straight passes—Will you never cease, man?
Carmen.
He's just a passing policeman.
(Josephs pulls in the winnings, all but his next stake.

Myrtle again fades him. Josephs throws the dice again.)

Josephs.
An eighter, sweet potater, from Decatur.
Frances.
Dice, now speak! How many days in the week?
Josephs.
(Shooting again.)
Great! There's my eight!
Myrtle.
(Picks up the dice and throws them away.)
To hell with this game!
He's got no sense of shame!
Frances.
(Producing a deck of cards.)
Let's tell fortunes.
Carmen.
Who can do it?
Frances.
Myrtle can.
Carmen.
(To Myrtle.)
Go to it.
(Myrtle takes the cards from Frances and lays some of them out in front of her.)
Myrtle.
A jack of spades.
Carmen.
What does that mean?
Myrtle.
That the next highest card is the queen.
Carmen.
Quit kidding and tell me my fate.
Myrtle.
(Laying out more cards.)
There's the six of clubs, and there's the eight. It means you are going on a long journey with an attorney named Ernie.
(Laying out more cards.)
But you will return with a party named Ed, who is dead, and riding in the baggage coach ahead.
(Carmen snatches up the cards, tears them and scatters the pieces.)
Carmen.
Enough of that stuff!
Let's us girls go and find
The men, Josephs here can stay behind
And warn us if the Federal agents come.
(To Josephs.)
Do you understand me or are you too dumb?

(Carmen, Myrtle and Frances start to exit in the direction taken by the bootleggers.)
Josephs.
But wait a minute, Carmen! Don't go yet!
Carmen.
Why not?
Josephs.
Because it's time for our duet.
(Frances and Myrtle exit, but Carmen comes back to Josephs.)

DUET—"ROSE SONG."

Josephs.
I have your flower close pressed against my heart.
Pretending it is you, not just a rose.
(Searches himself for the flower.)
So you are with me e'en when we're apart,
(Gives up search for the flower.)
Though now I've left you in my other clo'es.
Carmen.
You're very sentimental, I can see,
And really you look lovely when you sing,
So please tear off a rose song just for me.
Josephs.
I'd love to, but there ain't no such a thing.
Refrain (Waltz time):
Josephs.
1. You hear them sing of violets,
    Tulips and daffodils.
    Forget-me-nots are vocal pets
    And so are John O. Quills.
    But I am asking you tonight,
    Just why do you suppose
    Some extra bright young men don't write
    A song about a rose?
    Carmen.
2. That's something I'd not thought about before—
    How lyric writers overlook the rose,
    The flower above all flowers that I adore—
    A flower so pleasing to the eye and nose—
    Josephs.
    But really there is nothing we can do;
    It's something that we'd better just forget.
    What care I for a rose when I have you?

(Tries to caress her, but she wards him off.)
    Carmen.
    Wait, wait till we are through with our duet!
    Second refrain:
    Carmen and Josephs.
You hear them sing of violets,

Tulips and daffodils.
Forget-me-nots are vocal pets
And so are John O. Quills.
But I am asking you tonight,
Just why do you suppose
Some extra bright young men don't write
A song about a rose?

    Josephs.
It may be just an oversight.

    Carmen.
No, no! I'm sure it's just for spite
That not one bright young man will write
A song about a rose.

    Both.
A song about a rose.

    Carmen.
(Recitative.)
Now I must go and join the girls and men.

    Josephs.
All right, but kindly hurry back again.

(He tries to kiss her, but she eludes him and exits, following the direction taken by the girls and the bootleggers. The Battling Bam air, "Champion," is heard offstage on the opposite side. Josephs listens attentively. Bam enters and looks around as if in search of some one.)

    Josephs.
(Recitative.)
Here! Wait a minute, you!
Where are you going to?

    Bam.
I'm going where I choose!
Is't anything to youse?

    Josephs.
You don't know who I am!

    Bam.
Nor do I give a damn!
My name is Battling Bam.

    Josephs.
Not Battling Bam!

    Bam.
That's who I am!

    Josephs.
But why do you come here?

    Bam.
To see my sweetie dear.

    Josephs.
What is your sweetie's name?

    Bam.
Carmen.

    Josephs.
(Shouting.)
Carmen!

    Bam.
The same.

    Josephs.
But Carmen's mine!

    Bam.
Get off the line!

    Josephs.
(Rushing at him.)
I'll knock you for a gool!

    Bam.
(Avoiding Josephs' rushes.)
Keep cool! Don't be a fool!

(Carmen, Myrtle, Frances, Bloom, Grazzi, Mario and the bootleggers, alarmed by the commotion, rush on stage.)

    Carmen.
(Getting between Bam and Josephs.)
Boys! Fighting over me?
What children men can be!

    Bam.
(Standing aside.)
I didn't want no fight
With him, at least tonight.

    Carmen.
Are you scared of him? Are you yella?

    Bam.
Me scared of this here little fella!
Well, good-night, nurse!
But you'll never catch me fightin' when they ain't no purse.

    Josephs.
(Struggling to get at Bam.)
Let me loose for just a minute.

    Bam.
I don't box when they's nothin' in it.

    Bloom.
(To Bam.)
Would you mind beating it now?
If you stay here, it prolongs the row,
And this is no place for a riot.
Our work demands absolute quiet.

    Bam.
I'll go.
(To Carmen.)
But I'll see you again.
(To the others, except Josephs.)
And listen, you girls and you men:

How'd you like to come Saturday night
And see me and Kid Busby fight?
  All (Except Josephs.)
Oh, Bam, you're a regular peach!
  Bam.
The tickets will cost you $16.50 each.

(The bootleggers and girls look crestfallen.)
Good-night. See you at the fight.
(Bam exits to the air "Champion." Bootleggers and girls are about to exit in the opposite direction when Miss Michaels enters. She sees the crowd and is startled.)
  Josephs.
(Observing her.)
Jennie!
  Miss Michaels.
Dan!
  Carmen.
Well! What the hell!
  Josephs.
What are you doing here?
  Miss Michaels.
I've come from your mother dear.
She wants you to come home tout de suite.
She's having trouble with her feet.

ARIA—"COME BACK TO BINGHAMTON."

  Miss Michaels.
1. Besides, New York is not a place
    Where hicks should run around loose.
    At home you always were an ace;
    Down here you're just a deuce.
(Giving Carmen a dirty look.)
    This dame you're with, she's just a flirt.
(Carmen looks threateningly at her, but she stares her down.)
    'Twere best that you should part
    From her before she steals your shirt
    Like she has stole your heart.
  Refrain:
Come back to Bing-Bing-Bing-Binghamton.
We'll dance and sing, sing, sing and have our fun.
I know a place that's very wet;
I know a place where people pet.
The girls have all been miss-miss-missing you;
The girls will all be kiss-kiss-kissing you.
Oh, you handsome son-of-a-gun,
Come back to Bing-Bing-Binghamton!
2. When you arrive, you'll hear a cheer
    So loud 'twill drive you deef.

You're just a common cop down here;
    Up there you'll be the chief.
(Looking at Carmen.)
    I can't imagine how you picked
    As dumb a dame as she.
    Up home there's plenty got her licked
    To death, including me.
(Repeats refrain. All except Josephs join in the second time, Miss Michaels singing the same words as before and the others singing, "Go back, etc. You'll dance and sing, sing, sing and have your fun. She knows a place that's very wet; She knows a place where people pet, etc. Oh, you handsome son-of-a-gun, Go back to Bing-Bing-Bing-Binghamton!")
  Josephs.
(To Carmen, at the end of the song.)
Do you want me to go?
  Carmen.
Yes, go.
  Josephs.
But I don't want to go,
Oh, my girlie sweet!
Yet how can I say no,
If my ma's got trouble with her feet?
  Carmen.
Go! You can't say no.
(She turns away from him.)
  Miss Michaels.
(To Josephs.)
Come dearie. We can still catch the 4:10 on the Erie.
(She starts out and Josephs follows her rather reluctantly. He looks back at Carmen, but she pays no attention to him. The chorus repeats a refrain of "Binghamton," but as Josephs is disappearing the air of the Battling Bam song, "Champion," is heard offstage.)

ACT III

Scene 2.

The exterior of Madison Square Garden on the Madison Avenue side. Upstage center is the main entrance to the Garden. In front of it the covered sidewalk. On this are standing or walking around in confusion, Policemen, Men and Women in evening clothes, roughnecks, kids, vendors, gamblers, ticket speculators, etc. Every little while a policeman hits a perfectly innocent bystander over the head with a club or a blackjack and says, "Move on, youse!" It is about nine-thirty at night.

OPENING CHORUS—"NOTHING SOLD INSIDE THE GARDEN."

Vendors.

1. Nothing sold inside the Garden.
    Now's the time to get supplies.
    You will not be out till late;
    You'll be sorry if you wait.
    Buy from us if you are wise.
    Nothing sold inside the Garden.
    Can't get out when once you're in.
    Better buy refreshments here;
    These here fights may last a year.
    Buy, and you are sure to win.
    Cigar Vendors.

2. Buy cigars and cigarettes,
    Chewing gum and chick-o-lets,
    Sealed up tight—they cannot harden.
    Nothing sold inside the Garden.
    Popcorn Vendors.

3. Popcorn! Eat it while it's hot.
    It is better hot than not.

(They shove sacks of popcorn under the noses of prospective customers.)
Popcorn! No? I beg your pardon.
Nothing sold inside the Garden.
    Peanut and Candy Vendors.
    Roasted peanuts, crackerjack,
    Salted peanuts, dime a sack;
    "Cannies," choc'lates (Dolly Varden).
    Nothing sold inside the Garden.
    All Vendors.

4. Programme's long; may last all night.
    Don't go empty-handed, folks.
    No one can enjoy a fight
    If they ain't got eats and smokes.
    Nothing sold inside the Garden.
    Now's the time to get supplies.
    You'll be sorry if you wait.
    Buy from us if you are wise.
    Programme Vendors.

(Holding out "Programmes.")

5. Buy a programme of the scraps.
    See who's who among these chaps.

All their photographs are here.
Buy this handsome souvenir.
    Ticket Speculators.

(Showing tickets.)

6. Ringside seat? I've just the thing!
    You can nearly see the ring,
    And the price is very fair:
    Just a hundred bucks a pair.
    All Vendors.

7. Nothing sold inside the Garden.
    Buy from us if you are wise.
    You'll be sorry if you wait;
    You'll be sorry just too late.
    Buy from us poor sidewalk guys.

(End of Opening Chorus. A poorly dressed man tries to push his way through the crowd. The Policemen stop him and draw their guns and press them against his head. They search him and one of them finds a dollar.)
    First Policeman.
Ah! You had a dollar concealed, eh?
Well, that'll buy a ticket for the Policemen's Field Day.
(Hands the man a ticket and pockets the dollar. The man, unprotesting, shuffles along.)
    A Gambler.
(Addressing another gambler.)
How're you bettin' on the bout?
    Other Gambler.
Eight to five he knocks him out.
    Gambler.
Take you for eighty grand.
    Other Gambler.
Eighty thousand? Here's my hand.
(He extends his hand.)
    Gambler.
(Refusing the proffered hand.)
Wait a minute! That's too much!
Whichever lost would be in Dutch.
Let's just make it—
    Other Gambler.
Ssh! Don't holler!
    Gambler.
Eighty cents to half a dollar.
    Other Gambler.
Yes, but I am shy of dough.
    Gambler.
Never mind. I'll trust you, Joe.
(They shake hands and separate. A little man comes along the sidewalk and tries to enter the Garden.

From his coat lapel hangs a large pasteboard badge on which is inscribed "WORKING PRESS" in big letters. A policeman stops him roughly.)

Policeman.

What's that badge? Press?

Little Man.

(Quietly.)

Yes.

Policeman.

Where's your ticket?

Little Man.

(Quietly.)

Right here.

(Shows his ticket.)

Policeman.

Don't get smart or I'll bust you in the ear.

Little Man.

May I go in now, please?

Policeman.

No, you big cheese!

(Policeman hits the Little Man over the head with a blackjack and kills him. As the Little Man falls dead, Capt. Moran enters.)

Moran.

Here, here! What's this about?

(Looks at the dead man.)

My God! It's Larry Stout!

A high-up politician,

And on the police commission!

Who killed him?

Policeman.

Me, sir. I.

Moran.

But why? Tell me why!

Policeman.

I'm sorry, Captain Moran,

But I thought he was a newspaper man.

Moran.

Oh, if you made a mistake, all right.

Now get the body out of sight.

(The body is removed. Moran addresses a lieutenant of police.)

Have you arrested many people yet?

Lieutenant.

You bet.

We've pinched fifty little orphans from the Grand Street Mission.

Moran.

On what grounds?

Lieutenant.

On suspicion.

Moran.

Suspicion! Well, well—

Lieutenant.

We figured one of them might have killed Elwell.

Moran.

Good!

We've cleared up that case as I knew we would!

(Observes a slender Policeman.)

Hello, there, Hopper! How's the budding young copper?

Even your puny form looks good in our uniform.

SONG—"THE POLICE FORCE."

(This song should be in six-eight time, with a sailor lilt and hornpipe strains running through it. Sailor dances to follow the second refrain.)

Moran.

1. Some people say that miners in the mines where coal is mined

   Do lead a happier life than any class of men you'll find,

   While others think no working man can have it half as gay

   As he who calls on you and hauls the garbages away,

   But I cannot agree;

   It's always seemed to me

   That the life of a policeman is the greatest life there be.

   Refrain:

Yo-ho! Yoo-hoo!

Here's to the boys in blue!

Who wouldn't be a copper?

That's what I'm asking you.

What joy, what fun,

To always wear a gun

And use it any time, in any place, on anyone!

Heave-hoo! Heave-ho!

If I don't like you, bo,

It ain't no use to argue;

To prison you must go.

Oh, whether I drive a motorbike, or walk, or ride a horse,

I will be true and stick like glue to the po-lice force.

2. Some people claim nobody ever had as soft a snap

   As Dempsey's sparring partners when he's training for a scrap.

   Still others swear real blissfulness don't come to many men

Besides the ones inhabiting the death house in the pen.

I'll never b'lieve it's right;

I'll argue day and night

That the life of a policeman is the mecca of delight.

Second refrain:

Yo-ho! Yoo-hoo!

Here's to the boys in blue!

Who wouldn't be a copper?

That's what I'm asking you.

Oh, what a treat

To walk a city beat,

Attempting to forget the different things that ails your feet!

Heave-hoo! Heave-ho!

Small chance for heavy dough,

For some one's always snooping,

And to the chief they go,

And up on the mat, he'll tell you, "Pat,

Your work is much too coarse!"

Then with a sigh, you say good-bye to the po-lice force.

(Chorus repeats 2d. refrain and this is followed by a sailor dance.)

(At the end of the dance, Moran, the policemen and most of the crowd go offstage, leaving five or six young roughnecks talking together.)

First Roughneck.

Who do you think I seen go in?

Second Roughneck.

Who?

First Roughneck.

Ed Wynn.

Second Roughneck.

That's nothin'! Who do you think I saw?

First Roughneck.

Who?

Second Roughneck.

John McGraw.

Third Roughneck.

And who do you think I seen?

Fourth Roughneck.

Who?

Third Roughneck.

Tommy Meighan.

Fourth Roughneck.

Who was he with?

Third Roughneck.

Al Smith.

Fifth Roughneck.

I'll tell you who I seen first.

First Roughneck.

Who?

Fifth Roughneck.

Hearst.

First Rougneck.

That's nothin'! I seen Sullivan, old John L.

Second Roughneck.

You did like hell!

Third Roughneck.

He's dead.

First Roughneck.

He ain't! You lie!

Third Roughneck.

(Attacking him.)

I'll give you a bat in the eye!

(There is a general mix-up among the Roughnecks; it is interrupted when a loud automobile horn is heard offstage and the policemen, including Moran, and the rest of the crowd rush back on. Bam's air, "Champion," is played by the orchestra.)

Moran.

It's Battling Bam! Stand back, you bums!

All.

Here he comes! Here he comes!

(Battling Bam enters. He is wearing shoes, socks, trousers and a heavy, gaudy sweater. He is followed by Carmen, and a short distance behind her are Myrtle and Frances. The crowd cheers Bam wildly.)

All.

Speech! Speech!

(After the cheering has died down, Bam faces the crowd embarrassed.)

Bam.

(Recitative.)

I thank you for this reception, gents.

It's immense.

Between you and I,

I expect to stop this guy;

(Haltingly, as if unused to talking, and reaching for words.)

I expect to sock him.

I expect to knock him.

I will get him as soon as I can.

Some fellas might stall, but I ain't that kind of a man.

I may have to feel him out,

Like I done with Joe Bartlett in my last bout.

But the minute I see I can catch him with my right,

Good-night!

I've only one other thing to say, just one other—
I owe everything to my mother,
And as soon as I am through with this battle,
I am going to catch a train for Seattle.
(All cheer.)
          All.
Attaboy, Bam!
(Bam takes three fight tickets from his pocket and
hands them to Carmen.)
          Bam.
There's tickets for you and the other gals; ringside
     seats; pretty nifty.
And don't forget you owe me forty-nine-fifty.

(The crowd makes way and he enters the Garden.
The crowd follows him in, except the Roughnecks
and Vendors, who have no tickets, and Carmen,
Frances and Myrtle, who remain talking in a group.)
          Frances.
Listen, Carmen, you little flirt, you:
I know that Josephs is fixing to hurt you.
          Myrtle.
He seen you in Mouquin's, and the look he gave you!
If he ever gets a-hold of you, nothing can save you!
          Frances.
And he seen you in the taxi with Bam, and—Well,
If looks could kill, you'd be in hell!
          Myrtle.
So if you ain't just naturally dumb,
You'll keep away from that big bum.
          Carmen.
Listen, girls: I ain't afraid
Of any man God ever made!
(Hands them two of the tickets.)
You run inside and watch the scraps.
I'll have one of my own, perhaps.
          Frances and Myrtle.
No, no, Carmen! We'll stay with you!
          Carmen.
(Pushes them toward the entrance.)
No, no! I do not want you to!
          Frances and Myrtle.
(Entering the Garden.)
Well, then, so long. Let out a yelp
If you need anybody's help.
(They enter the Garden. Now and during the follow-
ing scene, the fans, inside, are heard shouting—"Bat-
tling Bam!" "Bust him, Battler!" "Kill him, Kid!"
"Come on, you Busby!" "That a boy, Bam!" Etc.
The Vendors and Roughnecks have dispersed. Car-
men looks up and down the walk. Presently Josephs

enters. He has been drinking and looks wild. He sees
Carmen and comes up to her menacingly.)
          Josephs.
So here you are! I've got you!
(Grabs her.)
          Carmen.
(Tearing herself loose.)
Hands off, you drunken sot, you!
          Josephs.
(Grabbing her again.)
Right here is where I swat you!
          Carmen.
(Breaking loose again.)
Well, go ahead; I'll watch you.
          Josephs.
(Pulls gun from his pocket.)
I think I'd better shoot you.
          Carmen.
Just do whatever suits you.
(As he is about to fire, Shorty, a terrible-looking
roughneck from the slums, about the size of Bill
Fields' Shorty, comes rushing out of the Garden;
inside there is now loud cheering.)
          Shorty.
Bam wins!—

(Sees Josephs aiming gun at Carmen; rushes up to
Josephs, knocks gun out of his hand and hits Josephs
in the jaw, knocking him down. All this time, the
Bam air, "Champion," is being played. Capt. Moran
and policemen come out of Garden. Moran sees
Josephs fall and makes a rush at Shorty. Shorty
knocks him down and out. Now the crowd comes
out of the Garden, carrying Bam, in his fighting
costume, on their shoulders. Bam sees Carmen, gets
loose from his admirers and rushes to her.)

          Bam.
My sweetheart!
(Shorty rushes between them and knocks Bam down
and out.)
          Carmen.
Help! Help!
          Shorty.
Don't worry, girlie, I won't hit you.
I'm wit' you.
          Carmen.
I'm wit' you, too. I think you're sweet!
          Shorty.
Let's go get somethin' to eat.
(They walk off together.)
                    Curtain.

Talking To Writers

*With varying success, a peripatetic journalist
interviews some great authors here and abroad*

By PHYLLIS MÉRAS

Illustrations by DANIEL MAFFIA

I was rummaging the other day in an old steamer trunk bought years ago in the flea market in Geneva, Switzerland. The lining is mottled, of course, stained by many seasons of exposure to dampness, and the smell when you open it is musty and evocative. In it are stored years of memories—notebooks that remind me that the French feminist, Simone de Beauvoir, once patted me gently on the head and murmured "Ma pauvre petite"; that I chatted with W. Somerset Maugham in his hotel suite in Vevey, Switzerland; that, in the presidential palace at Dakar, Senegal, the poet-president, Léopold Sédar Senghor, chided me about my French and explained his philosophy of negritude.

Twice I have toured Europe interviewing authors, assisted by a Swiss Government Exchange Fellowship, a French publisher 'cousin, and the *Providence* (Rhode Island) *Journal*. Once I have toured the United States talking with writers, with the help of a Pulitzer Fellowship in Critical Writing and the *New York Times*.

When I pulled out one of those old notebooks the other day—a yellowed tablet that says "Bloc Steno" on the cover and that seems to have been bought in Paris, I came across a brief notation of a week's interviews: "Tuesday, Richard Hughes," it said; "Wednesday, Leonard Woolf; Thursday, J. R. R. Tolkien." And below it, on undetermined days, it appears that I was to visit with mystery story writer Margery Allingham, novelist Elizabeth Goudge, and playwright Christopher Fry. For that series of interviews, I remember, I set out each morning from a damp room in the Knightsbridge section of London, where I was spending holidays.

I had quit a job as a reporter for the *Providence Journal* to accept the Swiss fellowship and was studying international affairs in Geneva. But at Wellesley College I had been an English major, and my enthusiasm for books and authors had not lapsed. From time to time I wrote book reviews for various publications. So my father suggested, as a means for exploring the Europe beyond Switzerland, that I look up authors abroad and contribute interviews with them to periodicals. *The International Who's Who* directed me to some; newspapers to others; and the cousin, Robert Laffont of Editions Laffont in Paris, supplied still others. Among the first names and addresses I had, I remember, were those of Simone

ANDRÉ MAUROIS

de Beauvoir, François Mauriac, André Maurois, Ignazio Silone, J. B. Priestley, and Romain Gary. In the bottom of the steamer trunk, I have found the graph paper on which Simone de Beauvoir wrote to agree that I might see her.

Of course, once the first few authors had said they would see me, I buoyed up subsequent requests with their names. It always seemed to me it would be more difficult, faced with a list that included Erich Maria Remarque, Ivy Compton-Burnett, Doris Lessing, et al, for some new writer to turn me down. In a somewhat random fashion, I have culled through some of these interviews, starting with the earliest in Europe and going on to a few later ones in America.

I cannot be sure now who it was I first saw, but I suspect it was André Maurois, for he lived in Paris, and I wanted to visit. I knew he had been in the United States, spoke English and would, therefore, be easier to talk with than a writer who didn't. French is my only other language, and I was not then secure in it. He suggested that I come by for a morning interview at his apartment overlooking the Bois de Boulogne. Nervously, I got there an hour early and ambled in the Bois, going over the questions I thought I might ask such a venerable man of letters. In preparation, I had read *Ariel*, his life of Shelley. The press of time between requesting the interview and having my request answered was such that there was no time to read more than that. But I needn't have worried. M. Maurois was a seasoned interviewee, and talked charmingly and effusively without my having to ask a single question. Perhaps, indeed, he launched me on what—ever afterwards—was to be my author-interviewing technique—to be prepared to ask questions, but not to ask them unless there were long silences. (The exception, of course, is that there should always be an opening inquiry like "When will your next book be out?" or "Do you use a typewriter?") When you are interviewing literate people, they will invariably talk literately. They will keep the conversational ball rolling if you look attentive and respond alertly. They may ramble, but in the ramblings of an intelligent mind is much of its richness. Specific, perfunctory questions result in perfunctory answers.

André Maurois received me in his gray-carpeted study with floor-to-ceiling bookshelves double-lined with morocco-bound volumes. It was one of three such rooms in the apartment, and I recall his saying when I remarked on it, "But you see, books are my life." He was elegantly dressed in a black suit. He always, he said, dressed properly to write. The biographer not only of Shelley, but of Disraeli, Balzac, Byron, Georges Sand, and Marcel Proust, M. Maurois, the father of the psychological biography in France, was at work on a biography of the discoverer of penicillin, Sir Alexander Fleming. On his desk lay sheafs of neatly written longhand.

"I do everything by hand," he said. "I get up at 8 a.m. every day and I write until one. Then, after lunch, I do lighter work." Lighter work for him then, he explained, was studying bacteriology at the Pasteur Institute to give him the proper feeling for the Fleming book. He was fascinated, he said, by the differences between authors and scientists—Fleming was the first scientist about whom he had ever written. "It is interesting," M. Maurois said, as he formed a church steeple with his long fingers, a characteristic gesture, it turned out, "there are always so many passions in an author's life; in a scientist's, I have found, there are few. Fleming, for example, only married once, and very happily. Contrast that with Byron."

M. Maurois talked of the influence of Freud on his biographies. "I certainly try to avoid making people a case," he said. "On the other hand, I cannot say that I would have written the same way without Freud. His ideas about sexual life are true. They are very important for the creative work of the writer."

Clearly a man of strong opinions, unhesitatingly expressed, M. Maurois pronounced unequivocally that "the literature is better in France today than anywhere else in the world." André Maurois was seventy-two when I saw him; his hair and mustache white, but his blue eyes still flashing intelligence undiminished by age. "You know," he said, "there has almost never been a time when there was not great literature in France. French people have fine taste about literature—about everything. They cannot help it because there is taste everywhere about them. The

girl going to work as a dressmaker passes the Louvre every day. She sees beauty. Pretty soon she has taste. Like our taxicab drivers." And he smilingly recalled how one, driving him to an appointment, had recognized him, and told him how eager he had been to make his acquaintance because he wanted to ask M. Maurois' opinion of a certain poet.

When the interview was over, and I was back in the Bois de Boulogne, I felt pleased with myself. The future as an author-interviewer looked promising. A few months later, I arranged to see Simone de Beauvoir. There, I had my first problem as a sophisticated interviewer of the celebrated.

Slender and black-haired, the author of *The Mandarins* and *Memories* led me into her ground-floor flat. She apologized that the interview could not be a long one, for a driver would be picking her up in half an hour for another appointment, but she was willing to talk briefly. Mainly, she discussd the literature of commitment, and said she felt it had superseded romantic literature. And she commented on the influence of French writers on the French people vs. that of American writers on Americans. "No one in the United States really takes the intellectual seriously," she said. "In France, listening to the intellectual is part of our tradition."

After a while, it was time to go, and we said goodbye at her flat door. It was not, it developed, a final goodbye. To leave many French apartment buildings, one must push a button to open the outside door. I pushed what I thought was the appropriate button, an elevator came. I pushed another button, a closet door swung open. Outside, a black limousine drove up. A black-hatted chauffeur stepped out and polished the windshield. Clearly (at least in my mind) he was awaiting Simone de Beauvoir. I hurried to the other end of the hallway where I saw a door into a garden. I looked out. Another apartment building backed onto the garden. Frantically, I dashed out among the flowers and into the adjoining building and began pushing buttons at the street door. An elevator came. A closet door opened. I returned to the de Beauvoir building. I was still pushing buttons when Simone de Beauvoir emerged from her flat. The "ma pauvre petite" comment followed as she pressed still a third button I had not noticed and let me out.

Since I had talked with Simone de Beauvoir about the responsibility of the writer to humanity, I wanted to learn more of it from her longtime friend, teacher, and exponent of commitment, Jean-Paul Sartre. I wrote to him. There was no reply, so, boldly, I went uninvited to his apartment on the rue Bonaparte to see about obtaining an interview. When I got to the floor where he lived, I knocked timidly, though. There was no response. I knocked more firmly. A tall, darkhaired young man answered. I mumbled in pidgin French that I was an American journalist seeking an interview. He was at least kind enough to let me in. (It turned out that he was Jean Cau, then M. Sartre's secretary, now a well-known author in his own right.) He led me into the living room where he was at work on a card table. I stumbled against it. The card table collapsed. Fluttering out apologies, I retrieved the papers I had spilled. Then I repeated my interview request.

Behind a closed door, I heard M. Sartre cough and clear his throat. There was a rattling that sounded like a chain. I wondered if he had a big dog he let loose on intruders. Jean Cau was very polite, but rather cool (understandably, as he tried to sort the file cards that had been tossed to the carpet). He proposed that I return about the same time the next day. He said he would put my request to M. Sartre. The following day I was back. I knocked. M. Cau opened the door a crack. "Il y a quelqu'un," he said quickly, closing the door. I tried again the next day at the same time, and he did not answer. I never did see Jean-Paul Sartre.

I have sometimes been chided by more scholarly friends for my eclectic tastes in literature. The volumes in my bookcase juxtapose Sarah Orne Jewett's *The Country of the Pointed Firs* with George Borrow's *Lavengro*, Christina Stead's *The Man Who Loved Children,* and Ralph Ellison's *The Invisible Man.* My selection of authors to interview has been similarly eclectic. In a night school course in African literature, I was introduced to the poetry of Léopold Sédar Senghor. The rhythms and melody of his verse, the rich imagery, the concepts of negritude made

Simone de Beauvoir

him seem a most appealing figure about whom to know more. The idea, too, of a poet-president in a world where arts too often play a minor role was impressive. I couched a letter saying I expected to be going to Dakar and wondered if he would have time to see me. (Actually, I was not planning to go unless I could have an interview. The distance was too far unless such a meeting was in prospect and writing a story about it could help to pay my way.)

I remember the day the cable came, setting the time for an appointment. I have not come across it yet in the trunk, but I am sure it is there somewhere, for it is the only correspondence I have ever had with the president of a country. I was awed and delighted. I quickly made the necessary travel arrangements. I found Dakar a city of gleaming white buildings and purple bougainvillaea tumbling over golden walls. It was hot the day I arrived. At midday, there was a downpour, and the streets swirled with water. But the rain notwithstanding, I made my way to the presidential palace. After two soldiers had verified at the gate house that I was, indeed, expected by President Senghor, I was directed up wide marble stairs and led into a gray-carpeted waiting room. A few minutes later, I was invited into the poet-president's office.

Bespectacled and professorial looking, M. Senghor shook hands warmly and apologized for having kept me waiting at all. He said he had spent the morning on the other side of the country inspecting a peanut plantation and the flight back had been slightly delayed. One of the leading poets of black Africa, and a prime exponent of the philosophy of negritude that insists that the creations of a black man are affected by his race, M. Senghor spoke of the need in the bustling industrial world for poetry and art and novels. "Here in Africa," he said, "perhaps we express ourselves more vibrantly, more vigorously than people elsewhere in the world because we have been struggling for so long for so many things."

The French that he spoke was swift and meticulous and there were times when I was obviously puzzled by it. He would shake his head severely at such moments and urge me to work harder at perfecting the language. "It is so clear and graceful a tongue," he said. "Our African languages are very rich, but they are, perhaps, too rich. They are emotional rather than intellectual. Learn your French well," he advised. And when, after he had pressed a buzzer under his desk, and a secretary had come, he asked for copies of some of his writings for me—*Chants d'Ombre* and *Liberté I: Négritude et Humanisme*—he asked that they be brought in French editions. "After all," he said, "they were written in French; it is in French that they should be read."

When I returned to Geneva, it was to the news in the *Tribune de Genève* that W. Somerset Maugham was expected shortly in neighboring Vevey. It was a far cry, indeed, from the poet-president of Senegal to the master English storyteller, but I was as enthusiastic about seeing the one as the other. When I wrote to seek an interview, Mr. Maugham's reply was "Come round Friday at 3."

I found Mr. Maugham sitting by the window of his suite looking out over the quiet waters of Lake Leman. Whenever his stutter interrupted his conversation, he would tap on the arm of his chair until the stuttering stopped. His voice—despite his age (he was eighty-four then) and the stutter—was a rich, resonant one. The author of, among others, *Of Human Bondage* and *The Moon and Sixpence,* said, however, that age was getting him down—that he had always written from ten until one in the past, but he was no longer putting in much more than an hour's work a day.

He described himself, as he had been doing for years, as "a very, very old party." He noted that he had written no fiction in more than ten years. "The power of invention," he said, "is something that young people have. As you grow old, you lose it. But I don't care," he added, "I've written over a hundred stories, twenty-five or twenty-six novels, so now I'm writing only for my own entertainment. I enjoy having something to think about."

He remarked that he was thinking of taking a "jaunt"—perhaps to Ceylon. "I expect that I've wandered pretty well through every sea in the world that there is to wander through," he said, "but when you get to my age, you no longer have the desire to embark on all sorts of adventures. You only ask not to have to do the same thing every day. Now you've

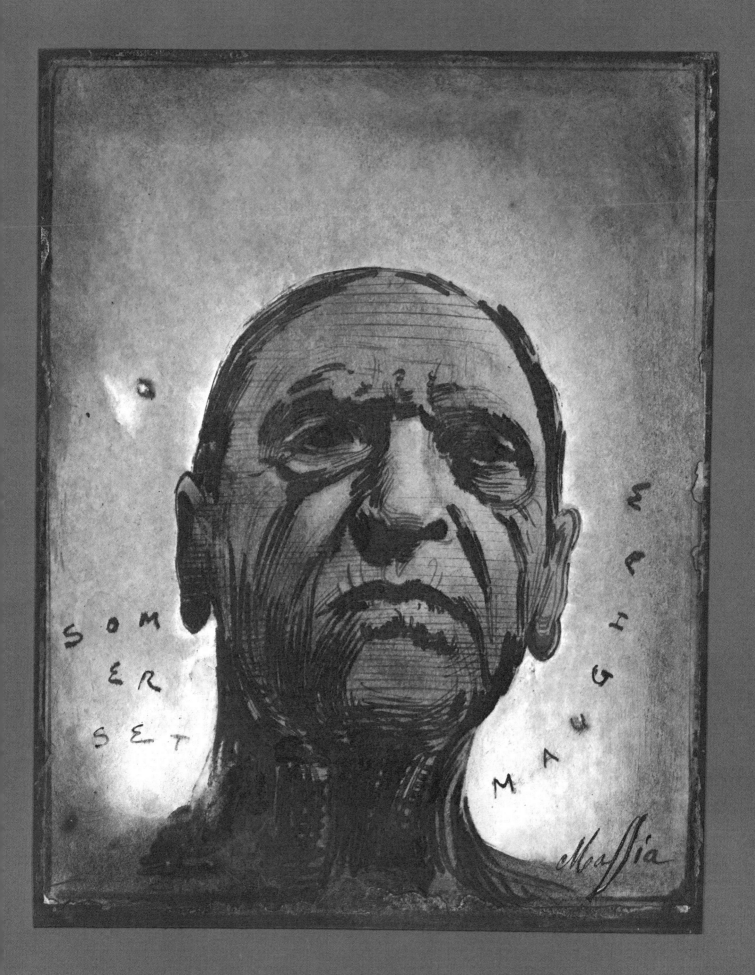

SOM
ER
SET

W
E
U
G
H

M
A
U
G

Maffia

asked all the questions I'm going to let you ask," he said in dismissing me. "For the rest, you can use your imagination."

On a day when the rain was pouring, I went to Oxford for a talk with J. R. R. Tolkien. I left London in the morning with two volumes of *The Lord of the Rings* trilogy under my arm, and I read with avidity all the way out.

We sat in Mr. Tolkien's garage-cum-study for our talk, and he paced so vigorously as he told stories of hobbits and Middle Earth that one might, indeed, have imagined that he was a hobbit himself, with tickling fur on his feet keeping him on the move. He watched the rain stream down the garage window-panes and soak into his garden and drench his trees, and remarked that if he hadn't been born a Christian, he would have been a tree-worshipper. "I've always had a theory," he said, "that a man isn't the same on the top of a hill as in a wood."

Tall, kindly and pipe-smoking, a vigorous talker and a superb storyteller, Mr. Tolkien was what students long to have all teachers be. He had the ability to enthrall and also to stimulate ideas. Middle English expert that he had been at Oxford for thirty-nine years, he almost convinced me in that brief meeting that I, too, should become a specialist in Middle English. But he talked mainly of his love of storytelling, and the trouble he had giving direction to his tales.

"You see, my problem always is to keep new chaps from cropping up. They keep coming in, and sometimes they say things I don't want them to say."

There were a half-dozen other good interviews in England that holiday-time. Four months later, when my next vacation occurred, I prepared to spend it, again, interviewing.

And in those later years when I traveled from country to country still seeking more authors, I found, with few exceptions, that writers are hospitable and generous. I might be scheduled for an hour-long visit, but more often than not, I would still be visiting two hours later.

I went to Wales to see Richard Hughes, and ended up spending most of a weekend with the Hughes family, strolling their land, crawling over their slate walls, helping to catch recalcitrant pet horses.

The weekend I arrived, there were two children, two grandchildren, and two house-guests in evidence. We lingered in the living room much of the morning—Mr. Hughes gruffly bearded, but not gruff at all; Mrs. Hughes infinitely maternal. It was a comfortable, unpretentious living room of worn leather chairs, animal skins, stuffed birds, and Picasso and Augustus John originals leaning casually against the wall baseboard. On the wall itself, in the place of honor, hung a primitive painting of a boat by an East Anglian fisherman.

The weekend was a foggy one, but it did not prevent Mr. Hughes from taking me on a tour of the property, where he would stop every now and then to smell honeysuckle or to point out where, on a clear day, Britain's highest mountain range—the Snowdonia Range—could be seen. The tour over, he nestled down in the biggest of the brown leather living room chairs, dug his hands deep into the pockets of his green tweed jacket, listened to the wind whistling down the chimney, and was reminded of his novel, *High Wind in Jamaica*. It had its beginnings, he said, when he was shown a few pages of a manuscript by an old woman who had been captured by pirates in 1822 when she was a child.

"She told in it how the pirates made a tremendous fuss over the children—and gave them too much crystallized ginger. And when I was reading that, I thought, suppose there had been some hitch and the pirates had gotten stuck with the children? And that was the way the book began."

Mr. Hughes puffed on his pipe and adjusted his feet in his maroon slippers as he remarked that he hadn't really known when he began writing the book where the story was going. "If I got the perfect synopsis on paper, I wouldn't want to write the book, would I? There would be no need. A novel has to grow like a tree instead of being built by me. I'm often completely taken by surprise when some things happen. I was, for example, in the scene where the children are giving the nativity play for the edification of the pirates and the boy loses his footing and breaks his neck. When I started out, I had no idea that the boy was going to break his neck."

Talking of his method of writing, he commented that the first draft is "almost like the seed, do you see; my first drafts are awful. In fact, it's in revising that I do most of my serious writing." Noting the contemporary fondness for nonfiction as opposed to the novel, he said he thought it suggested that "this is primarily a frivolous period, for nonfiction answers questions while fiction asks them, and that's harder for people to deal with."

His wife announced that Sunday dinner was ready, and introduced a newly arrived, unexpected guest who had come for information about Mr. Hughes's fellow Welshman, the poet Dylan Thomas. So, over a dinner of lobster and fresh, plump fruit from his garden, Mr. Hughes recounted anecdotes of Dylan Thomas. And when dinner was done, back around his property—"Mor Edris" (Murmur of the Seas) — we went to walk off our dinner. Over the walls and through the blackberry patches we climbed, with Mr. Hughes recalling the history of shipbuilding in Wales, and of slate quarrying, and showing off the gray castle of Harlech on a neighboring hill.

It began to grow dark. Back at the house, Mrs. Hughes was trying to catch her favorite horse and get him into his stall for the night. The two Hughes grandsons were just getting up from their naps. Mrs. Hughes stopped coaxing the horse long enough to remind her husband that it was his turn to read Evensong at church and to suggest that perhaps he should prepare.

Just as welcoming was Leonard Woolf, who suggested that I come down to Rodmell near Lewes in Sussex one late summer day when the pink and white roses were in bloom on the flint wall in front of his 400-year-old house. He was eighty-five, but he was hard at work with his pruning shears in the back yard. He had been a gardener all his life, he said, as he rescued a prickly ball of hedgehog from his dog and then led the way into his hot house where hydrangeas were growing.

We went from the hot house up the back stairs of the house to a sunlit landing, where he dislodged a Siamese cat from a chair and resettled her on his lap. His dog stretched out affectionately at his feet. He stroked the cat and talked of his work. "And after we've talked, would you like to see two kittens, and then we can have some tea, but would you mind if it's in the kitchen?"

Despite his advanced years, he was obviously not retired. He was, at the time, finishing the last volume of his autobiography, *Downhill All the Way,* the story of his life after the death of his wife, Virginia. He worked on it each morning, he said. "I should feel it was quite wrong to do anything else. My wife always wrote in the morning, too. And afternoons, and at other times, I have plenty of other things to do. I'm parish clerk here at Rodmell, and until last week I was a director of *The New Statesman,* but I don't think one ought to go on after the age of eighty as the director of a company—even if it is *The New Statesman.*"

Mr. Woolf was a spare man, with a long face and a slightly beaked nose. He talked briskly and made it clear that questions were not to be asked of him unless they were genuinely perceptive ones. It was evident that he was not a man for social chatter and small talk. He commented that he was still in London once a week to read manuscripts for the Hogarth Press that he and his wife had founded in 1917. "Now we're with Chatto and Windus—not identical, but together. We've done people like William Plomer and Iris Murdoch and, of course, all of Freud's psychoanalytic books in English." He reminisced a little about Freud. "He came over here during the war, and my wife and I got to know him. He was a very interesting sort of man even apart from his work. He was extremely courteous—rather formally courteous. I remember he presented my wife with a carnation, and he was very kind and nice. And he had a good sense of humor." When I left Leonard Woolf, he took me down to the garden gate and waved goodbye as I walked back toward the village..

I had a somewhat less felicitous reception from Arthur Koestler, to whom I wrote in London to say I was going to be there, and to ask if he had time for a chat. When there was no reply, I went to London all the same, and called him as soon as I got in—from cold, cavernous Victoria Station. His secretary said she was terribly sorry, but he had just left for Austria. He had meant to write telling me he wasn't free at that time for an interview. Now, she said, he was taking a much-needed rest in Austria. Sociably, I inquired where he liked to vacation in Austria. Sociably, she told me Alpbach. I went to the railway information center and asked how I could get to Alpbach, Austria. It took a while for the clerk to ferret out what I needed to know—that Alpbach was on no main rail route, but could probably be reached by post bus from Brixlegg, which, in turn, could be reached from Innsbruck, a regular stop on the Arlberg Express from Paris to Vienna. There was a train to Paris leaving in sixteen minutes, the clerk said, if I thought I could make it.

A day later, from the station in Innsbruck, I called Mr. Koestler between trains. His Austrian secretary said he really did not like being disturbed on his holiday. But the train to Brixlegg was leaving, and there was no time to change my plans. That afternoon, the post bus left me at Alpbach, a 3,300-foot-high village of velvet-brown weathered pine chalets with heart-and-vine decorations carved into them, and crosses and bell towers on their roofs.

This time when I called, Mr. Koestler himself picked up the phone. When I said I was in Alpbach, he sighed resignedly and we met at the village Gasthaus. A stocky man with shaggy gray hair, penetrating blue eyes and impatience with frivolity, he lacked the giving quality of most of the writers with whom I had talked. He made it clear he did not like being interviewed, and was not, in the Maurois way, willing to offer entertaining details of his life and writing methods. His replies were no more than polite. He told me he had said everything that he had to say about politics. "A political journalist and a politician must repeat themselves, but a writer shouldn't repeat himself. I've spent twenty-five years writing about politics—seven of them as a Communist, and I've written warnings enough. Now I am writing more abstractly," the author of *Darkness at Noon* said. And that was that, until I said wearily that, as

long as I was in Alpbach, I thought I would write a travel story about it.

Mr. Koestler beamed. It was evening, and he wanted to be on his way home, but he proposed that we meet again in the morning at the Gasthaus so he could tell me the story of Alpbach. And in the morning he did. He told me how legend had it that God created man and woman, and then the Alpbacher, and how proud Alpbachers are of the story. He said Alpbach architecture was considered the best in the Tyrol. Altogether, I had a lovely morning, even if I learned little of the beginnings of *Darkness at Noon* or *The Act of Creation*, which Mr. Koestler had just finished writing.

That spring, there was a welcome in Rungstedland, Denmark, from the Danish storyteller, Isak Dinesen. Thin and angular, her head in a turban, she chain-smoked cigarettes, drank tomato juice, and ate biscuits and imported honey toward dark one evening in her ancestral home overlooking the long, gray shore and the green-gray sea near Elsinore. She reminisced happily about her 300-year-old home, once an inn, and told how ivy had grown over its pink-white gables. When she returned to the house after her years in Africa, she was asked by the local fishermen one day if the ivy could be removed. They liked to steer their courses at night by her gables, they said. And she had the ivy cut down.

She told how long it took her to write. "I think," she said, "I am the world's greatest snail. Sometimes I find that I have written the same sentence ten or fifteen times. Often I wake up in the middle of the night and say to myself, 'That should be different.' I have to get up. I have no peace of mind till I get the change made."

For years, she said, all of her writing was in English. But when the Germans occupied Denmark in World War II and English was forbidden, she began writing in Danish again, but she always translated her work herself for English publication. "When you know a language, you can't stand to read someone else's translation," the author of *Out of Africa* said.

In the old trunk, too, I have found notes from interviews with American writers. Among them are

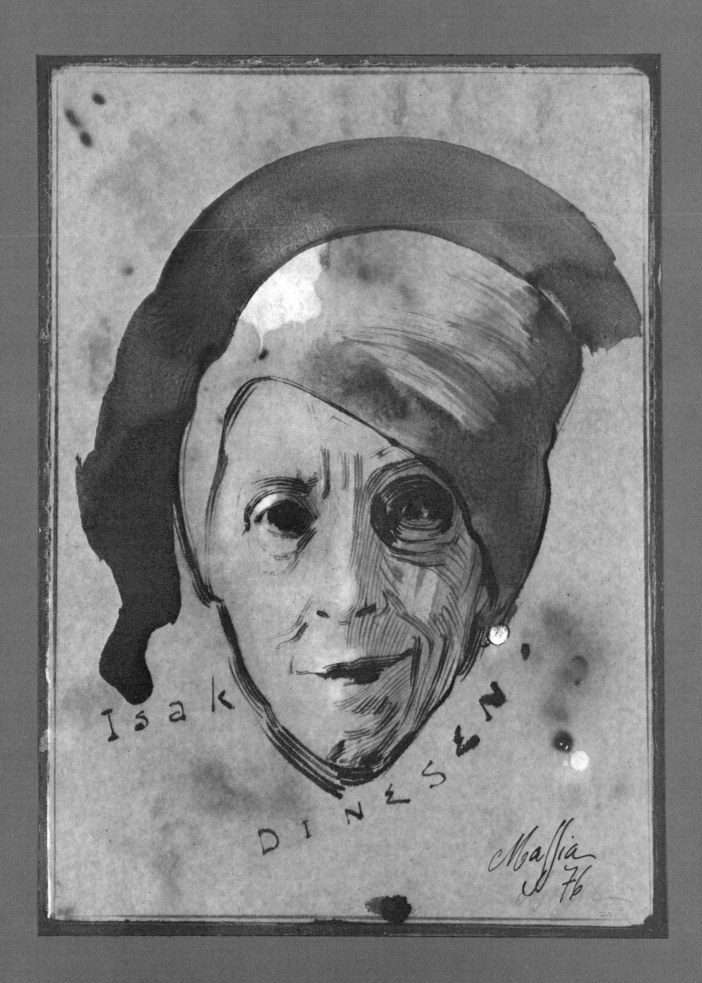

Isak DINESEN

Massia 76

jottings about John Barth and Leslie Fiedler (they let me see them twice when I lost my notes) ; William Styron, Bernard Malamud (he promptly and graciously answered all letters and phone calls, but only his agent could convince him to be interviewed); Vance Bourjailly, Terry Southern, and Kurt Vonnegut (all warm-hearted and welcoming); Reynolds Price and Walker Percy (Southern gentlemen); Lillian Smith and Carson McCullers (both gallant in the face of terminal illness); Norman Mailer, Mark Harris, James Jones (who didn't seem like a writer at all) ; John Updike, James T. Farrell (with the Irish gift of blarney).

For a long time, I kept two Flannery O'Connor peacock feathers in a black Chinese vase in my bookcase, and when I tried, myself, to write, they would remind me of her comments. I went to Milledgeville, Georgia, to see her, to Andalusia Farm, the sprawling hillside home where she lived with her mother, raised peacocks, wrote her extraordinary short stories rich in compassion and Catholic faith, and fought fiercely against the disease that killed her.

She said she thought good writing should have a concrete approach to life. That, she felt, was what made Southern writing powerful. "The Southerner doesn't approach life in abstractions," she said. "This is the Bible Belt, and the Bible makes the absolute concrete. God walks in the evening."

It was May of 1964, and she died in August, at thirty-nine of lupus, a disease that gradually paralyzed her. She was frail, but filled with a radiant joy, quietly welcoming. We met first for lunch at a local inn. Her mother was with her, and while we stood on the inn porch waiting to enter, passersby all nodded and greeted her. "All the old ladies in town are suspicious of me," she said, and her blue eyes smiled. "They're all very polite about my being a writer. They shake my hand. But none of them reads my books."

When we returned to the house, she sat at the end of the living room sofa, gave tips on the raising of peacocks for a while, and then turned to the business of writing. She said she felt the sensitive, Christian-oriented writer had a responsibility to make the "repugnant distortions" he finds in his life appear clearly as distortions to a world so accustomed to them that they seem natural. That, she said, was what she was after in her short stories and her novels like *Wise Blood* and *The Violent Bear It Away*.

She said, for her, fiction came from the small community. "I don't mean that I think fiction is small," she said. "It's not. To be good, it's got to be big. So much of our bad fiction is purely private experience. Fiction has to take in more than the personal. To write, you have to have something more than your own little birdcage of a head." But she said that in the small community, you could see people more clearly than in the large one. She explained that she liked writing short stories because they could be encompassed in one period of enthusiasm. As for a novel, "it's just like going through the Okeefenokee Swamp or the Sahara," she said.

Similarly preferring another form to the novel (though he is back writing them now) was Truman Capote who talked over brunch at the Plaza in New York about his preference for reportage. "Then I'm not on the rack all the time about this thing of taking a character, putting him in, then taking him out because he doesn't belong. And reporting gives me a feeling of total objectivity. I like feeling that something is happening beyond and about me that I can do nothing about. I like having the truth be the truth and I can't change it."

Today, Mr. Capote is rotund and balding, and a bête noir for the exposé of jet set society that will be his next book. But he was slight and boyish when I saw him in 1959, with a shock of blond hair that fell on his forehead. He looked fresh and ingenuous in a gray suit with a rosebud in the lapel, a white-collared blue shirt and a gray silk bow tie. He said he wrote slowly, "because one of my greatest interests is the texture of language. I have to rewrite all the time. Sometimes I think I don't even write; I just rewrite."

He commented that he always wrote a great deal, whether he foresaw publication or not, as he ordered vodka on the rocks, skimmed milk, scrambled eggs, and bacon. "When I wrote *Breakfast at Tiffany's* I simply put it away. For me, to publish is a great step. You should be at your best every time that you

publish. When I put that away it was about two-thirds finished, I guess. Then I didn't look at it again for several years. When I took it out, I liked it personally, but I wasn't sure about getting it printed. I finished it anyway, though, then took it out again. And now, in retrospect, I think I could rewrite it again."

He smoked while he awaited his brunch, and played with the handle of his walking stick. Mr. Capote's voice was light, with a pleasing intonation. He said writing made him anxious—that he never wrote for more than an hour or so without taking a walk. "I'm always in such a state of apprehension over what I'm writing. While I'm walking, I try to coax myself back into writing, but it's never really till about six o'clock that I get anything done. Then I suddenly feel quite calm. I think the reason is that I know the day is ending. At seven-thirty or so I know I'm going to have a drink and eat dinner. It's the prospect—the carrot in front of me—that gets me started then.

"You know, the real writers I know—like Katherine Anne Porter and Tennessee Williams and Carson McCullers—never seem to write freely. They all have that anxiousness I spoke of about what they do. And that's all right. You have no right to enjoy writing the way other people do if you're a real writer. Your writing is for your reader to enjoy, not you."

Katherine Anne Porter, however, seemed to feel differently about her art. When I went to see her, she was living on a quiet Georgetown street, in a house whose decor fairly burst with femininity. Her kitchen was pink.

"I don't pretend to have a serious mind," she said, almost by way of greeting. "I simply love writing. I'm an artist. I like Venice, not Florence. These intellectuals are always criticizing the way my mind

works. I am a working artist and a good cook, and I never pretended to be anything else." Whereupon she offered a glimpse of her pretty kitchen, and a Creole recipe for rice and saffron cooked in chicken broth with mushrooms and a little green pimiento "which is hot." "My friends say to me, 'What's a woman who can cook like you doing trying to write?' But I love to write. It's my pleasure and my fun."

She bustled into her living room then, a room of green, red, and violet velvet upholstered furniture. She fluffed her soft white hair with one hand and recounted how she had found her sofa "in chunks and pieces lying on a sidewalk in Brussels. It's Louis XV. It was in the rain and I was in a taxi. I said to the driver, 'Will you pick it up and put it in a sack for me?' And here it is!"

While she talked, she clasped and unclasped her hands animatedly, and rearranged red roses in a vase on the coffee table. Her fingernails were silver-polished. "You know," she said, "I don't choose my stories, they choose me. Things come to my mind. Sometimes it takes years and years for them to coalesce—it's like iron filings collecting on a magnet. Then, finally, it's a story, and when it's ready I usually write it only once. That wasn't true of *Ship of Fools,* I'll admit. With that, I'd be stopped sometimes for a year or two—sometimes in the middle of a sentence—I thought it was going to be like Grandma's patchwork quilt. But that was almost a one-time thing. Once I start to write, the stories are ordinarily written in one sitting. They take three or four hours sometimes, but they're completed in the course of a day. I don't write to correct morals. I bring no message. I am like Arthur Rimbaud. My whole motive is to write so that people will enjoy, and because I enjoy writing."

Then she chatted of herself and her forebears. She was born in Texas. "My mother's people came to America in 1648, to Virginia," she said, "and my father's in 1720, to Pennsylvania. They were all very literate people. When they went west over the Gap they carried their harps and violins and Greek and Latin grammars. I left Texas—let me see—in 1917. I was already 27, and you're pretty well what you're going to be by then. I went to Denver because they thought I had TB. I think the best thing a Southern writer can do is get out of the South and see the world. I love my Southern feelings and background, but I'm not a Southern writer, I'm simply a writer," Katherine Anne Porter said emphatically as she began to recall her start in writing.

"I was living in New York then. I had started thirty-five or forty stories, but I didn't finish them. I was like a horse taking a certain number of gulps, and then refusing the last. I'd stop every story and put it away. Finally I decided I'd finish one story if it killed me. I worked on it for seventeen days and nights, and I was just living on peanuts and bananas because I had heard they were nourishing. And my breakfast was grapes and a great big crusty roll and two cups of coffee. Anyway—I finished the story and that was 'Maria Conception.' I was thirty-two years old and it was the first story I'd ever turned out. Oh," she said, "you know I was just as happy then when I had to count my nickels to see if I had enough for a bar of Ivory soap and a bus ride uptown to see my editor, and a bunch of fresh green peas for my supper."

Of course, there were some interviews that went more easily than others. Aside from my aborted effort to see Jean-Paul Sartre, there is only one total failure I can remember. That was with the West Indian, V.S. Naipaul, and points out, I suppose, the perils of journalistic interviewing. I had read his *A House for Mr. Biswas,* and found it charming. I had dabbled in *An Area of Darkness,* the story of his leaving Trinidad to visit India—his family's place of origin. But, as was often the case, scurrying as I was from city to city and interview to interview, there simply had not been time to read more of his works.

The first question Mr. Naipaul asked, after he had let me into his London flat, was "What of mine have you read?" When I told him, his response was a cool one. "That puts you at a great disadvantage, doesn't it? You've done me a great discourtesy, haven't you, coming here without reading more than that?" Under the circumstances, he said he preferred not to talk at all about his works.

I begged and pleaded (tearfully, my notes recall). But he was firm. "I'll give you tea," he said, "but I won't talk to you about my writing."

"I'll talk about noise, if you like," he said. "Look at the amount of traffic this little road receives. London Airport is miles away, but we still get its noises. Silence, you know, is a prerequisite of civilization. Without silence, what we have ceases to be civilization and becomes a great monkey thing." He talked a while longer, but never about anything consequential. "Look, this is rather silly, isn't it?" he said finally. "You can't print this anyway."

Like their works, all writers are different. Sometimes, meeting the creator, one understands the writing better. One sees the author in it. But in other instances, it is hard to believe that the writer and his work bear any relation to each other.

There had always seemed to me to be a mysticism in the writing of Friedrich Dürrenmatt, author of *The Visit, The Judge and his Hangman.* Dürrenmatt, the man, proved far from mystical as he basked beside his swimming pool like any Swiss burgher, and admired the prospect of the Bernese Alps that his well-appointed house afforded.

It seemed unlikely that Shirley Jackson, supplying Band-Aids to her children in Bennington, Vermont, could be the author of that short story of human sacrifice, "The Lottery." It seemed more unlikely still that the idea for it had come when she was pushing her son to the store in his carriage.

On the other hand, Gore Vidal, a dashingly perfect host at a rooftop apartment in Rome, was exactly what I had imagined the sophisticated writer of *Washington, D.C.* to be.

Gentle, blue-eyed Isaac Bashevis Singer, with his ears like an elf's, recalling a Jewish boyhood in Poland in a softly bewitching voice, was the kindly Yiddish writer tales like "Gimpel the Fool" had led me to expect.

And Georges Simenon, with his owl-like eyes, his racks of pipes and neatly arranged cups of red and blue writing pencils, seemed just the organized sort to compose detective stories in his Swiss chateau.

The steamer trunk is deep, but one day I will take out all the notebooks and transcribe their contents in an orderly way.

Flying Blind

The acquisitions of an unsighted book collector

By R. L. SAMSELL

R. L. Samsell in his study:
"True, I don't read
the books on my shelves.
But I know they're there."

Everything you have heard about blind bibliomaniacs is true. Yes, the depletion of modern first editions from bookshops across America is due to the wizardry of blind collectors. Our cunning has become so notorious, and envied, that I have been asked to divulge just how I achieved my legendary library.

Of course, blind bibliomaniacs put others at a disadvantage, for, as everyone knows, the blind man's sixth sense affords him a reservoir of discernments, the capacity for classifying instantaneously whatever nuances hover about a transaction. And, contrary to popular belief, the blind collector enjoys another's compassion, even pity, particularly when that maudlin state effectuates the bargain purchase of a prime item.

I recall the campaign waged when I was after a fine, dust-jacketed copy of Sherwood Anderson's first book, *Windy McPherson's Son,* for sale at a local book store, at a robust price. I flanked the opposition by persuading a collector to choose that book store for the sale of his books; then I informed the dealer that the collector would be contacting him about his library. The dealer was generous with my friend, then generous with me, inviting me to lunch, informing me straight out that I could have *Windy McPherson's Son* at a sizable discount. Thus, dealer, friend, and I fared well.

As a blind lawyer, winning numberless cases out of sympathy, it was my good fortune to put book dealers in touch with estates wherein resided handsome volumes, and, in turn, the dealers have appreciatively remembered my want lists. Years ago, when I did not think that a deceased friend's library had been fairly appraised, I asked Jake Zeitlin, of Zeitlin & VerBrugge in Los Angeles, if he would take a look. When Jake had done so, his fair appraisal resulted in his purchase of the library, and, because of my advance information, I was able to purchase that library's H. L. Mencken collection.

Jake Zeitlin's integrity, by the way, generated one of the local bibliophilic legends, a legend in which I am the hero, Jake the willing victim. On Jake's shelf unobtrusively stood F. Scott Fitzgerald's *The*

Samsell and Jeanne Bennett at the Zeitlin & Ver Brugge bookshop, where they found the sleeper of *The Beautiful and Damned.* Opposite: "And damn the man who borrows this book." Samsell flanked the opposition to secure Sherwood Anderson's copy of *Windy McPherson's Son.*

Beautiful and Damned. My secretary, Jeanne Bennett, browsing while Jake and I exchanged pleasantries, pulled it from the shelf, and, before returning it—knowing that I already owned a copy in jacket —mentioned that someone had written something across the endpaper. Now, Fitzgerald's signature is strong and large, but is it bold and distinctive enough for a dimly-visioned zealot to identify? Let it be known that F. Scott Fitzgerald's signature can be authenticated by a man whose vision resembles yours when you are looking through a melting ice-cube. It was Scott Fitzgerald's signature, and this signature followed an inscription dated, "St. Paul,—March 2nd" which predates publication by two days. The book was priced $25.00, as though just anyone had scrawled on the endpaper. Turning to Jake, I told him I wished to purchase the book at its designated price, showing him, as I did, the inscription, which, as one might expect, brightened his attentions. Then, in quiet, professional tones, Jake said: "Fine, I'm very pleased for you." Fitzgerald's inscription refers to the *St. Paul Daily Dirge,* a parody newspaper he had published in January, 1922.

Because book collecting, blind or otherwise, parallels the joys, the torments of love affairs, perserverence may well carry the field. I have found that book dealers' nerves fairly unravel during the course of long-distance phone calls made with the regularity born of determination. Three thousand miles does have an effect—proof, I suppose, that modern man does not yet really take gadgetry for granted.

Thus, some of my best acquisitions have been made on the telephone, and this method can be especially effective just prior to the mailing of a book dealer's catalogue. All of those items marked *SOLD* were purchased by blind bibliomaniacs. Those books you wanted, I have. Conversely, local calls, lacking the enchantment of distance, are not as rewarding. But my calls from Los Angeles to Baltimore, New York, and Boston have garnered rarities: a review copy in dust jacket of Ring Lardner's *You Know Me Al,* letters of Zelda Fitzgerald, Sherwood Anderson's own copy—inscribed *And damn the man who borrows this book*—of *Winesburg, Ohio.*

Professors, too, can be easy marks. Generally, because they seldom fight in the arena, they are about as defenseless as St. Francis, and, despite their antimaterialism, they do enjoy a glimpse of the green. If you can catch a professor after his completion of a biography, the volumes he accepted from those who helped him along the way can often be bought for a song and a few dollars.

But book collecting friends, especially if they are sighted, can be the most difficult competitors, for they are the most possessive, stubbornly hard-hearted. Their cordial ambiguities rival those of politicians, and they can be just as amiably corrupt. I have known hard-hearted sighted book collectors, who, scorning a volume, would yet keep it from me. Indeed, the blind man's first rule is: Do not look to your collector friends for help. Only once in my memory have I prevailed over a possessive friend,

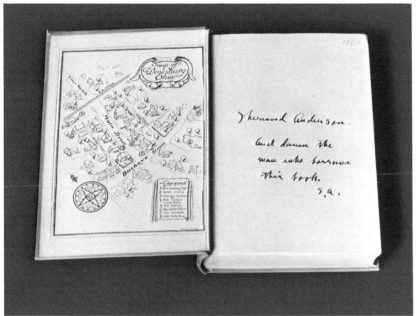

and that, with Nathanael West's *Miss Lonelyhearts,* was due to the calculating humor with which I softened up an otherwise flinty soul. Some years ago I offered the man who scoffed at his copy of *Miss Lonelyhearts* $25.00 for her. His braggadocio informed me he had picked her out one day on Hollywood Boulevard for a paltry sawbuck. Still, he would not part with her for $25.00. A year or so later, my price soared to the century mark. But he wasn't tempted. He knocked the book, sneered at me for wanting the book; but he kept it. I went to $150.00. The blackguard wouldn't so much as walk me up to his library. Then, around the Christmas holidays, which, parenthetically, is a good time for accomplishing anything devious, my secretary drove me to *Miss Lonelyhearts'* keeper, and, with bills stuffed in my pocket, I marched inside to wish my friend a Merry Christmas, and, incidentally, to make my ultimate attempt at the procurement of my love. I told this Joyce, Pound, and Faulkner collector that I was there to make my final offer: "My last offer is $151.00." And, with this sly flicker of jest, I brought my fat roll of one-dollar bills into view. When my antagonist made the mistake of laughing, I knew *Miss Lonelyhearts* was mine. Of course, the humor was alloyed with my extreme self-mortification. Another rule: Never let pride stand in your way. My *Miss Lonelyhearts* is, to my knowledge, one of the few inscribed, dust jacketed, first editions extant. She was worth the ordeal.

Finally, we come to what every bibliomaniac knows so well, that love, unbridled and loosed to its wildest heights, is the sublime magnetism of book collecting. Vision be damned. And that love, manifested by exuberance, desire, and determination, does take its toll on those exposed to it. Any serious collector surrounds himself with a nimbus, felt and envied by those who see him coming. A book dealer knows full well what the maniac is after. If you love dearly, the dealer remembers just as hard. And that love touches his humanity. He enjoys becoming a part of your affair. Dealers, friends, clients, or even acquaintances of theirs, have called to ask if I would be interested in a book. One day, a perfect stranger called to ask if I would care to buy an inscribed first printing of *The Great Gatsby.* On another occasion, a client called to say she had found a manuscript sheet of Frank Norris' *McTeague* in a discarded, rebound library book. This manuscript had actually been circulating inside the book through a public library for years. These purchases and many others were made possible only because my enthusiasm was communicated and transfused into the awarenesses of others. Eyesight, money, stamina, charm, cunning, .humor —yea, the totality of your projected personality—all these and more will fail you if your zeal is not fueled by love. A great book collection is the consequence of possessive passion generated by the love of words. The collection, its taste, is the mirror of what you are. True, I don't read the books on my shelves. But I know they're there. How very well I know they're there.

Scribbling, Writing, Publishing

By LARRY McMURTRY

There are, clearly, tens of thousands of unpublished writers in America, many of whom continue to pile up pages for most of their lifetimes without having the faintest idea as to why they keep at it.

We Americans may or may not be a nation of sheep, but we are certainly a nation of scribblers—of typewriter pounders, hunt-and-peckists, jotters of every description—in short, verbal dissolutes. Every young writer, as he struggles toward publication, may, in his lonely concentration, feel that he is the only person in the world who is trying to write; it is a natural thing to feel if one is serving one's literary apprenticeship, say, in a small town in North Dakota; but only let him make it—let him publish—and he will at once discover that he is only the tip of an iceberg, or a wavelet in a sea. Not only will he learn that almost everyone out there in the rest of America is writing books, but that nearly everyone in his small North Dakota town has been covertly writing them too, and merely waiting for him to publish and expose himself so they can start carting their manuscripts up to his garret.

When I began publishing books, fifteen years ago, I knew only a handful of writers—now I know only a handful of people who *aren't* writers, each of whom I cherish dearly. I scrutinize each new face I meet, wondering how long it will be before the face reappears, wearing an apologetic look, with an eighteen-pound manuscript in its hands. Right away I learned that one of my responsibilities, as a published writer, was to serve as a kind of conduit, a human aqueduct whose function was to funnel a portion of the great river of manuscripts—whose tributaries touch every village in the land—either off into safe backwaters or on toward the already overflowing reservoirs of the publishing houses of Boston and New York.

At first I welcomed this responsibility, happy that someone wanted my opinion. It was not long, however, before the novelty of reading the unreadable began to wear off; though I continued to accept manuscripts, I did so with waning enthusiasm. Finally, I attempted to check the flood entirely, only to find that I was dealing with a natural force too strong to be brooked. Do what I would, manuscripts somehow leaked in. I have only to glance across my study to see that five have leaked in during the last few weeks, don't ask me how.

On the top of the pile, at the moment, is a screenplay authored by the Algerian ambassador to Pakistan. I can't imagine what it might be about. Underneath that are several novels, one of which seems to be about football. Another, as near as I have been able to make out from a cursory perusal, is about dirty socks. It is getting so I can no longer perform even the most ordinary acts of life—like taking my son to the orthodontist—without turning up a manuscript: his orthodontist recently asked me if I could help him find a publisher for a book called *Orthodontistry for the Layman.*

So bizarre, indeed, have been the manuscripts that have come my way—and I am, remember, only one published writer out of thousands—that I often wish some well-funded organization would attempt a census of unpublished writings in America. Such a project would of course involve a door-to-door canvas of the whole nation, the results of which would require hundreds of volumes, even to list; but what fascinating statistics it might yield. We would know at last how many autobiographical novels of childhood, adolescence, and initiation lie hidden in America—my guess would be in the neighborhood of 200,000, considering that I've read nearly 200 myself in the last fifteen years.

Also, I believe, the door-to-door canvas would reveal many droll and curious writings, akin in spirit to those that are to be found in the home of a former doctor of mine, in Leesburg, Virginia. I say former because the good doctor is now deceased. We discovered that we were both writers one day when I went in to get some medicine for a sore throat—before I left I learned that the thing he liked best to do was to write rhymed couplets, in the manner of Pope. He had written other things—three historical novels and an attic-full of children's stories—but his real passion was for the couplet. In that form he had composed a 250-page biography of Robert E. Lee

It is only sensible, I think, to ask young writers to consider whether writing is really a healthy thing for a human being to spend a life at.

—a unique effort, I feel sure. He had also made an attempt at putting the Bible into couplets, but had given it up somewhere in Deuteronomy and had turned his attention, instead, to *The Outline of History*. The last time I saw him he told me he had put nearly 300 pages of *The Outline* into couplets and was, as he put it, "forging onward."

Among the unpublished writers I have known, the good doctor's gallantry and spirit were matched by that of only one man, a Czech emigrant who somehow, in the 1950s, wound up in Denton, Texas, where I happened to be going to school. This determined man had been writing for nineteen years on a vast, labrynthine novel—the story, I gathered, of his days —the pages of which literally filled his small apartment, leaving, as the saga continued, less and less room for him. I was allowed to rummage around in this effort, squeezing into the living room past the typewriter, which was virtually his only furniture. I rummaged now and then over a period of months, but all I could discover about the story was that every time the hero got in serious trouble his wife appeared from out of nowhere and poured a pot of hot coffee over the villains, such as they were. I saw no evidence of a wife, in the tiny apartment, but so recurrent was the coffee-pouring motif, if that's what it was, that I came to fear she might appear from out of nowhere and pour a pot over me, if I didn't immediately get my friend's manuscript published.

That, of course, I could not accomplish. If *Look Homeward, Angel* had required a trunk, this manuscript would have needed a railroad car. Nor could I have helped my doctor friend: if there's one thing they're not looking for, in New York and Boston, it's couplet biographies of Robert E. Lee—though on the whole I suspect they would have been even less responsive to the 20,000-page novel by the Czech emigrant. But, in determining one's position *vis-à-vis* manuscripts, the good doctor and the Czech emigrant don't really count, because in both cases the men had

long ceased to be dependent upon the fantasy of publication. They wrote because they liked or needed to write. It had become, for both men, a pure, self-perpetuating activity, and publication would only have muddied the water.

There are, clearly, tens of thousands of unpublished and unpublishable writers in America, many of whom continue to pile up pages for most of their lifetimes, without having the faintest idea as to why they keep at it. Some never try to publish—indeed, would be embarrassed it it were suggested that they try—but many do keep trying long after they know that the effort is futile; trying to publish becomes, evidently, a part of the cycle. It is as if the delusion that they are artists can only be sustained by simultaneously sustaining the illusion that they will someday be published and, in some measure, recognized. What happens to the individual ego when the dream finally dies I don't know, but it can't be nice. An editor of a major eastern publishing house told me recently that his firm received about 4,000 unsolicited book-length manuscripts a year, evidence of just how persistent this particular dream is.

The vast majority of these 4,000 unsolicited manuscripts are novels—just as the vast majority of the unsolicited manuscripts I read each year are novels. When I agree to look at a manuscript, and to attempt to decide whether to pass it on to my publisher, the problem ahead of me will involve more than literary judgment. It will involve, also, an individual ego, often a vulnerable, damageable one. The books that show no talent at all present the least problem, because in most cases the people who bring them in don't expect them to be passed on. Passing them on to *me* is the last act in the cycle, after which they are usually quite content to go off and produce another, equally hopeless book.

The manuscripts that pose the problems are those that, while probably not publishable themselves, contain at least a smidgen of promise. These manuscripts raise interesting questions—questions having to do with the nature of literary talent and its development. In my view talent is merely a seed, and not every seed will inevitably flower. Some talents, for lack of the right response at the right time, will remain merely seeds. Our culture at the present moment is a rich soil for fiction—that is, there is a lot to write about—but the climate above ground is terrible. Young short-story writers stand virtually no chance; the form is so hard to publish that it is quite

clearly dying. The day when Faulkner, Joyce, Hemingway, Fitzgerald, and Lawrence could grow up ambidextrous, writing the short story and the novel with equal ease, is a day that has passed. My own generation, for instance, has produced only two short-story writers of real originality: Donald Barthelme and Leonard Michaels.

The climate for novels is a little better, but not much. The number of first novels published in Amer-

Writing is not a full-time occupation. Larry McMurtry is also the proprietor of Booked Up, a Georgetown used-and-rare bookshop.

Young writers, will keep coming, and some of them will persist and find out for themselves what I'm talking about—but they aren't going to be able to accuse me of having encouraged them to it.

ica each year has dropped in recent decades from around eighty to around forty, and probably several thousand would-be novelists are competing for those forty slots. The slots, unhappily, are more likely to go to the luckiest than to the best—to those with contacts, who happen to know an editor, or to have somehow caught the eye of a powerful agent. One gets the sense that the major publishers have recently come to regard fiction as a necessary—or perhaps an unnecessary—evil; they are not really interested in promoting the talents they already have, much less in developing young talent, writers who stand no chance of paying off commercially for a book or two. Poets have been selling mostly to poets, and short-story writers to other short-story writers, for some time now, and it may not be long before the novel too becomes a mandarin form, something that publishers list for prestige reasons—or to convince themselves that they're still interested in literature.

As more and more publishers fall into the maw of conglomerates, as sales figures are scrutinized with colder and colder eyes, as the blockbuster syndrome in publishing becomes the rule rather than the exception, the squeeze on young fiction writers becomes ever more severe. Which editor wants to publish a sensitive first novel, by a kid who might pay off in ten years, when, with less effort, he can commission or orchestrate another *Jaws*? Who wants to publish fiction anyway, when non-fiction is outselling it so overwhelmingly?

It is there and not from television or the movies that the real threat to the novel comes. The real threat is the new or supra-journalism, that journalism that so often uses the techniques of fiction while retaining the sales-appeal of fact. Who needs a novel, say, about a man who builds birch-bark canoes, when John McPhee can actually go and find one and describe him and his passion with all the skill of a novelist? In short, who needs the second-rate novel, that great staple that kept much of the reading world happy throughout the 19th and part of the 20th centuries? Nobody—certainly not publishers. Documentary journalism has all but wiped it out.

What do I do, then, when I receive a novel that contains a few frail buds of talent? Do I stomp on them, tell the young writer to forget it, or do I send it my editor, to let him do the stomping? Do I tell the youngster to put this novel away and write another, hoping that inertia will then pull him into something safer, or, if not, that he will go off and write a book so strong and compelling that no publisher can reject it? Trouble is, there is virtually no such book. Publishers routinely reject novels nowadays that would have been as routinely accepted in the fifties and sixties. The pressure to be first rate, not with your third or fourth book but with your first, is more intense now than it ever has been.

Finally, and most seriously, what do I do about the real ones, the kid that is going to show up maybe once in a decade who is simply filled with talent? And who, besides talent, has energy, will, determination. I can of course tell him that publishers are an increasingly venal crew, and that it may take him eight or ten years to get published, and that he may have to write four or five books before it happens. That sort of discouragement the real ones will merely shrug off—they have nothing if not time.

To the real ones I think I would pose some rather stark questions, not so much to discourage them as to counter the kind of mindless, blanket encouragement which seems to be dished out in creative writing classes across the land. This encouragement often causes untalented people to attach their egos so tightly to the need to be a recognized writer that their egos get crushed if, as almost always happens, they fail—and besides which, it does not cause anyone, talented or otherwise, to give much thought to the nature of writing as an activity. Great and near-great writers, in their interviews and memoirs, have sounded warnings enough (indeed, their lives are warnings enough), but these remarks seem seldom to be remembered.

It is only sensible, I think, to ask young writers to consider whether writing is really a healthy thing for a human being to spend a life at. A lonely action in itself, is it not perhaps essentially introverting, essentially lonely-making? Does it bind the writer to mankind—or merely separate him from people? His working life, after all, will be spent in a corner putting pieces of paper through a strange machine, onto which the writer will have projected much of the best of himself—his emotional, intellectual, and imaginative resources. These are all resources which, if he thinks about it, he might rather give to some human or group of humans—a family, perhaps?

To which the kid might say, but I can do both. I can live and write too. And I will say, try an experiment. Read the biographies of any fifty writers—any fifty. How many did both well, satisfying both their muses and their loved ones? How many left behind them widespread human wreckage, along with one or two good books?

It is, after all, a question worth thinking about—and only one question of several that might be posed. Life is long, and the enthusiasm and responsiveness that produce a writer's first books bear the sort of relation to a *life* in writing that first love bears to marriage. To begin with, there is, in Chaucer's phrase, "the crafte so long to learne." You might learn it, but then again it might elude you. Then, if you do learn it, there is the marketplace to contend with—it may welcome you, but then again it may starve you, and your merits as a writer will have little to do with either eventuality.

Finally, and more crucially, there is the complex question of the psyche. Is not writing, in a sense, a form of self-cannibalism? The psyches of great writers, at the end, are like mines from which every seam of ore has been stripped, leaving, often enough, a hollow, propped up with a few shaky emotional supports. Often enough, the writer probes one time too many, or too deeply—for it is only through such probing that one gets better—and these supports collapse, leaving him nothing left to contemplate except the curious fact that he has somehow, over a lifetime, consumed himself.

There are, of course, satisfactions to writing, but these are as lonely, as incommunicable as the visions of Don Quixote, which for the most part even Sancho couldn't share. These satisfactions have little to do with the marketplace, with fame or money; they have little, for that matter, to do with publication. They come at odd moments in the writing itself, when you realize suddenly that you've turned a barber's basin into a golden helmet. Your readers will see and delight in the golden helmet; a few may even sense the barber's basin; but the moment of turning, wherein lies the true and perhaps the only self-satisfaction the artist gets from his work, is unsharable.

It is a chancy business, it seems to me, to blandly encourage the young to set out to devote a life to an activity of which only the product, never the process, can be shared. It is to advise them to become hunger artists, persons who fast over pages, not because they think there is virtue in fasting but because they have trained themselves to want a food that can only be found, in mouthfuls here and there, in the stoniest fields of human experience.

Young writers, of course, will keep coming, and some of them will persist and find out for themselves what I'm talking about—but they aren't going to be able to accuse me of having encouraged them to it. The Algerian ambassador to Pakistan will have to take his screenplay on to Karachi. The novel about dirty socks can, so far as I am concerned, live in a drawer, beneath the clean ones. What I hope is that some of those who take a simple pleasure in using words are as lucky as my old doctor, and find a kind of writing they can be pleased just to do—vilanelles, verse epics, or couplet biographies of noble soldiers. That, so far as anyone knows, can't hurt. But then, as Hemingway was fond of asking, how far can anyone know?

Southern Illinois University Press

By JOHN GARDNER

Press Director Vernon Sternberg in agonized supplication.

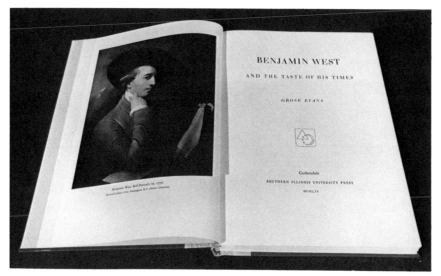

Fine bookmaking has been a hallmark of SIU Press from
its inception. This book was designed by Andor Braun.

No one familiar with the work of university presses would deny, I think, that among the smaller presses one of the best in the business—some would say the best—has for years been the press connected with Southern Illinois University, Director and Editor, Vernon Sternberg. Sternberg *is* the press, in effect. Though Sternberg cannot be made to say so, Southern Illinois University Press has never had anything like the support normally given by a university to the press that brandishes its name and promotes its respectability all over the world. Yet in an age when most university presses large and small have tended to play it safe, so that almost none are any longer "active and venturesome," as the late Lionel Trilling put it two years ago, the press at SIU remains one "that seems to have more liveliness than most."

The reason is largely that Vernon Sternberg, though a man not long on tact or patience, is the most intelligent, aggressive, and dedicated editor in the business. He knows what a university press ought to do, what books it ought to publish, how to go after them, and, even more important, how to keep an author, volume after volume, once he's been persuaded to publish with the SIU Press. One writer, philosopher Irwin C. Lieb, wrote fifteen years ago, after Sternberg had just brought out his award-winning *Experience, Existence, and the Good,* "You are an angular man who is difficult to deal with. But you certainly do know how to make a gorgeous book." In my own first dealings with the SIU Press I had that feeling any number of times, half anger and frustration, half astonishment and pride. But though Sternberg drives a hard bargain (tight press finances leave him no choice, and in the end his contracts prove competitive), and though his stubborn insistence on the standards that win awards would wring obscenities from a stone, one quickly discovers that nothing Vernon does is for personal glory, much less gain. He's a servant of good books, fiercely loyal and committed to his writers (who repay the compliment), an ingenious fox who regularly takes big risks, publishing works that larger, financially more comfortable houses would not touch for fear of loss or embarrassment—works like Paul Weiss's *Modes of Being,* a huge, brave study in metaphysics (629 pages) published when fashionable, small-minded philosophies (of the kind mocked in Tom Stoppard's *Jumpers*) had all but put metaphysicians out of business.

Modes of Being, published in 1958 after being declined by Chicago and Indiana, was a critical and financial success—it is still in print in paperback—and helped make Weiss Sterling Professor at Yale, later Heffer Professor of Philosophy at Catholic University. Along with Weiss's other books, nineteen titles in all, all published by Southern Illinois University Press, *Modes of Being* has helped establish Weiss as one of the most respected of modern American philosophers; and the publication of such books—ventures that took solid conviction and nerve —put Sternberg's press on the publishing map.

The risks have again and again paid off, making Sternberg a kind of specialist in the impossible. "But why?" the uninitiated may ask. "Who needs such books as" (glancing through the catalogue) *"The Giant Canada Goose,* or *Freedom of the Press: An*

Frances Walker, Head,
Order Processing

Beatrice Moore, Chief Editor

Teresa White, Assistant Editor

The People at the Press

Annotated Bibliography, or *One Hundred Nine-teenth-Century Rhyming Alphabets in English?"* It is not enough to answer that every one of those books, along with many others, has won for the SIU Press some major publishing award or, in some cases (for instance, *Freedom of the Press*), four or five such awards. What is it that a university press is supposed to do?

One thing a reputable university press is *not* set up to do, it should be mentioned at once, is publish the work of its own faculty. Except in the case of books commissioned by the press, every book, record, or film project is sent to judges outside the university (usually the work must receive at least two favorable reports), and in this process a writer from within the university has no advantage over anyone else. He may be, in fact, at a considerable disadvantage. If a press begins to look like a mere house organ, it loses its prestige, loses its ability to attract first-rate authors either outside *or* inside, and in the end loses money, without which—for a press not primarily funded by the university—there can be no publication.

A university press exists to publish work that com-mercial presses cannot publish, for financial reasons, or else do not have the high-mindedness or vision to

publish. Most of the books published at Southern Illinois University Press, as at other university presses, are aimed at a limited audience, one so small or spe-cialized as to be beneath the notice of a publisher whose chief concern is profit. The SIU Press pub-lishes, for instance, first-rate books likely to have only regional interest, like the beautifully written and photographed study of the southern Illinois area, *Land Between the Rivers;* and it publishes (more often) books intended mainly for scholars.

Both regional and scholarly functions are import-ant (the two are brought together in the press's monumental *Illustrated Flora of Illinois,* which, when complete, will run to forty volumes); but a good university press serves other important func-tions, including the publication of books which are of wide interest but have been ignored, dropped out of print, or foolishly turned down by commercial publishers. It seems incredible that the SIU Press should be needed for the publication, in Danish and English, of the tales of one of the finest writers of our century, Isak Dinesen (Baroness Karen Blixen), or for the futuristic explorations of R. Buckminster Fuller; yet it is so. And the press has of course pub-lished many other books of wide interest. It put back

Walter Kent, Assistant Director—Marketing

Lois Bursack, Advertising
and Promotion Assistant

Marilyn Hails, Production Editor

into print, after a lapse of many years, Thayer's great three-volume biography of Beethoven; it is one of the country's chief publishers of Spanish novels in English translation; and it has been widely praised for its rescue of forgotten American literature, from Zelda Fitzgerald's *Save Me the Waltz* to the titles in the Lost American Fiction series. The press, in fact, has saved more forgotten works than its catalogue shows. The word is out, and when Sternberg shows interest in the rights to a book that has long been out of print, the first reaction of those who own the rights is often to try it with a commercial publisher.

An occasional best seller is a matter of some importance to a press like SIU. The average sale of a book by a university press is about 1,300 copies over a five-year period, according to the *New York Times,* or about 2,000 overall. The sale of 5,000 copies of a title makes a book a best seller as far as university presses are concerned, and while it is common for some of the giant university presses (like Chicago) to sell over 100,000 copies of a work, 10,000 copies is a reasonable measure of solid success for a smaller press. SIU has had nine works which have sold in the above-10,000 range: four works by Buckminster Fuller, one novel (Fitzgerald's *Save Me the Waltz),*

two textbooks, a work in philosophy, and one work in Harry T. Moore's Crosscurrents/Modern Critiques series, Moore's *Contemporary American Novelists.* Only by "winning big" now and then can a press justify the high risks it must take to carry out its most ambitious projects or publish academically unfashionable or even iconoclastic books—books of a kind the SIU Press has repeatedly taken a chance on when nobody else would.

One way of showing the extent to which Sternberg has won by being venturesome, or willing to take risks, is to point out the contrast between what his press has to work with and the work it gets done. The press is funded by the university to the extent of housing and salaries for most of its staff on campus (but not for the freelance designers, artists, etc., on whom the press must depend for its design awards, among others its Printing Industries of Metropolitan New York awards for 1961-64, 1966, and 1973, and its American Institute of Graphic Arts awards of 1959 and 1967.) Capital and working cash have to come out of sales receipts, specific subsidies, and grants. Some $50,000 to $100,000 in outside funding is required each year to sustain the press, and here SIU has been at a striking disadvantage in comparison to other presses. Established in 1953 but not formally organized until 1956, the press came too late to win Ford money in the 1950s; and it was passed over for the Mellon Foundation grants in the 70s—a matter of astonishment to the SIU Press and to press watchers. Thus at SIU, sales must carry an unusual burden. And here, too, SIU is at a marked disadvantage.

There are probably a half-dozen to a dozen university presses with annual sales of over $1 million, and a few with sales in the $3 to $5 million range—not counting the super-giants, Oxford and Cambridge. With its severely limited capital available for advertising and promotion, Southern Illinois University Press brings in a sales income of about a half-million dollars a year. Yet despite these disadvantages, the press does remarkably well at bringing out a full and substantial book list. Again comparisons may help: the super-giant Oxford has sometimes published over 560 titles in a single year (679 in the peak year, 1971); the ordinary giants, such as Chicago, Harvard, or California, publish between 100 and, at most, 170 or so; and the annual list of the smaller but still long-established and well-heeled university giants—such as Yale, Johns Hopkins, Cornell, and Columbia—runs to between 50 and 100 titles. Southern Illinois publishes in the range of 50 to 60 titles each year, more than the number published by such old, established university presses as Stanford (about 35 titles each year), Minnesota (about 30) Illinois (about 50), and many others. In other words, working with less capital than most presses smaller than Southern Illinois University Press, Sternberg hits the lower range of the publishing giants.

The amount of money it takes to mount such a list is easily enough calculated. The average cost of a scholarly book today is approximately $5,000—for manufacturing alone. Non-manufacturing expenses add another $5,000 to the cost, making a total of approximately $600,000 for a list of 60 books. The figures of course include payment of royalty, and in some instances advances, which the Press pays on almost all the titles it publishes.

Sternberg manages to achieve high quality as well. The press has won scores of awards for both content and design and has achieved a number of publishing coups, among them such monumental reference works as *The London Stage, 1660-1800* (11 volumes) and *A Biographical Dictionary of Actors, Actresses . . . in London, 1660-1800* (projected to run 15 vol-

umes). Sternberg's press is responsible for, among other such things, the magnificent projected 15-or-so-volume work, *The Papers of Ulysses S. Grant* (six volumes now completed), the five-volume *Early Works of John Dewey* (published under the coveted Seal of the Center for Editions of American Authors [CEAA]), and this year will begin, under the same seal, its 15-volume *Middle Works of John Dewey*. The list of coups, of virtues and triumphs, could be expanded considerably.

But the point is just this: Southern Illinois University Press has achieved what it has because Vernon Sternberg is the "angular and difficult," original, aggressive, and tenacious man he is. He's as well known for sudden moves in startling new directions as for keeping his authors satisfied and clinging to quality. He told me once, "I'm perfectly resolved to come to the office every morning and tear up what I did yesterday. Change is a way of life for us here." It's true. In the all-too-often stodgy world of university publishing, Vernon Sternberg is one of the last of the swift, sly foxes.

The Southern Illinois University Press imprint was established in 1953, but regular publication began when Vernon Sternberg was hired to organize the Press in 1956. The Press celebrated the twentieth anniversary of its organization in January. Sternberg, a native of Wisconsin, was born 12 Aug. 1915 in Wausau, Wis. He is a graduate of the University of Wisconsin, B.A. 1941, M.A. 1946. He majored in English literature. He served in the U.S. Navy during World War II—to the wartime rank of Lt. (j.g.). He is a Lt. Cdr. USNR (Ret.). He taught at the University of North Dakota, 1947-50, and returned to Wisconsin for graduate work before joining the University of Wisconsin Press in 1953, where he was associate editor.

The Southern Illinois University Press publishes phonograph records and educational tests in addition to books. The records are distributed under the Pleiades Records label; the paperbacks under the Arcturus Books trademark. To date the Press has published 666 titles, 592 of them still in print. It has distributed slightly more than 1.2 million books and records since 1956.

Scholar-novelist John Gardner flourishes in the world of university presses and in the world of trade publishing. His books include *The Complete Poetry of Chaucer*, *The Sunlight Dialogues*, *Grendel*, and *The King's Indian*.

Ken Crowell, Warehousing Assistant Manager, (left) places palletized cartons in storage racks.

Maurice West, Warehousing and Shipping Department Manager, (below) checks orders and sends them down the wrapping table line.

View of a portion of the picking racks (bottom). Titles are set up on the racks in ascending order of International Standard Book Numbers.

Filling the Orders

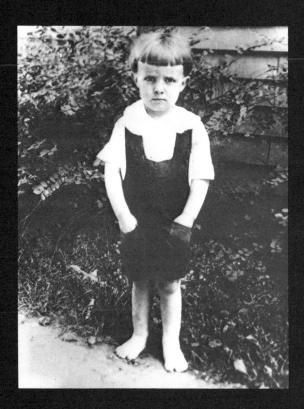

How I was always rich but was too dumb to know it

By RAY BRADBURY

At MGM some fifteen years ago I received a copy of a script I had worked on for six months with my name missing from the title page.

"How come!?" I yelled at the typing pool.

"Studio policy," was the reply.

"Well," said I, "Bradbury policy is to have his name on anything he has killed himself to finish. Retype the title page. I'll pay."

Which is the long way around to saying if no one cares if your name's on a script, who's going to care about a writer's finances? For that's what this article is going to be about: being poor at Pico and Western, Olympic and Norton, Figueroa and Temple, and out in Venice by the sea when I was living on apricot pie and Campbell's tomato soup and writing about rocket ships and Mars. I write this to show I came from somewhere and that place was halfway between the unemployment office and the L.A. riverbed in a dry season. Lacking money for an office, I typed my novel *Fahrenheit 451* in the library basement at UCLA, shoving dimes into the typing-machine every half hour and banging away like mad before the dime ran out.

But let's go back before that. I started writing when I was twelve, started submitting stories to *Esquire* and *Coronet,* the magazines for quality writers in America, when I was fifteen in 1935. When I graduated from L.A. High School in 1938, my family was on Relief, and I wore a suit an uncle of mine had been murdered in, with a bullet hole through the front and out the back, simply because we had no money to buy a new one for graduation.

Big deal? No. Everyone else was poor, too, so who noticed? I learned how to sneak into the back door of the Uptown Theatre where MGM held most of its important previews at least once a week. I saw everything MGM made, free, from 1934 up through 1940. The manager got so used to my sneaking in, he invited me through the front door.

When I was nineteen I sold newspapers for three years on the corner of Olympic and Norton, where I made ten bucks a week, and lived at home, writing in the living/bedroom with my Mom, Dad, brother, and a radio, all talking at once.

A picture of Ray Bradbury at 3 in 1923 set into a recent portrait of the author.

THE SIEVE AND THE SAND
Bradbury

WHICH IS LEAST
As I choose the ~~most~~ valuable?"

"~~But~~ Pick any old one."

What If I ~~hand in~~ a substitute and Beatty DOES knows
WHICH
the ~~title of the~~ book I stole, then he'll guess we've an
entire library here!"

Mildred's mouth twitched. ~~She sat and thought
about it, and moaned.~~ "See what you're doing? You'll
ruin us! ~~Did you steal that Bible last night? Hand it
to them.~~ Who's more important, me or that Bible?" She
was beginning to shriek now, sitting there like a wax
doll melting in its own heat.

could
He hears Beatty's voice. "Sit down, Montag.
Watch. Delicately, like the petals of a flower. Light
the first page, light the second page. Each becomes a
black butterfly. Beautiful, eh? Light ~~the second page
from the first and~~ the third page from the second and so
on, chain-smoking, ~~the entire book~~ chapter by chapter, all
~~of the words and all~~ the silly things the words mean, all
the false promises ~~and fantasies~~, all the secondhand
notions and timeworn philosophies." There sat Beatty,
perspiring gently, the floor littered with swarms of black
moths that had died in a single storm.

Mildred stopped screaming as quickly as she
started. ~~Because~~ Montag was not listening. "There's only
one thing to do," he said. "Some time before tonight when

In late 1940 I had my first story accepted by Rob Wagner's *Script* in Beverly Hills. Payment: a free subscription to the magazine. So, total income from writing in 1940: zero.

In 1941 I made my first real sale to *Super Science Stories,* with Henry Hasse as collaborator, for $35.00. Later that year I sold two more tales to *Thrilling Wonder Stories.* Net income for the year: $75.00.

In 1942 I skyrocketed to four sales. One, "The Candle," to *Weird Tales* for $16.00, another to *Thrilling Wonder Stories* for $33.00, and stories to *Astounding* and *Astonishing* at $30.00 and $25.00 respectively. Income for the year, an incredible: $104.00.

I could only go up from there. In 1943, I made so much money writing that I quit selling newspapers on that street corner. I sold one short story each month, most of them to *Weird Tales,* at $35.00 each for a year-end total of $503.00, just a trifle less than I made selling those infernal *Herald-Expresses.*

1944? You guessed it. I fell upward again. Twenty-three stories sold out of fifty-two submitted, for roughly $20.00 per week and a final income of $1064.00.

What I was doing, of course, was starting a short story every Monday morning and doing a first draft in one day. On Tuesday I revised the story. On Wednesday I did a second revision. On Thursday and Friday I did my third and fourth versions. On Saturday I typed a final copy and sent it out. The next Monday I started a new story. It went on that way for years, at the rate of fifty-two stories a year. I'm still on the same schedule, doing a story or an essay a week, or an equal amount of pages on a novel.

In 1945 I submitted more than sixty stories, sold only fifteen, but experienced a big jump in income and a grander jump into the quality field. In April I sold a story to *The American Mercury,* which later appeared in the *Best American Short Stories.* In the late summer, needing money, I sent three stories off to the slush piles of three magazines under the name of William Elliott, fearing that the editors of the quality magazines might not read stories by someone named Ray Bradbury who lived in Venice, California, and had his name on the cover of *Weird Tales.*

On August 18th I sold a story to *Charm.* On August 21st I sold "One Timeless Spring" to *Collier's.* On the 22nd, my 25th birthday, I sold "Invisible Boy" to *Mademoiselle.* The combined checks totalled $950. I telegraphed each magazine, confessing my real name. When the first check for $500 arrived from *Collier's* I asked my bank to give me five $100 bills,

"I write this to show that I came from somewhere and that place was halfway between the unemployment office and the L.A. riverbed in dry season...."

Opposite: original typescript for *Fahrenheit 451.* Above: dialogue for Ray Bradbury's *Moby-Dick* screenplay, written in London in 1954.

191

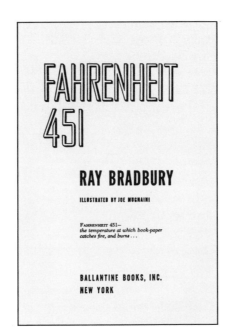

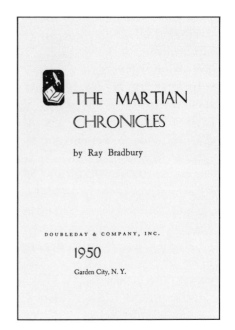

"I typed my novel Fahrenheit 451 in the library basement at UCLA, shoving dimes into the typing-machine every half hour and banging away like mad before the dime ran out."

Title pages from five Bradbury novels.

which I carried around for one day just to look at them, stunned. By the end of the year my income was about $40.00 a week, doubled again from the prior year to $2,100. It was my first tax year. I paid out forty-three bucks to the IRS, and celebrated.

In 1946 I sold eighteen stories for $2910.00, another rise.

In 1947 I sold twenty-seven stories for $3,174.00. Up, by God, to around $60.00 a week! But, beyond the sales, the money that I so dearly needed, what else was that year like?

It was like this . . .

Those were the summer nights when I'd pick Maggie McClure, my fiancee, up from where she clerked at Fowler Brothers Book Store down across from Pershing Square, have a hamburger, play a game of miniature golf at Gittelson Brothers Golf Course downtown, or out on Hollywood Blvd., and get home on the Venice Short Line street car at one in the morning in order to write another story about Mars and canals where only ancient dust ran along the empty bottoms and the far hills were strangely blue and clearly remembered.

That was the summer and the early fall, 1947, when, walking around Hollywood, on the streets with lights, and the streets with shadows, Maggie quoted Byron to me and I went home on the trolley and wrote "And the Moon Be Still as Bright," and she recited Sara Teasdale to me and I went home and clanked out "There Will Come Soft Rains."

I had a small room behind my Dad's garage with a fine view of an open meadow full of weeds extending all the way to Raymond Chandler's oilwells pumping all night every night near half-ruined bungalows and those old Venice canals full of shattered moons and strange seepages of dreams and a lot of old circus lion-cages someone had dumped and left for the sea to fill with stranger creatures than ever prowled Ringling's. I called it *all* Chandler country, because I was in love with not only California but the California Chandler himself had trapped with his mind and then with his typewriter.

I would sit half the night looking out at that meadow stretching off toward Chandler's flake-painted houses and lost desires, and write my own tales of people going mad on Venus or falling through space complaining of the velocity and losing touch when their rockets exploded. Around three in the morning I'd go look in the icebox, take out a slice of Mom's banana cake and a cold glass of milk and sit thinking about the great writer I someday just had to become. I was twenty-seven and time was running out. I made time run into my typewriter where I could keep it forever, or a few years, anyway, if I was lucky.

That was a good year because not only did my income go up to $60 a week, but my first book of stories, *Dark Carnival*, was published, got good reviews when it got any among the obits in the literary sections of the *Peoria Bugle* and the *Manassas Times*, and got me a $500 advance, which I sorely needed. That was the year I also called and wrote my hero Norman Corwin, told him he was the greatest writer/

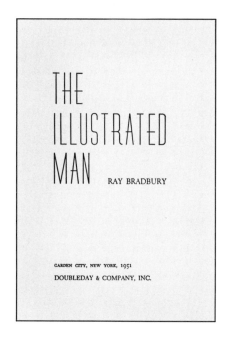

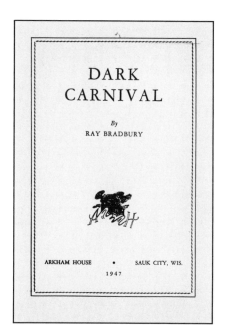

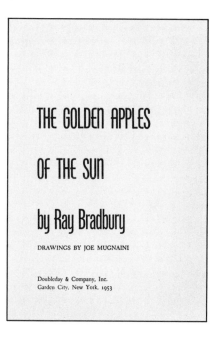

director/producer ever to broadcast on radio, sent him a book, and asked, if he liked it, could I buy him a drink some day. He telephoned a week later and said, "You're not buying *me* a drink. I'm buying *you* dinner." We spent a long grand talking evening together, he drove me back to Venice, near those old lion-cage canals at midnight, and we have been friends now, dear friends, for twenty-eight years.

1947 was so good that Maggie bullied me into getting married. I was frightened, of course, as I think all writers are, that somehow as soon as one got married, the world swallowed your income whole and you went down the drain, Underwood Standard and all. The day we married, in late September, I had ten dollars in the bank. I offered it to the minister who handed it back saying, "You're a writer, aren't you?" I nodded. "Then you'll need this more than I will," he said. Dear man.

The week after we bought our toothbrushes and settled in a $30-a-month apartment in Venice, I sold my one and only story to the *New Yorker* for $400, which was like getting a rainfall from God worth $3,000 in today's dollars. I had a feeling He was watching and staying in touch.

1948 upped me to $3,184 for the year plus Maggie's $2,564 earned working with Stanley Slotkin at Abbey Rents. We rode the tram down to Ocean Park every night, total cost coming and going forty cents, where we ate hot dogs, spent fifty or sixty cents in the penny arcade or took in a forty-cent movie and got home to bed at ten o'clock. Sometimes I stayed up late to commune with my Martians.

In 1949, God scared us. Maggie was pregnant. But God told Norman Corwin to tell me to get on the Greyhound Bus and go to New York, which I did, and stayed in the YMCA up on Central Park West for a buck a night, where I wrote an outline for a book called *The Martian Chronicles* and sold it to Doubleday the next day, along with *The Illustrated Man*. I took the Greyhound as far as Chicago, then said to hell with it and took the chair-car on the train the rest of the way, sitting up, and happy. By year's end, our first daughter was born, and God and Norman Corwin's advice had nailed our income up to $4,410.

It never went down again. With each of our four daughters our income doubled.

Our biggest leap was in 1953 when John Huston appeared on our doorstep and offered me a chance to write my first screenplay, *Moby Dick*. Huston, and that film, changed our lives forever. It made us employable when we needed to be employed. Our income has been constant ever since.

That's it. The years were long. The years were good. Even when we were poor we never knew it, because the family worked as a family, and our marriage, when it happened, worked as a marriage. When people ask me why I am genetically optimistic, the reasons are all here. Good friends like my wife, my daughters, my literary representative Don Congdon, and Norman Corwin. It turns out I was *always* rich, but too dumb to know it.

Maurice Sendak:
Grand Master Of Make~Believe

*An illustrator with near-total recall
of "the sounds and feelings and images of childhood"*

Text by SELMA G. LANES

"To me, illustrating means having a passionate affair with the words," Maurice Sendak has said. Frequently the author of the very words he sets to pictures, Sendak is virtually unchallenged as the pre-eminent children's book illustrator of our time.

Born in Brooklyn in 1928, Sendak had, one way or another, prepared for the career of illustrator since childhood. He and his brother, Jack, would draw pictures, often hand-lettering stories and binding little books of tales. "It was all I ever wanted to do," the artist says.

During his early teens, Sendak remembers spending "hundreds of hours sitting at my window, sketching neighborhood children at play. There is not a book I have written or a picture I have drawn that does not, in some way, owe them its existence." Certainly *A Hole Is To Dig,* his first collaboration with Ruth Krauss in 1952 and the work that brought him his earliest fame, is deeply indebted to this apprenticeship. Sendak fondly refers to the sketchbook drawings as "the only school that ever taught me anything."

Taking his own measure as an artist, Sendak denies that he writes or draws appreciably better than many others. "If I have an unusual gift," he has said, "it's that I remember the sounds and feelings and images of particular moments in childhood."

One such recollection, in fact, provided the inspiration for *Where The Wild Things Are* (1963), the picture book that won for Sendak the Caldecott Medal for the best-illustrated children's book of the year. "It was my re-creation of what it was like to be a small kid when adults came to the house—usually relatives with bad teeth who looked at you as though they were going to eat you up because you were so cute. These relatives of mine were probably the originals of the Wild Things."

They may have been originals, but a good deal of self-instruction enriched their ultimate Sendakian form. During the fifties and early sixties, the artist began studying the master illustrators of the 19th century—William Blake, Randolph Caldecott, Wilhelm Busch, and Ludwig Richter, among others—"borrowing techniques and trying to forge them into my own personal language." This personal language was soon characterized by Sendak's uncanny ability to make palpable the emotional reality of any tale. The artist confesses to "only two obsessive themes in all his work: One is a great curiosity about childhood as a state of being. The other has to do with how all children manage to get through childhood from one day to the next, how they defeat boredom, fear, pain and anxiety and find joy. It is a constant miracle to me that children manage to grow up."

He has pursued these themes in works as dissimilar as his stately two volumes of German folk tales, *The Juniper Tree and Other Tales from Grimm* (1973) and his comic-strip work about the perils of dog ownership, *Some Swell Pup* (1976). Maurice Sendak's achievements have won him the Hans Christian Andersen Award. He is the first American to receive this equivalent of the Nobel Prize for children's literature.

195

Nurse Jennie devours Baby's breakfast

The canine heroine, Jennie, of Sendak's most personal and mystifying tale, *Higglety Pigglety Pop* (1967), is not your garden-variety fictional heroine. In real life, Jennie was, for many years, the artist's beloved pet Sealyham. Not only is his own dog the central character, but the all-important supporting player, Baby (left) is taken almost exactly from a family-album photograph of Maurice Sendak as an infant. Characteristic of his best work, this dreamlike fairly tale draws upon memories from his own childhood in the nineteen-thirties. Sendak's meticulous pen-and-ink drawings, with their intricate cross-hatchings, emulate 19th-century English and German steel engravings.

Serving birthday soup to three best friends is Sendak's ursine hero, lovingly created for Else Holmelund Minarik's *Little Bear* (1957). Between 1959 and 1966, four popular sequels followed. Sendak's forte was to make palpable the warmth of Little Bear's relationships with parents, grandparents, and assorted friends. The artist's tender—but never cloying— portrayal of childhood happiness and security has assured the quintet a permanent place among this century's nursery classics.

An unmistakeable Sendakian rage launches *In The Night Kitchen* (1970), as it did *Where The Wild Things Are* (1963), the two picture books closest to the artist's heart. The pajama-ed Mickey (below) has been rudely awakened by things that go bump in the night. This, in turn, triggers a wild and triumphal dream about the Night Kitchen (following pages), its three mysterious bakers, and "Mickey the Pilot" who makes a daring flight "over the top of the Milky Way."

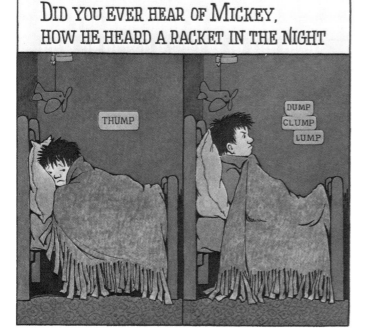

The lion of truth sets a trap destined
to fail in "The Twelve Huntsmen."

Tales from Grimm

Of his 27 intense and highly distilled illustrations
for *The Juniper Tree and Other Tales from Grimm*
(1973) , Sendak has said: "I was looking to catch the
moment in each fairy tale when the tension between
the storyline and the emotion is at its greatest."

Dumbkin confides his problem to
a magical fat toad in "The Three Feathers."

The Devil is forced to keep a bargain
with his intended victim in "Bearskin."

The unsuspecting groom discovers his love's treachery in "Rabbit's Bride."

King of all the Wild Things

At the climax of Sendak's best-known work, *Where The Wild Things Are*, the beasts crown Max their king. One of the artist's many pint-sized alter egos (Sendak has a penchant for heroes with names that, like his own, begin with the letter M), Max presides at an orgy of Wild Things until—temper tantrum against his mother abated—he begins to miss home and to long for his supper. Though many parents and educators shied away from the fantasy when it first appeared in 1963, fearing it would terrify small children, its popularity among the nursery set is by now legendary.

Just Down The Road From "Ragtime"

Paperback publishing is not all
multi-million-dollar deals
with glamorous name authors;
for Patrick O'Connor at Popular Library
it's an opportunity
to publish books he likes
by selling plenty
of what other people like

By JOHN F. BAKER

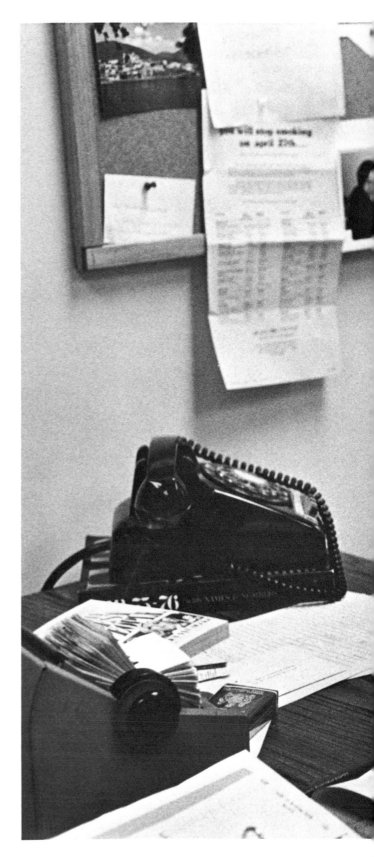

Big money always makes big news, and when word came last year that Bantam Books had paid $1,850,000 for the paperback rights to E. L. Doctorow's novel *Ragtime,* even people who never think much about books or author royalties were startled. At one blow the author of a critically admired but not, one would have thought, overwhelmingly saleable novel had earned what many of the world's greatest authors had never made in a lifetime of *successful* writing. And although the *Ragtime* sale was the crowning statistic that put paperback sales on the news pages, there have been enough extraordinarily large sums paid for paperback rights in re-

Patrick O'Connor, Editor-in-Chief at Popular Library:
"You're not an editor, you're a merchandizer!"

cent years to indicate that such sales are no more immune to inflation than the contents of the grocery basket. Just in the last two or three years, $1.5 million for the rights to that perennial favorite *The Joy of Cooking*, $1-million-plus for Woodward and Bernstein's *All the President's Men* and James Michener's *Centennial*—and, currently, $700,000 for a new novel, *Interview with the Vampire*, that wasn't even *published* yet, and which the people who frantically bid against each other to reach that figure had only read in manuscript (copies they had apparently managed to sneak out of the offices of Knopf, the book's hardcover publisher).

Just how typical are these huge prices—and the big and important movie sales that usually follow or accompany them—in modern paperback publishing? Has it really become big business on *that* vast a scale, or are such spectacular deals very much the exception rather than the rule? To answer such questions, the basic nature of the paperback industry must be understood. For a start, it is profoundly different from hardcover publishing, not necessarily because the sums involved are so much larger, but also because the very nature of the product, and the ways in which it is distributed, set paperbacking decisively apart.

The best analogy might be with the film industry. There, too, you have the big prestige pictures, carefully booked into the right theaters, perhaps even with reserved-seat prices, and with a carefully orchestrated publicity campaign—the equivalent of the big best sellers by name authors, which are ordered by booksellers on the basis of enthusiasm for the author's track record, or the publisher's promotional promises. At the same time, you have hundreds of lesser pictures, usually opened with no publicity or critical fanfare at all, which form the bills at drive-in theaters and quickly get sold to TV to help fill in the gaps between the soap operas on long viewing afternoons—the equivalent of the regular monthly carton of books from the paperback publisher, which aims to please certain well-defined tastes, which no bookseller actually *asks* for, but which just serves to fill the racks in the paperback book outlet—often for about as long as the minor movie fills the screen at the local drive-in.

For what many outsiders do not realize is that the mass-market paperbacks found in your average airport bookstall or drugstore—or even, increasingly, supermarket—are not *chosen* by anybody. Each publisher has his quota of racks in the store, which are filled up at regular intervals by the guy who drives the truck for the distributor of the publisher's books. For the important titles, perhaps as long as six weeks or two months in the sun; for most others, out with the old lot and in with the new every time the driver makes a delivery. It is obviously very important for a paperback publisher to maintain his quantity of output, otherwise he would slip behind in the amount of rack space available to him—or, even worse, those racks would be full of the same old books, week after week.

Product, then, is of the essence to the paperback publisher, just as it is to the small-budget movie company (or, perhaps a better analogy these days, the producer of the weekly or monthly TV situation comedy or cops-and-robbers action thriller). He cannot hope to fill his lists just by reprinting successful novels or gardening or cookery books from the hardcover publishers' lists; there are simply not enough of them to go around, particularly when you realize that each promising title is being competed for by about a dozen paperback publishers. The answer, then, is obviously to publish plenty of original books—and, although their economics are generally a long way away from those of the big blockbuster titles, such originals are still the backbone of most of the mass paperback operations.

At this point it might be as well to examine in close-up the operation of one typical mass-market paperback publisher. I have chosen to look at Popular Library, partly because in size and scope it is most typical, falling midway between such mammoth companies as Bantam and Fawcett and such comparatively unknown and insignificant ones as Ace, Pinnacle, and Pyramid; but even more because its editor-in-chief is one of the liveliest, most outspoken and original figures on the paperback scene.

Patrick O'Connor came late to publishing ("I was 35 before I grew up"), having dabbled in earlier days in movie and TV production and authorship; he remains a balletomane whose dance reviews appear regularly in ballet magazines. He had been in turn associate editor and senior editor at Popular Library before going off as editor-in-chief of another paperback line, Curtis Books. Two years ago Curtis folded and Popular, which had recently been taken over as a subsidiary of CBS, asked O'Connor back to head the imprint.

Popular Library itself is one of the oldest paperback companies, originally created in 1943 as an all-fiction spinoff from the magazines of its parent corporation, Pines Publications. Right from the start, with the "Saint" books of Leslie Charteris, the thrillers of John Dickson Carr and the romantic mysteries of Mary Roberts Rinehart, it set its sights on popular genre books. And although today, as at most other houses, Popular's monthly carton contains its share of reprints—perhaps a third of the total—the genre fiction with which it began its life remains an essential element.

One of his assistants once said of Patrick O'Connor that "He has a hell of a lot of taste—good and bad." It is an observation that delights him, and that he constantly lives up to in the exercise of his power over Popular's list. For one thing, he has his own very special tastes in literature, and, unlike most of us, he is in a position to indulge those tastes and give readers a chance to share them; on the other hand, he is also well aware that his own tastes are rarefied compared to those of most of his likely customers, and that to publish only books that he personally admires would be economic suicide. He accepts this equably, and reserves his keenest impatience for intellectual snobs who would impose their own mandarin standards on the entire reading public. "In this business you have to give up the idea that you can raise people's level. Why not just let everyone enjoy what they enjoy?"

In a typical month, Popular Library issues about twenty books, though in coming months this is expected to rise to about twenty-four, which, O'Connor notes, "will enable us all to stay later at the office." Of those twenty-odd monthly books, two will be conventional Westerns, probably originating with pulp-magazine authors, selling (still) for 95¢ and in printings sometimes as low as 30,000 or 40,000. (It is astonishing how Westerns linger on; even big-time Bantam offers as its biggest selling author Louis L'Amour, who has written dozens of them.) These books, O'Connor notes, are seldom observed by the tastemakers because "They are not sold in New York." In the same category there will be a monthly novel in what O'Connor calls the Frontier genre:

"This has a woman holding a gun on the cover, and goes for $1.25. There are some quite classy authors who do these—David Lavender, for instance—and they can be literary."

Science fiction is very much on the upswing these days, and O'Connor likes to do a couple a month when he can find them; but that's becoming increasingly difficult, partly because of the competition (everyone acknowledges that Ballantine has the greatest expertise in this area and invariably gets first to the best) and partly because it has a very demanding audience. O'Connor calls the science fiction audience, in fact, "the most discriminating readers in America today."

On Westerns and science fiction he has his own specialists among his three regular editors; the next category, the mysteries, he picks himself. One will be standard sex-and-violence, two will be what he calls "Ladies' Mysteries" (more exactly classified at Doubleday as "Ladies in Distress" titles), which can on occasion be of high quality: the English mystery writer P.D. James he puts in this category.

Each month will see at least one book on plants or some aspect of gardening, another rapid-growth category in which O'Connor claims Popular was a pioneer. These are all either written or acquired by the house's regular expert, Elvin McDonald.

Gothics—that category of fiction in which young women, frequently governesses or poor relations, are romantically terrorized by the brutal but handsome owners of sinister English mansions—are the *spécialité de la maison* at Popular. O'Connor publishes no fewer than five of them a month, in a variety of classifications: one will be a large-type, easy-to-read one, very popular with the older women who are a major part of the readership; there will probably be a couple of Queen-size, of 70,000 to 90,000 words; and one bigger-budget Empress, up to 150,000 words.

All the genre Gothics are written to order by free-lance writers, whom O'Connor describes as "indentured slaves." They get $3000 to $5000 for one of the shorter books, perhaps $8000 or more for a longer one. They are fantastically productive—one of O'Connor's regulars, a Canadian, can turn out a 90,000-word manuscript in three weeks — and he speaks of them fondly. "I'm probably crazy to say this, but these journeyman writers, and please note that I will not call them hacks, are very much underpaid. They were getting $3000 for a manuscript ten years ago, and they're still getting it today, though everything else has doubled in that time. And they're

Meeting in Patrick O'Connor's office. Left to right:
Kate Duffy and Karen Solem, editors; Charlotte Gordon, Senior Editor;
Dudley Frasier, Executive Editor.

real professionals. I don't have time to deal with amateurs. When you've only got three editors you can't afford to have to pencil-edit each manuscript. They get one reading in the house once they've been approved by our outside readers, then they go straight to copy editing."

Despite his title, in fact, O'Connor acknowledges the truth of what someone once told him at a party: "You're not an editor, you're a merchandizer!" His chief concerns, indeed, apart from deciding what books the house will publish in the first place, are with covers, with sales plans, and with the presentation of the monthly list to the salesmen. That list, of course, will include a number of general-interest, as opposed to genre, books, bought in the regular way from hardcover houses, and this is the area where O'Connor is able to display the good side of his taste.

"I like to have at least one book on the list each month that I can give away with pride to friends and relatives," he says, and cannot resist adding: "Not that it does them much good. I send my sisters in Pennsylvania their monthly Gothic allowance, and every now and again I'll slip in a Katherine Anne Porter and tell them they have to read this in order to get their Gothics. But it doesn't work."

Books that O'Connor likes to give away with pride reflect a catholic taste, with a leaning toward some of the more recondite English contemporary authors. Nancy Mitford's *Love in a Cold Climate* and *The Pursuit of Love,* for instance, are his favorite books. "I have to have them always in print." As a result he has also sought out lesser-known Mitford works and brought them back. When Jean Rhys, an elderly English author whose economical studies of feminine despair had been virtually forgotten, was the subject of a critical reassessment not long ago, O'Connor was first on the scene with reprints.

Anthony Powell, another O'Connor idol, has been

leisurely compiling his huge "A Dance to the Music of Time" saga for the last twenty-five years, and this spring the last volume, *Hearing Secret Harmonies,* was published. O'Connor was very anxious to secure that last book so that he could issue the entire sequence in a set of four big volumes in the coming year. But he knew that, being Powell's last book in the series, it would receive more than usual attention and he would have more than the usual trouble securing it at auction; it did, and he did, but it would never have occurred to him not to complete the series.

Most paperback houses like to be able to offer the collected works of certain authors (Fawcett, for instance, although known largely for its big women's novels, has all of James Michener, John Updike, and Joyce Carol Oates on its list) and O'Connor is no exception. His tastes being what they are, his definitive authors' list includes Cornelius Ryan (he had to bid unusually high for Popular, $400,000, to get the last, *A Bridge Too Far,* but that was part of a package that enabled him to reprint *The Longest Day* and *The Last Battle* as well); Angus Wilson; Elizabeth Taylor; the thriller-writer Mignon Eberhart; the Catholic philosopher and sociologist Dorothy Day; and the highly experimental early twentieth-century English novelist Dorothy Richardson, whose books are as unknown today as her appearances in literary histories are inevitable. He also has, as probably the commercial crown of his collection, the complete works of John O'Hara, which Popular secured in an exclusive package deal from O'Hara's hardcover publisher, Random House.

There are other favorites O'Connor would like to publish exclusively in paperback. Doris Lessing is one, but although he has half-a-dozen of her books in print, others went to other houses, and "now it's a standoff." He is also a warm admirer of English novelist Margaret Drabble, and when last seen was exultant at having secured *The Realms of Gold* for $30,000; he thinks he can probably get most of her books without too much difficulty since, despite a high critical reputation, she is not as yet a major seller.

It is highly unusual when a mass-market paperback house like Popular Library buys anything from a university press, but that is what O'Connor did recently, in furtherance of another of his tastes for unappreciated corners of literature. For the past three years the Southern Illinois University Press has been publishing a series it calls Lost American Fiction, consisting of notable novels that are long out of print. This is a subject that fascinates O'Connor and he even suggested a possible title to the editors of that series; so when they were seeking a paperback publisher for the whole line, he naturally and gladly came forward. The list contains such unusual titles as *The Cubical City* by Janet Flanner, the well-known *New Yorker* writer, a famous forgotten novel, *Weeds,* by Edith Summers Kelley, an only novel called *Dry Martini* by John Thomas—a book much admired by John O'Hara—another novel by a *New Yorker* writer, Robert M. Coates's *Yesterday's Burdens,* and a grim Depression novel called *They Don't Dance Much* by a Southern newspaperman, James Ross, whose only book it was.

Most of the books that O'Connor buys in accordance with his personal taste have to be purchased at auction from the hardcover house that originally published them. The auction is a feature of paperback publishing that is comparatively new, and works on the same principle as an agent's auction of a book by a popular writer who has no regular publisher. The subsidiary rights director of the hardcover publisher will supply interested parties at the various paperback houses with proofs of the book (the important auctions usually occur *before* official hardcover publication, though not inevitably) and then set a date at which bids can be accepted. Frequently, as in furniture or cattle auctions, there will be a "floor" for the bidding. The sale is normally accomplished by phone rather than face-to-face, and particularly hard-fought auctions have been known to continue for several days of frantic back-and-forth telephoning and consultation before a price is finally agreed upon.

Most paperback houses, including Popular Library, will have carefully calculated in advance of an auction what a book will probably fetch, and will also have decided, in consultation with the business and sales managers, how many copies they are going to have to sell to enable them to pay that price. They therefore enter the lists with a firm idea of how much they are prepared to spend. "Once you get in an auction, though, fever takes over," says O'Connor, "and no matter what ceiling you've set yourself, or what rules you're playing by, you'll overbid when it comes to the crunch, for something you very much want."

Most paperback houses have a formula by which

In a typical month Popular Library issues 20 titles, including these categories: westerns, Sci-Fi, Gothics, mysteries (sex-and-violence and "ladies' mysteries") , and plant books. Popular also publishes the Lost American Fiction series and Anthony Powell's *Dance to the Music of Time* cycle.

they decide how much they should spend on an advance for a book in order to enable them to make a profit on a predetermined number of copies, but paperback executives are highly secretive about such formulas, and O'Connor is no exception. "When you move around, as I have, you get to know several different formulas," he says. "They're all different, and everyone guards them jealously, but of course none of them really work. They just let you think you've got it all figured out." One thing that remains fairly constant, however, is that hardcover publisher and author generally split the paperback advance 50-50; author royalties on paperback sales are calculated on a sliding scale, based on all sorts of imponderables like weeks spent on best seller lists, sale of movie rights, and so on. They can start as low as 8% and go as high as 20% but for most authors of most books most of the time they average out at around 12%.

The really big sums for paperback rights—and even today anything over half a million dollars is still regarded as a big sum—inevitably emerge from a bidding situation. Most of the figures in that stratosphere, however, are paid by Bantam, Fawcett, Pocket Books, Ballantine (and more latterly Warner Books, whose corporate parents have been spending freely to put their company into the big time); Popular goes into six figures quite seldom. "I estimate that of the 10 big auctions in any month there'll be just one book that I like and that I think has good sales potential as well," says O'Connor.

But such a cautious approach does not mean he has not splurged in his time. Popular's all-time best seller (in fact probably *anyone's* all-time paperback best seller) is the paper version of *Webster's New World Dictionary,* and the house bought rights to it sixteen years ago, paying a hefty $750,000 "at a time when people were paying peanuts for paperback rights." It still sells a million-plus copies a year, and is in fact the book on which Popular has ordered its largest-ever press run—one million copies. The record payment for a book at Popular since O'Connor has been in charge was the aforementioned $400,000 for *A Bridge Too Far,* and since an all-star movie has recently been announced of this property, it is likely to turn out to have been money well spent.

Unlike some of the larger houses, in which professional support for a title is automatic, but in which it often goes no further than professionalism, Popular, O'Connor feels, exerts energy in the sale of one of its books "in direct proportion to the real enthusiasm of the editor for that book—and that translates itself into sales enthusiasm." For that reason he likes his editors to follow their books all the way, from the time when the purchase is first conceived, through the auction (he prefers to let the bidding be done by an editor fired up about a book rather than a specialist in rights purchases) and to the final sales and cover meetings. "In the end the editor's chief concern is with the cover, and with the presentation to the salesmen." The cover of a paperback is, of course, all-important, and by far the most expensive element in the production; but O'Connor is proud of the production quality of his books all down the line. "We spend enormous amounts of money on quality control, although the average reader probably never thinks about it. How often do you see typos or misspellings in a paperback?"

The sort of sales success on which Popular, and Patrick O'Connor, thrive, enabling them both to pursue their more intellectual endeavors with impunity, was scored not long ago by a book called *The Heart Listens* by Helen Van Slyke. This was a warmly written "woman's novel" that had made no particular splash in hardcover and O'Connor, his ear ever to the ground in such matters, first became aware of its potential when he heard from one of his Pennsylvania sisters that she couldn't get it out of her local library because there was such a long waiting list for it. That kind of word-of-mouth, among that kind of readership, spells certain success, and O'Connor quickly got hold of a copy and was convinced his sister was right to want the book. He snapped it up for almost nothing ($17,500), then, going on the principle that "you go all out for something you believe in," spent $75,000 on advertising and promotion. At last count the book had a million copies in print, and another Van Slyke novel (its title changed from the hardcover *All Visitors Must Be Announced* to the much snappier *The Best People*) is about to be sold with a barrage of TV advertising. Another recent purchase shows an even wider

margin between price and promotion expenditure. A novel called *The Hollow Mountains* came in as an unsolicited manuscript ("over the transom," as publishers say), and the Popular people spotted in it the makings of one of those big Western family sagas that seem to be particularly appealing to Americans in their Bicentennial year. That too is getting a sendoff that will cost many, many times as much as the original book did ($3000). Also in the coming season O'Connor is taking a fling on a Nazi-past thriller that was a big success in Europe, but which no American publisher had tried out in translation: *The Caesar Code* by Johannes Mario Simmel. It's a calculated risk, but it could be another Frederick Forsyth, and meanwhile no enormous sums are at stake.

And that, in essence, is at the root of O'Connor's publishing philosophy. Never buy extravagantly—no matter how exciting the auction pressure; carefully calculate probable sales, and print conservatively (he cannot suggest an *average* printing of one of his titles, because they vary so enormously, from as low as 30,000 to as high as 500,000); and, when a book warrants it, go all out in promotion, especially on TV, where he feels much of his readership is.

Last summer, a novel called *Looking For Mr. Goodbar* by Judith Rossner, who had written several previous novels, in rather similar vein but with singular lack of success, was published by Simon and Schuster and adroitly promoted to major best-seller status. As befits a book of such promise, it was sold to paperback, after a hectic auction with a $100,000 floor, for just over $300,000. It will probably do very well in paperback. But meanwhile O'Connor had in his deep-freeze one of Rossner's earlier novels, *To the Precipice,* which its disappointed hardcover publisher was glad to give away for paperback at $1500. That book will shortly appear on the Popular Library list with a new cover, a coverline tactfully reminding readers that here is another novel by the author of *Goodbar*—and in a printing of 500,000 copies.

It isn't exactly *Ragtime* and $1,850,000, or *Jaws* and 9,000,000 copies, but it's a highly workable approach—and it enables Patrick O'Connor to look forward with pride to the fact that when he brings out the four volumes in Anthony Powell's great cycle this summer and fall, "We'll be giving it the works—a real die-cut cover, the most expensive we've ever given anything."

Log of a Screen Writer

*Vampires and Giant Frogs, Walking Dead
and Psychic Detectives, Robot Housewives
and Sex-Starved Teenagers...*

By WILLIAM F. NOLAN

When people ask me about my screen work I casually tell them that I wrote a film script for director William Friedkin long before he made *The French Connection* or *The Exorcist*. Having hooked their interest, I add: "That was after he almost killed me."

We met in September of 1966 in Friedkin's phone-booth-sized office at Paramount Studios. When I came in he was slouched back in a swivel chair, his feet propped on a weathered wooden desk, sipping Scotch from a dented paper cup. He looked young and intense. Freshly graduated from the overcrowded directorial ranks of TV, he had just completed his first motion picture, starring Sonny and Cher (which bombed at the box office), and was "in the market" for another project.

I pitched my idea: a Dean-type rebel called DePompa (I took the name from a man who'd painted

my car) becomes sexually involved with a bizarre older woman whose kinky habits eventually destroy him. Heavy stuff for 1966!

"Let's *do* it," snapped Friedkin.

I'd need a guarantee of ten thousand dollars for a first-draft screenplay, more if the project jelled. No problems. "You'll have your guarantee by tomorrow night."

It was Thursday.

By Friday Steve Broidy of Motion Pictures International had agreed to finance "DePompa," and my agent began drawing up the contracts.

Which is when Friedkin almost killed me.

I had suggested to Friedkin that the remote Mexican coastal fishing village of San Felipe might make an ideal location site. My exotic description of the place excited him. "We'll fly down this weekend," he told me.

The weather looked bad; storm warnings were out. But Friedkin was determined. He talked Broidy's son, Art, into piloting us down to Calexico in the pro-

Nolan as a member of Machine-Gun Kelly's mob in *Melvin Purvis, G-man*.

ducer's four-passenger Cessna. I liked *big* planes, didn't trust small ones. Was Art any good as a pilot? "Terrific," Friedkin assured me. "No problems." (Which was one of his favored expressions.)

The flight down to Calexico was okay. Gray skies. Rain sprinkles. Nothing worse. We took a rented car across the border into Mexico, drove down to San Felipe on the Gulf of California, scouted the small fishing village, then headed back for the airport at Calexico. When we got there the bad weather was closing in fast, and the local flight dispatcher warned us not to attempt a takeoff. But Friedkin shrugged the warning aside. "No problems," he said—and we soared skyward once again.

Shortly thereafter, God told us we'd made a big mistake. We ran smack into the middle of a teeth-grinding rainstorm—with Art fighting to maintain something approaching level flight. Friedkin had curled up in one corner of the tiny cabin, eyes closed. "Wake me when we land," he said, yawning.

"Billy can sleep through anything," Art declared, thrusting a folded sheet of paper toward me. "Storm's getting worse. I'll try to get us down at the airport in Palm Springs. Spread the map against the window and let's find out where it is."

Art checked the map, then peered below. "See any lights down there?"

"I can't see a bloody thing!" I said.

He shrugged. "Airport's got to be around here *somewhere*."

My stomach jumped into my throat as a huge gust

of wind slapped us sideways. The Cessna dropped several hundred feet as Broidy fought the stick. I was a dead man. "DIRECTOR AND PRODUCER'S SON DIE IN AIR CRASH," the headlines would read. And under them, in much smaller type, "Writer Also Aboard."

Well, we made Palm Springs, and I went on to write my first-draft script on "DePompa"—but the film was never made. Billy got nervous and hopped away to New York to direct another picture. I got my ten thou, plus a few gray hairs from that storm-tossed night in the air over Palm Springs—and I was off to another assignment.

In twenty-three years as a writer I've tackled scripts about vampires and giant frogs, walking dead men and psychic detectives, robot housewives and sex-starved teenagers, helicopter cops and undercover ladies, Tommy gun-toting G-men and Gothic ghosts, dirt-track daredevils and damsels in distress. . . . But, from the outset, my prime career ambition was to sell a novel to Hollywood for a fat, six-figure check. First, however, I had to write one.

In 1965 a science fiction idea took shape for me. Working with a fellow TV-writer, George Clayton Johnson, I completed a futuristic chase-adventure dealing with an overpopulated death-at-21 society. We called it *Logan's Run,* and by October of '66 the novel had been optioned by producer Stan Canter for the sum of $10,000 against a total pick-up of $100,000. Canter had twelve months to come up with the full option price. . . .

Dissolve to: October 1967. Canter appeared at our agent's office—but *not* with the other $90,000. He waved a check at us for $40,000. "I couldn't raise any more," he told us. "But, counting the ten you got last year, this will give you fifty thousand for your book. I think that's a very fair film price for a first novel."

No, we calmly told Stan; our price was a flat hundred grand, and we were not going to sell our book for a penny less. He blinked at us. "You mean, you're turning *down* a check for forty thousand dollars?"

"That's right," we said.

His face tight with anger, Canter slowly tore the check into tiny pieces, dropping them one-by-one into the wastebasket at his feet. He held up the final piece, bearing his signature, and as we watched he *ate* it! Then, without another word, he walked out of the office. We never heard from him again.

But, suddenly, MGM was interested in buying *Logan.* One Friday morning in late November they offered $60,000, take it or leave it. We said we'd leave it; our price was $100,000. They said they'd have a final decision by Monday. We were sweating a lot. That weekend seemed to last several months—but on Monday morning, as promised, MGM was back with an option offer of $15,000 down and an additional pick-up, in November of '68, of the other $85,000. We gulped and said yes—and, sure enough, by the following November the studio picked up their option and paid us our full price.

But it took MGM seven years to get around to producing our book—and once it was sold I turned my attention to other projects. From '68 into mid-1972 I concentrated on novels and biographies—but in July of '72 producer-director Dan Curtis entered my life—and I made my move into prime-time TV with my first solo-written 90-minute Movie of the Week, a horror tale of a walking dead man pursued by a psychic detective. Title: *The Norliss Tapes.*

I have a special fondness for this show, mainly because it has grossed more money for me than any other television script I've written—a grand (and glorious) total of $22,457.22!

When we met in '72 Dan Curtis was newly-arrived from New York, having moved his offices to the West Coast, and had just bought a large house with thirteen bathrooms in Beverly Hills. (Large houses are obligatory to successful producers.) He had scored heavily with his freakish, off-trail vampire soap-opera, *Dark Shadows,* and his *Night Stalker* had also racked up incredible Nielsen ratings. Thus, Dan was looking for more horror-oriented material. *The Norliss Tapes* began as a brief, thinly-plotted outline by Fred Mustard Stewart—and a writer was needed to develop it into an NBC Mystery Movie. Curtis hired me for the job. A tall, curly-haired, fierce-eyed man with a toothy wolf's smile, Curtis thrives on crisis, and much of what he says is delivered in a shout. He bellows over a phone, yells down the hall at his secretary, shouts at his writers.

The stars of *Norliss* were Angie Dickinson and Roy Thinnes—and during an outdoor night sequence in Culver City, at the same lot where *Gone With the Wind* was made, we almost lost them both. My script called for a demon to be set afire by Roy inside the studio of Angie's dead husband. Roy grabs her hand, and they rush out to safety as the place begins to burn behind them. Dan rehearsed the scene as the crew prepared to torch the "studio." (Actually a wooden falsefront with ignitable material packed around and within it.) At the last minute, Dan decided to have them exit fast, running directly down to the road—a change from his original plan to have them hesitate on the porch. Angie and Roy are alive today because of this change. A mistake was made in firing the studio—and the *entire* area, porch and all, exploded into gouting fire within seconds after the two stars had cleared the door. Had they hesitated on the porch they would have been instantly engulfed in flame.

During this same period American International Pictures got a bright idea: they wanted to enter the television arena with an AIP-financed Movie of the Week—and they prevailed upon John Milius to write a script, which would be a spin-off of his *Dillinger* pic. He came up with a teleplay he titled *Purvis: FBI*—and Dan Curtis was hired to direct and produce. Dan read the script and bellowed. It was not shootable. It needed a great deal of work. It was no damn good. The AIP people were apoplectic; they had their locations all rented in the Sacramento area; the actors were ready to be hired; shooting was to begin in ten days. Which is when Dan called me in on a "re-write" basis, meaning I'd get only $5,000 for the job of actually turning out a whole new teleplay.

Now, my usual habit is to write at home (or in long-hand at coffee shops), but due to our pressing deadline I took the office next to Dan's at AIP—and while I wrote each new scene he'd revise the previous one. The entire crew (numbering over seventy-five men and women) was set to leave for Sacramento to begin filming on Monday—and by Friday afternoon our new

Nolan in *The Intruder,* on location in Missouri.

A trade-paper ad for *Melvin Purvis, G-man.*

teleplay was only half-written. I agreed to work at Dan's home. The weekend was one of incredible pressure. AIP's chief of production paced the hallway outside Dan's study as we worked, popping in every half hour to ask, "How you guys comin' along?" When I left the house that Saturday night Curtis walked me to the door, looking defeated. "We need forty more pages," he groaned. "There's no *way* we're going to be able to finish this mother by Monday."

"We'll see," I said.

I bought three felt-tip pens, a fresh pad of paper, and—late that night—settled into a 24-hour coffee shop in the Valley.

And I wrote.

The next morning Dan met me at the door. "Get anything done?" he wanted to know. I sighed, said nothing. We entered his study and Curtis slumped down on the black-leather couch. "Hell, I *know* you didn't. Not after working all day yesterday. I can't expect miracles."

"Sure you can," I said, grinning, and handed him the forty new pages. The script was finished. He

couldn't believe it, just flat could not believe it. This was, in fact, the fastest writing I'd ever done, and I've never matched it since.

The next morning, with *Melvin Purvis, G-Man* in mimeo, we all took off for Sacramento.

There's a postscript to this one: I got to exercise my frustrated acting talent in *Purvis* by taking the role of a gun-crazed member of Machine Gun Kelly's mob. I was shot down on the roof of the gang's hideout by G-Man Purvis himself (played by Dale Robertson)—dying with a smoking Tommy gun in my hand. Ah, but the ham was ripe in Sacramento!

My final script job in 1974 turned out to be another Melvin Purvis epic, *The Kansas City Massacre,* a highly-fictionalized version of the famed 1933 shoot-out in Kansas City's Union Station (which was actually filmed in Pasadena, California!).

Both of these Purvis productions had gained strong network approval, and ABC wanted more of the same. Dan assigned a third Purvis to me—and I agreed to a deal wherein I was to be paid by ABC when they okayed the story outline. I *should* have arranged for advance step-payments from Curtis Productions to finance the project, but I figured that Dan and I could agree on a basic outline and that there would be no real problem with money. How wrong I was!

My first outline was called "The Tri-State Terror" and pitted Melvin P. against the hillbilly outlaw Wilbur Underhill. Dan read it, then flipped the manuscript across the desk at me. "It won't do. Nobody cares about Underhill. Give me Nelson. We could do a *lot* with Baby Face Nelson."

So I gave him Nelson—in an outline I called "Bullets for Baby Face." The first thing he said was, "I *hate* the title!" Then, after reading it, he declared: "I was all wrong about Nelson. We should concentrate on John Dillinger."

So I wrote one called "The Great Dillinger Manhunt." Dan read it and shook his head. "Dillinger's not enough. We still need Nelson. Go back and put in Nelson."

So I wrote a whole new outline called "The Great Dillinger-Nelson Manhunt." Dan read it, sighed. "Nope. Now there's too much about Nelson. Let's switch the main emphasis back to Dillinger."

"I need some money, Dan," I said quietly. "I've done four complete outlines and have been at this for three months without a dime coming in. I figure you owe me."

He bellowed out something to the effect that ABC

would pay the money, not Dan Curtis, and until he was personally satisfied with the outline it wouldn't *go* to ABC. Which is when I told him I was withdrawing from the project. "No writer ever walked out on me!" Curtis yelled. "This one just has," I said—and walked.

For me, the big news of 1975 was *Logan's Run*. After seven years MGM had taken my novel off the shelf and was investing eight million good American dollars in its production. Saul (*Fantastic Voyage*) David to produce, Michael (*Around the World in 80 Days*) Anderson to direct—and featuring British star Michael (*The Three Musketeers*) York as Logan.

A few changes had been made: the mandatory death age had been moved up from 21 to 30, and one of the central characters had been removed, but Mr. Logan still made his run for life, chased by the Sandmen of the future.

I flew to Dallas in the heat of a Texas summer to watch it all come together on location. One of the more intensely visual sequences—representing "total sex" in a Love Shop of Tomorrow—was filmed inside a zonky night-spot on the outskirts of Dallas known as "The Oz Club." The place was wild to begin with, but by the time the MGM boys were through "dressing" it you felt that you were indeed in a twenty-third-century sex palace. A dozen young couples were hired from Dallas to strip to the buff and writhe in simulated passion while Logan is pursued by an enemy Sandman through the weirdly-lit Love Shop. (In the finished film, this entire sequence happens in tantalizing slow motion.)

I spent two weeks in the Dallas area watching them shoot *Logan's Run* and people kept asking about the sequel.

"What sequel?" I'd say. "There's no sequel."

"There's *got* to be a sequel," they'd tell me.

And when I returned to California I began to think about it. I let the idea take root and, by February of 1976, I'd written "Logan's World."

Whether or not MGM ever films it is another matter. I wrote it for myself, to see if I could actually *do* a sequel. It was a challenge, and it was *fun*.

God knows, the frustrations are monumental; the pace is killing; and creative dreams often turn into cliché-brimming nightmares. But sometimes it all works.

A page from Nolan's teleplay, *The Norliss Tapes*, with a trade ad for the TV movie.

TONIGHT AT 8:30
NBC-TV
"the norliss tapes"

A terrifying trip into the world of the supernatural. Breathtaking! A shocking suspense-packed feature film for television starring Roy Thinnes and Don Porter with guest stars Angie Dickinson, Claude Akins, Michele Carey, Vonetta McGee and Hurd Hatfield. Produced and directed by Dan Curtis. Teleplay by William F. Nolan from a story by Fred Mustard Stewart. Executive Producer Charles W. Fries, Associate Producer Robert Singer.

METROMEDIA PRODUCERS CORPORATION
A DAN CURTIS PRODUCTION

CONTINUED:

Now Cort drops to his knees and begins a weird CH

                    CORT
               (in his reedy
                rasp of a voice)
        Ngar... absorath... yenab...
     akazar...

The WIND increases.

CLOSE ON FACE OF DEMON SCULPTURE

as the eyes open, glowing with an evil yellow light (SPECIAL EFFECT) as the red clay begins to SHIMMER i moving life.

FULL SHOT - FEATURING THE DEMON

as the wind, now higher in volume, WHIPS UP the cape demon figure. He raises his muscled arms high, clawe hands flexing. Cort, still on his knees, stares up a thing he has released -- then, in abject worship, touc his forehead to the floor, remaining in this position.

ANGLE ON NORLISS AND ELLEN

as Norliss pushes down the girl -- and springs toward t circle, lighter in hand, thumbing flame into the wick.

CLOSE ON THE CIRCLE

as the hand of Norliss tosses the lighter to Instantly, as the tip of light of the circle i

Recovering
The Author's Intentions

It may come as a shock to the general reader that just about every edition of the literary classics sold to him is corrupt, with departures from what the author actually wrote that may swell into the thousands in small details, but with enough major corruption in the words themselves to distort the sense and give cause for serious concern. In no other field is the reproduction of the original so careless. The tape or phonograph record of a symphony in two competing versions is scrupulously rehearsed and played from a score that does not significantly vary. But a book is another matter. The readers of our literary heritage unknowingly accept editions that are peppered with words that are not the author's and with styling that may bear only a faint resemblance to how he himself wrote the manuscript, or to the earliest publication. It is quite simply the truth that the reader of the average edition of our great literature is getting short-changed by publishing standards that are scandalous.

The question is how untrustworthy are these reproductions? The general rule is that texts do not improve with age: they deteriorate. A current edition of a Victorian novel masterpiece has passed through close to a hundred years of accumulated textual corruption, the piling up of printers' errors, fancied editorial 'improvements,' and general tampering. Moreover, the odds are that the first edition was not entirely accurate to begin with, given the usual publisher's treatment of an author's manuscript. When an artist finishes a painting and puts it up for sale, it is finished. The gallery does not hire a hack artist to repaint the background or main figures before the purchaser comes along. But when a writer finishes a book, he is only at the start of a succession of typists, editors, printers who deliberately or accidentally alter what he has written. By the time the author sees the proof, it is too late to make more than very small changes, and far too expensive to demand a return to his original. Moreover, he will seldom these days be given a chance to check whether the changes that he re-

No iocond health that Denmarke drinkes to day,
But the great Cannon to the cloudes shall tell.
And the Kings rowse the heauen shall brute againe,
Respeaking earthly thunder; come away.   *Florish.*
    Ham. O that this too too sallied flesh would melt,   *Exeunt all, but Hamlet.*
Thaw and resolue it selfe into a dewe,
Or that the euerlasting had not fixt
His cannon gainst seale slaughter, ô God, God,
How wary, stale, flat, and vnprofitable
Seeme to me all the vses of this world?
Fie on't, ah fie, tis an vnweeded garden
That growes to seede, things rancke and grose in nature;
Possesse it meerely that it should come thus
                    C.   But

Hamlet, Act I, Scene 2 (Second Quarto, 1604-5).

By FREDSON BOWERS

quested have actually been made and if so whether in the form he wanted and without error elsewhere in the line. In some book contracts a modern author must sign away his rights to make *any* changes at all in publisher-styled proof except for the correction of misprints.

What happens to a first edition is bad enough, but when a literary text goes through a series of publishers over the course of several generations, the accumulation of error on error may be truly mountainous. The record of reading editions and anthologies, including the popular paperbacks, is a dismal one. No attention is ordinarily paid to the history and transmission of the text to discover whether one early edition is better than another to reprint. Instead, one paperback sits on the shoulders of the last, the earliest popular edition on some earlier text, usually one printed years after the author had died and subject to all the vicissitudes of time. Each new publication adds to the corruption. Statements of origin cannot always be believed. In England a paperback of Mrs. Gaskell's *Wives and Daughters* represented itself as reprinting the original 1864-66 serialization but was proved instead to have been drawn from a debased tradition starting with a faulty 1891 edition. In the United States a reprint of Nathaniel Hawthorne's *Scarlet Letter* alleged it was based on the author-revised third edition of 1850. Hawthorne revised no edition of this novel, and the cheap edition was in fact derived from an 1884 late edition, one of the most corrupt ever published.

At this point the reader may well ask if it really matters that much, especially in a novel of many thousand words, whether a few words are changed. There are several answers to such a question. One is that the corruption and debasement of texts in their transmission from edition to edition will not change the plot of a novel—if that is all one wants, as in a detective story. Jude the Obscure will still be defeated at the end; David Copperfield will not turn out to be a woman in disguise. But to be the passive victim of a whole se-

> Respeaking earthly Thunder. Come away.   *Exeunt*
> *Manet Hamlet.*
>
> *Ham.* Oh that this too too solid Flesh, would melt,
> Thaw, and resolue it selfe into a Dew :
> Or that the Euerlasting had not fixt
> His Cannon 'gainst Selfe-slaughter. O God, O God!
> How weary, stale, flat, and vnprofitable
> Seemes to me all the vses of this world ?
> Fie on't ? Oh fie, fie, 'tis an vnweeded Garden
> That growes to Seed : Things rank, and grosse in Nature
> Possesse it meerely. That it should come to this :
> But two months dead : Nay, not so much; not two,

Hamlet, Act I, Scene 2 (First Folio, 1623).

ries of careless publishing and printing operations is as unnecessary as it would be to keep a phonograph record of the Eroica Symphony in which that magic entry of the horn with the Eroica theme recapitulated in a remote key were burbled and palpably flat, or—a better analogy—entered in a more conventional key that Beethoven never intended. If every note counts in a symphony, so every word and even every signpost of punctuation has a cumulative effect that matters in a literary masterpiece.

A great writer knows exactly what he is doing, and to have his intentions changed by a succession of human carelessnesses is distracting and can be maddening. In *The House of the Seven Gables* (1851) it makes a difference for a stylist like Hawthorne whether one reads *humanity* or *humility*, *drop* or *droop*, *tested* or *tasted*, the good old-fashioned idiom *barn-door fowl* or the sophisticated *barn-yard fowl*. It makes a difference whether in modern reprints of Laurence Sterne's *Tristram Shandy* (1759-67) one reads *clause* or *cause*, *port* or *post*, *timber* or *tinder*, *catching* or *catechising*, and *caravans* or *caverns*. In editions of Tobias Smollett it changes the sense here and there that a careless modernizing editor confused the London prison called the *Fleet* with maritime *fleet* and made the prison into a collection of ships. Until a year or two ago, no reading edition of Henry Fielding's masterpiece *Tom Jones* (1749) took account of his extensive revisions in the fourth edition. Only a few years ago was a misplaced whole chapter in the standard edition of Henry James's *The Ambassadors* (1903) finally put in its proper position. Most modern reprints of Lewis Carroll's *Alice in Wonderland* (1865) and *Through the Looking Glass* (1871) ignore his final revisions, one

popular reprint even providing only four lines of " 'Tis the voice of the lobster" that he later expanded.

Another answer is that the extent of the damage to the author's intentions depends in part (but not exclusively) on which words are affected. A single word in a long passage can be crucial to the meaning of the work. In a technical work real damage can be done, as whether William James in a mathematical discussion is stating that numbers are *finite* or whether they are *infinite*. But artistic works are subject to equal distortion. Extravagant critical praise based on misprints is not uncommon. In Herman Melville's *White-Jacket* (1850) the midshipman falls into the sea from the yardarm. F. O. Matthiessen unfortunately used a reprint of Melville which read:

I wondered whether I was yet dead or still dying. But of a sudden some fashionless form brushed my side— some inert, soiled fish of the sea; the thrill of being alive again tingled in my nerves, and the strong shunning of death shocked me through.

Commenting on these lines the critic wrote:

But then this second trance is shattered by a twist of imagery of the sort that was to become peculiarly Melville's. He is startled back into a sense of being alive by grazing an inert form; hardly anyone but Melville could have created the shudder that results from calling this frightening vagueness some 'soiled fish of the sea.' The discordia concors, *the unexpected linking of the medium of cleanliness with filth, could only have sprung from an imagination that apprehended the terrors of the deep, of the immaterial deep as well as the physical.*

The only difficulty with this critical *frisson* about Melville's imagination, and with undemonstrable generaliza-

tion such as "hardly anyone but Melville could have created the shudder," and so on, is the cruel fact that what Melville wrote was "*coiled* fish of the sea," and Matthiessen had puffed up a misprint to extraordinarily inflated proportions.

The wearing away of the stone is even more impressive within the concentrated texture of poetry. Is Hamlet's flesh *sallied* (i.e. *sullied*) or *solid*? did the Ghost appear in the *dead vast and middle of the night* or in the *dead waste*? did Hamlet first address Gertrude as *good mother* or as *cold mother*? according to Polonius are Hamlet's vows *pious bonds* or *pious bawds*? Such matters are of more than casual interest. It is of moment whether in "Among School Children" (1927) William Butler Yeats speaks of *solider Aristotle* or of *soldier Aristotle*—or in his "Byzantium" (1929) whether *a starlit or a moonlit dome disdains all that man* or *distains*. Whether in "Ash Wednesday" (1930) T. S. Eliot wrote *Against the World the unstilled world whirled* or *Against the word*.

The more technical the work, the more essential it is that the author's precise meaning be preserved. In William James's *Some Problems of Philosophy* (1911) one should care whether in his discussion of Being he wrote that the maximum of being has seemed to some philosophers the *easiest* or the *earliest* to accept; whether one gets farther and farther away from *the mere perceptual datum* or from *the perceptual type of experience*. In short, in a book on arithmetic if two plus two equals five, the reader has been deceived about the arithmetician's intent.

In contrast to the downhill road taken by modern popular editions, scholars have these days developed techniques for producing truly definitive editions with what can be called established texts. A definitive edition is authoritative and accurate. It recovers the author's full intentions in every possible detail and establishes a text from the original documents that should never need to be re-edited. The immediate intent is to produce a tool for teachers of literature, for scholars, and for critics, since the use of unreliable texts leads to unreliable interpretation, as with Melville's *White Jacket*. But the definitive edition is not just for the learned: it is the best text for everybody, and once published in scholarly form it can be given the widest dissemination, with all scholarly apparatus removed, as the best text that there is for the general public to read.

The ordinary reader, thus, can rightly be interested in what is happening in this present age of editing, for not only is most of the great literature of the distant past now available in correct new editions but the texts of almost every prominent author in subsequent English and American literature have been redone in the twentieth century, many of these in our times. Even modern authors are being examined by the new editorial methods to establish their best texts. Joseph Conrad and D. H. Lawrence editions are about to start, for example, and discussions are underway to establish the true texts of James Joyce, starting with *Ulysses*. Although the original forms of such editions may be too expensive or too technical in their function for the usual reader, they can be expected to appear shortly in cheaper editions, without the technical material but with appropriate informative introductions so that good texts can be made available to anyone in the future at a reasonable price.

Ideally, we may say that a "definitive edition" is one that never needs to be done again because the known materials that should make up the text have been exhausted. Practically, there is some truth in this assertion if one recognizes that not all problems may ever be solved. For instance, no one can identify with any certainty what Shakespeare actually wrote that got itself printed in *Measure for Measure* as "Some run from brakes of ice and answer none" (I.ii.29), or in *All's Well That Ends Well,* "I see that men make ropes in such a scarre That we'll forsake ourselves" (I.i.38-39). Two editors could differ whether to print some desperate guess or to give up and leave the original; but either way the 'definitiveness' of the edition need not be endangered.

Although a series of unnecessary, ignorant, and untimely emendations might affect one's view of the end results, usually the foundation of a definitive text lies elsewhere than in an editor's alteration of the original. For instance, no text can pretend to be a permanent one that has not made use of every textual document —manuscript or printed—that has some direct relation with the author. An editor of Henry Fielding's *Tom Jones* must consult not only the first edition, his basic text, but also know that the second edition and most of the third were not touched by Fielding but that Fielding thoroughly revised the fourth edition. He must then ignore the posthumous fifth, or so-called Murphy edition, although practically every popular editor has reprinted that, or somebody's text deriving at a distance from it.

From the true authorities an editor must, then, select the one closest to the author's own original form and therefore the one that has undergone the least corruption in passing through the hands of a succession of typists, editors, and printers. These author's revisions must be incorporated (but not the unauthorial corruptions in the same edition), for a definitive text must come as close as the fullest evidence suggests to the author's complete and final intentions for every last detail of his writing. In short, an editor bases his text on the original source documents and so is not misled by second-hand evidence. A definitive edition, thus, is a primary edition that goes back directly to the original sources for its evidence, and it is also a comprehensive edition since it makes use of every source that has the slightest bearing on determining what the author actually wrote.

The scholarly form of such an edition will be expensive because the research and checking has cost some thousands of dollars; moreover, it will contain a full apparatus in which every change is recorded that the editor has made from his basic source and also a list of all the variants in every other text that has some claim to authenticity. The scholar making use of this elaborate documentation finds all the editor's cards on the table—face up. But the general reader does not need this elaborate analysis and documentary evidence. What he wants is the trustworthy text that emerged as a result of the research and scholarship. This can be made available at ordinary commercial rates in cheap editions once the big research job has been done. Instead of a weak and second-hand text that for convenience and cheapness prints any form of the text that is out of copyright, the modern reader can read in paperback the same thoroughly researched

of perception. "I told yeh so, didn't I? We're goin' up
th' river, cut across, an' come around in behint 'em."

"Huh," said ~~Wilson~~ the ~~blatant~~ *loud* soldier.

Some of ~~Conklin's~~ *the tall one's* companions cried with emphasis
that they too had evolved the same thing and they congratulated themselves upon it. But there were others
who said that ~~Conklin's~~ *the tall one's* plan was not the true one at
all. They persisted with other theories. There was
a vigorous discussion.

The youth.
~~Fleming~~ took no part in them. As he walked
along in careless line, he was engaged with his own
eternal debate. He could not hinder himself from
dwelling upon it. He was despondent and sullen, and

and authentic text present in the expensive scholarly edition and can hear the author speak directly to him, not through the veils of corruption that surround every text of the past and many of the present in their usual careless form.

The attempt of modern editing to get things right has become big business and has fostered a whole new discipline of scholarship scarcely dreamed of fifty or even twenty-five years ago. This is how it works.

In the simplest cases a writer published only one edition with which he had anything to do, and no manuscripts, typescripts, and the like are preserved. Here the main problem is to make sure that the copy of the first edition chosen is the best one for the purpose, and then to re-print it with no more correction than is essential, unless everything like spelling, punctuation, capitalization, word-division are to be modernized, a process scarcely necessary after the start of the nineteenth century. Modernization of early literature, like Shakespeare, may be a necessity for general reading, but it is a process to be approached with caution because of the booby-traps encountered at every turn: for instance, in *The Tempest* (III.iii.15) when Antonio proposes to kill Alonzo and his adherents "now they are oppress'd with travaile," does he mean when they are sleeping, tired out with *travel* (i.e. with the journey to the isle and their shipwreck) or with *travail* (i.e., their labor in searching the isle for the missing Ferdinand)? The Elizabethan *travaile* could mean either one, but the reader of a modernized text, which usually reads *travel* (in my opinion wrongly), does not know the existence of the alternative.

Of course, an editor must make sure that an author's first edition was never revised; hence if it were published in more than one printing he must compare all later forms word for word and comma for comma to burst into praises of what he thought to be his powers of perception.

Some of the tall one's companions cried with emphasis that they, too, had evolved the same thing, and they congratulated themselves upon it. But there were others who said that the tall one's plan was not the true one at all. They persisted with other theories. There was a vigorous discussion.

The youth took no part in them. As he walked along in careless line he was engaged with his own eternal debate. He could not hinder himself from dwelling upon it. He was despondent and sullen, and threw shifting glances about him. He looked ahead, often ex̲p̲e̲c̲t̲i̲n̲g̲ t̲o̲ hear from the advance the rattle of firi̲

But the long serpents crawled s̲ hill to hill without bluster of smoke. ̲ ored cloud of dust floated away to̲ The sky overhead was of a fairy blue.̲

The youth studied the faces of ̲ ions, ever on the watch to detect k̲ tions. He suffered disappointment.̲ of the air which was causing the ̲ mands to move with glee—almost ̲ had infected the new regiment. Th̲ to speak of victory as of a thing ̲ Also, the tall soldier received his̲

Opposite page: *The Red Badge of Courage* (manuscript, University of Virginia). At left: *The Red Badge of Courage* (first edition—New York: Appleton, 1895). Below: *The Red Badge of Courage* (*The University of Virginia Edition of the Works of Stephen Crane,* ed. Fredson Bowers, 1975).

make certain that the author never did alter anything in the text. This comparison or collation can be done by a special superimposing machine whenever the type has not been reset; but every different typesetting calls for handwork, although computer comparison is possible. This comparison was not done by the early editors of *The Scarlet Letter,* or the myth that its third edition had been revised would never have started: evidence, not hearsay is required. Moreover, in early books, as in Shakespeare's day, every preserved copy of the first edition must be scrupulously collated by machine or by hand, for it is well known

16 · The Red Badge of Courage

The men stumbled along still muttering speculations. There was a subdued debate. Once, a man fell down and as he reached for his rifle, a comrade, unseeing, trod upon his hand. He of the injured fingers swore bitterly and aloud. A low, tittering laugh went among his fellows.

Presently, they passed into a road-way and marched forward with easy strides. A dark regiment moved before them, and, from behind, also, came the tinkle of equipments on the bodies of marching men.

The rushing yellow of the developing day went on behind their backs. When the sun-rays at last struck full and mellowingly upon the earth, the youth saw that the landscape was streaked with two long, thin, black columns which disappeared on the brow of a hill in front and rearward vanished in a wood. They were like two serpents crawling from the cavern of the night.

The river was not in view. The tall soldier burst into praises of what he thought to be his powers of perception. "I told yeh so. didn't I?"

"Huh," said the loud soldier.

Some of the tall one's companions cried with emphasis that they too had evolved the same thing and they congratulated themselves upon it. But there were others who said that the tall one's plan was not the true one at all. They persisted with other theories. There was a vigorous discussion.

The youth took no part in them. As he walked along in careless line, he was engaged with his own eternal debate. He could not hinder himself from dwelling upon it. He was despondent and sullen and threw shifting glances about him. He looked ahead, often, expecting to hear from the advance the rattle of firing.

But the long serpents crawled slowly from hill to hill without bluster of smoke. A dun-colored cloud of dust floated away to the right. The sky over-head was of a fairy blue.

The youth studied the faces of his companions, ever on the watch to detect kindred emotions. He suffered disappointment. Some ardor of the air which was causing the veteran commands to move with glee, almost with song, had infected the new regiment. The men began to speak of victory as of a thing they that at that time proofreading and changes in text were usually made during the course of printing a sheet so that later copies of the same pages through the press may differ from earlier ones. An editor must know which is which, because if it were not the author who made the changes during the printing, any alteration must be viewed with suspicion. It is quite literally true that no two copies of the Shakespeare First Folio (1623) are textually identical.

By the nineteenth century the only point in the comparison of copies of the same printing of the first edition when the book is not plated is to see if minor errors occurred during the course of the working of the sheets, for text was seldom changed then except by accident and its repair. The optical machine that superimposes two copies —the Hinman collator—is very useful for this task since a researcher can make a minute comparison of two copies of a book in a day, if he is quick. This machine is also of use in detecting changes made in the stereotype or electrotype plates of later printings, whether authorial or not, for minor changes in the text are common between printings from plates, some of them unhappy ones if damage were repaired without proofreading.

Problems arise with a simple edition if the manuscript or typescript has been preserved. An editor will want to know whether such documents are drafts or whether they represent the author's final intentions except for whatever changes he may have made in the proof when the text was typeset. Drafts may be useful to ferret out possible errors in the typesetting, but they also give an editor some insight into the author's characteristic punctuation, spelling, and word-division, what can be called the *formal* features of a text; these are likely to have been styled away from the author's idiosyncratic habits by publishers and printers. However, when a manuscript is preserved—as with Hawthorne's *House of the Seven Gables* —that can be shown to be the actual printer's copy, then its authority is manifestly superior in every respect to the printed edition manufactured from it, except for whatever changes the author may have made by alterations in the lost proof.

The identification of these important authorial proof-changes is crucial but often difficult, and the technique adopted to make the identification may differ from case to case. For *The House of the Seven Gables* each of the eight compositors had marked his share on the manuscript itself. Thus it was possible to make a statistical study of the variation between manuscript and first edition according to each compositor, guided by what was known of Hawthorne's own characteristics. As a result, only a handful of the several thousand *formal* variants, representing the book styling, were accepted by the editor, and the new text for the Centenary Edition, based on the manuscript, for the first time reproduced Hawthorne's own complex parenthetical marking of his syntax that shows the way he wanted it to be read. The difference in effect of such a text with several thousand such variants is incalculable. For the verbal variants—what may be called the *material* features of the text— only about one-third passed the stringent bibliographical tests for authenticity: the rest were the printer's words, not Hawthorne's. As a consequence of this rigorous analysis, in the new edition an almost one hundred per cent reproduction was possible of what Hawthorne wrote in every detail, supplemented by the identification and incorporation in the manuscript version of the revisions that he had made in proof. This new text replaces the usual reprint of the first edition, which represents chiefly what the printer thought Hawthorne should have written in several thousand cases.

Some books have a more complicated history. Stephen Crane's *The Red Badge of Courage* (1895) has been widely reprinted, but always from the first edition or from some copy of a copy of that edition. In fact, because of its checkered transmission, the text of the first edition represents a distinctly faulty picture of what Crane actually wrote. The manuscript has been preserved, showing two main stages of revision. In the first, covering about a fifth of the manuscript, Crane not only refined his style but also generalized his narrative and its characters by adopting a set group of descriptive phrases instead of names, which were retained only in dialogue. Thus Henry Fleming became *the youth,* Conklin *the tall soldier,* and Wilson first *the blatant* and then *the loud soldier* until the important point where he proves his maturity and becomes simply the youth's *friend.* Crane showed his manuscript to the prominent critic Hamlin Garland, who objected to the fact that all of Crane's characters spoke in a thick country dialect. Crane then began another revision, changing all the dialect to relatively normal speech, continuing and developing the use of the generalized descriptive phrases for the characters' names, altering the endings of some chapters, omitting a part of a battle scene, and so on. But then about two-thirds of the way through this revision he changed his mind about Garland's advice. Although he still altered the youth's rustic speech to normal colloquial idiom, he left in the original country dialect for the other soldiers. The intention of the manuscript is clear as to the names (although he missed a few that an editor must alter for him), but Crane never bothered to go back to make his use of dialect speech consistent.

From this manuscript the publisher made a typescript, now lost. One copy was sold to a newspaper syndicate that distributed it in a cut and much rewritten version, yet one from which an editor can recover important details about the underlying typescript. The other copy was hastily revised in New Orleans, where Crane had paused on his way to Mexico. From this copy of the lost typescript the first edition was set up. Here the problem is complicated by the intervention of the typescript, for the typist made a number of errors that Crane—a notoriously careless rereader of typescript and proof—never caught. These are numerous and sometimes serious, as when on two occasions the typist mistook Garland's marking of dialect passages as deletions, so that they were omitted in the book (see the illustration). With some help from the newspapers an editor can go a long way toward identifying the typist's errors by direct comparison of book against the basic manuscript; the newspapers (which did not contain the New Orleans revisions) are also a help in what is the central problem, to distinguish among the numerous differences between book and manuscript the authorial revisions made in New Orleans, since all other variants will represent either typist's or printer's error plus some amount of publisher's smooth-

ing of Crane's craggy syntax and idiom. From this body of analyzed evidence an editor for the first time can base a new text on the authoritative manuscript, as in the University Press of Virginia's edition. Then on the evidence within this manuscript of the types of revision that Crane wanted made, the editor can project authorial intention into a finished product superior to anything in the faulty first edition, which for instance still keeps the imperfect adjustment of dialect that Crane had not bothered to correct in the manuscript or typescript. In the first edition the youth's companions talk good English at the start and then later lapse into country speech, an anomaly that no editor had either noticed or tried to explain from the evidence of the manuscript.

In some cases an author may revise later editions. Henry Fielding revised the second, third, and fourth editions of *Joseph Andrews* (1742). For his *Tom Jones* he did not touch the second edition, and made changes in only one chapter of the third, but he did thoroughly revise the fourth. This novel presents a classic case of what is called the theory of copy-text; that is, the edition on which an editor should base his new text. In earlier and innocent days it was customary to take the last edition in an author's lifetime as the model in case it had contained authorial revisions—this without troubling to find out whether revisions were actually present. Later critics worked on the principle of unified authority—of establishing which edition was a revision, and reprinting that as it stood. But twenty-five years ago the distinguished English scholar Sir Walter Greg promulgated his "rationale of copy-text." In brief, he pointed out that, especially in early literature, every new edition represents a printer's

restyling. Thus although the fourth edition of *Joseph Andrews* would contain Fielding's final choice of words, yet its whole texture of spelling, punctuation, and so on—the *formal* features—were very far from those of the author since the texture of the first edition (closest to the lost manuscript) had been restyled by three other printers. It followed that revised texts do not have unified authority but instead that authority is split between the texture of the first edition closest to manuscript (or the manuscript itself, of course) and the latest revised wording. A text, Greg urged, should combine both authorities to form an ideal new version.

One can see how this works with *Tom Jones*. The third edition reset the six volumes of the first in a cheaper four-volume format. Except for one episode of the Man of the Hill, Fielding made no revisions; hence all of the third edition's other differences in wording from the first are printer's errors. For the fourth edition, the publisher provided Fielding with a copy of the four-volume text since the fourth edition was to be a page-for-page reprint of the third. Fielding thoroughly revised this text; but he was unaware of the third-edition corruptions, and except for a few misprints all of these are passed on to the revised fourth-edition text. Applying Greg's rationale of copy-text, an editor takes the *formal* texture of the first edition, and into this he inserts all of Fielding's identifiable revisions in the fourth but omitting the reproduction in the fourth of the third-edition changes in words, and all of the innumerable differences in punctuation, spelling, capitalization, and so on. The result combines the two highest authorities and, in fact, reprints what would have been the actual revised marked copy if Fielding had been given the first instead of the third edition in which to write his revisions. This is new and revolutionary editorial theory, but it produces the best text, the closest to what Fielding actually intended, far nearer than would have been the case if unified authority had been applied and an editor had based his text on that of the fourth edition, even though weeding out the third edition's departures from setting-copy.

Even more revolutionary, though now advanced beyond the experimental stage, is the treatment of what can be called *radiating authority*. In the examples already mentioned *linear* authority has· been present because editions descended from other editions and eventually from manuscript in a straight line, one reprinting another. In *radiating* texts, different versions are set from a common original, so that all have, technically, equal authority. The editorial problem is to recover from the multiple evidence as much as possible of the lost originals in back of the preserved editions. When two or more radiating texts are present, the document can be reconstructed from which they independently derive. The more texts, the higher the degree of accuracy in the recovery. For example, of six newspaper versions of Stephen Crane's novel *The Third Violet* (1897) the common copy can be positively recovered in any reading in which all agree, and so on down the scale to lesser certainty. For *The Third Violet* it turns out that in certain respects the common newspaper version that can be recovered is more faithful to some of Crane's characteristics than the greatly smoothed-out first edition with which the publisher had tinkered, even though Crane revised its typescript at a date later than the setting of the newspaper version from the other typescript copy. Hence by combining the two authorities, an editor can recover a maximum amount of Crane's true text of

this novel, freed from the interference and the errors found in the first edition.

This process of multiple authority reaches its most classic expression in Stephen Crane's short story "Death and the Child" (1898), which has been anthologized as one of his best pieces. Bibliographical analysis demonstrates that its initial publication in an English magazine and then in the English edition of the collection *The Open Boat* (1898) derived from a lost typescript and its carbon made from the lost manuscript. Correspondingly, analysis shows that the initial publication in the United States, in a magazine and in the American edition of *The Open Boat,* derived from a different lost typescript and carbon made at another time from the same manuscript. When one compares the English texts, their agreements show what the typescript was like from which they were set, and so with the two American texts. Each lost typescript, then, can be partially reconstructed. Now when one compares all four printed texts in the same scrupulous manner, the agreement of any three —and thus of the two different typescripts—shows what was the reading of the manuscript from which both basic typescripts were made. Although the most commonly reprinted form of the text—that in the American *Open Boat* collection—has more faulty verbal differences than any other version, the real variation between the two typescripts can be reduced by this statistical study from dozens to only ten words, enough to show that no authorial revision had taken place and that one or the other of these ten variants, all taken separately, must represent the typescript or the manuscript; and on this basis some decision can be reached as to what Crane was most likely to have written. Thus a lost document, in this case the manuscript, can be reconstructed almost verbatim for its authorial words, or *material* features, and these can be set in a text

of recovered *formal* features that is perhaps seventy-five per cent accurate to what the manuscript must have read in punctuation, word-division, spelling. The new methods of editorial skill can scarcely go further than in this example, which from four individually faulty printed texts can recover for the general reader almost verbatim what Crane's lost manuscript read, two stages back in the transmission.

Some of the editorial techniques for these scholarly editions have been developed as a direct consequence of the research support given to the Center for Editions of American Authors (CEAA) by the National Endowment for the Humanities. These editions guarantee for the future better reading texts for popular consumption, whenever a publisher has the conscience to base his reading edition on the scholarly foundation that has been built by more research and expertise than could ever be paid for in commercial terms. The CEAA required that its texts be made available to any publisher for a small fee, so that the university press editions with full scholarly apparatus may be followed by the text alone in paperback or cheap hard-cover. If, as is proposed for the new Conrad edition in England, the direct leasing system can be extended, then any literary classic can be made available to the public not in the usual faulty and debased version but in the purity guaranteed by every technique available to advanced scholarship. Cleared of its footnotes and textual apparatus essential in the scholarly edition, there is nothing intimidating about a first-rate text properly introduced in a popular edition. Anything else is a cheat, for a paperback can be cured.

A passage from the copy of *A Farewell to Arms* Ernest Hemingway presented to James Joyce, in which Hemingway supplied the unprintable words.

looked up. She looked perhaps a year younger. Aymo put his hand on the elder girl's thigh and she pushed it away. He laughed at her.

"Good man," he pointed at himself. "Good man," he pointed at me. "Don't you worry." The girl looked at him fiercely. The pair of them were like two wild birds.

"What does she ride with me for if she doesn't like me?" Aymo asked. "They got right up in the car the minute I motioned to them." He turned to the girl. "Don't worry," he said. "No danger of ———," using the vulgar word. "No place for ———." I could see she understood the word and that was all. Her eyes looked at him very scared. She pulled the shawl tight. "Car all full," Aymo said. "No danger of ———. No place for ———." Every time he said the word the girl stiffened a little. Then sitting stiffly and looking at him she began to cry. I saw her lips working and then tears came down her plump cheeks. Her sister, not looking up, took her hand and they sat there together. The older one, who had been so fierce, began to sob.

"I guess I scared her," Aymo said. "I didn't mean to scare her."

Bartolomeo brought out his knapsack and cut off two pieces of cheese. "Here," he said. "Stop crying."

The older girl shook her head and still cried, but the younger girl took the cheese and commenced to eat. After a while the younger girl gave her sister the second piece of cheese and they both ate. The older sister still sobbed a little.

"She'll be all right after a while," Aymo said.

An idea came to him. "Virgin?" he asked the girl next to him. She nodded her head vigorously. "Virgin too?" he pointed to the sister. Both the girls nod-

You May Have To Take It With You

*Current tax law prevents writers
from claiming deductions for donating
their manuscripts to libraries.*

By WILLIAM R. CAGLE

When the United States Congress, in its greater wisdom, wrote the Tax Reform Act of 1969 with an eye to closing loopholes made conspicuous by the gift of papers of certain public figures for tax credit, it also closed the door on a major source of benefaction for the nation's libraries and museums. The area of revision which struck most deeply at these institutions was that defining "self-created materials" —works of art created by the donor, a manuscript written by the donor, letters and memorandums prepared by or for (i.e., sent to) the donor—as "ordinary income property" rather than as "capital gains property." The distinction is crucial: "ordinary income property" may be claimed only at its adjusted basis— that is, at what it actually cost the creator; "capital gains property" may be claimed on the basis of its current market value. (Fair market value is determined by the price at which similar material has recently been sold, or by the price a reputable dealer could expect to obtain for it.) In effect, this law means a writer, a politician, an actor, a scientist, or other person who wishes to present his papers, drawings, paintings, manuscripts, or the letters he has

received to a museum or library may claim an adjustment to his taxable income only for his cost in materials—ink, paper, paint, or canvas—a nominal sum and wholly unrelated to the actual value of the gift. The result is easily foretold: contributions of this type have all but come to a halt.

Let us consider, as an example, a publishing company which had given a portion of its archives to a university library. The archive contains letters and manuscripts of major authors as well as other materials of importance to literary scholars and, therefore, is a major resource for the university. Prior to 25 July 1969 the publisher was allowed to give these archives and receive a tax benefit for the gift based on the actual market value of the material given. Under the reformed law a corporate archive is self-created and therefore the only value which may be claimed is to be determined by the "cost of paper and ink" formula. Now when a backlog of no-longer-current files has accumulated in the publisher's office, the tax incentive is gone, and the publisher hesitates to make his gift. His attorney advises a wait-and-see attitude. Who knows, someday the tax law may again

be revised. What is true on the corporate level also applies to individual authors, artists, and public figures. They also are waiting to see. And libraries and museums wait with them.

This situation is not helped by the confusion which exists in the minds of both potential donors and potential recipients about what constitutes "self-created material." A painter's canvas, an author's manuscript, the scientist's notebook recording the experiments which won him recognition are all clearly "self-created," but the law also includes items created "for" the donor. If a congressman has in his files letters to him from, let us say, Presidents Kennedy and Johnson are these self-created by the congressman—that is, were they generated by the congressman's position—and, if so, is no tax credit allowable for their gift to a library in as much as they cost the congressman nothing?

If the creator may not himself give his work and receive credit for its market value may he give it to his wife or child to donate for their tax advantage? No, not if the materials are a gift. However, if they are inherited they may be treated as capital gains property and given for credit at full market value.

Inevitably, the more confusing the rules, the more numerous are the experts. Librarians, museum directors, curators, and appraisers are all available to give the donor the tax advice he should get from a tax attorney. Recently, as an illustration, a university library was given the papers of a deceased public figure by his widow, and an appraiser was called in. "As she is a member of the immediate family, she can only claim the value of the autographs," the expert advised. "Nothing can be allowed for the content of the material." And the appraisal was submitted on that basis. Clearly, the appraiser, who was completely competent to determine the market value of the papers, was not a tax expert. Neither was the librarian who forwarded the appraisal to his donor. Under paragraph 1.174A-4, the tax law recognizes only two categories of appeciated property: "ordinary income property" which may be given at the value of the cost in materials to the donor and "capital gains property" which may be given at its full market value. There is no middle ground which would allow valuation at a portion of market value, in the above case the going price for the autographs in the papers. An appraiser should be asked to do only that for which his expertise qualifies him: to establish the fair market value of the items appraised. The donor's attorney should then advise him whether his gift qualifies as "capital gains property" or as "ordinary income property."

Even then, the amount of the value which may be allowed for tax purposes may need further scrutinizing. A further provision of the 1969 Tax Reform Act differentiates between gifts of tangible personal property related to the recipient institution's functions and those which are unrelated. In the case of the latter the deduction is reduced by 50% (62½% in the case of a corporation). The example given in the code, paragraph 1.170A-4 (b) (3) (i) is as follows:

. . . if a painting contributed to an educational institution is used by that organization for educational purposes by being placed in its library for display and study by art students, the use is not an unrelated use; but if the painting is sold and the proceeds used by the organization for educational purposes, the use of the property is an unrelated use.

The burden of proof lies with the donor who must establish, before claiming the deduction, that the property is not in fact being put to an unrelated use or that, at the time of the contribution, it is reasonable to anticipate the property will not be put to an unrelated use.

Thus, if a museum is given a painting, and the directors of the museum decide it is outside the scope of their collection and sell the painting, the donor may claim only 50% of the appraised value of his gift. If a library is given a collection of books and finds some of these to be duplicates of copies it already owns and sells these duplicates and they represent anything more than what the IRS regulation terms an "insubstantial portion" of the whole gift, the donor may claim full value only for the books kept and half the value for those sold.

Related versus unrelated use raises several questions to which answers will not be available until some test cases have been tried and precedents have been established. How long must related use of a gift continue? If a museum sells a painting several years after receiving it as a gift, is the donor required to file an amended tax return, reducing the value of his gift by fifty percent? Probably not, but as the statute of limitations on IRS audits is three years, it would be advisable for a donor to know to what use his gift is to be put for at least that period.

The revised tax law also requires that for a contribution by an individual of property other than money the donor must provide with his tax form "the terms of any agreement or understanding entered into by or on behalf of the taxpayer which relates to the use, sale or disposition of the property contributed. . . ." It has been suggested to me by one tax authority that restrictions placed on the use of a gift by a donor, as, for example, limiting access to a collection of papers could cause such a gift to be considered as being put to an unrelated use.

In all cases concerning related or unrelated use it is the responsibility of the recipient institution to inform the donor how his gift is to be used and for the donor to ask his attorney whether such a use qualifies as related or unrelated.

The framers of the 1969 Tax Reform Act sought to correct real and, sometimes, flagrant abuses of what one writer has termed "the art of charitable giving." Amounts of some appraisals raised eyebrows, and the stories of clever impositions on the IRS could fill a book, like the one about the collector who sent a painting to auction, had it bid up to an astonishing figure, bought it in himself and then, having established the value of a canvas by this artist, gave forty of them to a museum for an enormous tax benefit. Of course, that is not relevant to gifts of "self-created materials," but it was part of the climate which prompted the review of the tax laws with respect to charitable giving. Perhaps the single most important factor in prompting the 1969 Tax Reform Act was the huge private tax deductions allowed to public officials for the gift of their papers to libraries. It was at these gifts the "self-created materials" section of the law was aimed. Unfortunately, what should have been a sniper's shot became a broadside, and a law aimed at preventing public figures from gaining tax advantages through the gift of what many regard as already public papers, created in public service and at public expense, went beyond its reasonable intent and eliminated fair tax credit for gifts of their own works by writers and artists to our museums and libraries. It is to be hoped that, when next the tax law is revised, the nation's librarians and museum directors will come forward to make their case known to the lawmakers.

POSTSCRIPT: *In June 1976, legislation that would allow writers, artists, and musicians to deduct the value of works donated by them to museums or libraries was introduced in Congress. The bill was sponsored by Senators Jacob Javits, Claiborne Pell, and Abraham Ribicoff.*

"The Sun Has an Ill-Natured Pleasure, I Believe, in Making Me Look as Old as Himself"

In February of 1862 Nathaniel Hawthorne's Bowdoin College classmate and lifelong friend, Horatio Bridge, then Paymaster General of the Navy, invited the author to come to Washington. During the visit Hawthorne took an excursion to Harper's Ferry, inspected Fortess Monroe, observed General McClellan, had his portrait painted, posed for a photograph by Matthew Brady, and called upon President Lincoln. Hawthorne also met Joseph Henry, Secretary of the Smithsonian Institute, to whom the author of *The Scarlet Letter* sent a carte de visite photograph made from the Brady negative.

The letter and Brady photograph are shown here actual size.

Rugby House, April 3d [1862]

My dear Sir,

I hope you will inform the ladies that my hair is not actually quite so white as these photographs would make it appear. The sun has an ill-natured pleasure, I believe, in making me look as old as himself.

I beg to remind you that you promised me, in exchange for my photograph, something much more valuable—viz. your own.

Sincerely &
Respectfully yours,
Nath *Hawthorne*

If you want to write for TV...

Don't.

And I'll explain that in a few minutes.

We all know the two major clichés about television dramas. First, that they constitute a vast Wasteland. Second, that they chew up material at a greater rate than any other medium. Both clichés are true. On the other hand, the ratings-comparison of commercial with public TV shows that the populace toward whom TV drama is directed likes it just fine. I could never get too upset about the Wasteland aspects of TV, anyway. I tend to be one of those people who commit censorship: when a show I don't like is on the tube, I switch to another channel.

The second cliché doesn't disappear so easily. Producers acknowledge there is a desperate continuing need for dramatic material, yet there are hundreds of writers panting to write for TV and finding it totally impossible to break in. What goes on?

What goes on essentially is that producers use writers whom they can rely on and whom they trust to do the sort of material they want for their series. This means using professionals. I started out as a short story writer and moved on to the novel in 1969; I fully intended to stay there. If anyone had told me eighteen months ago I would be a regular writer for the Sunday-night CBS police drama *Kojak,* I would have said he was nuts. But—barring the unforseen— by the time you read this (as opposed to when I wrote it), at least five of my *Kojak* dramas will have been on the air.

So when I got tapped for *Kojak* I was not a scenarist, but I was a pro; and I was asked to write for them because one of the producers, Jack Laird, had read a couple of my detective novels titled *Dead Skip* and *Final Notice.* He felt I wrote the sort of dialogue the *Kojak* concept could use.

So he called my Hollywood agent Gordon Molson (my New York agent is Henry Morrison) to see if I would be interested, and Gordon asked me, and thus I was launched into my TV-writing career.

Well, not quite. Before you can write for TV, you have to learn HOW to write for TV. I quickly discovered there are four things a writer can do for a weekly dramatic show.

1. He can furnish a story-line (Treatment) which is then developed into a script by other writers.

2. He can *be* one of those other writers, doing scripts to somebody else's story-line.

3. He can *rewrite* that other writer's script from that first writer's Treatment. This sort of work, however, doesn't come along too often. It is usually done by the show's Story Editor or one of the producers —most of them have long lists of writing credits on their own.

4. Or he can do it all. Treatment, First Draft Script, and Polish (i.e., revise the First Draft along suggested lines) . In the process he will make ALL of the scripting money (yeah, I'll talk about money in a few minutes, too).

Naturally, any writer would prefer to do (4) . Producers, too, would *prefer* that writers do (4) , because that way fewer seams are likely to show in the finished product.

Treatment. First Draft. Polish.

A Treatment is nothing more than an old-fashioned Narrative Outline given a new name. Here is an example from one of mine.

Muggers, McNeil is yelling at Kojak behind Kojak's closed door. What do you mean, muggers? I mean, Frank, says Kojak patiently, that's why we can't get a warrant for Harms. But he assaulted a police officer. . . . *Two* police officers, says Kojak. But he didn't give 'em

Kojak (Telly Savalas) to Captain McNeil (Dan Frazer) : *He suckered 'em, Frank.... They followed him into the alley, and* wham! *Instant encounter group.*

By JOE GORES

time to *say* they were police officers. He didn't give them time to get their badges out. Just—*whoomp!* So all he has to say is he thought they were muggers, following him down an alley that way, and how you gonna make an arrest stick?

A "qualified" writer who works regularly for a show might, instead of this carefully worked-out exposition, be just giving them one-liners to mark out the area in which he wants to work. But a fully developed Treatment makes the work of scripting that much easier. Here, done to standard TV script format, is a First Draft script segment of this paragraph of Treatment. Note the location has been switched from Kojak's to McNeil's office, but otherwise the broad outlines of the Treatment are faithfully developed.

84 INT. MC NEIL'S OFFICE – DAY   84
The camera is tight on a McNeil who is yelling, his eyes popping with rage.
    Mc Neil: *Muggers!*
The camera pulls back to a looser shot including Kojak. He is smoking a thin cigar and looking bemused. McNeil is just crushing a report in an excess of ire, and hurls the ball of paper on his desk.
    Mc Neil: What the hell do they mean, muggers?
    Kojak: (imperturbably) That's the way Communications got the report, Frank.
    Mc Neil: (less hysterical) He assaulted a police officer while in pursuit of his du - -
    Kojak: *Two* police officers, but who counts? (beat) The point is that he phoned it in and said they were muggers.
    Mc Neil: They must have flashed their tin. . . .

85 NEW ANGLE   85
Kojak interrupts him to go over and perch on the corner of McNeil's desk. He takes matches off the desk

and relights his cigar, then speaks around it.
    Kojak: He suckered 'em, Frank. (removes cigar) He made 'em think he was going down the alley to sneak into a bar the back way. . . .
McNeil has cooled down sufficiently to retrieve the crumpled report and begin trying to flatten it out again.
    Kojak: They followed him into the alley, and *wham!* Instant encounter group.
    Mc Neil: So he gets away with it. And all we can do is hope he and Shotgun Willie don't get together. Because if they do. . . .
Kojak looks at his watch, stands up as he grinds out his cigar in McNeil's ashtray.
    Kojak: Yeah. If they do, we'll be scraping what's left off the sidewalk and into one of the coroner's little fold-lock bags.

The Polish is where everyone else's views of the above get final expression. In this case, both the Technical Advisor (an NYPD detective) and Telly Savalas objected to the concept of the Bad Dude beating up on a couple of police officers. So in the shooting version, Harms makes the detectives think he has gone through the back door of the bar, but it is really a clandestine massage parlor. When they open the door, he shoves them through it and slams it, and the attacking is done by the girls inside. As in this case, hacking up of your script at the Polish level is usually done for technical or production reasons.

But meanwhile, we left me wanting to be a (4) and do all these things and make all the money. I was still pre-Treatment, and so was still dealing exclusively with the Story Editor. Pre-Treatment your ideas can get killed without payment, and often are —because once they commission a Treatment, they have to pay for it whether they like the delivered product or not. I wasn't worried about that, however, because Jack had *asked* me for a story-line.

Kojak (Telly Savalas) and The Bad Dude (Rosey Grier) square off. The Bad Dude is being considered for a spin-off series by the network (CBS). Crocker (Kevin Dobson) looks on.

Acceptance was automatic.

Oh, yeah? Here's Jack's reaction to my first story idea:

Your story, WHAT SORT OF WOMAN, is not right for us. For a 60-minute episode, it is far too simplistic. Its ironic tag is a gimmick incorporated in a TV script I wrote 20 years ago (and I make no claim that it was original with me). Although traditional, there is nothing basically wrong with the *concept* of the story (e.g., trying to track down a murder witness before she is eliminated), but in escalating incident it is insufficiently complex, and it lacks the potential for interesting character and surprise developments we would wish for our episodes (judge us not by our failures but by our successes).

Well, sir! Crying for material, were they? Could it be . . . hey, in the midst of this schlock TV Wasteland—could it be they actually expected me to *write* for my supper? I decided that, to be on the safe side, next time I'd hit Jack with *two* brilliant ideas. The first came out of that week's newspaper headlines.

A Spanish-American girl is convicted of murder after shooting down one of two men who'd raped her. The girl is bright but illiterate, foul-mouthed but religious, physically alluring but spiritually chaste. And the whole thing raises a hell of an issue in today's world: at what point is killing by a rape victim justified?

The second also was from real-life, given to me on the sly by a psychologist who worked at rehabilitating spaced-out people.

A case which never came to trial, a small-town minister whom the police are convinced murdered his wife, but on whom they have no evidence. He's since remarried. My friend ran a P.S.E. (Psychological Stress Evaluator) analysis of his voice prints, and he came out guilty. Again, this raises somewhat larger questions than the usual murder, because of the minister

angle, man of God, all of that.

Jack's response to these came back Special Delivery:

There's no question but what you've selected two fresh and dramatically viable plot areas, but at the risk of being a pain-in-the-ass I must express pessimism concerning their practicality as KOJAK episodes. As sociological exercises or sturdy anthological fare, they are eminently topical . . . but in terms of *our* needs, each contains a built-in bobby-trap: each requires the author to hand over the bulk of the plot to the point-of-view perpetrators. I am obliged to ask, "What is Kojak's role in the piece? How involved is he? What are the ongoing complexities of the investigative processes? How substantial, intimidating, and even *dangerous* are the antagonistic forces?" As a guiding rule of thumb, we prefer stories in which Kojak has a heavy and forcefully motivated involvement, which comfortably permits him and/or his "troops" to be on-screen for the majority of our playing time.

Wow, gee whiz, and whew! I *still* didn't have it. This time I hit Jack with "areas" rather than worked-out stories.

First, bailbondsmen, and the fellows they hire as sort of bounty hunters to go out looking for people who have jumped bail and left them holding the bag.

Again, I had a second idea also. Again, based on fact.

In San Francisco last year, a local dress manufacturer sold out to a wealthy guy who sort of appeared from nowhere. This cat milked the firm dry, then was uncovered as a Mafia informer from the east coast who had been given a new social security number and identity by the feds. The point is that, although he had a new identity, he was still a thug.

It was this second notion which grabbed Jack's fancy.

Later for the bounty hunter notion. I like your dress

Horse-trading with the censor: The Bad Dude is allowed to slam another man up against a wall, after script-writer Gores agrees to delete offscreen sounds of violence in another scene.

manufacturer idea. Very much. I feel it's the one we should go with on your first outing. The kickoff incident should be of a size or nature which would logically and believably warrant the attention of a Lieutenant of detectives with an entire squad under his command. I really haven't anything else to say to you. It's your move, compadre.

At this point I did my first Treatment, a 20-page outline for a show I called *No Immunity for Murder*. The Executive Producer approved; they bought; and I was hired for First Draft and, subsequently, Polish. The show was first run about a year ago.

My second Treatment was built around the bail-bondsman bounty hunter idea. I called it *Bad Dude*, and ex-L.A. Ram Rosey Grier played the title character. Apart from the *Kojak* regulars, it had an all-black cast. The show was first shown in January.

I did a third show which will probably be aired next year; meanwhile, my relationship with the show had crystallized. I was given a commitment for three more scripts, one to be a two-hour shot probably to be used as the season opener this fall. Despite a pretty full schedule of novel- and feature-film work, I have ended up a part-time writer for series drama on television.

Before going into some of the good things this can mean, I ought to mention some of the drawbacks from a writer's point of view which are inherent in this sort of work.

First, you are not your own man. And this goes deeper than having to write scripts around characters created by someone else. It means, on the *Kojak* show, for instance, that Treatment and then First Draft must be looked at, commented upon, and approved by: the executive producer; the producer; the supervising producer; the story editor; the technical advisor (that NYPD detective); and the CBS censor. The director chosen to do the show, as well as Telly Savalas, also can make suggestions concerning the finished script.

Apart from the many changes, shifts, and subtle alterations always demanded by the exigencies of actual filming, changes are demanded on a whole shifting galaxy of grounds: artistic, financial, production problems, censorship demands.

Censor stories are fun, especially in an election year when the networks are running in terror of a Congress panting for splashy issues like Sex and Violence on the tube which can be cynically exploited for votes. One result has been the thought-control of necessity inherent in the Family-Viewing-Hour idea. A second lesser, and more amusing result, has been the informal setting of quotas for swear-words on TV drama. At the moment, an hour show is allowed two hells and one damn. Earl Holliman likes to tell the story of trading a bloody arm for an extra hell on *Police Woman*. In one of my *Kojak* episodes, the censor offered me a deal: if I would drop the off-screen sounds of a fist fight in another room, I could retain on-screen a character getting slammed up against a wall by another character.

Another interesting result is that the networks are deadly afraid of Sexual Innuendo. Johnny Carson can casually drop more unbleeped zingers in one evening on the *Tonight* show than I can sneak into a year's worth of *Kojak* scripts. Every now and then, however, we manage to beat the system. Consider the following bit for my First Draft of *Bad Dude:*

Kojak is taking a big roll of bills out of Delia May's purse. She has bounced out of the car and is trying to grab for the money. He easily keeps it away from her. She finally desists.

DELIA MAY (Dee Timberlake): *That's my bread, mister. I earned it.*
KOJAK: *How?*
DELIA MAY: *Taking care of business.*
KOJAK (fanning the bills) : *The Eighth Army in town?*

DELIA MAY: That's my bread, mister. I earned it.
KOJAK: How?
DELIA MAY: Taking care of business.
KOJAK: (fanning the bills) You could have taken care of half the tourists in Manhattan for this.

Oh my, did the censor scream! Kojak's line, "You could have taken care of half the tourists in Manhattan for this" was, in his words, "unnecessarily explicit in this situation." Well, did he have any ideas of what might be substituted?

How about a classically simple, dignified, "Uh huh"?

Well, what the hell (which leaves me one hell and one damn to go) ? Why not? "Uh huh" it became. But Telly Savalas has a grand sense of drama and an inventive mind. He played it thus:

DELIA MAY: That's my bread, mister. I earned it.
KOJAK: How?
DELIA MAY: Taking care of business.
KOJAK: (fanning the bills) The Eighth Army in town?

Over such things do censors lose their pencils. Or the lead therein.

What all of this does is illustrate a point: if you're the sort of writer who can't stand anyone laying a finger on your work—forget it. You aren't for TV. Because changed your work is going to be.

Second drawback: because you are an employee of the studio, your paycheck is subject to withholding. But because tax is computed as if you earned whatever your script garners in a single week, the tax bite (plus your agent's commission) takes out just about fifty cents on the dollar.

Third: you must join Writers Guild of America, West. You are not given the option; you *have to.* WGA demands a $200 initiation fee, plus $40 a year (payable quarterly) in dues, *plus* a total of *one per-*

cent of your gross income from scripting. There are many benefits, obviously, to Guild membership, but this compulsory money bite is still a big one.

Plusses?

For me, script-writing's a hell (whoops! But I still have my damn left) of a lot of fun. I've been treated wonderfully by the *Kojak* production people; and a one-hour show requires about a sixty-page script, which takes me only about the same length of time that writing and polishing a 5,000-word short story takes. The pay is just incredibly better.

Because, let's face it, script-writing is lucrative. Up until April 1st, the minimums required under the industry/Guild contract (I *told* you there were benefits to WGA membership) for a sixty-minute dramatic show were as follows:

For Treatment	$1559
For First Draft Teleplay	2432
For Polish	509
TOTAL	$4500

Even if other writers are subsequently brought in to second-guess you, the originating writer gets full payment for those portions of the whole which he did. And beyond this $4500 package is the bonus paid to "qualified" writers (generally defined as those who have completed and sold three or more prime-time episodic television scripts). This is substantial, $1900 for a one-hour teleplay, or a grand total of $6400. A heavy reputation outside the TV-writing field might get the three-script stricture for bonus waived.

And it all was sweetened considerably last April, when minimums for story, teleplay, and revisions (plus qualified writer's bonus) on prime-time drama went up:

30-minute programs: from $4,500 to $5,000

Saperstein (Mark Russell), Stavros (George Savalas), and Crocker (Kevin Dobson) put the arm on Shotgun Willie Baines (Charles Weldon) before he can put the blast on The Bad Dude.

60-minute programs: from $6,400 to $7,400

90-minute programs: from $9,400 to $10,000

If all of this has given you an uncontrollable urge to write for episodic TV dramatic shows, let me return to my opening word of advice:

DON'T.

Why not? You afraid of the competition, Gores?

No. Because you don't *own* anything. The studio owns it all—your story, your treatment, your teleplay, your characters. In part, the pay is good because you aren't ever going to get any more (except for modest sums at rerun time).

Your best script gamble today is feature film scripts. IF you hit, you hit big. Why is that IF so big? Competition, baby. That's what makes it a gamble.

Next best bet, Movie of the Week scripts. Again, a gamble, because these are *very very difficult to sell* these days. Why? Because the networks are demanding much stronger, more artistic, harder-hitting stories than they used to. This, in turn, is because they can't count on recouping their investment by showing the movies in theaters in Europe as they used to be able to do. There is too much competition from made-in-Europe movies aimed at this theater audience.

So, what can I tell you? If you insist on trying to write for television, a few tips:

1. MOVE TO HOLLYWOOD

I'm not kidding. My agent could think of only *four* (and two of them were a husband-and-wife team) TV writers who broke into TV while living elsewhere.

2. GET A GOOD AGENT

How? Your problem, baby, but you have to do it. NO network show will consider unagented material (except in the rare cases where it is recommended by one of their own writers). Period. As to how one gets noticed by a good agent or a producer . . . why do you think you moved to Hollywood? Get out and hustle, use your contacts, use your wiles, use every trick you know to get your material read by SOMEONE.

3. WATCH THE SHOWS YOU WANT TO WRITE FOR

So obvious it hardly needs saying. But *study* them. Get to know the characters, the basic situation, the strengths and weaknesses of the actors who appear every week.

4. STUDY ALL THE TV SCRIPTS YOU CAN LAY HANDS ON

Classes in TV writing? To hell (oh oh! exceeded my quota!) with them. NOBODY can teach you to write, only WRITING can do that. But a dozen hours of script study can teach you the format.

5. THINK VISUALLY

How *many* writers find this impossible! *Use* the medium. *Use* the camera. Avoid stories which really are just a mess of people sitting around and talking in front of a camera.

6. PLOT YOUR DRAMAS FULLY

Thin material shows: Characters spend half their time walking up and down driveways, getting in and out of cars, opening and closing doors. Oddly enough, you must avoid OVERPLOTTING too, when it takes the form of *too much backstory* (i.e., where so much has gone on before our drama opens that lengthy explanations are necessary at the end). Too much plot of this sort also results in a mess of people sitting around and talking in front of a camera.

Did I forget anything? Oh, yeah. One final point:

7. WHY DON'T YOU CONSIDER SOME OTHER LINE OF WORK?

How I Design a Dust Jacket (when dust is a secondary consideration)

By GARY GORE

Explain the title of this article. There is lots of dust in my society. What does it mean?

I suppose I just couldn't resist the comment that a dust jacket no longer exists just to protect the book.

If the jacket isn't to protect the book, then what you are saying is that it is a marketing tool, right? Isn't it just another form of packaging, like the detergent box?

That won't wash. It is true that on some books the jacket is a package to attract attention in the bookstore. This is especially true of paperback covers. But the hardcover jacket has many functions, and some of them have little to do with the bookstore. Although not in any order of importance, here are some of the reasons for a dust jacket:

To please the author.
To attract the reviewer. This is very important.
To exist as an art form, as an esthetic visual statement of the book.
To provide a vehicle for the flap copy and the back ad, and for information about the author or a photograph.
To cover slight damage a book sustains in transit.
To sell the book.

Let's talk about designing a jacket. Where do you get your ideas or information? Do you read the book?

I read the flap copy. If it is well done, that is usually enough. In the case of fiction, it is often necessary to read the book. Sometimes the jacket merely illustrates the title. In other cases, it is the designer's interpretation of the book's central idea, or one of its ideas.

Aren't you assuming a lot by putting your interpretation of the book on the jacket?

Somebody has got to interpret it visually in order to get a visual statement. Besides, the danger isn't so much misinterpretation as it is too liberal interpretation. The key to successful jacket design is to say one thing, and say it well. For instance, I just designed a book on movies as an educational tool. The design consisted of a movie film, rolled up in the shape of an apple. Now, this was a vast oversimplification of the book and the title, but a useful one. I could have said much more —but it would have complicated the design so much that it would destroy it. Another example: for a book on welfare in the United States, I did a jacket showing a stylized flag, but the stars were hearts. Although you can take issue with this editorially, it made a strong statement. It said one thing, was a little bit jarring because it presented a familiar object in an unfamiliar way, and did well as a jacket. Nobody who looked at that jacket really expected to read about hearts on a flag—jacket design is often highly symbolic.

When you design a book, I assume you keep the reader in mind.

It's a little like designing a fishing bait. It would be nice to design it for the fish, but it is the fisherman who buys the bait. In this case, the fisherman who buys the jacket design is the publisher. But ultimately, yes, I keep the reader in mind.

Speaking of publishers, what is your relationship with them?

It varies greatly. Sometimes I work with the editors, sometimes with the production manager, sometimes with the sales manager. Sometimes a committee is involved, I'm afraid.

Do you prefer to be given specific directions, or merely suggestions?

I prefer to be given the manuscript, or the dust-

Movies: Universal Language (Notre Dame, Ind.: Fides, 1967) This design oversimplifies the book, but a jacket should express one idea well.

A Novel
by Edith Summers Kelley

Introduction by Matthew J. Bruccoli

Weeds (Southern Illinois University Press, 1972—Lost American Fiction Series). The lettering was designed to suggest a weed.

jacket flap copy, and work out my own solution. The less instruction necessary, the more likely it is that a good design results.

What is the greatest detriment to a good jacket design?

Fear. Any strong visual statement can be criticized and rejected for a number of reasons. The very thing that makes a jacket strong may trouble a publisher because he is afraid—afraid that it is too simple, too pat, or too much distillation. Often, a jacket design is rejected because it tells only one side of the book, or one point in the book. The result then is a revision that tells so many things that you can't see any of them—when everybody shouts, nobody listens. Or, ironically, the solution becomes a typographical treatment which doesn't say anything.

Do you mean that an all-type jacket can't be effective?

No, sorry, I didn't mean that. It can be very effective and is a legitimate solution to many jacket-design problems. But it can be a cop-out, too. It works best with short titles, and then the type face itself becomes part of the design. The typeface used in *Weeds* looks vaguely like a weed and is extremely effective. They are damned difficult to do, by the way.

Should the author approve the jacket design?
Lord, no.

You sound very positive. Doesn't he know more about the book than anybody else?

Yes, but jacket design is not his field. He often doesn't understand the needs of the marketplace, the system of reviewers, or the printing problems involved. He nearly always wants his favorite colors used, along

with a complex group of elements that will tell his whole story, if only the designer is clever enough to express the author's ideas. Chaos is the result. Often, a good writer is simply not a visual person—he handles words well but tends to be unsophisticated in design matters. Very often his approach to a jacket design is similar to that of the political cartoonist—contrive a complex situation that will illustrate a particular point of view. The result may tell you what is in the author's mind, but that isn't the purpose of the jacket. The book is there to tell you what is in the author's mind; the jacket is there to get the book reviewed or sold or picked up. It gets attention, if it is a selling jacket.

Are there times when a jacket is not a marketing device?

I think so. In the case of the fine edition, for instance, it may be simply a tasteful addendum to the book; an artful placement of type and visual elements to enhance the book. It may be there just to look and feel good.

The term design has several meanings. Can you define it?

"Problem solving" is a fair definition. That includes technical, editorial, and visual problem solving.

What are these exact problems, and how do you solve them?

There are two kinds of problems, really: those set by the publisher and those set by the designer. The limitations that the publisher sets include the schedule, the number of colors of ink available in the budget, the trim size of the book, the length of the title, and the fee. The publisher might add other limitations in the form of taboos or suggestions. And, of course, there always exist the basic limitations of working on a flat surface, and in a vertical format. I'm using the word "limitations" in place of "problems" now. A limitation is a

The Stream of Consciousness and Beyond in 'Ulysses' (University of Pittsburgh Press, 1974) Another Magic Marker job, with strong blacks.

Lake Songs and Other Fears (University of Pittsburgh Press, 1974) Enlarged old engravings used as cover art.

problem to solve. It actually helps to design the jacket, because when I consider all the limitations together, the jacket begins to design itself. For instance, if the publisher reminds me that the author's name will sell books, then my mind starts to consider a large typeface. If the author's name is also very long, then we have a conflict—so a condensed typeface begins to suggest itself.

Then there are the limitations that I have as a designer. There are things I can't do well, or can do well only with great difficulty. For instance, illustration of people in realistic poses, such as are found on paperback covers are difficult for me. I can do them, but with effort, and I work best in other directions. However, stylized illustration is easy for me. Faces are easier than bodies for me. How to explain to a customer that I can draw faces but not bodies is something I haven't learned yet. They simply don't believe me. On the other hand, I am totally at home with type, photography, and highly symbolic design elements.

So it is natural that a designer consider each problem in the light of what he can do best. How I approach a problem is a rather complex mixture of the limitations of the job and my own limitations. When I do illustrate, my illustration relies heavily on technique. By this I mean that the interesting textures, shapes, and designs are derived from the technique. For instance, sometimes I draw with ink on a paper towel. The spreading and blotching of the ink adds interest to the drawing if properly controlled and at the same time covers up minor flaws. In the process, it makes the printing process less critical and can save the customer money in plate costs. It is an especially nice feeling to solve several problems all at once—visual, editorial, and budgetary—by application of the right technique.

The typical jacket assignment comes to me in the mail, from an established customer or somebody who has heard of me through a referral. It usually includes the jacket blurb, and if it is a new customer some mention of fee is made. Sometimes the publisher sets the fee; sometimes the designer. The fees are higher for big-budget books, or for books of special importance. An expensive, mass-market book jacket will carry a larger fee than a slender volume of poetry, because there is more money in the budget to work with.

Money does control the jacket appearance at times. I have a small local publisher who can pay only a small fee for a jacket. But he realizes that this is a limitation, and so I do things for him that are very fast, and he trusts me enough so that I don't prepare a comprehensive (jargon for "sketch for approval") beforehand. I simply do a finished mechanical for him in a way that doesn't eat up a lot of chargeable hours. That relationship is based on confidence.

Technique is all-important. Designing a jacket for a romantic novel with, say, a woodcut technique is a bit like trying to write a romantic limerick. It can be done, but it strains the process to its limits. A water color, or some other visual equivalent of the sonnet, would be better for that job. But if only one or two colors of ink is available because of the budget, then a water color is not as practical as a woodcut. So things begin to intermix, and I begin to search for a third solution.

The jacket is a rather expensive part of a book. It isn't unusual for a $10 book to cost $1.80 print, and of this the jacket might account for 30¢. By the time everybody adds his mark-up—the publisher, the wholesaler, the bookstore—that 30¢ is multiplied by a factor of five or six and could add $1.50 to the price of the book.

Dynamics of Institutional Change (University of Pittsburgh Press, 1973) Arrows to suggest change.

Blue-collar Aristocrats (University of Wisconsin Press, 1975) The model was a printing salesman.

Now and then, I get an assignment that has no real budget limitations. A typical example of this would be a four-color jacket for a cookbook with a large promotion budget. At these times the jacket can be a terribly expensive item. The following budget, although hypothetical, is possible:

Model fee	$ 75.00
Props—food and kitchen items	75.00
Film and processing	30.00
Presentation sketch	100.00
Travel expense	300.00
Time spent in photographing, gathering props, designing jacket, preparing materials, travel	600.00
Color plates	500.00
Printing and paper	600.00
Plastic coating	200.00
	$2480.00

If you printed only 1,000 of these jackets, the cost would be $2.48 each—obviously impractical. But if you printed 10,000 the cost would be only a few hundred dollars more, and the price would go down to 30¢ or so. If you printed 100,000, the price would drop much further. So you can see that the design approach for a university press book is quite different from a mass-market, expensive edition.

For years the book jacket has usually been printed on coated paper and varnished. The reasons for this practice are obscure, but I suspect that they stem from the fact that the coated paper worked best with letterpress printing. Coated paper—it is usually glossy—needs varnish because the surface is clay, and the ink will rub off if it is not varnished after the ink is applied. But today offset printing is the common process, and it can print well on soft laid or text papers which require no varnish. Clear shrink-wrapping is used more and more to protect the jacket from soil. The jacket, which used to protect the book, is now being protected by a 7-cent shrink-wrap. So far no one has learned how to print an advertisement on the shrink-wrap.

I am asked, from time to time, what the trend in jacket design will be. My comments will haunt me ten years from now, but I think we will see the following things happen:

First, a trend toward unusual papers such as kraft, newsprint, tissue, and other stock which have more character than the coated sheet.

Second, more books bound in material (cloth or non-woven substitutes) which has been printed with artwork or illustration in the manner of a jacket. Textbooks are often done this way now. It effectively eliminates the jacket without eliminating the design.

And third, a return to jacketless bindings that are highly decorated in the grand manner and protected with shrink-wrapping or plastic film.

Assuming that you are right—that dust-jacket design is an art form—why do publishers spend the stockholders' money to put art on their books?

Because they can feel. Because they aren't selling deodorant—that's a book under the jacket.

Gary Gore has been designing books and their dust jackets for sixteen years. He has won design awards from the American Institute of Graphic Arts, the Chicago Book Clinic, the Association of American University Presses, the Virginia Museum, the Art Director's Club, and has had a one-man show at the American Institute of Graphic Arts in New York. He is Publications Director for the American Association for State and Local History.

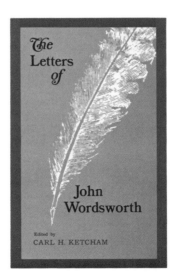

The Letters of John Wordsworth (Cornell University Press, 1971) This feather was photographed, then run through an office copier.

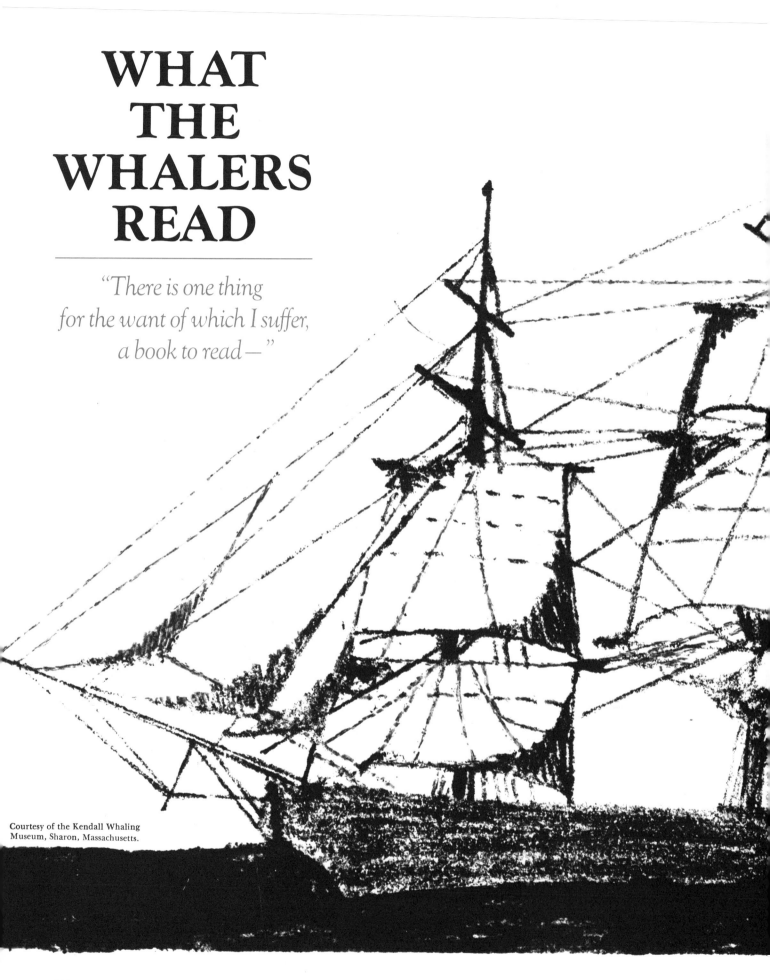

WHAT
THE
WHALERS
READ

*"There is one thing
for the want of which I suffer,
a book to read—"*

Courtesy of the Kendall Whaling
Museum, Sharon, Massachusetts.

By PAMELA A. MILLER

Sketch of the New Bedford bark *Wave*.

During the years of American whaling, which began almost as soon as America herself and lasted until the 1920s, approximately 14,000 whaling voyages were made. For each of these voyages, an official daily record, or log, was kept, usually by the first mate. In addition, private records, or journals, were often written by other officers as well as members of the crew.

Very few of these records have survived. Many journals were taken home and used as scrap paper or scrapbooks, with neswpaper articles, poems, or pictures pasted over the pages. Many were used as sketchbooks by the very young. Many were simply thrown away. In the mid-1920s, for example, whaling logs and journals were sold as scrap paper for as little as a nickel a pound.

Approximately 3,500 whaling logbooks and journals still exist in thirteen major public collections in America. Some of these, like the Kendall Whaling Museum in Sharon, Massachusetts, and the Nicholson Collection in Providence, Rhode Island, are the work of deliberate and knowledgeable connoisseurs. Most of the others are the result of bequests to local historical societies. The scarcity of available material would seem to make generalization difficult. However, what does exist is often surprisingly consistent.

Whaling was one of America's dirtiest and dreariest exploitations of labor, especially in its latter days. During frequent and lengthy periods on every whaleship, absolutely nothing happened except the appearance of depressingly monotonous, unhealthy, and scanty meals. On these long voyages (four years was a typical cruise, and seven years was not unusual), ships often sailed for months without lowering after a whale. Blank time was filled with scrimshawing, singing, unspeakable (or at least unrecordable) practices, and reading.

Very few whaleships had any library as such. Francis Olmstead, in his *Incidents of a Whaling Voyage* (1841), describes a remarkable exception:

The forecastle of the North America is much larger than those of most ships of her tonnage, and is scrubbed out regularly every morning. There is a table and a lamp, so that

the men have conveniences for reading and writing if they choose to avail themselves of them; and many of them are practising writing every day or learning how to write. Their stationery they purchase out of the ship's stores, and then come to one of the officers or myself for copies, or to have their pens mended. When not otherwise occupied, they draw books from the library in the cabin, and read; or if they do not know how, get some one to teach them. We have a good library on board, consisting of about two hundred volumes. . . .

Olmstead believed many other whalers resembled the *North America,* but he was greatly mistaken. The *Charles and Henry* had a small ship's library of thirty-nine titles. But these vessels were exceptions to the general rule.

For most whalemen, reading was limited to what they brought with them or what they could borrow. J. Ross Browne, in his *Etchings of a Whaling Cruise* (1846), describes the usual situation:

As to reading, I was necessarily compelled to read whatever I could get. Unfortunately, I had brought neither books nor papers with me, so that I had to depend entirely upon the officers, none of whom were troubled with a literary taste. Mr. D____, the first mate, who was very friendly toward me, had a bundle of old Philadelphia weeklies, which I read over a dozen times, advertisements and all. The cooper, a young man from New Bedford, was by far the most intelligent man aft. His stock of literature consisted of a temperance book, a few Mormon tracts, and Lady Dacre's Diary of a Chaperone. . . . One of my shipmates had a Bible; another, the first volume of Cooper's Pilot; a third, the Songster's own Book; a fourth, the Complete Letter Writer; and a fifth claimed, as his total literary stock, a copy of the Flash newspaper, published in New York. . . . I read and reread all these. Every week I was obliged to commence on the stale reading, placing the last read away till I systematically arrived at them again. . . .

What whalemen read depended to a great extent on when they were reading. Two fairly distinct periods appear, the mid-point falling about 1830.

As Hohman says in *The American Whaleman* (1928)—probably the best and most complete book available on American whaling—until about 1830 the majority of American whaling crews were homogenous. Very often, small towns sent out a ship or ships as a joint venture. Entire crews were friends or neighbors united in financial endeavor. Many young men eager to make good signed on before the mast, including sons of local merchants and the well-to-do.

After 1830, though, whaling became industrialized, with fewer firms sending out more ships. Large towns like New Bedford became the centers, and crews became much more heterogeneous. Well-educated and intelligent young men still staffed the officers' quarters. However, the character of the crew changed dramatically. Few men shipped on more than one voyage, unless incapable psychologically, physically, or legally, of working on shore. Crews were increasingly immoral, badly trained, lacking in morale. As more than one director of a whaling museum has said to me, these crews were the dregs of society, frequently signing on under false names to escape prosecution. More and more, foreigners took the majority of the bunks in the forecastle. In 1850, in *The Whale and His Captors,* Henry Cheever described the usual conditions: there, "with no possibility of classification and separate quarters, with few or no books, or opportunity to use them if they were possessed, with the constant din of roystering disorder, superabundant profanity, and teeming lasciviousness of conversation and songs . . . three-fourths of their forty months' absence are passed."

The amount and quality of what was read on whaleships naturally reflect the quality of shipboard life as well as the general reading trends of the day. Until about 1830, the authors mentioned in logs or journals are those that were popular on land as well. Quotations appear quite frequently, especially from the Bible, Shakespeare, Thomson's "The Seasons," Young's "Night Thoughts." Contemporary popular songs and ballads were also often copied out in full.

After 1830, the change in emotional and intellectual climate produced marked changes in reading, abetted by the increased availability of printed matter such as newspapers and inexpensive novels. Many of the post-1830 logs and journals contain clippings or copies of scraps of facile newspaper verse, generally of the most bathetic sort. Thoughts of home, God, loved ones, and death predominate in the characteristic Victorian mode. In addition, many tantalizingly vague references are made to reading in general. Clearly, many whalemen did read, and read a great deal. In fact, cheap bookstalls on many wharves served last-minute customers.

Despite the general lack of specific detail, seven compulsive list-makers, all but one an officer, left full records of their shipboard reading. Further, the entire library list of the *Charles and Henry* in 1840 has been published recently by Wilson Heflin in *Historic Nantucket*. Most of these lists are extensive. The titles often overlap, but the lists reveal a great deal about their compilers despite the difficulties of deciphering handwriting, bad spelling, and inaccurate titles.

The earliest of these list-makers was John Provost, who was probably mate of the *Alexander* in 1827. His journal is in the collection of the Peter Foulger Museum on Nantucket. Provost made several lists, including what he had borrowed from shipmates, what he had lent, and what he had bought in Valparaiso. Altogether he records about eighty titles, some more than once. About one quarter of his list is made up of novels, several of them well known: Smollett's *Roderick Random* and *Peregrine Pickle;* Scott's *The Tales of My Landlord;* and, on a lower artistic level, Rowson's *Charlotte Temple;* Porter's *Thaddeus of Warsaw;* Roche's *Children of the Abbey;* and Jackson's *Alonzo and Melissa.* Provost's list includes poets typical of the pre-1830 period (Thomson and Young)

as well as Johnson's *Lives of the Poets* and *The Rambler.* And, like almost all his fellow list-makers, Provost read moral and religious works. Among these fifteen titles is Thomas à Kempis' *Imitation of Christ.* Altogether, John Provost was an active reader, obviously borrowing and lending as much as possible. Like most of the whalemen who kept reading lists, he seems preoccupied with both escape and morality.

Half of the eight lists are from the early 1840s. One, also in the Peter Foulger Museum, that stands out is that of the ship's library of the *Charles and Henry* (Melville came aboard at Eimeo). As Heflin notes, its library was "a rarity in whaleships of the time—put aboard her by the Coffin owners. It consisted of thirty-seven books and two magazines (presumably bound copies of several issues)." For their $16.24, the thrifty Quakers were able to supply nine histories and miscellanies, and twelve moral and religious works. Of the five naval titles supplied, one was "entertaining": Marryat's *Poor Jack;* one was "moral": Cardell's story of *Jack Halyard, the Sailor Boy, or, The Virtuous Family.* And, as Heflin points out, three narratives on the dreadful consequences of shipwreck may have been "chosen . . . to dissuade their whalemen from deserting on savage Pacific isles." Nantucket Quakers were noted for craft and business ability as well as piety.

The other three lists from the early 1840s are equally revealing.

A scramble for "salt junk" at mess time.

Tying the baleen from whales' upper jaws.

W. B. Howes, first mate (and later captain) of the *Nimrod,* recorded forty titles in his journal now at Mystic Seaport. He seems an eminently practical man: ten navigation aids; thirteen moral and religious works, including Methodist and Episcopal hymnals and an Episcopal prayerbook; four works on arithmetic, geometry, and such; and three medical guides. Howes dismisses the rest of his library as "Histories etc.," other than Goldsmith's *History of Greece* and *The Poetical Works of Mrs. Felicia Hemans.* It is a working captain's library, equipped for all emergencies, including Mrs. Hemans for moments of leisure.

Varamus Smith, captain of the *Ohio* in 1841, lists about forty-five titles, including those belonging to others, in another of Mystic Seaport's whaling journals. Smith was strong on morality and self-improvement, though not on spelling. He took three aids to navigation; fifteen moral and religious works; and twenty titles of histories, memoirs, arithmetics, and readers. However, besides Baxter's *A Call to the Unconverted* and *The Saint's Everlasting Rest* and "Bunion's" works, he read three novels and *The Pirates Own Book.*

As Dorothy Brewington of Mystic Seaport com-

mented to me, James C. Osborn, mate in 1841 on the first voyage of the *Charles W. Morgan,* "was obviously bucking for captain." Mystic Seaport owns his beautifully illustrated and informative journal which records his fondness for fiction. He read twenty-two of Marryat's works, twelve of Bulwer's, and twenty-five others, including *The Pathfinder, The Bravo, Mercedes of Castile, Pamela,* and *Humphry Clinker.* In addition, he chose eight histories or essay collections, three moral works, and two health guides. One more of his interesting choices deserves mention: Joseph C. Hart's *Miriam Coffin or the Whale Fishermen* (1835), one of the first novels about whaling and a probable source for *Moby-Dick.*

Two lists appear in journals from the 1850s.

Benjamin Boodry, second mate on the *Arnolda* in 1852, was another reader of novels. His journal, in the Old Dartmouth Whaling Museum in New Bedford, includes only five histories or miscellanies in his list of sixty-seven titles. (He ignored more practical works, at least in his reading.) His handwriting and spelling are major obstacles, but his choices are interesting. He read two of Dickens' novels, three by G. P. R. James, five by Cooper, five by Marryat, *Jane Eyre, Afloat and Ashore,* and *Uncle Tom's Cabin*—besides being the only unpublished whaleman journalist to mention "*Mober Dick.*" He seemed interested in the evils of city life, too, reading Vose's *Seven Nights in Gotham* and Nunes' *Aristocracy; or Life Among the "Upper Ten"*—exposés of New York and Philadelphia.

William R. Potter, captain of the *Mt. Wollaston* in 1853, cited an astounding number of works: 132 titles. In this journal, now owned by the New Bedford Free Public Library, he lists forty-four novels; twenty-two histories or miscellanies; twenty-one works on arithmetic, astronomy, geography, or grammar; ten religious or moral works, including two copies of the Bible; eight works of poetry; and five aids to navigation. Potter's list includes well-known names and titles from many areas: Gibbon's *Decline and Fall,* Prescott's *Ferdinand and Isabella;* Byron, Keats, Scott, Shakespeare; Griswold's *Poets and Poetry of America;* and novels by Irving, Cooper, Bulwer, Anne Brontë, Charlotte Brontë, Dickens, Marryat, and Benjamin D'Israeli. On a less classic level, he shows a fondness for Timothy Shay Arthur (three titles, but not *Ten Nights in a Barroom*), and read Mary H. Eastman's response to Harriet Beecher Stowe, *Aunt Phillis' Cabin.*

The most recent list located was compiled by Frederick H. Russell, a crew member on the *Pioneer* in the 1870s. He shows great interest in fiction, to the exclusion of all else, listing fifty-nine novels and nine "Stories I have read in the ledger" as his reading. His journal is now in the Yale University Library. While he did read such works as *The Black Tulip, The Woman in White, Oliver Twist,* and *Our Mutual Friend,* most of Russell's list is comprised of dime novels or their equivalent. At least eight items are from Beadle's series, and many have titles like *Adelaide the Avenger* and *Chenga the Cheyenne.* One wonders whether Russell was aware that to those who knew nothing of the harsh realities of life on a whaleship, *his* life was romantic and exciting. His reading provided necessary escape from the frequent tedium and constant bad food and hard work. Interestingly, Russell escaped boredom in yet another way: he was a collaborator on "The Frozzen Limb," a ballad which was the only original pornographic work to appear in all 3,500 logs and journals.

During the entire era of American whaling, reading was very much a part of life on board ship. Until the 1830s, the quality of shipboard life was such that reading there seems to have followed closely the same patterns as on shore. As the whaling business became more industrialized and life on board more emotionally isolating, escape literature began to predominate as the preferred form. In many ways, Frederick Russell's reading list of the 1870s is a culminating point, an illustration of trends that gradually eliminated the standard works of navigation, education, morality, and even of fiction, in favor of melodramatic escape literature. The later the list, the larger the proportion of deservedly forgotten writers.

After Russell's time, few logbooks or journals were written that contain much of interest other than to whaling historians. The process begun about 1830 moved to its inevitable close, and the last whaling records kept aboard ship are often pencilled and irregular scrawls. In earlier days, however, many inquiring and contemplative young men kept lengthy, literate journals, and read all they could find. One, William D. Buel of New York City, sailed on the *Wave* in 1856, unable to afford the 75¢ he needed for a copy of Washington Irving's *Wolfert's Roost.* He was killed at sea after a brawl, but his journal, now at the Providence Public Library, preserves a lament many whalemen could have voiced: "There is one thing for the want of which I suffer, a book to read—"

Book list from the log kept in 1841
by Captain Varamus Smith of *The Ohio.*

Jericho: The Marketing Story

By BETTY ANN JONES

Photo: Carl Fischer

The book-publishing industry, like most other industries, is feeling the results of the recession. Reports from New York tell of staff cuts at the biggest houses; editors inform their authors that the days of the big advance are past; some publishers even murmur about cutting the royalty percentage their authors ordinarily receive. All drastic measures, of course—but made necessary, we are assured, because books just aren't selling as they used to, production expenses are up, paper costs are heading through the roof, etc., etc.

But that's not the way we feel about book publishing in Birmingham, Alabama. Oxmoor House, the five-year-old book publishing division of The Progressive Farmer Company, publishes books that *do* sell. Indeed, *Jericho: The South Beheld* is probably the biggest success in recent publishing.

Jericho is a 6½-pound volume which measures 12½ x 16 inches, contains 168 pages and includes over 100 Hubert Shuptrine art reproductions, 75 in full color. The paintings are accompanied by a text written by the poet and novelist, James Dickey. This numbered first edition of *Jericho* is printed on 65-pound cover stock and is custom-bound (partially by hand) in the best buckram and sailcloth available. The first printing was 150,000 copies — the largest first printing of any quality book in the history of publishing.

The publication of this volume is probably the most ambitious literary achievement to come from the South in this century. In *Jericho,* two Southerners turn their talents to their land and their people—Shuptrine

Above: The New Puppy.
Opposite: Patient Turn.

visually, and Dickey by a poetic process. The paintings should be looked at for themselves, and the prose passages read for themselves, as part of the concept that Dickey calls "Jericho"—the Promised Land.

Jericho has been called an event, a happening, a once-in-a-lifetime thing, and Oxmoor House pulled it off when the house had been in business for only four years.

When it was published on October 1, 1974, *Jericho* was priced at $39.95. On January 1, 1975 the price was raised to $60.00, as is the custom with gift books. Before the price went up, 158,000 copies were sold.

How did a small, almost unheard-of publisher achieve these sales? That's the question the New York publishers have been asking. And the question this article hopes to answer. Les Adams, director of Oxmoor House, summed it up like this: "The book's success is due to a number of factors not usually counted on to sell books: 1) a painstakingly tested and executed direct-mail program; 2) the intensely personal regional pride of the Southerner; 3) the growing national trend of nostalgia and the desire to return to the land."

In April 1974 we conducted our initial direct-mail marketing tests to determine the retail price of the book, the marketing techniques to use, and the number of books to be printed. 140,000 packages were mailed to fourteen 10,000-name segments of *Southern Living* subscribers. The chart below describes these tests.

APRIL 1974 INITIAL JERICHO DIRECT MAIL TEST

1. *Jericho* at price "A"—green 9″ x 12″ (control package)
2. *Jericho* at price "B" (price test)

3. *Jericho* at price "C" (price test)
4. *Jericho* at price "D" (price test)
5. *Jericho* at price "E" (price test)
6. *Jericho* at $39.95 with free art reproduction (premium/price test)
7. *Jericho* at price "A" with repurchase certificate (offer test)
8. *Jericho* at price "A" with installment credit (offer test)
9. *Jericho* at price "A" with free art reproduction (premium test)
10. *Jericho* at price "A"—mustard-colored package with 16-page booklet (package test)
11. *Jericho* at price "A"—6″ x 9″ version of control package (package test)
12. *Jericho* at price "A"—6″ x 9″ package with no copy on envelope (envelope test)
13. *Jericho* at price "A"—6″ x 9″ package with window on envelope and perforated return token on order card (offer test)
14. *Jericho* at price "A"—#10 first-class envelope (package test)

Obviously, there were many other tests that we could have conducted, but chose not to because testing is expensive. For example, we did not test the title (after discussions with the author and after discarding many title suggestions, we felt the word "Jericho" was right); we didn't test the jacket art (we knew it fit the title); we didn't test numbering the books (it had to be a plus); we did not test the size and format of the book (that was determined by the art and manufacturing requirements).

The test results showed that the token (#13), the

The media and the message. The ad that ran in *U.S. News and World Report,* and *Southern Living*. Center: Ingredients of a winning package include letters from Director Les Adams and *Southern Living* Editor Gary McCalla, color brochure, one-year repurchase warranty, premium slip for art reproduction, all mailed in envelope below.

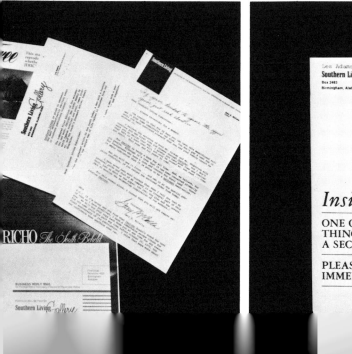

Hubert Shuptrine sketching.

16-page booklet (#10), and first-class mail (#14) did *not* increase orders. But most important, the higher price pulled just as well as lower prices, in combination with the total package. The 6″ x 9″ package did *not* pull as well as the 9″ x 12″ package, but the larger-size package cost much more to manufacture and mail.

When test results were read in early May 1974, we made the following decisions:

1. The price would be $39.95.
2. We would give away a free art reproduction as a premium with each book.
3. We would offer installment credit.
4. We would offer a 12-month repurchase guarantee (we've never heard of any other publisher making this guarantee) .
5. We would mail the 6″ x 9″ version of the control package.
6. We would print 150,000 books!

At this point, we fully realized the magnitude of our commitment and knew that this book would be the biggest publishing coup of 1974 and perhaps of this century.

We hired a full-time publicist to work exclusively on this book. His job was to get public exposure for the book and its author and artist. He scheduled national and local TV appearances, radio and newspaper interviews, civic and art club speaking appointments, art shows and receptions.

Jericho was a featured alternate selection of the Book-of-the-Month Club and was excerpted in *Playboy, Southern Living,* and *Progressive Farmer* magazines. James Dickey appeared on the "Tonight Show"; Dickey and Hubert Shuptrine appeared together on "Dinah Shore Show," "Book Beat," and almost every significant local TV talk show in the South.

We scheduled major media advertisements in *Publishers Weekly, The New York Times, U.S. News and World Report, Wall Street Journal, American Artist, Art in America* and, of course, our own *Southern Living* and *Progressive Farmer.* We sent out over 500 review copies of the book to newspapers, magazines, TV and radio reviewers. Our trade sales force made up of independent sales representatives began calling on bookstores and libraries throughout the United States and Canada.

After building this momentum we were ready for the direct-mail campaign. Here's a summary of our campaign:

July 3, 1974
1,007,574 packages to *Southern Living* subscribers
  269,831 packages to 27 other lists (list tests)
1,277,405 packages mailed
Sold 26,295 books

July 17, 1974
1,007,574 packages to *Southern Living* subscribers
 (same names mailed to on July 3)
Sold 12,642 books

September 10, 1974
  343,460 packages to 35 other lists (list tests)
Sold 4,102 books

October 1, 1974
  983,584 packages to *Southern Living* subscribers
  636,422 packages to lists tested in July
1,620,006 packages mailed
Sold 14,126 books

October 21, 1974
  983,584 packages to *Southern Living* subscribers
 (same names mailed on October 1)
Sold 5,599 books

November 8, 1974
  610,843 packages to lists tested in September
Sold 9,020 books

December 10, 1974

62,423 packages to new *Southern Living* subscribers

Sold 2,498

Were we successful?

Initial test sold	3,640 copies
Direct-mail campaign sold	74,282 copies
Media advertising sold	21,614 copies
The trade sold	58,000 copies

157,536 (with returns
of less than 12%)

Oxmoor House won the Carey-Thomas Award for Creative Book Publishing for *Jericho*. Oxmoor House won the DMMA's (Direct Mail Marketing Association) Silver Mailbox Award for *Jericho*. And samples of the materials used in the test and campaign are now used as direct mail teaching aids throughout this country and abroad.

We were successful and believe that we will continue to be successful. Maybe not in *Jericho* proportions every year, but it is Oxmoor House's firm conviction that people will buy good books if they know about them and if they are readily available. We know that many small towns have no bookstores at all and that many potential customers who live in large cities never have time—or the desire—to browse through a bookstore, so we've learned we have to take our books to the consumer—through radio, television, and newspaper publicity, through magazine and newspaper advertising, and through direct mail.

Instead of printing 5,000 copies of 100 or 200 or 300 new titles each year and allocating almost no advertising and promotion budget to each, we plan to publish only six or eight or ten new titles and print 25,000 to 75,000 of each and allocate enough money to sell them, to reprint them, and to continue to sell them for years to come. Because we are not publishing hundreds of new titles each year we know we have to be very selective in the titles we do decide to publish. That we have to stand behind each book with our convictions, enthusiasm, and our money.

That's our plan. *Jericho* proved it will work.

Inspected books on skids at bindery.

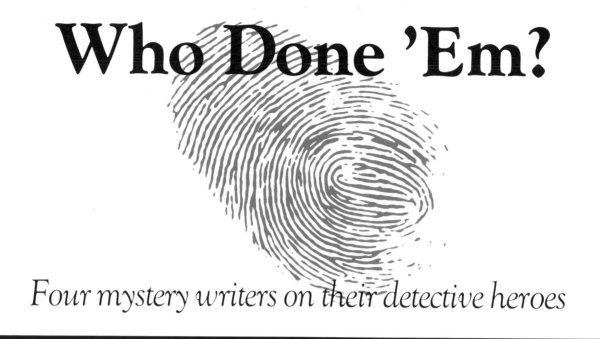

Who Done 'Em?

Four mystery writers on their detective heroes

MR. AND MRS. NORTH

By RICHARD LOCKRIDGE

There is an irresistible appeal to the scatterbrained young woman who finds herself in the unlikeliest situations, never quite knowing how she got into such a mess and only miraculously escaping some horrible fate. Detective fiction is full of them. While they are as exasperating as real-life women, they still have a mad charm that can squeeze affection out of the grouchiest reader. No one better exemplifies this personality than Pamela North, the delightful albatross around Jerry North's neck. Perhaps the most likable couple in mystery fiction (along with Nick and Nora Charles), the Norths made their detectival debut in The Norths Meet Murder *(1940). This is how they were born:*

Mr. and Mrs. North had been fictional, or semi-fictional, characters for several years before they first met murder (I paraphrase the title of the first mystery novel about them—*The Norths Meet Murder*). I had written many pieces about them for *The New Yorker*—not short stories, precisely, but what *The New Yorker* then called "casuals." Brief domestic comedies, I suppose they were. And they were based, sometimes closely, on things which had happened to my wife, Frances, and me.

I wrote, and the magazine bought, a good many of these pieces, and eventually they were collected in a book called *Mr. and Mrs. North*. The publisher, rather ill-advisedly, called this collection "a novel." Several reviewers snorted and so, in a mild way, did I. Novels, like short stories, require plots, and I, then, was plotless: And the Norths, in the early *New Yorker* pieces, were without first names.

The surname was easy. It was merely lifted from the somewhat amorphous, and frequently inept, people who played the North hands in bridge problems. In *The New Yorker*, in their early appearances, they were merely "Mr." and "Mrs." But midway of one piece, it became necessary for Mr. North to call his wife in another room of their apartment. It seemed unlikely that he would call out, "Hey, Mrs. North." So, on the spur of the moment, he called for "Fran." I do not remember that I had ever called Frances that, although, among other things, I did call her "Francie."

When proofs—*The New Yorker* always sent proofs—came back, the "Fran" stuck out. The spur of the moment had, clearly, struck too close to home. As a one-time printer, I could count spaces, so that only one line would have to be reset. (I had been, a few years earlier, the printer in the Kansas City, Missouri, post office. I had learned to set type in a "journalism" course at Kansas City Junior College, where journalism certainly started with the fundamentals. I was taught to run a job press at the post office by an elderly man, who really was a printer and was retiring. He lacked the two fingers on his right hand which were conventional for

Edited by OTTO PENZLER

The popularity of mystery fiction is undisputed. In recent years there has been increasing willingness to accept its literary excellence, when it is present, and to treat it without the condescension formerly accorded to it almost reflexively. W. Somerset Maugham once wrote that detective fiction is the most significant literary achievement of the twentieth century.

One criterion of a superior work of literary creation is the introduction and development of memorable characters. It is not difficult to tick off the handful of characters that have leapt from the pages of books to take up permanent residence in the world of living people, known to every literate person (not to mention those who didn't read the book but loved the movie).

Robinson Crusoe is such a figure, and so is Alice, and Oliver Twist, and Anna Karenina, and Tom Jones.

Detective fiction has provided more than its share of living personalities to the world. Is there an artist, or a general, or a head of state as recognizable throughout the world as Sherlock Holmes? Can anyone hear the name of Dr. Fu Manchu without knowing he represents evil incarnate? Isn't there a universal ring of familiarity to such names as Charlie Chan, James Bond, and Ellery Queen?

Meet some of the most extraordinary detectives. What characteristics have separated them from the ordinary to make their names widely recognizable? Perhaps these brief profiles, written by the authors who created the characters, will help explain the phenomena.

Richard Lockridge

long-time operators of job presses. I did manage to retain mine.)

Anyway, I counted spaces, and "Pam" came close enough, and Mrs. North became Pamela, "Pam" for that line of type. I have no idea how her husband became "Jerry" or, for that matter, how he became a publisher. In *The New Yorker* stories he had no occupation, so far as I can remember. Except, of course, that of being foil, straight man, to his wife.

Actually, the Norths did not first appear in *The New Yorker,* although that was the first time they had names.

When we first went to New York to stay, the *New York Sun* devoted that part of its back page not occupied by John Wanamaker to a department called "The Sun Rays." It consisted of very short, preferably humorous, pieces, and fragments of verse. We were broke; flat broke is not excessive. Frances got a job reckoning payments due from people who were buying on time—buying electric generators, as I recall. She was paid twenty-five dol-

The dust jacket for the first Mr. and Mrs. North book.

lars a week. It was a job for which she was totally unsuited, and which she did very well. We paid twenty dollars a week for a large room with a bath and a gas plate at one end. I, for some months, had no job at all, although I kept applying to all the city's newspapers, which then were numerous. So I started submitting pieces to "The Sun Rays."

Most of them were about "the babes in the studio apartment." In retrospect, the "babes" seem to me unbearably cute. The description was also inaccurate. We were both experienced newspaper reporters, Frances much more experienced than I. But we *were* babes in Manhattan, and had fallen into the habit of eating. "The Sun Rays" pieces helped us sustain the habit. They also helped me, finally, to get a job on the city staff of the *Sun*.

The "babes" were the Norths in embryo. And the time was fifty years ago. You could buy twenty-five-cents-worth of stew meat and make it do for two dinners. If, of course, the stew

didn't spoil between meals; we had no refrigeration in the studio.

I kept on writing North stories while I was doing rewrite, and covering murder trials, on the *Sun*. We seemed to spend more than our combined salaries, although by then Frances had found a job more suited to her skills, and somewhat better paid. *The New Yorker* kept on buying. And we both, from time to time, read detective stories—mystery novels, novels of suspense, whatever publishers care to call them. (My own preference is for "detective stories," or the variants which I think of as "chases." Chases are more likely to become 'one-shots in magazines, or did before general magazines shrank so drastically in size and, of course, in numbers.)

It was Frances who first decided to write a detective story of her own. For several days her typewriter clicked happily. Then it stopped clicking. Then she came to me. There was one point with which she was having

a little trouble, and perhaps I could help.

I read the dozen or so pages and it seemed to me to start very well. Then there was a scene, obviously crucial. A rowboat, apparently with nobody in it, was crossing a lake in the moonlight. I recognized the lake; we were renting a summer cabin on just such a lake. The rowboat came ashore. There was a body lying in it.

"Fine," I said. "Very good scene. Foreboding. Only, with only this dead man in it, what made the boat move? You say it was a still night; no wind to blow it ashore. So?"

"Yes," she said, "that's the point I'm having trouble with. I thought maybe you could help. After all, you were in the Navy."

I had been. On a battleship which had spent most of 1918 in what was then the Brooklyn Navy Yard. New engines were being installed. With new engines she could move herself. In fact, she did move while I was still aboard. Across water in the Yard and, with a considerable bang, into a pier. The *USS North Dakota* managed, later, to steam to a drydock for junking.

None of this seemed to have much to do with a rowboat, occupied only by the dead, moving across a quiet lake under a full moon.

Frances was disappointed. I promised her we would work on it.

We did work on it. And we got nowhere. I still think about it now and then. I still get nowhere.

But then we got the idea of collaborating on a mystery, without the magical boat, but with Mr. and Mrs. North, already established characters.

The way we worked together, on that and subsequent books in what became a series, was to have story conferences. Who will we kill this time? Male or female? And who will do the killing, and why?

We would talk things out, making notes, coming up — usually slowly — with ideas, each of us accepting, or rejecting, the other's notions.

After some hours of this, each of us

would type up a synopsis of the book and of individual scenes in it. We would name the characters, which is often a tricky business. We would, finally, jumble it all together. Then I would write the story, drawing on our outlines and my experience, not very extensive, as a police reporter. And also my experience in covering murder trials, which was greater. (Hall-Mills, Snyder-Gray and others celebrated in the now-distant past. Newspapers went all out for trials in those days. Some rented houses to lodge their covering staffs. The *Sun* made do with three of us and, now and then, as in the Browning separation suit, with only two.)

I did all the writing on all our books. Frances summed it up neatly in one speaking appearance we made together: "I think up interesting characters and Dick kills them off."

The Norths themselves almost got killed off before, as detectives, they were ever born. Somebody, and I am afraid it was the late George Bye, my agent and close friend, suggested that they be renamed—perhaps become the Souths, or maybe the Wests.

It would be too much to say that by then the Norths had a following. But they were known to *The New Yorker* readers. The suggestion that this perhaps minimal advantage be thrown away was hooted down, mostly by me, but also by the editors.

When Frances died very suddenly and I kept on writing, several re-viewers searched diligently for changes in our style. One or two found it, which I thought very astute of them.

I wrote no more Mr. and Mrs. North stories after Frances' death, partly because, in my mind, she had always been Pamela North; partly because the spontaneity seemed to be ebbing from them.

People used to ask me what Pam and Jerry looked like. I could never tell them. I have always avoided detailed physical descriptions of characters. It is better, it seems to me, to let readers form their own conceptions. (This attitude of mine may stem from the days when I was a boy and my mother read Dickens to me. She read from heavy volumes of an edition set two columns to the page in six point. There were sketches of the characters. None of them ever looked remotely like the people I had learned to know so intimately from Dickens' words.)

So Inspector Heimrich is a big man who thinks he looks like a hippopotomas; Lieutenant Shapiro is tall and thin. He wears gray suits which need pressing and has a long sad face. Readers can take it from there.

They have taken Pam North a good many places. Nobody ever seemed to care much about what Jerry looked like. When the collection of North stories was published in England, the publishers decided they needed to be sketched as chapter headings. Pam was matronly; Jerry smoked a pipe. Neither was in the least what I had, vaguely, imagined.

I suppose I had thought, insofar as I thought of it at all, that Pam was small and quick and blonde. I had no quarrel with the casting of her in either the play or the television series. Either Peggy Conklin in the play or Barbara Britton in the television series was all right with me. (During rehearsals of Owen Davis' play, Miss Conklin used to crouch in the wings, for all the world like a runner preparing for the hundred-yard dash, and make her entrances at a runner's speed—which was, to my mind, entirely appropriate.) Gracie Allen, in the movie, seemed to me a triumph of miscasting.

Pam's mind is another matter. It seemed to me to glint. Its logic was darting, now and then bewildering, but always acute. The female mind is often like that. Owen Davis once told me that Pam North was what every well-married man likes to think his wife is.

I have been most lucky to be twice married to women with minds like that, which is obviously more than any man deserves. Men plod their ways on paths of logic, and laboriously reach conclusions to find women sitting on them, patient as they wait for the laggards.

Men like to call this superior mental alacrity "womanly intuition."

MICHAEL SHAYNE

By BRETT HALLIDAY

Private detective stories traditionally involve tough guys who aren't afraid to use their guns or their fists, who spend most of their time drinking and sexing, and who are more often than not steeped deeply in the cauldron of cynicism. Mike Shayne, the big red-head with the fists of a Paul Bunyan, breaks that stereotypical mold. Although he uses his fists in virtually every one of his more than sixty cases, he seldom uses his gun, and most often uses his brain. A strong partiality to cognac is a trifle unusual for a breed that generally prefers whiskey, but it somehow seems to fit the good-humored Shayne. Where did Brett Halliday get the idea for such a character?

I first saw the man I have named

Michael Shayne in Tampico, Mexico many, many years ago. I was a mere lad working on a coastwise oil tanker as a deckhand when we tied up at Tampico to take on a load of crude oil. After supper a small group of sailors went ashore to see the sights of a foreign port. I was among that group.

We didn't get very far from the ship, turning in at the first *cantina* we came to. We were all lined up at the bar sampling their *tequila* when I noticed a redheaded American seated alone at a small table overlooking the crowded room with a bottle of cognac, a small shot-glass, and a larger glass of ice water on the table in front of him. He was tall and rangy and had craggy features with bleak gray eyes which surveyed the scene with a sort of quizzical amusement. He appeared to be in his early twenties, and while I watched him he lifted the shot-glass to his mouth and took a small sip of cognac, washing it down with a swallow of ice water.

I don't know what caused me to observe him so closely. Perhaps there was a quality of aloneness about him in that crowded *cantina*. He was a part of the scene, but apart from it. There was a Mexican playing an accordion in the middle of the room and several couples were dancing. There were gaily dressed *senoritas* seated about on the sidelines, and some of the sailors went to them to request a dance.

I don't know what started the fracas. Possibly one of the sailors asked the wrong girl for a dance. Suddenly there was a melee which quickly spread to encompass the small room. There were curses and shouts and the glitter of exposed knives. We were badly outnumbered and getting much the worst of the fight when suddenly out of the corner of my eye I saw the redheaded American shove the table away from him and get into the fight with big fists swinging.

Each time he struck, a Mexican went down—and generally stayed down. I was struck over the head by a beer bottle and was trampled on by the fighting men. I must have lost consciousness for a moment because I was abruptly conscious that the fight had subsided and I was lying in the middle of a tangle of bodies with blood streaming down my face from a broken head. Then I was dragged out of the tangle and set on my feet by the American redhead. He gave me a shove through the swinging doors and I stumbled and went down, to be picked up by my comrades who were streaming out the door behind me.

We got away from there fast, back to the ship where we patched up broken heads and minor knife cuts.

We went to sea the next morning and none of us knew what happened to the redhead after we left the *cantina*.

I didn't see him again until many years later in New Orleans. I had quit the sea as a means of livelihood and was barely eking out a precarious living by writing circulating library novels.

I stopped by a smoke-filled bar in the French Quarter for a drink and I glanced back over the rest of the room as I ordered a drink at the bar.

There I saw him! Sitting alone at a booth halfway down the room with a shot-glass and a larger glass of ice water before him.

There could be no question that it was he, several years older and with broader shoulders than I remembered but with the same look of aloneness in his bleak gray eyes.

I paid for my drink and carried it back to his booth with me. He looked puzzled when I slid into the booth opposite him, and I quickly reminded him of the fight on the Tampico waterfront and told him I was the sailor whom he had dragged out of the fight and shoved outdoors.

A wide grin came over his face and he started to say something when a sudden chill came over his features. He was looking past me at the front door and I turned my head to see what he was seeing.

Two men had entered the bar and were making their way toward us. He tossed off his cognac and slid out of the booth as they stopped beside us. He said harshly to me, "Stay here," and started down the aisle with one burly man leading the way and the other following close behind. They disappeared in the French Quarter, and I've never seen him again.

But I have never forgotten him.

Years later when I decided to try my hand at a mystery novel, there was never any question as to who my hero would be. I gave him the name of Michael Shayne because it seemed to fit somehow, and wrote *Dividend on Death* and began sending it out to publishers and getting it back with a rejection slip.

All and all, it was rejected by twenty-two publishers before I gave up on it and laid it aside on a shelf.

In the meantime I had written another mystery novel under the pseudonym of Asa Baker. It was titled *Mum's the Word for Murder* and was written in the first person, laid in El Paso. It was rejected by only seventeen publishers before Frederick Stokes brought it out.

Then came one of those coincidences that do occur in real life. Soon after *Mum's the Word for Murder* was published I was visited by a salesman from Stokes who had my book in stock. He was accompanied to Denver, where I was then living, by a salesman from Henry Holt and Company (one of the few publishers who had not had the opportunity to reject *Dividend on Death*). I invited the two of them out to my home for dinner that night, and during the course of a mildly alcoholic evening I was congratulated by both of them on *Mum's the Word for Murder*.

I thanked them but told them I had a much better mystery written and laid away after twenty-two rejections. The Holt salesman told me that Henry Holt was just starting a new mystery line and suggested that I send *Dividend on Death* to them. I did so, and Bill Sloane (then editor of Henry

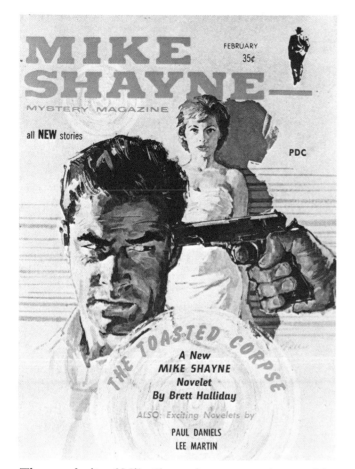

The popularity of Mike Shayne has generated a monthly mystery magazine.

Holt) liked it and sent me a contract.

Thus, Michael Shayne was finally launched.

I had not thought of it as the first of a series when I wrote it, but Bill Sloane wrote and asked me for a second book using the same set of characters, and I did *The Private Practice of Michael Shayne.*

The first book had been the story of Phyllis Brighton, a very young and very lovely girl who was accused of murdering her mother. She fell in love with Shayne during the course of the book and tried to make love to him as it ended. Shayne was many years older than she, and he patted her paternally on the shoulder and advised her to come back after she had grown up.

I used her as a subsidiary character in the second book, and they were engaged to be married as the book ended.

Twentieth Century-Fox bought

The Private Practice of Michael Shayne as a movie to star Lloyd Nolan and gave me a contract for a series of movies starring Nolan as Shayne. For this they paid me a certain fee for each picture starring Shayne, promising me an additional sum for each book of mine used in the series.

But they didn't use any of my stories in the movies. Instead, they went out and bought books from my competitors, changing the name of the lead character to Michael Shayne. I was surprised and chagrined by this because I thought my books were as good or better than the ones they bought from others, and I was losing a substantial sum of money each time they made a picture. I finally inquired as to the reason and was told it was because Shayne and Phyllis were married and it was against their policy to use a married detective.

Faced with this fact of life, I decided to kill off Phyllis to leave

Shayne a free man for succeeding movies. This I did between *Murder Wears a Mummer's Mask* and *Blood on the Black Market* (later reprinted in soft cover as *Heads You Lose*). I had her die in childbirth between the two books, but alas! Fox decided to drop the series of movies before *Blood on the Black Market* was published, and the death of Phyllis had been in vain.

With the movies no longer a factor, in my next book, *Michael Shayne's Long Chance,* I took Shayne on a case to New Orleans where he met Lucile Hamilton, and she took the place of Phyllis as a female companion. I brought her back to Miami with Shayne as his secretary, and in that position she has remained since.

I don't know exactly what the situation is between Shayne and Lucy Hamilton. They are good comrades, and she works with him in most of his cases, but I don't think Shayne will ever marry again. He often takes Lucy out to dinner and stops by her apartment for a drink and to talk, and she always keeps a bottle of his special cognac on hand.

He has only one real friend in Miami—Timothy Rourke, crime reporter on one of the Miami papers. Rourke is tall, lean, and slightly disheveled-appearing, a boon drinking companion for Shayne. He accompanies Shayne on most of his cases, hoping to get an exclusive story after the case is ended. Shayne is also on good terms with Will Gentry, Miami's chief of police. Gentry likes and admires Shayne, and is inclined to look the other way when Shayne oversteps the strict letter of the law in solving a case. On the other hand, Shayne's sworn enemy is Peter Painter, chief of detectives of Miami Beach, across Biscayne Bay from Miami. They have had numerous clashes when a case takes Shayne into Painter's territory, from which Painter always emerges as second-best.

I know nothing whatever about Shayne's background. As far as I am concerned he came into being in Tampico, Mexico some forty years ago. I don't know where or when he was born, what sort of childhood and upbringing he had. It is my impression that he is not a college man, although he is well educated, has a good vocabulary and is articulate on a variety of subjects.

He has no special or esoteric knowledge to help him solve his cases. A reader can identify with him because he is an ordinary guy like the reader himself. He solves his cases by using plain common sense, a lot of perseverance, and absolute fearlessness. When confronted with a problem, he assesses it from a practical viewpoint, following out each lead doggedly until coming up against a stone wall, then dropping that lead and following up the next one until it peters out. He seldom carries a gun, trusting to his fists to get him out of any trouble he gets into. As a result he has taken some bad beatings as he goes along, thrusting himself into danger.

In several of my books I have mentioned that Shayne was an operative for a large detective agency before setting up in Miami on his own, and as a result he has friends in different cities throughout the country on whom he can call for information or help if a case requires it. He is well known and trusted by the criminals in Miami who respect his close-mouthed integrity and are willing to pass on information not available to the police. He depends on no special gadgets or devices such as those James Bond uses, depending on his fists and an occasional hand-gun to carry him through.

On all of his cases, I try to give the reader exactly the same facts and information as Shayne possesses at any one time.

That just about sums up Michael Shayne as he has been depicted in sixty-odd books.

VIRGIL TIBBS

By JOHN BALL

In the Heat of the Night *won the Edgar Allan Poe Award of the Mystery Writers of America as the best first novel of the year in 1965. It subsequently became the first of three popular motion pictures starring Sidney Poitier as the quiet, determined detective on the Pasadena, California, police force. John Ball recounts his adventures, often to the embarrassment of the modest homicide expert. While it is often difficult to get personal information from one as self-effacing as Mr. Tibbs, his close friend, John Ball, has managed to do it. Here, he recreates the circumstances:*

Mrs. Diane Stone, secretary to Chief Robert McGowan of the Pasadena Police Department, was on the phone. "The chief has approved the release to you of the details concerning the Morales murder," she told me. "He has authorized you to go ahead with it at any time, if you want to."

Of course I wanted to: the unraveling of the case via the patient, intelligent investigation work of the department in general, and Virgil Tibbs in particular, would need no embellishment in the telling. As I always do in such instances, I called Virgil and suggested a meeting. Two nights later we sat down to dine together in one of Pasadena's very fine restaurants.

The atmosphere was conducive to the conversation despite the fact that the lights were so dim the menus should have been offered in braille. By the time that the main course had been put in front of us we had gone over the Morales case in detail and Virgil had filled me in on several points which had not previously been made public. As always, I agreed to publish nothing until the department had read the manuscript and had given it an official approval. This procedure helped to eliminate possible errors and also ensured the department that no confidential information was included.

"When did you first know that it was murder?" I asked.

"When I found that the TV set was tuned to the wrong channel," Tibbs

John Ball

answered. "The UCLA basketball game had been on at the time of Morales's death. That appeared all right on the surface, but when I checked on the point, I learned that he had no interest at all in basketball and didn't understand the game. A show that he was known to watch regularly was on another channel at the same time, so something was obviously wrong."

The waitress brought iced tea and I stirred my glass. "I have a letter from Otto Penzler," I said.

Virgil nodded recognition. "The co-author with Chris Steinbrunner of the *Encyclopedia of Mystery and Detection*? I have a copy."

"Otto has asked me for a piece about your background. How much may I tell him?"

I should insert a footnote here. Virgil Tibbs is a basically quiet, sometimes almost self-effacing man. He is genuinely modest. He has mentioned to me more than once that my ac-

counts of some of his cases have proven somewhat embarrassing to him. However, Chief McGowan feels that these books help to explain the police function to the citizenry at large and to show how modern, enlightened police departments function. The outcome of that difference of opinion is predictable.

"I know that you have McGowan behind you on this," Tibbs said. "Otherwise I'd ask you to drop it, our personal friendship aside. All right: I was born in the Deep South as you know. I was about five, as I recall, when my father sat down with me and on a fine spring afternoon explained that we were Negroes and therefore I could expect to face prejudice, dislike, distrust, and even hatred during all of my life. It was the greatest shock I have ever known; I lay awake all that night wondering why God had made me different when I hadn't asked Him to. When I finally got con-

trol of myself, I began to understand some things I had already noticed.

"Then dad had another talk with me. He explained that things were getting better, slowly but definitely. His great hope for me was that I would have some opportunities, particularly in education, that had been denied to him. He spoke of Dr. Carver, Walter White, John Hammond, and other influential people who were helping. This is before Ralph Bunche and Martin Luther King became prominent, of course."

The attractive waitress came and refilled Virgil's coffee cup. Her pleasant manner attested that times had indeed changed, and for her as well: she was Korean-American.

"When I was about seventeen," Virgil continued, "one of my friends was murdered—because of his color. When that happened I didn't rant and rave, but I did feel a terrible determination. I made up my mind that if I ever could, I would try to do what I could to stop such senseless violence and to deal with those who were responsible for it."

"You certainly accomplished that," I noted. "You've already taken a number of murderers out of circulation. Not to mention drug dealers and the like. But please go on."

Tibbs ate a little before he continued. I knew that I was putting him over the hurdles, exhuming some painful memories in his mind.

"I came to California and managed to get into the university. I worked my way through, washing dishes, doing some janitor work, shampooing cars, and whatever else I could find. I took up social sciences principally, and other subjects that might prepare me for my goal. I wanted to be a policeman."

As he ate a little more, I paid attention to my own plate and said nothing. I knew that he would continue when he was ready.

"When I was still a freshman I was worried that I wouldn't be able to make the weight requirements; I was quite thin. One day some members of

In the Heat of the Night. Sidney Poitier as Virgil Tibbs
with Rod Steiger in the background.

the All-America Karate Federation
gave a demonstration on campus. I
was tremendously impressed and
went down to see about lessons. I had
very little extra money and wanted
to find out if I could work out my
tuition in some way. John, I think
that was the first time in my life that
I met a group of people, talked with
them, and was never conscious of the
fact that we had different ethnic origins. Most of them were Japanese, of
course, and they understood. They
gave me a scholarship. Two years later
I was chosen for a special class; it was

taught at first by George Takahashi,
then, later, by Master Nishiyama himself. You know his standing."

"The best in the world," I commented.

"Believe it," Tibbs said. "What he
did to us I don't think I could live
through again, but I reached the
brown belt level and went into competition under his direction. The art
suited me; physically and mentally I
responded to its disciplines and the
things that we were taught. Nine years
after the first day that I walked in,
Nishiyama gave me my black belt.

"That's about it, John. I graduated,
took my degree, and then looked for a
police department where a Negro ap-
plicant would be acceptable. Pasadena was having an examination and
I took it."

The girl came again, charmed us
both with a smile, and took away the
dinner plates. Virgil had some more
coffee.

"Is that enough?" he asked me.

"Yes," I answered. "The rest is
pretty well known."

"One thing," Virgil added. "You
can put this in for me, if you want to.

If people want to call me black I don't mind, but I prefer something else. My first choice is to have my origins ignored and within the department, that's the way that it is. I don't like the idea of sorting people out by colors; if I called Jim Lonetree 'red,' he'd probably slug me. And if anybody called my partner, Bob Nakamura, 'yellow,' I'd resent it very much. If I have to be classified, then call me a Negro. It's a dignified, proud word—my father taught me that."

I signaled for the check. "Thank you," I said. "I'll pass this on to Otto, and let him take it from there."

We stopped together on the parking lot outside before we said good night. Tibbs looked around him, taking in the pinpointed sky overhead and then the clusters of vehicles that were parked in orderly rows. As he did so I looked at my friend again. Still in his thirties, five feet nine, weight not a great deal over a hundred and sixty. Although I was dressed informally, he had on a subdued Italian silk suit and a tie that

had come from one of the best shops. Despite his dark complexion, his features were aquiline in their molding; his nose was straight and well defined, his lips were slightly on the thin side. At one time I had suspected that his heritage might be mixed, but he had denied that. He had known all four of his grandparents and there had been no question of their origins.

"There's something I wish you would put into your story," he said, breaking the silence. "So many people overlook it. Police work is a team effort, from relatively simple matters up to major investigations. We don't have any room for prima donnas, and none of us work in a vacuum.

"It's a ceaseless war that we're engaged in, and some of the people we fight for, and take our chances for in some pretty dangerous situations, hate our guts in return for what we do."

"I know it," I said.

We shook hands and parted, leaving in our respective cars. I hit the west-bound freeway and headed back for Encino.

Fifteen minutes out of Pasadena I tuned the radio to the all-news station to find out what, if anything, was going on. Or, more properly, what was going on that had been made public. The two are seldom if ever the same. After a few minutes the announcer broke into the steady flow of his edited copy to air something that had just come in. A body had been found in an alley in the western section of Pasadena, where most of the thrift shops were congregated.

I was going home for what remained of an essentially quiet evening. The body could be an OD, an alcohol pass-out, or even natural causes. But there was, of course, the possibility of foul play, a very old and time-worn expression that could be compressed into the single fatal word *murder*.

Before long I would be comfortable and deep in the pages of a good book. Virgil Tibbs might not have that privilege, much as I knew he would value it. If indeed it was murder, then in all probability he was already back at work.

THE SHADOW

By MAXWELL GRANT

"Who knows what evil lurks in the hearts of men? The Shadow knows!"

No lines in the history of radio are more recognizable than those. And no character chilled the bones of evildoers more thoroughly than The Shadow. The phantom crimefighter appeared in more than 300 pulp magazine novels, of which 283 were written by a single man during a stretch of more than fifteen years. During that time, Walter B. Gibson, using the Street & Smith house name of Maxwell Grant, wrote more than a million words a year about The Shadow. During those golden years of

pulp fiction, several hundred pulp characters battled crime. The Shadow towered above them all. Why? Walter B. Gibson tells the store here:

If ever a mystery character created himself in his own image, that character was The Shadow. From a nebulous nothing he materialized into a substantial something, then merged with enshrouding darkness like a figment of the night itself—terms that were to be used to describe his comings and goings in some 300 novels that were dedicated exclusively to his adventures over a span of more than

fifteen consecutive years.

To say that The Shadow sprang spontaneously into being would be putting it not only mildly, but exactly. As a factual writer with an eye toward fiction, I had been thinking in terms of a mysterious personage who would inject himself into the affairs of lesser folk, aiding friends who would do his bidding and balking foemen who tried to thwart his aims. So when I learned that an editor was looking for a writer to do a story about a so-far undefined character to be known as The Shadow, it marked a meeting of the minds.

From then on The Shadow took over, both in a literal and a literary sense. In order to assure his own evolution and give it plausibility, The Shadow needed an amanuensis to transcribe his annals into a palatable, popular form. That, of course, demanded The Shadow's own official sanction, hence the opening paragraph was attributed to the leading character himself. It ran:

This is to certify that I have made careful examination of the manuscript known as The Living Shadow as set down by Mr. Maxwell Grant, my raconteur, and do find it a true account of my activities upon that occasion. I have therefore arranged that Mr. Grant shall have exclusive privilege to such further of my exploits as may be considered of interest to the American public.

THE SHADOW

With such a send-off the story just couldn't miss. As Maxwell Grant, a pen name which was concocted for use with The Shadow stories only, I was ostensibly under The Shadow's orders as much as the agents who obeyed his bidding or as well as the hapless victims of conniving criminals whom only The Shadow could rescue from the brink of doom. Even the title of the first story, "The Living Shadow," established The Shadow as an actual personage and the central theme in the minds of avidly susceptible readers. The titles of the next two novels, "The Eyes of The Shadow" and "The Shadow Laughs," continued the same motif.

In those early stories The Shadow moved in and out of the affairs of friend and foe, not only as a cloaked figure but as a master of disguise who could adopt various personalities, even doubling as a crook in order to confuse other criminals. Actually there was nothing that The Shadow couldn't do, which made it all the easier to describe the things he did do. From those he developed not only his own personality but his own background. Whatever he had to have, he saw to it that he had it and Maxwell Grant said so.

Early in the game it became evident that The Shadow, whoever he was, needed a million dollars or more to knock down criminals who were thriving during the depression. So he identified himself as a wealthy resident of suburban New Jersey answering to the name of Lamont Cranston. Then, when even Maxwell Grant was convinced that The Shadow had disclosed his actual identity, it turned out that he was simply doubling for Lamont Cranston when the millionaire was taking extended trips abroad. By switching from Cranston to other identities, including his cloaked self, he continually kept enemies off his trail.

This, however, could cause complications whenever Cranston returned home, but The Shadow offset those by switching to the personality of George Clarendon, a man-about-town whose favorite habitat was Manhattan's exclusive Cobalt Club. He played that role long enough to lure crooks along a false trail from which he vanished, never to reappear as Clarendon. Until then The Shadow had often visited police headquarters, doubling for a dull-mannered janitor named Fritz, in order to listen in on the reports of Joe Cardona, an ace detective. But with Clarendon permanently gone from the Cobalt Club, Cranston was free to appear there and cultivate the acquaintance of Police Commissioner Weston, a regular member, who frequently summoned Joe Cardona to confer on crime developments after the ace detective had been promoted to inspector.

Meanwhile The Shadow conducted his own investigations in the seclusion of a black-walled room that served as his sanctum. Under the glow of a bluish light, his hands opened reports from agents and inscribed orders that they were to follow. His identifying token, a scintillating girasol, or fire opal, gleamed from the third finger of his left hand, flashing rays that exerted a hypnotic effect upon many persons whom he encountered while on the rove.

One analyst who read The Shadow novels closely came up with the opinion that the somber, eerie, isolated atmosphere of the sanctum undoubtedly aided The Shadow in reasoning out his brilliant deductions and battle plans with no fear of secret watchers who might attack him. This analysis was dated back to The Shadow's role as a spy in World War I when, as an American air ace called the Dark Eagle, he pretended to be shot down over Germany and using disguises by day and black garb at night he worked his way back to the Allied lines, releasing many prisoners and guiding them along the route to safety.

From this the analyst assumed that The Shadow "had to work out his plans in out of the way places or at night; and the constant fear of being seen or found out no doubt left a major impact on his way of thinking or manner of working." Hence The Shadow's need for a secure sanctum when he returned to the United States and decided to combat the postwar crime wave that was rampant there.

Actually this shows the remarkable impact that The Shadow, through Maxwell Grant, had upon the constant readers of his chronicles. Among the millions of words devoted to his current adventures there were probably only several hundred referring directly to his earlier career. Those formed a separate section of The Shadow's archives, to which Maxwell Grant had only occasional access; hence analytical readers were forced to form their own theories. But in this instance it went wide on two counts.

First, The Shadow had recourse to his sanctum only when operating within range of his fixed base in Manhattan; never when adventures carried him far afield. Again in none of his numerous adventures was the word "fear" ever applied personally to The Shadow; indeed he could be well described as totally unemotional throughout. It was The Shadow's

Is it Lamont Cranston staring from the jacket of *The Living Shadow?*

utter impassivity that won him loyal agents who supported him in his campaigns against crime. As his forays expanded The Shadow came into conflict with formidable antagonists whose own cryptic identities became titles for the stories in which most of them met their deserved doom, notably, "The Silent Seven," "The Black Master," "The Crime Cult," "The Blackmail Ring," "The Ghost Makers," "Kings of Crime," and "Six Men of Evil."

These involved spy rings, murder cults, mad scientists, and haunted houses, which in turn brought new agents and specialists into The Shadow's fold. At times The Shadow's exploits became topical: when New York police were baffled by a real-life terrorist who signed himself "Three X," The Shadow met and conquered his fictional counterpart in the form of "Double Z." These themes could prove prophetic, too: "The Black Hush" foreshadowed New York City's "blackout" by thirty years, while another novel, "The Star of Delhi," called the turn on a jewel robbery that occurred two decades later.

Most important, however, were the supervillains who developed during The Shadow's saga. The mere turning of "shadow into substance" produced new prospects, most notably a parade of intermittent rivals, such as the Cobra, the Python, the Condor, the Green Hoods, the Hydra, and the Voodoo Master. During most of this expansive period, which included a total of 125 novels written during a six-year period, The Shadow so identified himself as Lamont Cranston that their personalities virtually merged. This gradually lessened the value of other identities that The Shadow assumed whenever occasion demanded, but when matters neared a crux, he was ready with the answer.

In a novel titled "The Shadow Unmasks," the real Lamont Cranston was injured in a British air crash, forcing The Shadow to revert to his real self, that of an aviator named Kent Allard who had disappeared in a flight over the Guatemalan jungle years before. The Shadow took off secretly for Yucatan and emerged from the wilds with two bodyguards from a tribe of Xinca Indians who had presumably worshipped him as a "bird god" during those lost years, though actually he had been combatting crime as The Shadow all that while.

In due course The Shadow reverted to the Cranston guise but occasionally switched to Allard, one advantage being that he could team with the real Cranston, who by now was familiar with The Shadow's ways and always willing to go along with them. The Shadow reverted more and more to the Cranston role, so that Allard became almost forgotten, except on rare occasions when his identity could prove helpful in diverting crooks from Cranston's trail. In the opinion of some readers The Shadow apparently "felt more comfortable when he was Cranston," but perhaps it was the readers who felt that way. Whichever the case, it worked out as intended.

This tied in with the initial concept of The Shadow, a feature which was preserved throughout the series. Always his traits and purposes were defined through the observations or reactions of persons with whom he came in contact, which meant that the reader formed his opinion from theirs. Since The Shadow's motto was "Crime does not pay," that convinced the readers—like The Shadow's own agents—that he could do no wrong. That in simpler terms meant that although he might be misinformed or unaware of certain circumstances, he never made mistakes. By the old rule "What is sauce for the goose is sauce for the gander," whatever applied to the reader applied to the writer. It was up to Maxwell Grant to maintain The Shadow's image constantly in mind and portray it faithfully and consistently.

Thanks to the frequency with which the novels appeared—twice a month for ten consecutive years!—the reactions of readers were both rapid and frequent, thereby serving as guidelines for future novels. Many stories involved a "proxy hero," whose fate was a bone of contention between The Shadow and the villains with whom he was currently concerned. Therefore no fixed style of writing was required, since the "proxy" rather than The Shadow was temporarily the central character. Keen analysts have classified The Shadow novels in three patterns—the "classic," the "thriller," and the "hard-boiled"—and these frequently could be used in combination, producing a diversity of types which kept up the tempo and sustained reader interest through a constant expectancy that usually resulted in the unexpected.

This gave The Shadow a marked advantage over mystery characters who were forced to maintain fixed patterns; and that, in turn, made it easy to write about him. There was never need for lengthy debate regarding what The Shadow should do next, or what course he should follow to keep in character. He could meet any exigency on the spur of the moment, and if he suddenly acted in a manner totally opposed to his usual custom, it could always be explained later by The Shadow himself, through the facile pen of Maxwell Grant.

A noteworthy example was the question of The Shadow's girasol. It was constantly described as "a magnificent fire opal, unmatched in all the world," and in an early novel The Shadow stated that it had come from a collection of rare gems long owned by the Russian czars. In a later novel this was countered by a claim that the girasol was the eye of a Xinca idol given to The Shadow when he landed in the jungle as Kent Allard. Serious-minded readers were prompt to point out the discrepancy in these conflicting tales, but the answer was readily found by a search of The Shadow's archives.

Fire opals are found only in Mexico and since an idol normally has two eyes, it was obvious that one could have been stolen, thus finding its way into the czarist collection from which The Shadow obtained it. Arriving in Yucatan as Allard, the Shadow, by showing the mate to the remaining eye, naturally won the loyalty of the Xinca tribe and was given the idol's left-over eye. So he actually had *two* girasols, each "unmatched" as it is practically impossible to find two opals that are exactly the same. Hence each story was correct, according to which girasol The Shadow happened to be wearing at the time.

The Shadow's very versatility opened a vast vista of story prospects from the start of the series onward. In the earlier stories he was described as a "phantom," an "avenger," and a "superman," so he could play any such parts and still be quite in character. In fact, all three of those terms were borrowed by other writers to serve as titles for other characters who flourished in what might aptly be styled "The Shadow Era." Almost any situation involving crime could be adapted to The Shadow's purposes, hence the novels ran the gamut from forthright "whodunit" plots to forays into the field of science fiction. The most inimitable of The Shadow's features was his laugh, which could be weird, eerie, chilling, ghostly, taunting, mocking, gibing, sinister, sardonic, trailing, fading, or triumphant.

Often, when a story ended on such a note, the very echoes of The Shadow's mirth would set up the pattern for the next novel. It might involve unfinished business, or some theme suggested during the development of the story, or a way by which surviving crooks might think they could turn the tables on the victorious master. Always, in the finishing chapter of a story, The Shadow was really on the go, so that new situations naturally sprang to mind and unfinished plots would readily crystallize. Also, from my recollections as an author, I can definitely say that at the climax of a story, the mood that I adopted when writing as Maxwell Grant was in-

Walter B. Gibson, AKA Maxwell Grant, creator of The Shadow.

variably at a peak.

The final rule was this: Put The Shadow anywhere, in any locale, among friends or associates, even in a place of absolute security and almost immediately, crime, menace, or mystery would begin to swirl about him, either threatening him personally or gathering him in its vortex to carry him off to fields where antagonists awaited. Always when The Shadow defeated some monstrous scheme he would be spurred on to tackle something bigger; while, conversely, master criminals, learning that one of their ilk had been eliminated, would logically profit by that loss and devise something more powerful to thwart The Shadow.

In the story of "The Crime Master," one supercriminal actually made all thoughts of evil profit or ill-gotten gains subordinate to his real purpose, which was to obliterate The Shadow and thus win the everlasting acclaim of crimedom. In all his well-calculated schemes of robbery and murder, he left loopholes that would enable The

Shadow to counteract the impending crime but only at the risk of putting himself in traps from which escape would prove impossible.

To set up the snares the Crime Master used a large board with hundreds of squares representing the scene of the crime-to-be, with dozens of men of various colors representing police, detectives, criminals, lookouts, and victims. When the board was all set, he added a single black piece to represent The Shadow; then from there he worked out moves and countermoves, like a chess game in reverse, since the king was already in check at the start; and the purpose was to keep him from getting out of it rather than merely adding stronger checks toward an ultimate mate.

Needless to say, The Shadow did get out. That was his forte throughout all his adventures. Always his escapes were worked out beforehand, so that they would never exceed the bounds of plausibility when detailed in narrative form. And that was the great secret of The Shadow.

Auld Lang Syne

The manuscript of the most widely known poem in the English language

By G. ROSS ROY

"Auld Lang Syne" has become the song of friendship and parting particularly in the English-speaking world, although it is also sung throughout most of Europe and in places as distant as India and Japan. The words are associated in the popular mind with Robert Burns, but there are earlier inferior versions; one of these was taken from a broadside and published by William Watson in his *Choice Collection of Comic and Serious Scots Poems* (1711). Another appeared in a work which Burns knew well, Allan Ramsay's *Tea-Table Miscellany,* an immensely popular compilation of songs which was published in four volumes between 1723 and 1737, with "Auld Lang Syne" contained in the first volume.

These earlier songs bear little resemblance to that which Burns fashioned. In fact the only elements

common to all of them are the line "Should auld acquaintance be forgot" and the expression "Auld lang Syne." The poet was somewhat vague about his knowledge of these earlier versions, claiming at one point that the work had "never been in print, nor even in manuscript, until I took it down from an old man's singing," and adding the comment to the version published here, "Light be the turf on the breast of the heaven-inspired Poet who composed this Fragment!" Elsewhere in the letter in which this comment appears Burns speaks of it as "an old song & tune which has often thrilled thro' my soul." Finally we have a comment by Burns about Ramsay's ver-

---

At right, the only copy of the poem in the hand of Robert Burns. Above, a version from Tin Pan Alley.

Auld lang Syne ———————

Should auld acquaintance be forgot,
　　And never thought upon?
Let's hae a waught o' Malaga,
　　For auld lang syne.
　　　　　Chorus
　　For auld lang syne, my jo,
　　　　For auld lang syne;
Let's hae a waught o' Malaga,
　　　　For auld lang syne. ———

And surely ye'll be your pint-stoup!
　　And surely I'll be mine!
And we'll tak a cup o' kindness yet,
　　For auld lang syne. ———
　　　　　For auld &c.

We twa hae run about the braes,
　　And pou't the gowans fine;
But we've wander'd many a weary foot
　　Sin auld lang syne. ———
　　　　　For auld &c.

We twa hae paidl't i' the burn
Frae morning-sun till dine;
But seas between us braid hae roar'd,
Sin auld lang syne. —
      For auld &c.

And there's a han', my trusty fiere,
      And gie's a han' o' thine;
And we'll tak a right gudewilly waught,
      For auld lang syne. —

    †   †   †   †   †   †   †

Light be the turf on the breast of the heaven-inspired
Poet who composed this glorious Fragment! There
is more of the fire of native genius ~~there~~ in it, than in
half a dozen of modern English Bacchanalians. —
Now I am on my Hobby-horse, I cannot help inserting
two other old Stanzas which please me mightily. —

      Go fetch to me a pint o' wine,
            And fill it in a silver tassie;
      That I may drink before I go
            A service to my bonie lassie: —

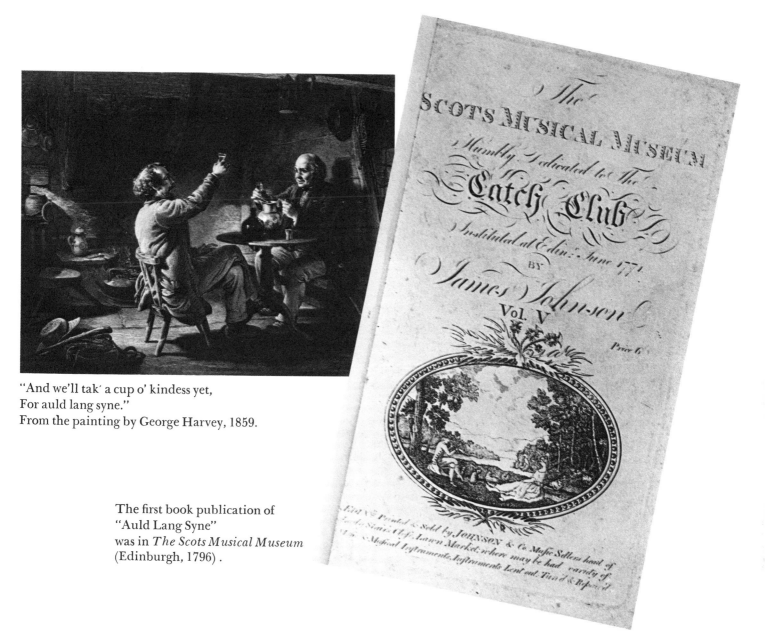

"And we'll tak' a cup o' kindess yet,
For auld lang syne."
From the painting by George Harvey, 1859.

The first book publication of
"Auld Lang Syne"
was in *The Scots Musical Museum*
(Edinburgh, 1796) .

sion of the song, "The original and by much the best set of the words of this song is as follows:" and the poet proceeds to copy his own words.

The letter in question was written December 7, 1788, to his friend Mrs. Frances Dunlop and is the earliest known MS. of the song. Although it was probably sent to James Johnson at about this time, "Auld Lang Syne" was not published until 1796 in Volume V of his *Scots Musical Museum* in slightly altered form from the present text. Burns also sent the song to George Thomson (September 1793) who published it in his *Select Collection of Original Scotish* [sic] *Airs* (1799), a series to which Burns contributed well over a hundred songs and which contained airs by Haydn and Beethoven. The tunes

printed with "Auld Lang Syne" in Johnson and Thomson are quite distinct, with the latter version now universally used. It serves today also as the tune for the national anthem of Sudan.

One of Burns's greatest achievements was as a writer of songs. He wrote new words to old airs, he wrote songs for tunes which had none, he revised and borrowed when it pleased him, leaving Scotland and the world a legacy of song almost without peer. In answer to Thomson's suggestion that he contribute to the *Select Collection* and offering to pay "any reasonable price," the poet replied that his songs would be "either *above*, or *below* price." How far above price "Auld Lang Syne" was to be even he could not have guessed.

Profile of a Book Collector:
Charles E. Feinberg

"My life would have been a desert without books."

How can anyone sum up Charles Feinberg in any few words? For the more than thirty years that I have known Charlie well, and worked with him on Walt Whitman and other aspects of collecting books, manuscripts, and letters, I have come to appreciate his genuine and ever-present enthusiasm for the materials of literature, especially American. But that's not all, for there are two other qualities: the tremendous fund of information he has at his finger tips, and the eager willingness he has to make both the published and the unpublished matter in his collection available to scholars.

Many private collectors and indeed institutions preserve and hoard their manuscripts and rare items for their favored few scholars, for their own prestige, or even for investment reasons. But Charlie Feinberg has said repeatedly to me and to others that he does not wish to compete with scholars and does not consider himself a scholar—though many who have heard him know how interestingly and vitally he writes and tells the stories about authors and their books and their writing—and that his primary reason for collecting is to make available in one place what these authors have written.

If it were not for Charles Feinberg I would never have edited the Walt Whitman Review, *which I have done for twenty-two years with his considerable help and support. I would never have edited the* Daybooks and Notebooks, *two fat volumes in the New York University Press edition of* The Collected Writings of Walt Whitman. *And I would never have written all the other books and articles and notes—based on manuscripts and printed matter in his great collection—on Whitman, Thoreau, Mark Twain, Henry James, Emerson, James Joyce, Dylan Thomas, D. H. Lawrence, Sir William Osler, Hemingway, John Ciardi, Karl Shapiro, and the others.*

However, it's not just that the books and magazines and letters and manuscripts are there in the Feinberg Collection—as they would be mute and boxed and shelved in any private collection or private library—it's that Charlie Feinberg is there, too: weekly and even daily with enthusiastic suggestions, encouraging advice and eager support for a wide variety of scholarly projects. "Why don't we do this? Why don't we do that? What do you think about this? When can we get started on that?" Thus, for someone with my own enthusiasms, interests and energy, and needing not too much in the way of suggestion and encouragement, my thirty-year relationship with such a friend has been the most important professional influence on my academic and scholarly life.

There are no figures to add up my debt to Charles E. Feinberg.

—William White

PAGES: Mr. Feinberg, no satisfactory history of American book collectors can be written without a lengthy chapter devoted to your accomplishments. Even more than your generous support of libraries here and

Charles E. Feinberg holding the copy of *American Poems* inscribed by Walt Whitman to Dr. R. M. Bucke.

abroad, your determination to build the greatest possible collection of *all* material by and about *one author* helped bring a new rationale to collecting. Your immense contribution to Whitman scholarship clearly demonstrates the essential interdependence between the collector and scholar. You've said it has been a challenging career. Mr. Feinberg, where did it all begin?

FEINBERG: I think it all began about 1910 when I was eleven years old and going to Ogden School in Toronto. We had a Miss McNaughton—that's the story of my life. Miss McNaughton was a marvelous sixth-grade (senior third in Canada) teacher, and those days, of course, the teacher taught all the subjects. This is the amazing part of it, this is where it started—eleven years old. Miss McNaughton used to read to us. She had a book called *American Poems,* published in England, I think, about 1872 by Edward Moxon. The editor was William Michael Rossetti—it meant nothing to me at that time. It included Longfellow, Whittier, Lowell, Poe, Whitman, many others; but it was dedicated to Walt Whitman, and I remember . . . I went to her and asked the meaning of the word "dedication," and she told me to look it up in the dictionary. I didn't know about dictionaries—she introduced me to them. Every Friday afternoon Miss McNaughton would include a period during which we would read poetry and a pupil would be assigned a poem to recite the following week—she once gave me such an assignment from *American Poems*. It's hard to remember why you are stopped by a word or a line or a page, but that was the beginning of my interest in Walt Whitman. We moved to Peterborough in August. There I had my first man teacher in the junior fourth, a man by the name of Neil. He played baseball with the boys after school. I could never play after school. Once in a while, I'd stay for a football game, but usually in between Hebrew lessons, because when you got through school, you had to come home to take Hebrew lessons. But the end of that school year I got a job.

PAGES: The junior fourth was your last year of formal schooling?

FEINBERG: Yes, that's right. There was this ad for a boy to work in a wallpaper shop. Wallpaper and china, and they also sold school supplies, if they got the contract. There were three school-supply stores, and this contract sort of rotated, even though they all bid—but somehow it seemed to be understood, if you didn't get it one year, you had a chance on the next. Apparently, this year they had the contract, and there was one con-

dition for the boy they hired: he wasn't to go back to school in September. I remember I came home and I told my father and mother I had a chance for this job. I think it was $2.50 a week for delivering china and wallpaper and schoolbooks. But I couldn't go back to school, and I had to give them a promise, and I had to have the consent of my parents or they wouldn't hire me. Well, there was the question. The need wasn't that great. We were never poor. We were struggling, but my father bought a house the following year or so; we never owned the land. Somebody made the decision that I would work. I used to give my mother the $2.50; she would give me back a quarter. With that quarter, I could do anything I wanted. I would come home every day for lunch; we lived just around the corner. I used to buy stamps and sell them; I used to trade. I shined shoes at night. Shines used to be a nickel for black, ten cents for brown, and we were paid a cent for the black and two cents for the brown and tips. I ran into Mr. Neil, the teacher, who wanted to know what I was doing. There was no night school. We didn't have a night school in those days . . . there was a high school, but no night school—no place where I could go to school after work. This was the terrible thing, so he wanted to know what I was doing and I told him. He said, "Well, you know there's a public library." I didn't know anything about libraries, so he took me down to the public library. Andrew Carnegie had given $3,000 to the town, and they opened this place over the marketplace. Neil used to guide my reading. When the question of who was going to be responsible for me was asked, he spoke up. He said, "Well, the boy has got a father; his father will sign. But I'll sign, let him take out the first books." I got to the point where I could take three books home at a time.

PAGES: What kind of books did you read?

FEINBERG: Neil started me on biography. One of the biographies that existed, I think, in every public library in Canada was Dr. R. M. Bucke's biography of Walt Whitman. It hadn't sold, and Bucke had hundreds of copies left. I think he gave copies to every public and university library in Canada because we had two copies in Peterborough. I remembered the name Walt Whitman because of the poetry that Miss McNaughton had read to us, and I remembered my question on the dedication. It was one of the books I took home, and since Bucke was a Canadian, I suppose that influenced me. I think I read it twice, and I re-

Charles Feinberg at 15½;
Peterborough, Ontario, 1915.

member saying to the librarian, "Where do I find a book of poems?" I don't recall whether they had a book or they got it for me, but they produced *American Poems*. Later I bought a copy of the book; it cost me ten cents.

PAGES: How did you go about buying books in those days?

FEINBERG: I got it one day when I was taking back some paperbacks to the second-hand dealer, who by that time knew me well enough to call me by my first name; he knew my father. He used to trade with my father. Well, he had wash boilers full of these books, and while I was looking through them, he comes along with this book of poems. He said, "You once asked for a book of poetry. It will cost you a dime, but if you don't like it, I'll give you your whole dime back." Well, in any event, when I bought my first copy of *American Poems* I couldn't have been much more than thirteen. The second-hand store used to sell boys' books—Frank Merriwell and Dick Merriwell, Horatio Alger—and they were in paperback mostly. He sold them for a nickel. You brought them back, you got a three-cent trade-in, so for two cents you got another book. You could buy a lot for a nickel—a movie, a dish of ice cream, a large chocolate bar with nuts in it, a *Saturday Evening Post*.

PAGES: Was your purchase of *American Poems* the beginning of your Whitman Collection?

FEINBERG: I still have the copy I bought for a dime, my first Whitman volume. Well, actually it isn't Whitman, it's merely dedicated to Whitman. I didn't start out to be a Whitman collector. I had no idea of being a collector. I didn't know what a collector meant.

PAGES: But isn't it important that you were to preserve that copy, that you kept it?

FEINBERG: My mother kept it, along with other books that I bought when I was quite young.

PAGES: What other books did you buy?

FEINBERG: Books I was reading trying to improve my mind. Biography, I still have the copy of the *Life of Lord Strathcona*. I have other books of that type. I was always trying to get an education, you see.

PAGES: How were you really hooked on Whitman, how did it happen to you, or did you do it to yourself?

FEINBERG: I was seventeen when the family moved back to Toronto. I had registered for the war and was waiting to be called and assigned. No firm wanted to hire you on such a temporary basis, but I finally got a job. I continued to pick up books by Whitman, and in Britnell's Book Store on Yonge Street there I found a first edition of *Good-Bye My Fancy,* with the signature of Professor James Mavor. Mavor had been a professor of economics at the University of Toronto and a great friend of Dr. Bucke. And wherever Dr. Bucke went in the academic world they had Whitman books. Bucke was one of the three Whitman literary executors and disposed of his share of what remained of unsold new books in Whitman's study at the time he died in 1892. Bucke used to advertise Whitman books and sell them to friends or people that he knew or strangers. *Good-Bye My Fancy, November Boughs,* and an 1876 edition of *Leaves of Grass* were sold, and there are grandchildren of Bucke who still have copies of the 1876 Centennial Edition with the unsigned title page—that's because Whitman would never sign a title page until he sold the book. I came into Britnell's a few times and one day they asked me if I would be interested in a Whitman letter. They brought out a letter, and I bought it. I just had my pay. I was making $22.50 at

The *Memorbuch* of the Jewish Community of Frankfurt, buried by the last
rabbi of Frankfurt. Presented to the Hebrew University by Charles Feinberg.

the time clerking, and they asked me $7.50. What was
important was not that it was a third of my pay. It was
the emotional impact. There was nothing in my background that readied me to understand or to compre-
hend that this was the paper that Whitman had held
in his hands, these were the words that he had written.
It didn't matter that the letter may not have been important, I don't think it was more than "Dear Sirs," or
an acknowledgment. It was only a one-page letter, but
it was a very emotional thing to me, nothing had prepared me for it. I don't know why . . . it hadn't occurred to me to visualize that a writer was a living human
being who wrote the same as I did, who used a pen
the same as I would. Then I had to explain it to my
mother who found it very difficult to understand why
I had paid $7.50 for the letter. This letter had been
written by a stranger who had written a book that I
seemed to think was tremendously important, but she
accepted it. About 1923 I had a job offer in the United
States, and I came to Detroit—I was the first one in my

family to come to the United States. I got a job in a
shoe store.

PAGES: Could you buy books in Detroit in 1923, the
kind you were looking for?

FEINBERG: Oh, yes, oh, yes. B. C. Claes worked for a
man down at the foot of Woodward who was the mean-
est person I ever knew in the book business, where
there aren't many unpleasant people. He should never
have been a bookman. He used to have some first editions locked in a display case, and I would say I wanted
to look at them. What was his name? Had it on the
tip of my tongue a moment ago. Higgins. Higgins'
Book Shop right near Jefferson Avenue. But I got to
know Claes very well. He was a nice, friendly Dutch-
man, and he loved books. He loved them. Higgins
wouldn't unlock the case. He said, "Are you going to
buy them?" I would say, "Let me look at them." "Not
if you're not going to buy them." An impasse. I had
a hard time with him, but Claes was very friendly, and

he would show me the books when Higgins wasn't around. Claes had to go to the hospital, and when he got out of the hospital, Higgins wouldn't hire him back. In any event, Claes, who had started to sell books from his home, got in touch with me. He could find books. Later on I underwrote his first trip to Chicago by giving him a number of bids when he went to an auction sale of a newspaperman by the name of Clyde Beck in the early thirties, and my only condition was that he give me first choice of whatever he bought with no stipulation as to price, no percentage. Claes could set his own price, but I was to have first refusal. Claes was always a good bookman. Claes was the kind of a dealer who bought a book for two dollars that he knew was worth five dollars, but he would sell it for three dollars. He made a profit, turned his money over very quickly. That was one place where I bought books and still do. Another place used to have an upstairs sales table, Sheehan's Book Shop. John Sheehan's Book Shop was in the fifteen hundred block on Woodward where the Eaton Tower is.

PAGES: Were rare books expensive in those days? Where did you get the money to buy books?

FEINBERG: I was working at the Regal Shoe Store. I started as an assistant manager and window dresser. I was always good at windows. If it came to a choice between a book and lunch—for the cost of lunch, you could have a banana and a cup of coffee and buy a book. I was a regular frequenter of the bookstores—I lived there and evenings at the Main Public Library. They had a poetry room on the second floor, just a nook really, with easy chairs. Small but very satisfying.

PAGES: When did you know you were a serious Whitman collector?

FEINBERG: I don't think I ever knew I was a collector until Dick Sessler, the Philadelphia dealer, once walked into my home in the thirties, took a look at the shelves, first time he'd ever been to my home, and said, "I didn't know you were a Whitman collector." I said, "I'm not." He said, "Look what you have on Whitman." I said, "I'm not a collector." A collector to me had meant somebody possibly a little wealthier —oh, I would have placed it more on a level with well-to-do people. You see, what I think I'm emotionally touched by is the remembrance of my obsession for reading. And I suppose it's not understood by young people: the necessity for reading, the obsession with reading, because of the lack of formal education. It's

a thing you've got to do, not when you have nothing else to do, but the thing you've got to do, to find time to do no matter what else you're doing for a living. There's a tremendous difference.

PAGES: Well, then, what makes a serious collector?

FEINBERG: I think dealers, of course, helped tremendously, and this is why I laugh at all of this business of people buying, or being advised to collect an author or to buy a manuscript because the price is going up or because it might turn out to be a good investment. I've even heard some foolish people say, "Well, I included it in my investment portfolio." How can anybody buy something like that and include it in an investment portfolio? They didn't buy it because they were interested.

I remember this fellow, Thornton—R. V. Thornton of Chicago—who retired to Tucson. Once I tried to buy his Whitman collection and *bought* it, then found that John Kohn had gone in and bid thousands more. I had bought it, offered him five thousand dollars as a deposit until I could get home, and he would send me a list. I didn't take anything with me—that was a great mistake. He urged me to but, I, very stupidly, didn't take anything. In defense of both John Kohn and his client, Waller Barrett, John had gone to Thornton to buy his Robert Frost collection and found he also had the Whitman books, manuscripts and some letters. I don't believe Thornton told John that he had sold them on a handshake and it was to be finalized as soon as the list of items was completed and sent to me. I wrote Thornton when I saw a couple of the items exhibited at the opening of the Barrett Library in 1960, but never got an answer. Later I realized he had used my purchase price to get a higher offer. I went to Arizona especially for the collection, took Mrs. Feinberg with me, just for the Thornton trip, at his request. I had corresponded with Thornton for five to six years. Apparently he'd had a heart attack and his doctors had said he had to slow down and quit business. He went to the bank for advice, and he bought a lot of things. Margie Cohn had advised him on Frost. He was a large buyer at the Bernheimer Sale. He was the one who owned the only copy of *Twilight,* before Waller Barrett bought it. I was interested in the sale which is why I remembered, but that's another story. I had owned a copy of *A Boy's Will* and I had given it and my first edition of *North of Boston* to the Hebrew University in 1960 or 1961. I had come down to the University of Virginia that time when Waller Barrett was opening his library and Frost said to me, "I'm sorry you're not going to be at Breadloaf." I said, "Why aren't I going to be at Breadloaf?" "I understand you're going to Israel." "Well, I'm not going there until October." "Oh," he said, "I was told it was August. I've always wanted to go to Israel." "Well," I said, "why don't you?" "Never been invited." I said, "Would you like to go to Jerusalem at the invitation of the Hebrew University? After all, I'm a member of the board, national chairman of the library committee. When do you want to go?" So he called Kay over—Kay Morrison. "When could I go to Jerusalem?" "Well, not before next March." "Well, give me a date," I said. She said, "You'll have to write me." I said, "I'll write you, send you a formal invitation, we'll pay expenses—or I'll pay. On top of that, I'll have a Frost collection there for you." Well, I started. I couldn't buy a first edition of *North of Boston* at the time. I got everything else, and I didn't want to give them my presentation copy of *North of Boston*. But I finally took the inscribed copy I had and presented it to the Jewish National and University Library on the occasion of Mr. Frost's visit. Anyway, we gave him a luncheon in New York. About twenty to thirty people. I remember I took Mrs. Isaac Stern there. I invited Isaac, but he had to be in San Francisco. The representative of the Mayor of New York presented Frost with a medal. I don't know who the hell the mayor was. Wagner, I think. And, I gave Frost this *North of Boston* as a token of the collection that was already waiting for him in Jerusalem. He wouldn't let go of it. He carried it with him on the plane. He additionally inscribed it when he gave it to them, and he signed the register of the University, and he had the most marvelous time. I remember Chet Huntley and David Brinkley ran a fifteen-minute film on Frost's visit to Jerusalem. He toured the country. "Greatest spiritual experience of my life. I walked the streets where Jesus walked," he said.

Collectors usually wind up getting acquainted with a dealer early in their career who gives them some guidance. I did not limit myself to one dealer until the early thirties. I forget when I first met Dave Kirschenbaum. It's now about forty-five years, but that brings me in just about the Depression years, 1930, and that'd be about right, 1929-1930. I first met Alfred Goldsmith. Goldsmith gave me some of my biggest bargains. I came uptown, I bought some things from Barnet Beyer. Beyer died, and the Whitman manuscripts that he had —one of them was the Bucke manuscript of his book on Whitman, much of it dictated and written by Whitman, recently printed in facsimile by New York University Press, by this fellow who's a member of the

Grolier Club, who used to be the head, and probably still is, of some safe company in New York (Diebold, I think). His name is Dan Maggin. There are three Bucke manuscripts, corrected by Whitman with words added to each, and we don't know in what sequence. I think I have the most complete one. Of these manuscripts, Duke has one, Maggin has one that he bought from the brothers of Beyer, and my copy now at the Library of Congress. I wanted to have the three manuscripts compared by scholars. Maggin insisted on printing his alone. This was an example of a lost opportunity to produce an important scholarly work of lasting value. The book Maggin underwrote was beautifully printed, but future scholars will require that the work be completely redone.

PAGES: What is it that serious collectors are really trying to accomplish? What is your rationale for collecting —in particular, for building a one-author collection?

FEINBERG: I'll tell you what I am trying to accomplish. It was in the early thirties when Dick Sessler came to the house. Those were bad years. I had bought some etchings from Dick and some paintings, and I wondered if I could raise money on them. It was a bad time for Rembrandt prints, and it was a bad time for my Dürer. The only thing Dick ended up with—I had some letters by T. E. Lawrence, in which he wrote to the publisher denying the reports that his manuscript of *The Seven Pillars of Wisdom* had ever been lost or stolen. That was the only item of any importance, that Dick said he had a ready market for. I don't think anybody who didn't live through that particular period, those years, could quite understand how difficult it was. I didn't want to touch any of my Whitman. I had a number of Whitman letters, and he wanted to buy them. I said, "No, Dick." He said, "But you said it wasn't a collection." I said, "I don't know what you mean by a collection because I didn't start out to be a collector." He said, "What did you start out to do?" I said, "First, I had my own interest in Whitman, as a poet. I found I could live with Whitman." He said, "Why? I've never bothered about Whitman. I'm familiar with some of his poems. You know, we're right in Philadelphia, and we're right in the heart of Whitman country. I know A. Edward Newton, whose father-in-law was a collector of Whitman." I said, "I started out first because of Whitman's poetry, but since then I have been trying to buy, within my limits." "But," he said, "you buy anything you can. Why?" I said, "In the first place, I wanted to disprove something I had

Robert Frost in Charles Feinberg's library.

read a long time ago, because I don't know how periods of a man's life can be dropped, as if he never lived, when he must have been active. He must have written things, he must have tried to get them published, and I found a number of things having to do with years that nobody seems to have paid any attention to." And he said, "How do you do that?" And I said, "Well, Mabel Zahn has sold me a couple of things that come from the Harned family that helped me with some of the days." "Oh," he said, "Harned was a literary executor." I said, "But Harned never sold anything of which he was a literary executor. Harned only sold things that he had bought. The other things he had given to his children, or to institutions. The bulk of

his collection is at the Library of Congress." I think I was imbued more with the denial of Holloway's account of certain aspects of Whitman's life. Holloway always kept on looking for facts of Whitman's life that I don't think ever existed, and later on in life, certainly not in the beginnings. I don't think I knew enough about the whole question of homosexuality. Holloway had only been looking, not at homosexuality as much as, supposedly, Whitman's sexuality. He had been focusing on the women in New Orleans, the possible octoroon, or somehow that Whitman had fathered a number of children, six children according to Whitman's own statement, which I think was a figment of Whitman's imagination after being charged with being a homosexual. He reacted in the only way he could think of, as an older man would react after he has been accused of not having any strength to show how virile he is. He overdoes it, and that's what Whitman did when John Addington Symonds wrote and said, "Aren't you like me?" After all, Symonds was an avowed homosexual when he made the statement.

PAGES: Why do you collect Whitman the way you do; why do you collect an author so completely; why do you go after not only letters, but what other collectors ordinarily disdain—envelopes, newspaper clippings, photographs, odds and ends?

FEINBERG: I think I can tell you that better if I explain some of the things that I have become involved in chasing, always with the hope that if I'm able to find them, I can put them together with the other things which are now destined to be available to scholars for all time, at the Library of Congress. Primarily, I think I learned from other collectors. I mentioned Waller Barrett before. Waller first told me of what he was trying to do —collect American literature, manuscripts, letters, first editions to present to the University of Virginia. I admired tremendously the purpose for which a collector could collect unselfishly because most of us collect for possession and not to give away. I think that helped me to formulate some of the ideas of pursuing things to complete a picture which I knew could never be completed, and which I could not do alone. The complete works of Walt Whitman was published in 1902, in ten volumes. Today material is available that was also available at that time but was not sought out and was not brought together for one reason or another, so that the complete works of Walt Whitman were not complete, either in poetry or prose. Even though now, seventy-odd years later, we still haven't got a complete Whitman, we have already published five volumes of the letters, and we're now in the process of getting together the supplement covering material which has been found since the fifth volume of letters was completed. In manuscripts, I can make my point by telling you about a manuscript that I never knew existed until I acquired it about two weeks ago: a check, which to most people will seem like a souvenir of a past age, which was written by Whitman for a definite purpose —it confirms Whitman's financial support of his younger brother, Edward, where it had previously only been suggested—which ties up with his life and his attitude towards other members of his family in a way that I consider tremendously important to such an ex-

tent that it may even be included in a publication which is now being readied in proof and will be published later this year—so that we continue to add to a picture that is not complete. I was resolved to bring together as much as I possibly could, and this I have done, occasionally not being able to acquire what I wanted only because I've lacked the money at the particular time the item was available and made the mistake of *not* going into debt.

PAGES: You're speaking now about the perils of buying at auction. Do you have any rules you follow when you buy at auction?

FEINBERG: Auction rules are something else. Of course, I suppose one learns by mistakes and one learns by experience—experiences which are good and bad. You've got to make up your mind before the auction how badly you want an item. Regardless of what the appraisals give you as an indication of what you may have to spend, you, in your own mind, have to decide just what limits you can afford. The only regrets I have are for the items I could have bought and didn't or the items I bid on and didn't bid high enough. The ones I didn't get. The ones that got away. This is especially true of manuscripts or letters. Very rarely can you compare them to a book, of which there are a number of copies and where you can hope for another copy if you didn't get the first copy—unless, of course, it was a unique copy. But ordinarily even a presentation copy, if you don't get one presentation copy, there may be another one come along in two years, ten years, twenty years. But very rarely do you ever get a second opportunity for a letter or a manuscript that you've lost. I would go a step further to say that every envelope that contained a letter carried the proof that a letter was written or something was written to be enclosed in the envelope because the envelope had a stamp, had a postmark, had a place where it came from, proving that the sender or the writer of that envelope was in a particular place at a certain time on a certain date and that in itself, even though the letter itself may not exist, is of sufficient importance to a scholar writing of a certain period of an author's life, or of any historical figure for that matter. It may only be of importance to six people and the collector —but what of that—it doesn't have to be important to everybody.

PAGES: Has anyone ever offered to buy your collection?

FEINBERG: Yes, many times. Let me give you an example. A dealer I knew represented a large university came to me to say he wanted to buy my collection. The dealer wasn't in the house ten minutes and he says, "I'll give you a million and a half for everything in the house." I said, "What would you leave me with?" He said, "A million and a half." I said, "You're only talking of money. What would I live with?" He said, "A million and a half." I said, "Have you ever lived with money? I don't live that way. You came here to talk about Whitman, you want to talk about Whitman? Don't talk about my house. Nobody is leaving me with an empty house as long as I'm alive." I called up the head of the university. I said, "You may want to buy my collection, but you'll never buy it the way you are going about it. Never send that man back here again." "What's the matter, didn't he offer you enough?" I said, "The offer was fine, I've no quarrel with the money. In the first place, he came here to buy one thing, and he offered me something else, and I wasn't even interested in what he came for. That was one thing. Why, it's insulting to walk into a man's home to buy everything in the house that he lives with. What the hell does he think I am?" He said, "I'll be over to see you." He came three weeks later. He was all right. He came here to offer me a million dollars for the Whitman. I have it in writing. I said, "It isn't the money. It isn't the terms; terms are all right." He wanted to give it to me in three years. If I insisted, I could have it in cash. "Well," I said, "if I was selling for cash, I'd rather have the cash, because the cash, after all, would be fifty to sixty thousand a year. Makes no difference; that wasn't what I wanted." He said to me, "Ed Hanley always said you would sell for a million dollars." I said, "I didn't know Ed was my agent." Ed had called me up the night Ed sold his collection. He said, "Charlie, your collection and my collection make the greatest collection of Whitman in the world." I felt like saying, "Ed, my collection without your collection is the greatest collection of Whitman in the world."

PAGES: When does a collector begin to worry about what he is going to do with his collection, how he is going to dispose of it?

FEINBERG: I think he begins to worry about it the moment he knows he has a collection, and the responsibility of the collector depends on his responsibilities to family, as to his financial situation in the world. I think it is a simple thing for one of wealth to merely consider it as something that he has to leave behind,

"I greet you at the beginning of a great career. . . ." Ralph Waldo Emerson's response to *Leaves of Grass*, 21 July 1855. Whitman printed this phrase on the spine of the second edition of *Leaves of Grass*. From the Feinberg Collection, Library of Congress.

all the rest of plate stet (is to be used for pocket bindings small edn of L of G. morocco gilt)

Leaves of Grass

Including

SANDS AT SEVENTY...*1st Annex*,
GOOD-BYE MY FANCY...*2d Annex*,
A BACKWARD GLANCE O'ER TRAVEL'D ROADS,
Portraits from Life and Autograph.

COME, said my Soul,
Such verses for my Body let us write, (for we are one,)
That should I after death invisibly return,
Or, long, long hence, in other spheres,
There to some group of mates the chants resuming,
(Tallying Earth's soil, trees, winds, tumultuous waves,)
Ever with pleased smile I may keep on,
Ever and ever yet the verses owning—as, first, I here and now,
Signing for Soul and Body, set to them my name,

Emendation in plate at bottom of page

Author's Edn ... (less than 200 pub'd) ... revised, authenticated, completed ... cumulus of 36 years (fm 1855 to date) ... the present Vol. personally handled by W W ... price $5 ... Camden. N. J.

1892

antique or black in long italic at bottom say l/p

hanging ind'l $.50 C their courier as you think best —close

Trial title page with Whitman's directions for the printer (Philadelphia: McKay, 1891-2).
From the Feinberg Collection, Library of Congress.

And by one great pitchy torch,
stationary, with a wild flame,
& much smoke,

Crowds, groups of forms, I see,
on the floor, and some in the
pews laid down;

At my feet a soldier, a mere
lad, in danger of bleeding to
death—(he is shot in the ab-
domen,)

I stanch the blood temporarily,
(the youngster's face is white
as a lily;)

Then before I depart I sweep
my eyes o'er the scene around
fain—I am fain to absorb
it all,

Faces, varieties, postures beyond
description, some in obscurity,
some of the dead.

"Of Abraham Lincoln bearing testimony twenty-five years after his death – and of that death – I am now my friends before you. Few realize the great days, the great historic and esthetic personalities with him in the centre, we pass'd through. Abraham Lincoln, familiar, our own, an Illinoisan, modern, yet tallying ancient Moses, Joshua, Ulysses, or later Cromwell – and grander in some respects than any of them; Abraham Lincoln, that makes the like of Homer, Plutarch, Shakspere, eligible our day or any day. My subject this evening for 40 or 50 minutes' talk is the death of this man, and how that death will really filter into America. I am not going to tell you any thing new; and it is doubtless nearly altogether because I ardently wish to commemorate the hour and martyrdom and name I am here. Oft as the reeling years bring back this hour, let it again however briefly, be dwelt upon. For my own part I hope and intend till my own dying day, whenever the 14th or 15th of April comes, to annually gather a few friends and hold its tragic reminiscence. No narrow or sectional reminiscence. It belongs to These States in their entirety – not the North only, but the South – perhaps belongs most tenderly and devoutly to the South, of all; for there really this man's birth-stock; there and thence his antecedent stamp. Why should I not say that thence his manliest traits, his universality, his canny, easy ways and words upon the surface – his inflexible determination at heart? Have you ever realized it, my friends, that Lincoln, though grafted on the West, is essentially in personnel and character a Southern contribution?"

Keep Carefully

Lincoln's Picture
one of the latest taken
before he was shot —
the most satisfactory
picture of A. L. I have
ever seen, (and I have seen
hundreds of different ones) — looks
just like I saw him last on the balcony
of the National Hotel

At left: Whitman's manuscript for his 1890 lecture on Lincoln.
Above: Whitman's note on his favorite Lincoln picture.
From the Feinberg Collection, Library of Congress.

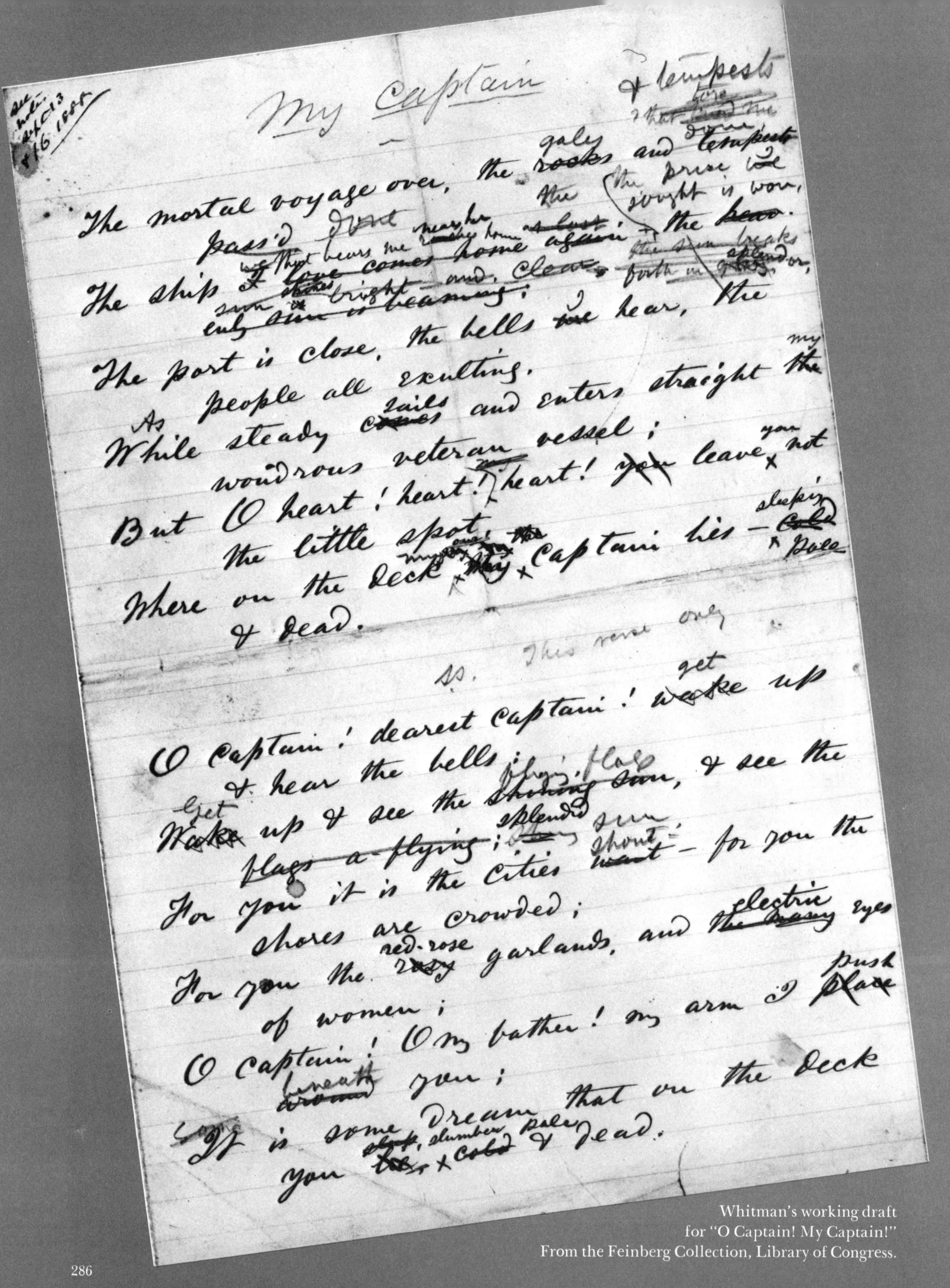

My Captain
The mortal voyage over, the gales and tempests pass'd
The ship that bears me nearing home again — the prize we sought is won,
The port is close, the bells I hear, the people all exulting,
As steady sails and enters straight the wondrous veteran vessel;
But O heart! heart! heart! you leave not the little spot,
Where on the deck my Captain lies — pale & dead.
This verse only
O captain! dearest captain! get up & hear the bells;
Get up & see the flying flag, & see the splendid sun;
For you it is the cities shout — for you the shores are crowded;
For you the red-rose garlands, and the electric eyes of women;
O captain! O my father! my arm I push beneath you;
It is some dream that on the deck you slumber, pale & dead.

Whitman's working draft
for "O Captain! My Captain!"
From the Feinberg Collection, Library of Congress.

and he's only interested in its disposition either as a memorial or as a gift to a school he may have gone to, or an institution to which he may feel close, or if he feels that he would like to be remembered by a catalogue, even an auction catalogue, which can be memorial enough for most families. I had a certain idea because Whitman was the kind of a man he was—I think he contributed much to American idealism, American thought. I've always loved his lines, "born of parents born here, their parents the same, their parents the same." And though I'm of immigrant parents, I've certainly admired the idealism of American democracy and the opportunity that it affords all people of other countries, of other parts of the world, and so to me the solution was much easier than it might be for most: I wanted my collection of this great American poet to be in an American institution, even though foreign institutions told me of their desire to give it a home. I wanted it in an institution that did not belong to one section of the country, but belonged to the entire country. And there was only one such institution, and that is our own national library, the Library of Congress. I was perfectly willing to overcome the difficulties and to meet any condition that was imposed in order to see that the collection ended where I wanted it—at the Library of Congress. Where, I'm grateful to be able to say, it will repose for all time.

PAGES: You've encountered great difficulty in accomplishing your wish, have you not? It hasn't been easy dealing with the Library of Congress?

FEINBERG: No, it hasn't. Peculiar circumstances have made it quite difficult. The failure of the country to provide money to the Library of Congress for building collections, to enable it to purchase things, to enable it to expand. It builds a building; somebody else wants that building for some other branch of government. Unfortunately, things at the Library of Congress are very inadequately housed. We lack exhibition space. I think our librarians have been handicapped by administrations who have at times interfered because the Library of Congress is administered by members of Congress who are not sufficiently detached from political situations. The period of McCarthy was a situation that embarrassed us. It prevented the appointment of a man who had been trained for a position of executive ability as the Librarian of the Library of Congress. I'm speaking of Vernor Clapp, who should have been Librarian and was prevented by McCarthy, which resulted in the appointment of another man.

PAGES: Did this change in administration have any effect on your plans?

FEINBERG: Yes, over a period of many years, they were naturally affected because originally, I had already spoken to librarians as far back as over thirty years ago. I had some definite ideas. One of my ideas—of course, it was a dream—I even proposed it to a member of the Mellon family—was the proposition that an exhibition hall be built for the National Library and eventually merged with the Library of Congress, so that we would have a new name under the merger as the National Library and the Library of Congress of the United States. I feel that most foreign countries know that the Library of Congress, although it is budgeted and provided for by Congress, belongs to the American people and is our national library. But the words "National Library and the Library of Congress" have been mentioned only occasionally. No one has yet dared to sponsor such a name because of Congress. It would require the approval of Congress as well as the provision, possibly, of outside money contributed by outside people, which is one of the reasons why I approached the Mellon family to do for the library what their father had done for the arts. I was not successful. That goes back at least twenty-five to thirty years, but it's still a dream. Our Library of Congress should be re-named as our National Library and the Library of Congress.

PAGES: But your Whitman Collection is now "officially" on deposit at the Library of Congress.

FEINBERG: Yes, about ninety-five percent of my collection up to the present time is already deposited at the Library of Congress. The rest of it is going there, and it will soon be there in its entirety.

PAGES: Does your interest in the collection—or in collecting—diminish any when you see your material deposited elsewhere, no longer in your own library?

FEINBERG: This is something I've never been able to understand about other collectors. I can only speak for myself. I've never been able to understand how interest in a collection can stop merely because it is no longer housed in your own home. My interest continues, and it has continued for the years that most of my collection has already been at the Library of Congress. I continue to purchase when the opportunity offers. I have made money available each year. I've made money available for the future so that the Library of Congress will be able to continue to add to the collection, long after I'm gone. I do not believe that any collection should come to a dead end merely because it is no longer owned or possessed by its original collector. There are the precedents of other collectors. I'm thinking of Lessing Rosenwald who has for many years given of his collection to the Library of Congress. I think the balance of his collection has been willed to the Library of Congress. He continues to add to his collections—both at the Library and his own personal collection—knowing that it will all eventually go to the people of the United States. I think this is the true spirit of any collection that is formed if the individual who collects feels close to his collection and wants to see that its use is continued and made available to scholars, both in this country and abroad. In Whitman's case, this is tremendously important because of the many translations that have been made, some from original material; but most of the translations have been made from other translations without access to original material. Now that my collection is at the Library of Congress, all of it is available to scholars, even while I'm still alive.

PAGES: What advice would you have for a beginning collector today?

FEINBERG: Make sure you only collect what you like and what you can afford to buy and collect something that is of particular interest to you without worrying about whether it's going to be worth a dollar more or a dollar less at any time. No one can take away from me the fifty or sixty years that I have lived with my books, my letters, my manuscripts, my collecting. It's been part of my life. I wouldn't have wanted it any other way. I am most grateful for the years and the understanding that is necessary if you have a married life. The understanding of a wife. I came to married life with a collection—small, but it was already definite. It has continued all these years with Mrs. Feinberg's acquiescence. Without it life could have been difficult.

PAGES: Collecting takes a large part of your life in terms of time, does it not?

FEINBERG: Yes, well, you have to make up your mind which road you want to take. What it is you want out of life. I wanted education. I wanted some knowledge. I think that was more important to me than just merely working. Making money was important, but not all the money. I've never been able to understand what people can do with two million dollars that they can't do with

one million and why people have to continue beyond what a reasonable amount might be for a comfortable living.

PAGES: What do you remember as the single most exciting acquisition in your years as a collector?

FEINBERG: An item I would never own. An item that came into my possession as a result of the Nazi holocaust. A *Memorbuch* of the Jewish community of Frankfurt, buried by the last rabbi of that community who himself was imprisoned in Theresienstadt. Dug up after the war, sold for the benefit of Youth Aliva—which is the taking of refugee children to Israel. I knew when I bought it that I was buying a piece of history I would never own. It should never belong to an individual. I microfilmed it, sent microfilms to the Library of Congress, the Bibliothèque nationale, the British Museum, the National Library in Canada, and the Hebrew University in Jerusalem. Eventually, it was given anonymously to the Hebrew University in the memory of three great pioneers who were instrumental in the rebuilding of Israel. It's exhibited in the rotunda of the Jewish National and University Library of Jerusalem. It's one of their historical treasures, as it should be. Originally started about 1626, all the entries written by hand of all the communities that were destroyed, beginning with that period and with the death of some of the most prominent of the Jewish families of the German community of Frankfurt, right down to the last Baron Wilhelm von Rothschild. There was a second volume started after 1900. That's disappeared.

PAGES: As you finally look around at your library and hear all of the bindings and the cases speaking back to you, what, what do they say?

FEINBERG: Oh, I've had a lot of fun. I had a lot of experiences. I've made friends I would have never met. I've talked to people from all over. I've received welcomes and honors. I've had a full life, but I've had a lot of fun chasing things. I've had a lot of fun coming to me from things that I have bought, given a lot of pleasure, and I guess I've acquired a bit of knowledge. I think the Whitman manuscript page from *Leaves of Grass* that came up at auction—well, it has a mysterious background. To this day, we don't know its provenance. But we have an idea how it survived. The only surviving page that we know of, up to this time, of the original manuscript of Whitman's *Leaves of Grass,* one page. It came to the attention of the auction house in 1954, I think. And when Dave Kirschenbaum, my dealer, heard of it, brought it to my attention, the first thing that came up was how sure was I that the manuscript was destroyed. I was able to turn to Whitman himself and I quoted Whitman, who had told Traubel that it was destroyed by fire, an accident at the printers. I hadn't known any page or anything had ever survived, but I had an idea what it might look like if it had survived. There was a question. How many more pages there might be if one survived; how did we know that there weren't ten? Arthur Swann called me at the time—he was the head of the book and manuscript department of Parke Bernet—and he told me the experience of the Gutenberg Bible when it was sold leaf by leaf from a broken copy. How were the people sure that there wouldn't be more leaves that would go at a cheaper price? The truth of the matter is that it was brought out at several hundred dollars and never, even in the Depression years, did it ever sell less than the publication price. I said, "But, Arthur, what if there were a number of different heirs and somebody else may have pages?" He said, "I think my Gutenberg experience is the answer. I don't think it will ever go less than whatever this page will bring." I remember the day of the auction, we all had lunch together, Sessler, Barry from New Haven and a chap who's now out in Los Angeles. There were half a dozen people, more maybe, around the table, and the question was how much it would bring—and, of course, there's always the question of an underbidder. Kirschenbaum said, "I don't know, my buyer hasn't told me yet how much he's going to bid." I hadn't really. I was asked and I said, "Well, I'm involved in it, and I've no idea." We didn't know. We really didn't know. The truth of the matter is the competition was a rather peculiar thing. One competitive collector from London came up to me and said, "I don't want to upset anything, but you know there're half a dozen of these pages at Duke University." I didn't say anything, but I knew that everything that was at Duke was pieces, not a page—wasn't one page. Ed Hanley was at the sale, and I was glad that that was his opinion because he didn't bid. I bought it for very little money because the underbidder was a man who was merely collecting autographs and he didn't have anything of Whitman's. He thought it would be nice to have something that had already received so much publicity. What was nice about it was not only the fact that I bought it—I paid $1,500 plus ten percent. Dave Randall came up to me after the sale and he said, "Charlie, I'm authorized to offer you $5,000 for that page." I said, "Dave, that's silly. You were here, why didn't you bid?" He said,

"When you bought it you authenticated it." I said, "Dave, thank you for the compliment." "Don't thank me," he said, "thank my clients. Will you take it?" I said, "No." "Will you put a price on it?" I said, "No, I haven't bought a page; I bought a cornerstone for my collection."

PAGES: May I ask you, was making money easier than collecting?

FEINBERG: Oh, I think at times. I'll put it another way. I think most people can make money in a number of different ways. The making of money is open to more people. I really think it is easier to make money if you set your mind to it and block out most of the other things in life. I can't do that. I couldn't do it when I was younger; I can't do it now. We're taught a number of things in life, and if I've been taught anything, I've either learned from my parents or I've learned from books, and I've certainly learned from my faith. I don't mean to be trite, and I don't mean to quote clichés: money is not the important thing in life. I had to decide that somewhere in the early years of my life. I'm not sure that I was altogether right, but I think I've tried to be fair with my family, my children and myself. I don't think I've ever hurt anyone by my collecting. I've enriched my own life, and I've tried to enrich the lives of everyone that I've come in contact with. Yes, I've shared. I don't know how you can go through life without sharing if you have the things that you want to share with others. I don't mean necessarily the actual things, the items themselves, but the knowledge that the items bring you, the friendships that they bring you. As you get older, you find that the friendships are tremendously important. I continue to speak at institutions—it's nice at my time of life that I'm invited. I only insist on one thing—that I be permitted when I go to any institution that has classes in American Literature, or in American Studies, that I be permitted to talk to students, in addition to being possibly an after-dinner speaker to an older audience, or to initiate a group of Phi Beta Kappas, which I'm asked to do by the United Chapters. I have been allowed to enjoy life. I've been endowed; I've been allowed to enjoy some of what I've had, and to give away some of what I've had, and to repay to the libraries some of what libraries have done for me. I'm a product of public libraries, and I bless the memory of that little Scotsman, Andrew Carnegie, for the tremendous help that he must have given to so many others in providing a world of books in areas where books had not been available. My life would have been a desert without books.

Adaline D. T. Whitney.

Sarah Orne Jewett.

QUEENS OF LITERATURE

POPULAR EDITION.

Elizabeth Stuart Ph

the Gates Ajar.
Hed

Char
In the T
The Prop

Harriet Beecher Stowe.

Uncle Tom's Cabin.
The Pearl of Orr's Island.
Sam Lawson's Fireside Stories.

Lucy Larcom.

Wild Roses of Cape Ann.
An Idyl of Work.
Breathings of the Better Life.

Charlotte Bronte.
"CURRER BELL."

Jane Eyre.   Shirley.   Villett

Original box and author cards
for the "Queens of Literature"
card game (1886).

Queens of Literature

*Some of the names in the game
have quietly disappeared —
others are still remembered and read*

By MADELEINE B. STERN

The rise and fall of princes is a theme that for centuries has served the historian and delighted the moralist. In this International Women's Year it seems appropriate that, even in such a context, the place of princes be pre-empted by queens. If those queens turn out to be literary instead of historical, they provide us with a fascinating variation on the theme. And when those queens of literature happen to be served up in a deck of nineteenth-century cards, what a prize package we have: a seminar in feminism and in literature; a game of reputations; speculations on the changing tides of taste; an answer to that tantalizing query—which queens, if any, still reign?

In 1886 when John McLoughlin, Jr., New York publisher of toy books and novelty items, manufactured the card game entitled QUEENS OF LITERATURE, the American reading public was devouring three best sellers: *Little Lord Fauntleroy, King Solomon's Mines, War and Peace.* The startling diversity of those titles and the complementary diversity of public taste are matched by the diversity of McLoughlin's literary queens. Of the eight scribbling women whose portraits and autographs adorn his author cards, four have passed peaceably into comparative oblivion and are remembered chiefly in scholarly bibliographies or doctoral dissertations. The other four still have a claim to fame.

One of the four forgotten queens, *Mary N. Murfree,* whose pen-name was Charles Egbert Craddock,

291

Literary queens and their cards:
Elizabeth Barrett Browning

has been neglected by the general public but not by the serious literary student. A southern writer associated with Tennessee, Miss Murfree, small, vivacious, and lame, never married. Her stories, written at first to beguile the time and to read to her family, were tales of local color, mountain people, moonshiners, preachers, blacksmiths. With *In the Tennessee Mountains* (1884) the pseudonymous Charles Egbert Craddock hit the literary jackpot. Her short stories became a sensation and were followed by another twenty-five volumes of local color or historical romances. We are told—and we can see—that Miss Murfree's handwriting was "bold and masculine, her fictional themes not feminine." When her real name and sex were revealed the disclosure electrified not only her editor, Thomas Bailey Aldrich of the *Atlantic,* but the nation. When McLoughlin shuffled his cards in 1886, Mary N. Murfree of the Tennessee mountains was in her apogee. Although she has fallen from that height, some of her books have been reprinted for use in local-color courses, and perhaps, having been introduced to the academic curriculum, Miss Murfree will one day be restored to the national consciousness.

If Mary Murfree gained a brilliant though short-lived acclaim for local-color stories narrated in "virile" style, her queenly companion of the deck, *Adeline D. T. Whitney,* owed her reputation to moral and sentimental homilies of domestic life. The former Miss Train of Massachusetts had at the age of nineteen married Seth Dunbar Whitney, a forty-

year-old trader in wool and leather. After her children had gone to school, Mrs. Whitney took up her pen and in 1863 produced in *Faith Gartney's Girlhood* an immediate success that went into twenty editions. Her idyls of hearth and home—her "Real Folks Series"—appealed to that extensive segment of the population who held with the author that girls should be satisfied with life at the fireside, that home was the true center of a woman's world and that suffrage was not. For almost half a century Mrs. A. D. T. Whitney relayed her unemancipated message to her unemancipated public and found herself immortalized among McLoughlin's QUEENS OF LITERATURE.

Mrs. Whitney at one time wrote a tribute to a sister queen, *Lucy Larcom,* who shared not only her status as a McLoughlin queen but her lack of interest in woman suffrage. Lucy, a Massachusetts mill girl, had been born to what she called the "privilege of poverty." Conservative and retiring, religious and domestic, she never married but devoted herself to those "Breathings of the Better Life" of which she wrote. An abolitionist in her youth, she was a lifelong friend of John Greenleaf Whittier. Yet when she composed a blank-verse narrative entitled *An Idyl of Work,* in 1875, chronicling the trials of three mill girls, she placed herself on the side not of the labor agitators but of the mill owners. General appreciation of her scenes of domesticity in New England, her rural characters, her sentiment and spiritual uplift was sufficient to crown her with regional fame. In 1885 a Household Edition of her poems was pub-

Felicia Hemans

lished and the next year she ascended to a throne in the McLoughlin kingdom of cards.

Like Lucy Larcom, *Elizabeth Stuart Phelps* hailed from Massachusetts. The daughter of an Andover professor, she grew up a motherless child in the center of New England theology, and her disdain of worldliness was a natural inheritance. The Civil War disrupted her life. She lost her suitor and resolved never to marry—a resolve she did not keep, for in 1888 at the age of forty-four she married a twenty-seven-year-old writer with whom she collaborated on three Biblical romances. Meanwhile, loathing domestic tasks, Mrs. Phelps abandoned the kitchen for the study, or rather the barn or attic where, wrapped in an old fur cape, she wrote *The Gates Ajar* (1868). In a series of conversations between Mary Cabot and her aunt, the author elaborated the idea that heaven offers the best of earth. "If," as she put it, "the Bible tells us there will be harps in heaven, why should we not also hope for pianos?" On the heels of the Civil War, *The Gates Ajar* became an immediate success in America and Britain and, translated into at least four languages, this epitome of uplift and optimism made its creator famous and independent. Unlike Mrs. Whitney and Lucy Larcom, Elizabeth Stuart Phelps did champion women's rights, advocating suffrage, dress reform, and wider employment for women. Her *Hedged In* (1870) defended fallen women and factory girls; *The Story of Avis* (1877) pondered the problem of combining marriage with a career; and *Doctor Zay* (1882) focussed on women

in medicine. Mrs. Phelps—an insomniac—was the author of fifty-seven books. It is devoutly to be hoped that she found pianos in heaven, for she was definitely on the side of the angels.

If half of McLoughlin's literary octet were merely queens of a day, the other half had longer reigns. Although *George Eliot* was once described as "a writer whose fame is menaced," today she is ranked among the major novelists of her century and her books are the subject of serious scholarship. Nonetheless, no one would call her *Adam Bede* (1859) the "finest thing since Shakespeare," as Charles Reade did. The lifelessness of some of her characters, her tendency toward didacticism, and her doctrinaire philosophy may pall, but Mary Ann Evans connects strongly with modern readers both as a writer and as a woman. Her intellectual power shines through her work: *Romola* (1863), a historical narrative of the time of Savonarola; *Daniel Deronda* (1876), her last novel, a tale of the Jewish people. George Eliot herself has much in common with the New Eve. The daughter of Puritan parents, she emancipated herself, becoming the disciple of Spencer and Comte. Her objection to the "indelibility of the marriage tie" was strong enough for her to act upon, and she lived with George Henry Lewes without benefit of church or state from 1854 until his death in 1878. The feminists of the twentieth century would not have been uncomfortable at her Sunday receptions in the Priory, and those among them who write books would appreciate the comment she made about

Louisa May Alcott

Romola. She began it, she said, "a young woman— she finished it an old woman." A generation of readers had enjoyed it before McLoughlin elevated its author posthumously to the royal line of QUEENS OF LITERATURE. In that line she still stands tall, a giant of her century.

Harriet Beecher Stowe was still alive when she was so elevated but her books had made their appearance more than a generation before. Harriet Beecher had grown up, as she said, in "a kind of moral heaven, replete with moral oxygen—full charged with intellectual electricity." She had injected much of that moral oxygen and intellectual electricity into *Uncle Tom's Cabin* (1852), a book that began in a vision and made history. After her marriage to Calvin Stowe and the birth of five children during seven years, Harriet dashed off a tale now and then so that she could hire household help. She had read of the atrocities of slavery, and when the Fugitive Slave Law spurred her to action she was metamorphosed into the "instrument" of the Lord who created an "epic of Negro bondage," a narrative of damnation and salvation. *Uncle Tom's Cabin* made its author famous overnight, sold 300,000 copies within a year, inspired a spate of anti-Uncle Tom novels, and won the praise of such diverse critics as Longfellow and Henry James. Between 1862, when she reworked her New England childhood into *The Pearl of Orr's Island,* and 1884 Mrs. Stowe produced at least a book a year, providing for her family, educating her children, sustaining an alcoholic son. Despite the inde-

pendence her pen had won her, she continued to sermonize against the emancipated woman who indulged in tobacco. She was accurately described by one biographer as a "Crusader in Crinoline." Her crinolines have become period pieces, her crusade historic. Yet she helped to document and advance that crusade, and although *Uncle Tom's Cabin* is no longer widely read, it will be remembered.

Charlotte Brontë was in a sense the oldest of McLoughlin's literary queens for she had died in 1855 and been a bestseller of the mid-century. In this instance, and with the gift of hindsight, the manufacturer of games had chosen well, for surely Charlotte Brontë must remain a perennial bestseller. The girl who had been raised in a bleak and remote Yorkshire parsonage with Emily, Anne, and Branwell, who had written stories in a minuscule hand, served as a governess and co-authored *Poems* by Currer, Ellis, and Acton Bell, still fires the imagination. When she published *Jane Eyre* (1847) its "freshness and vigor . . . took the world by storm." This romance of governess and married man conveyed and still conveys the passion of romanticism tinged with the discipline of stoicism, the violence of emotion balanced by a sober reserve. For all of its Gothic borrowings and ignorance of life, it is imaginative and strong, and *Jane Eyre,* almost one hundred thirty years old, is still very much alive.

In his final pictured queen Mr. McLoughlin was prophetic, for *Sarah Orne Jewett* had not yet created her masterpiece when he placed her likeness on a play-

Margaret Fuller Ossoli

ing card. The stately dignified woman who had grown up in South Berwick, Maine, the daughter of a country doctor—"the best and wisest man I ever knew"—sketched in her first book, *Deephaven* (1877), vigorous and perceptive portraits of the country people she knew. Her father, who served as subject of her novel *A Country Doctor* (1884), had advised her, "Don't try to write *about* things: write the things themselves just as they are." This she had done and would do, most notably when in 1896 she came to write *The Country of the Pointed Firs,* "one of the unquestioned classics of American prose writing," according to Warner Berthoff, her biographer in *Notable American Women.*

Sarah Orne Jewett described the writer as "the only artist who must be a solitary, and yet needs the widest outlook upon the world." It was the narrowness of their talent as well as of their outlook that has relegated to obscurity at least four of McLoughlin's literary queens. Perhaps to compensate for such an eventuality, the publisher included in his card deck the writings but not the portraits of various other women. There are cards inscribed with *The Dial, At Home and Abroad, Woman in the Nineteenth Century*—works of that indomitable citizen of the world *Margaret Fuller* who bequeathed a legacy to feminism because she was a lover of humanity. Finally, there are cards marked with the titles: *Flower Fables, Hospital Sketches* and *Little Women.* Such is the nature of her immortality that no one need be reminded of their author's name.

She was, as Emerson remarked, a "natural source of stories" and the family history she recorded is a domestic narrative that will endure as long as families endure. Indeed *Louisa May Alcott* is the only Queen of Literature whose portrait adorns the *Authors* card game of today. She resides in a goodly company for there, with Shakespeare and Scott, Dickens and Tennyson, Cooper and Irving, Stevenson and Longfellow, Hawthorne and Mark Twain, the Concord Scheherazade sits enthroned.

A good case can be made for half of McLoughlin's deck. But we may wonder at his omissions—where are Jane Austen and George Sand, and especially where is Emily Brontë? Ann Stephens, author of *Malaeska,* the first Beadle Dime Novel, might have been a more interesting choice than Mrs. A. D. T. Whitney. The nominations could become interminable.

Many of McLoughlin's Queens of Literature served an escapist purpose in those "good old days" when capital and labor, rich and poor, man and woman were discovering that each had rights as well as needs. But the struggles of yesterday gather dust. What was original in 1886 fails to sustain its freshness or its impact in 1976. What seemed universal becomes provincial. It is remarkable, not that half of McLoughlin's literary queens have dropped out of the deck, but that, in one way or another, half survive. What Queens of Literature would we nominate today and how long would they be remembered? We shuffle the cards; the pendulum swings; and time keeps score.

'Tropic Of Cancer' On Trial

The correspondence of Henry Miller and Elmer Gertz

Edited by FELICE FLANNERY LEWIS

In June 1961, Barney Rosset of Grove Press published the first American edition of Henry Miller's Tropic of Cancer, *which had been banned as obscene by Customs ever since its 1934 publication in France. To allay the natural concern of booksellers, Rosset let it be known that Grove would come to their assistance should obscenity charges be forthcoming, regardless of whether there was a legal obligation to do so. Elmer Gertz, well-known as a civil rights advocate and trial lawyer, was selected to handle any difficulties that might arise in the Chicago area by Charles Rembar, who served as Grove's general counsel in the more than sixty court tests that eventually developed across the nation.*

By October 1961, police officials in Chicago and adjacent villages had begun a systematic campaign against Grove's recently-released paperback edition of the book, intimidating booksellers and in some instances arresting clerks. Gertz took action when a suit was filed against those officials, on behalf of prospective purchasers but under the auspices of the American Civil Liberties Union, to restrain them from interfering with the sale of Cancer. *As he said later in* A Handful of Clients *(Chicago: Follett, 1965), "I thought it*

Elmer Gertz (left) and Henry Miller (right) at their first meeting, November 1962, in Chicago.

Felice Flannery Lewis, author of *Literature, Obscenity, and Law* (Carbondale: Southern Illinois University Press, 1976), is Dean of Liberal Arts and Sciences, Long Island University/Brooklyn Center.

would be better if the publisher and author intervened in the proceeding and sought not only a restraining order on the police but a finding that the book was not obscene."

As part of his preparation for this and other anticipated Cancer *litigation, Gertz read everything by and about Miller that he could locate. Since literary criticism had long been one of his avocations (he had co-authored a Frank Harris biography while still a law student), Gertz read with more than the usual care and interest as he looked for material that might prove useful in court. A minor detail in Alfred Perlès'* My Friend Henry Miller — *that Miller had habitually worn an "ancient Yemenite talisman" — led to the lasting Miller-Gertz friendship and their copious, intimate correspondence. Gertz asked Edward Schwartz of Minneapolis, founder of The Henry Miller Literary Society, whether he could supply more information about the amulet, and Miller himself replied on 3 January 1962.*

Some forty-nine days later the two men exchanged exultant telegrams in celebration of Gertz's victory in the action against Chicago and suburban police officials. But Cancer *litigation in Illinois and in other states ended only after a favorable 1964 United States Supreme Court decision in a Florida case; and the Miller-Gertz correspondence — fed by their shared passion for eclectic reading, the arts, philosophic problems, and social inequities — was only beginning.*

—F.F.L.

January 4, 1962

Dear Mr. Miller:

I was pleased, almost beyond words, to receive your letter of January 3. (An attorney, like a clergyman, is never really at a loss for words. Albert Einstein once told us that he inherited his brevity from his young son; but my not-too-young son is as verbose as I am.)

Eddie Schwartz asked the question with respect to the talisman in these circumstances. I was interviewing a very interesting young Lutheran minister, who is a great admirer of your writing. I intend to use him as a witness in the case which is to be tried before Judge Samuel B. Epstein of our Superior Court, commencing January 10. This clergyman found certain definite religious aspects to your work, almost in the spirit of what you have said in your book "The World of Sex." I was intrigued by what he had to say and explored the ins and outs of the subject, sometimes dwelling upon the important and sometimes upon the unimportant. At the moment, the talisman with the Hebrew text seemed of great interest and possibly of significance. Having read your letter, I now see it in the proper light. I assure you that the minister's testimony will be on a high and persuasive level.

I once heard Supreme Court Justice Cardozo say that the purpose of the law is to preserve the ancestral smell. Certainly, there is something ritualistic about it, particularly trial work. Still, it is a good way of arriving at the truth on occasion; and I think that we are going to be able to persuade the court to enter a decree in our favor. My feeling is that we are putting more into the evidence than is usual; this for the purpose of creating an atmosphere in which the judge will find it irresistible to decide in your favor.

Incidentally, Judge Epstein is the son of the late Dean of Orthodox Rabbis in Chicago and the brother of a rabbi in Boston. He is far better than most judges. That is one reason that I have a great amount of optimism.

Our Chicago situation is rather complicated. There are three prosecutions brought against booksellers, as well as one in a neighboring village. In addition, we have the suit pending in the Superior Court which is going to trial on January 10, in which we seek what is called a declaratory judgment that the book is not obscene and a restraining order and damages as to various police chiefs for interfering with the sale of the book. Finally, we have a case pending in the United States District Court pursuant to the Federal Civil Rights Act. The significant thing about our situation is that, for the first time, we have taken the initiative. Usually, all that a publisher or author can do is to sit back and await the outcome of prosecutions brought by the police. Through the two proceedings that I have mentioned, we are making the police chiefs understand that book censorship can be dangerous to them. If we should prevail, then it will be extremely unlikely in the future that they will act with such haste and unlawfulness, as in the present situation.

I was much interested to read in one of your books that Frank Harris was the first great writer you ever met. One of the sins of my youth is that I wrote a book about him over thirty years ago.[1] I wrote it while supposedly taking notes in some of my law school classes. Have you ever seen the book? You might even survive the reading of it.

I hope that the New Year brings you and yours good health, victories over the blue-noses and abundant joy.

Sincerely yours,
Elmer Gertz

1. I. Tobin and Elmer Gertz, *Frank Harris: A Study in Black and White* (1931).

Jan. 6th 1962

Dear Mr. Gertz —

I am sending you from here these —

1.) My Friend H.M.
2.) The Smile
3.) Night Life Brochure
4.) Reprint of appendix — Books in My Life

The others will come from Big Sur. It's possible I may not have any more of "Of, By + About".

Funny, but I was about to send you the Appendix from "Books in My Life"—thought it might interest you.

Was delighted to see your text on Frank Harris. He had invited me to come and stay at his place in Nice but I was too shy to take him up on it. How wonderful he looks in that photo! So vigorous. I loved him. He once took a text of mine for the magazine he took over —from McClure, I think. But I can't trace it down. Forget title and every thing.

I think it's wonderful that you can introduce so much "evidence"—usually the judge rules it out, no? I never could picture myself in court answering yes or no, or answering anything to any one's satisfaction. I go to Mallorca end of April to act as member of the jury for the Formentor Prize. Hard put to think of any American writers I can nominate—must be fiction writers. I'm going to fight hard to give it to John Cowper Powys. Remember him?

If you win in this fight you will have accomplished a very big thing—for writers *and* readers. I think the time is ripe—and I have a hunch you are the man to do it.

I often wonder about Leopold or Loeb—what he is doing with himself now that he is free.[1]

Should I ever pass through Chicago I would like to see you and have a good talk with you.

Meanwhile all the best.
Sincerely,
Henry Miller

P.S. I feel a bit ashamed to take your check, but I don't want to embarrass you by returning it. If you don't have the "Monographic" by Rowohlt Verlag, let me send you one. It's a documentary book, full of interesting photos. The text is dull—written by the President of [   ].

P.S. I wonder too if Judge Epstein knows Erich Gutkind's books!

1. Gertz successfully represented Nathan Leopold in his 1958 bid for parole.

Dear Mr. Gertz —

The books and brochures are coming to you in instalments.

Enclosed is something I wrote in 1953 for the lawyer—Maître Sev, Paris—who defended *Sexus*. I had appeared, with him, before the Juge d'Instruction (for which we have no equivalent here) . Then he (Sev) asked me to write something which he could use in the forthcoming trial. But there never was a trial. The case was dropped. I was given a wonderful hearing by that Judge—almost as if I were another Baudelaire, Balzac, Zola.

In any case, a friend of mine recently showed me this script. I had forgotten about it completely. And, so far as I know, it was never published any where, which is rather mysterious, as every thing I write usually finds its way into print.

Now then, this friend had copies made and asked my permission to place it for me in some magazine. (He wants nothing for his services—just thinks it ought to be known.)

Meanwhile it occurred to me that it might be of use to you now, or parts of it. I don't know, but I felt you ought to see it. Naturally, I wouldn't want it to be given to the newspapers or a magazine—not yet anyway. I leave it to your discretion.

In one of the packages you will receive you will find the Rowohlt "Monographic" I mentioned. I feel sure you don't own a copy.

Enough. I am holding that Frank Harris text, unless you wish it back. Must get back to work soon on Nexus —Vol. II.

By the way, I assume you have Plexus and Nexus (Vol. 1.) If not, I'll have my French publisher send you copies—in English.

One of the books I like—and which is almost impossible to find now—is Hamlet (in 2 Vols.—almost 1,000 pages) written with Michael Fraenkel. Do you know of it? *You* would enjoy it, I'm sure.

Sincerely,
Henry Miller

Jan. 14th 1962

Dear Mr. Gertz —

Here is another text of mine, which just appeared in "Elle" (Paris) but in mutilated form and in a weak translation. Again, please do not give any part of it to an editor of a newspaper or magazine. (I am trying to

From the forthcoming *Correspondence of Henry Miller and Elmer Gertz*, ed. Felice Flannery Lewis. © Southern Illinois University Press.

decide where to place it in America.) But I thought it would interest you, because of the subject.

I am slowly going through the issues of "The Paper"[1] you sent me. Can't take all that jazz at one gulp! Liked very much your review of "Le Balcon" (Genet). He's a writer I can't seem to read. I was also much impressed by Wm. Packard's article on Patchen in the Dec. 31, 1960 issue.

I am wondering how effective might be an open letter from me—along Packard's lines—to the editors of such mags as "The New Republic," The Nation, The Saturday Review, Esquire, Playboy—and others. And if I dare write them all at once. The few lines I addressed to the New Republic in 1942 or '43, on my own behalf, worked wonders.

But don't bother your head about such matters now. Just put it aside until after the trials. You need all your powers of concentration, I imagine, to win this battle. And I feel certain you will! It's so unusual (in this country, at least) to find a lawyer who is also a literary man. More, *who can write*.

Do let me know the outcome of the trial (s) soon as possible, or even a little word as to which way the wind is blowing.

> Sincerely,
> Henry Miller

1. A periodical published by Gertz.

January 17, 1962

Dear Mr. Miller:

Of course, I am working day and night on the case now on trial before Judge Epstein, but it is always a delight to interrupt it to read letters from you and to respond. I am more pleased than I can say by your reactions. I hope that not simply out of politeness, but out of interest, you will read the remaining articles and, if you are so minded, give me your views of them. I am thick-skinned enough to accept any sort of judgment.

Let me sum up the situation in the current trial. We have been offering evidence for five days—not the entire time, but substantial portions of each day. We have virtually completed our case and there is a two-day respite. On Friday the defendants will offer their evidence. I have learned through the grapevine that they are having difficulty in getting experts of any kind, but there is no point in assuming anything. It is my task to anticipate what they will offer and to arrange for evidence to overcome it.

We offered the testimony of Richard Ellmann, who is a well-known professor at Northwestern University and the author of a prize-winning book about James Joyce; Barney Rosset of Grove press; Hoke Norris, the literary editor of the Chicago Sun-Times; and Frank Ball, the regional sales supervisor of McFadden Publications. All of these witnesses were truly wonderful. The more they were cross-examined by the defense, the better they were. In addition, we were able to get into evidence the depositions of the various police chiefs against whose unlawful conduct we have complained. Then we were able to get into evidence a vast number of favorable book reviews, magazine articles, books and other material, showing your distinction as a writer and the high qualities of "Tropic of Cancer."

The one respect at which the Court balked at our testimony was in connection with the material that we have offered to show the community standards on sexual writing. We had a vast amount of so-called literature that is readily sold everywhere here, including the City Hall. We will have to content ourselves with a so-called offer of proof as to this material. That is really quite enough for our purposes.

I decided not to use the Lutheran minister at this time, but to save him for rebuttal, because it was clear that the Court felt that we had offered more than enough evidence and that it was now up to the defense to show what they have. If I could guess at this time, I would say that our rebuttal will consist of the Lutheran minister and a sociologist and, perhaps, some more documentary evidence. I think that the case is likely to be concluded next week. Then all of the attorneys will have to file briefs and the Court will probably take a couple of weeks thereafter to prepare an opinion. I think it may be a favorable one, but one never can tell.

There are so many other matters that I want to discuss with you and, perhaps, by the end of the day I will supplement this letter.

I want to thank you for all of the material that you have sent to me. Do, please, send on whatever you think will interest me. I have one trait at least in common with you. When I get absorbed in a subject I have an insatiable appetite for everything about it and at this time I am absorbed in you.

Sincerely yours,
Elmer Gertz

P.S. To my surprise, I was able to get the parties to agree to the Court's taking judicial notice of the facts with respect to Chicago's cultural position. The enclosed document is unlike anything that I have ever filed in court. I suspect that it may be unique.

Jan. 19th 1962

Dear Elmer Gertz —

Sitting here over breakfast pondering your request to say something about your writing, as revealed in "The Paper." Read a half-dozen or more in bed last night. (Liked very much the one on Tesla, whom I always venerated and never learned enuf about. Great man, yes!)

That you can express yourself is obvious. The sole question is—do you want to give yourself to it wholly or only in part? The character of your writing would change once you devoted yourself to it completely. Now and then—you know who I mean—we have good writers who are also doctors, lawyers, surgeons (even) and so on. Usually Europeans. Usually their professional pursuits took second place.

As I see it, what you have done is to "write about". *To write (penkt!)* is another matter. You then become involved—and *responsible* in a different way. Responsible, perhaps, to God, let us say. You invite defeat, humiliation, rejection, misunderstanding—You speak solely as the "unique" being you are, not as a member of society. Do I make sense? Am I answering as you wish me to? "The Paper" itself, while interesting enough, is of no great consequence. It serves to feed the various egos involved. Once seriously engaged, the ego falls away. You are happy—and blessed—just to be an "instrument."

In my mind a writer or any sort of artist is, in the last

analysis, no more important than a ditch-digger or garbage collector. We are all, no matter what our function or capacity, but instruments in the divine orchestra called humanity. Each one, however humble his task, is necessary. If we understood that we would take joy in fulfilling our respective roles. And the role of artist would then be seen to be the greatest privilege, simply because it permitted the "maker" (poet) the greatest freedom, the greatest joy.

Sincerely,
Henry Miller

Jan. 25th 1962

Dear Elmer Gertz —

Here's a fast one, probably too late and probably "irrelevant" and all that—in the eyes of the judge. Have you ever thought to make reference, when defending the "obscene," to the famous Hindu manuals of love, like the "Kama Sutra" and the "Ananga-Ranga"? or to present photos (enlarged) to the court, showing the erotic (but religious) sculpture from the caves and temples of India?

I was just thumbing through a brochure (with illustrations) the other night—called "Erotic Aspects of Hindu Sculpture" by Lawrence E. Gichner—probably an acquaintance of yours. (You seem to know about everybody of any importance in this world.) It was privately published in 1949—no address given.

Anyway, it's a shot in the dark. Better far than any Lutheran's testimony. *The works,* what!

Henry Miller

January 26, 1962

Dear Henry Miller:

There is so much that you have written to me, about which I want to comment. I am deeply grateful to you for this very wonderful exchange of views. As soon as the case is out of the way, I shall catch up with all of the loose ends.

Now, I simply want to tell you that the trial before Judge Samuel B. Epstein has been completed and that all day Monday, and perhaps Tuesday, the legal arguments will be heard. I open and close, and the defendants speak in between. I have been preparing my notes for the argument very carefully, and I hope it will give a good account of myself. Of course, the turn in argument depends a good deal upon the Judge. He may interrupt with comments and questions. It is very fortunate that we have a judge who, despite an innate prudery, is an honorable man through and through, who will decide on what he thinks the law and facts are, even if it hurts him. This is in marked contrast with some of the judges elsewhere. In Philadelphia, for example, I understand that the judge has been expressing his views about the "smut" in the book, in the course of interrupting witnesses who express other views; this, despite the fact that the Philadelphia Bar Association has intervened in your behalf. One does not like to generalize, but I am afraid that some judges, because of their particular religious upbringing, are incapable of acting in a judicial manner when books are involved.

So far as I can gather as of this moment, Judge Epstein believes that the obscenity laws, as interpreted by the Supreme Court, are directed only against hard-core pornography. The Judge personally is opposed to censorship. At the same time, he thinks that two or three passages in "Tropic of Cancer" are inexcusable. He has read the law on the subject matter each night until about midnight and says that this case has been of more concern to him than any during the fifteen years he has been on the bench. He is about a year older than you, a man of financial means, not a professional politician, a cultured gentleman, despite his strain of prudery. This means that we have a better than even chance of winning, but I would not be absolutely certain until the result is announced.

You will hear from me soon.

Faithfully yours,
Elmer Gertz

February 1, 1962

Dear Henry Miller:

Late yesterday, we concluded the final arguments in the case pending before Judge Epstein, and he said that he would prepare a written opinion within two weeks. I think the chances are good of our prevailing, but one can never tell. I was assured by everyone that my final arguments were excellent. The defense argu-

ments were not particularly persuasive. If there should be an adverse ruling, it will not be because of them, but because the Judge cannot conquer any temperamental antipathy that he may have for sexual explicitness. As I see it, he is struggling now with certain forces within him. He is utterly opposed to censorship, book banning, and the like. At the same time, he has a dislike, I think, for your kind of candor. He seems to feel that there can be obscenity convictions only in the case of hard-core pornography and he does not seem to regard your book in that light. He has been subjected to a lot of pressure both ways, and has been honest enough to tell us about these pressures. My closing note was that one cannot be opposed to censorship in general; one must be opposed to it in specific instances. I stressed to the Judge that he ought to show the courage of Judges Woolsey, Hand and Bryan,[1] and give encouragement to all creative artists by declaring your book non-obscene and restraining police interference with it. I am hopeful that, in the end, he will recognize this. In his opinion, he may condemn portions of the book and regret that he cannot expunge them, but I think that, in the end, he will find with us. If not, there are higher courts.

Always yours,
Elmer Gertz

1. In 1933, Judge John M. Woolsey of the Southern District of New York ruled that James Joyce's *Ulysses* was not obscene. His decision was upheld by Judges Augustus and Learned Hand in the Circuit Court of Appeals. Judge Frederick vanPelt Bryan cleared *Lady Chatterley's Lover* in 1959.

[21 February 1962]
GLORY BE. WE HAVE WON.
ELMER GERTZ

[21 February 1962]
CONGRATULATIONS. JUST MARVELOUS. NO ONE BUT YOU COULD HAVE DONE IT.
HENRY MILLER.

February 22, 1962

Dear Henry Miller:

The morning after our great triumph finds me fatigued, but extremely happy. I had not realized how worn out I am. I am going to see if, somehow, I can get a little relaxation. Whatever the wear and tear, it has certainly been worth it. The telegrams from you, Barney Rosset and others helped add to my joy. When you get a copy of the opinion, as you will in a few days, you will be happy all over again.

As I told you, the Judge summoned us to appear in his courtroom 12 o'clock noon and there was a surprisingly large attendance, including newspapermen, several members of my family, my secretary, some of my law associates and others. Promptly at 12 o'clock noon, the Judge opened the session, made a few appropriate remarks and then read the opinion, interpolating additional remarks now and then. After it was over, there was a receiving line in court of those congratulating me. I told the Judge that he had written an historic opinion. Laughingly, he said, "You would, of course, think so." But I told him that I believed it without regard to the fact that I had won; indeed, I do think that this is the most important decision in its way since Judge Woolsey's classic statement in the "Ulysses" case. In many respects, this goes beond the "Ulysses" decision. I hope the Judge's words are widely reprinted, as he deserves the acclaim.

Now that the case is over, I will tell him about your compassionate viewpoint with respect to him while the case was pending.

There is one additional way in which you can reward me, and that is to send me a copy of the cloth-bound edition of "Tropic of Cancer" with an inscription by you. You can date it as of February 21, when we won our great victory. Four years and a day prior thereto, I won my victory in the Leopold case. Of course, I have won other cases since then, but this one gives me the most satisfaction.

I am returning the various drafts of the Preface to "Stand Still Like the Hummingbird," except for the one that you have stated that I can keep. It is a fascinating thing, watching the progression from draft to draft. I don't wonder that your daughter wants the originals. For my own gratification, I have made photostats of the first and second drafts so that I may have them as a memento.

There seems to be no end of material by and about you that I am eager to get. I have gotten many things through New Directions and Grove Press, most of which are exhibits in the case, and I have purchased other items from the Gotham Book Mart, Bern Porter and others. I am sending herewith a list of some of the things that I yet lack. I would love to get them from you, if they are available and if you tell me how much I must pay. I do not want to put you to any undue expense.

With respect to the allegations in the Federal case about the book "Tropic of Cancer" being copyrighted, I was in error, and the allegations were corrected in the complaint in the case before Judge Epstein. We are going to have a running battle with pirates because of the lack of copyright on some of your books and it may be that we will have to work out devices to protect you. There are also other legal problems that may arise when the vigilante groups get after the book in the absence of police interference. These matters, too, I will discuss with you.

Monday night I was on a television program, on the subject "Should Broadcasters Be Free." One of the participants was Virgil Mitchell of CBS, who told me, privately, many interesting things about you. He has a tremendous admiration for you and for Emil White. I shall write Emil about it.

I shall certainly take your advice with respect to reading the "Maurizius Trilogy" and I shall write the Leopold story, as you suggest. Right now, I would like to kick over the traces and just meander around without aim or destination. Of course, I won't do this, knowing my own exigent nature.

This will have to do for today.

Always yours,
Elmer Gertz

Inscribed in the copy of *Tropic of Cancer* given to Gertz by Miller:
For Elmer Gertz—

A lover of freedom, truth and justice, a loyal friend, a lover of books and a peerless barrister. May Heaven protect him ever!

In gratitude and admiration —
Henry Miller
2/21/62

On the eve of the great decision. *"Victory."*

Acknowledgments

P. 130   "Carmen": Michigan Historical Collections, Bentley Historical Society, The University of Michigan. Copyright © Ring Lardner, Jr.

242   "What the Whalers Read": Delivered in an earlier form at the 1976 New England Modern Language Association meeting.

188   "How I Was Always Rich But Was Too Dumb To Know It": From *Journal*, © 1975 by Ray Bradbury.

296   " 'Tropic Of Cancer' On Trial": Copyright © Southern Illinois University Press.

Photo Credits

P. 28-29   Caroliniana Library, University of South Carolina

30-31   David E. Scherman. Time-Life Picture Agency. © Time, Inc.

32   Caroliniana Library, University of South Carolina

35   Alfred Eisenstaedt. Time-Life Picture Agency. © Time, Inc.

36   Caroliniana Library, University of South Carolina

43   Caroliniana Library, University of South Carolina

55   Sotheby Parke Bernet & Co.

58-59   Beinecke Rare Book and Manuscript Library, Yale University

65   Performing Arts Research Center, The New York Public Library at Lincoln Center

67   Wide World Photos

68   Performing Arts Research Center, The New York Public Library at Lincoln Center

71   Edward Hausner/NYT Pictures

72   UPI

85-87   F. Scott Fitzgerald Papers, Princeton University Library

88-89   Bruccoli Collection

90-91   Berea College Appalachian Museum Photographic Archive

92-98   Author's Collection

102   Photo by Allan Kain

104-115   All photos courtesy American Antiquarian Society

116-117   l. to r. Culver Pictures Inc.; Culver Pictures Inc.; New York Public Library; New York Public Library; Culver Pictures Inc.; *New York Times*, October 22, 1926

118-119   l. to r. *New York Times*, October 22, 1926; Culver Pictures Inc.; Culver Pictures Inc.; Culver Pictures Inc.

120-121   l. to r. Culver Pictures Inc.; Culver Pictures Inc.; New York Public Library; Culver Pictures Inc.; *New York Times*, October 22, 1926; Culver Pictures Inc.

122-123   l. to r. Wide World Photos; Wide World Photos; *New York Times*, October 22, 1926; *New York Times*, October 22, 1926; Charles Scribner's Sons, Courtesy Mary Hemingway.

124-125   Photo courtesy of Random House

126-129   All: The Pennsylvania State University Still Photography Services

133   Culver Pictures Inc.

172-175   All: Long Photography, Inc.

179   Photo by Diana H. Walker

182-187   All: Photos by Robert Stokes

188   Photo by Ralph Nelson

189   Collection of the Author

190-193   From *The Ray Bradbury Companion* (Detroit: Gale Research, 1974).

194-195   Illustrations from *Where the Wild Things Are*. Copyright © 1963 by Maurice Sendak. By permission of Harper & Row, Publishers, Inc.

196   Illustration from *Higglety, Piggelty Pop! or There Must Be More to Life*. Copyright © 1967 by Maurice Sendak. By permission of Harper & Row, Publishers, Inc.

197   Top. Illustrations by Maurice Sendak from *Little Bear* by Else Holmelund Minarik. Illustrations copyright © 1957 by Maurice Sendak. By permission of Harper & Row, Publishers, Inc.

197   Bottom. Illustration from *In the Night Kitchen*. Copyright © 1970 by Maurice Sendak. By permission of Harper & Row, Publishers, Inc.

198-199   Illustration from *In the Night Kitchen*. Copyright © 1970 by Maurice Sendak. By permission of Harper & Row, Publishers, Inc.

200-201   Illustrations reproduced with the permission of Farrar, Straus & Giroux, Inc. from *The Juniper Tree and Other Tales from Grimm* selected by Lore Segal and Maurice Sendak, illustrated by Maurice Sendak, Illustrations Copyright © 1973 by Maurice Sendak.

202-203   Illustration from *Where the Wild Things Are*. Copyright © 1963 by Maurice Sendak. By permission of Harper & Row, Publishers, Inc.

204-210   All photos by Nancy Crampton

212-217   All: Author's Collection

227   Reproduced with permission, The Joyce Collection of the Lockwood Memorial Library, State University of New York at Buffalo.

231   Collection of C. E. Frazer Clark, Jr.

233-237   All: Courtesy Universal Studios

242-243   Courtesy of the Kendall Whaling Museum, Sharon, Mass.

244   Courtesy of the Kendall Whaling Museum, Sharon, Mass.

245   J. Ross Browne, *Etchings of a Whaling Cruise*, 1846. New York Public Library

246   Courtesy of the Kendall Whaling Museum, Sharon, Mass.

247   Marine Historical Association, Inc. Mystic Seaport, Mystic, Conn.

252   Photo by Gerald Crawford

255   Photo by Mario Borras

262   Collection of John Cocchi

269   Manuscripts Department, Lilly Library, Indiana University

270   Manuscripts Department, Lilly Library, Indiana University

271   Roy Collection

273   Photo by John Henderson Studios

275   Photo by V. L. Vincent

276   Manning Bros.

279   Photo by Joe Clark

292-295   All photos of "Queens": Culver Pictures Inc.

296   Southern Illinois University, Morris Library, Special Collections

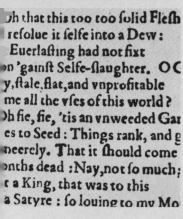

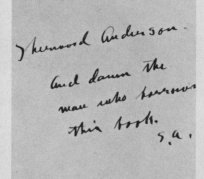